WEYERHAEUSER ENVIRONMENTAL BOOKS

Paul S. Sutter, Editor

WEYERHAEUSER ENVIRONMENTAL BOOKS explore human relationships with natural environments in all their variety and complexity. They seek to cast new light on the ways that natural systems affect human communities, the ways that people affect the environments of which they are a part, and the ways that different cultural conceptions of nature profoundly shape our sense of the world around us. A complete list of the books in the series appears at the end of this book.

FIR AND EMPIRE

*The Transformation of Forests in
Early Modern China*

IAN M. MILLER

UNIVERSITY OF WASHINGTON PRESS
Seattle

Fir and Empire is published with the assistance of a grant from the Weyerhaeuser Environmental Books Endowment, established by the Weyerhaeuser Company Foundation, members of the Weyerhaeuser family, and Janet and Jack Creighton.

Additional support was provided by the Association for Asian Studies First Book Subvention Program, the Chiang Ching-kuo Foundation for International Scholarly Exchange, and the James P. Geiss and Margaret Y. Hsu Foundation.

Copyright © 2020 by the University of Washington Press

Composed in Minion Pro, typeface designed by Robert Slimbach
Maps by Pease Press Cartography, www.peasepress.com

All rights reserved. No part of this publication may be reproduced or transmitted in any form or by any means, electronic or mechanical, including photocopy, recording, or any information storage or retrieval system, without permission in writing from the publisher.

UNIVERSITY OF WASHINGTON PRESS
uwapress.uw.edu

LIBRARY OF CONGRESS CATALOGING-IN-PUBLICATION DATA
Names: Miller, Ian Matthew, author.
Title: Fir and empire : the transformation of forests in early modern China / Ian Matthew Miller.
Description: 1st. | Seattle : University of Washington Press, [2020] | Series: Weyerhaeuser environmental books | Includes bibliographical references and index.
Identifiers: LCCN 2019046834 (print) | LCCN 2019046835 (ebook) | ISBN 9780295747330 (hardcover) | ISBN 9780295747347 (ebook)
Subjects: LCSH: Deforestation—China—History—960-1644. | Forest management—China—History—960-1644.
Classification: LCC SD418.3.C6 M55 2020 (print) | LCC SD418.3.C6 (ebook) | DDC 333.750951—dc23
LC record available at https://lccn.loc.gov/2019046834
LC ebook record available at https://lccn.loc.gov/2019046835

ISBN 9780295752877 (paperback)

The paper used in this publication is acid free and meets the minimum requirements of American National Standard for Information Sciences—Permanence of Paper for Printed Library Materials, ANSI Z39.48-1984.∞

For my grandparents

CONTENTS

Foreword: The Great Reforestation, by Paul S. Sutter ix
Acknowledgments xv
List of Maps, Figures, and Tables xix
Naming Conventions xxi

INTRODUCTION 3

ONE.   The End of Abundance 21

TWO.   Boundaries, Taxes, and Property Rights 37

THREE.   Hunting Households and Sojourner Families 58

FOUR.   Deeds, Shares, and Pettifoggers 77

FIVE.   Wood and Water, Part I: Tariff Timber 97

SIX.   Wood and Water, Part II: Naval Timber 117

SEVEN.   Beijing Palaces and the Ends of Empire 140

CONCLUSION 160

Appendix A: Forests in Tax Data 171
Appendix B: Note on Sources 177
Glossary 181

Notes 189
Bibliography 227
Index 257

FOREWORD
The Great Reforestation

PAUL S. SUTTER

As the field of environmental history has internationalized during the past two decades, few world areas have seen as rich a florescence of scholarship as has China. The attractions of China as a subject for environmental historians are obvious. One is an archival record stretching back for millennia, a record that, presuming one has the requisite language skills, can open up deep histories of human-environmental interaction that are difficult to recreate for most other parts of the world. Another, paradoxically, is a contemporary history of rapidly accelerating environmental change that has cemented China's central place in an emerging Anthropocene narrative. As even a casual observer today quickly realizes—as I did when I first visited in the summer of 2019—China is at once a staggeringly old and a startlingly new place. Any satisfying history of China's dramatic recent transformations, including its profound environmental transformations, must build upon an understanding of its deep history.

No historian has done more to establish a dominant environmental narrative for China's deep history than Mark Elvin, whose magisterial *The Retreat of the Elephants: An Environmental History of China* (2004) used the decline of wild elephant populations as proxy evidence for what he saw as the defining trend in China's environmental history: "long-term deforestation and the removal of original vegetation cover." In 5000 BCE, Asian elephants inhabited almost all of forested China, but the disappearance of forest cover has forced their withdrawal to a few refugia in the southwest, hard against the borders with Burma and Laos, today. Elvin called this process "the Great Deforestation." While he recognized that there were distinctive pulses of deforestation in Chinese history, including one during what he called the "medieval economic revolution" of a thousand years ago and another beginning in the seventeenth century that accelerated through the nineteenth century, he nonetheless assumed "the Great Deforestation" to have been relatively continuous across several millennia. And like the retreat of Asian elephants who relied on this forest cover for their survival, this "great deforestation" had a southerly direction.

Enter Ian M. Miller, who has produced a masterpiece of historical detective work that fundamentally transforms our understanding of China's early modern environmental history. In *Fir and Empire*, Miller revises Elvin's narrative of steady premodern deforestation in China by making innovative use of sources, many local and mundane, that provide him with indirect but nonetheless substantial access to the land use and land cover changes that marked South China's forest history. In doing so, he shows that the dominant trend in the region between 1000 and 1600 CE—between the forest crisis of Elvin's "medieval economic revolution" and the onset of profound changes beginning in the seventeenth century that led to another full-blown forest crisis in the nineteenth century—was, in fact, *afforestation*. Rather than Elvin's "Great Deforestation," Miller reveals, the period was marked by what we might call a "Great Reforestation."

Before getting to the fascinating specifics that undergird this sweeping revision, it is important to make clear what Miller is *not* arguing. He does not dispute that a defining long-term trend in China's environmental history has been the removal of what Elvin called "original vegetation cover," a process that accompanied the spread of Han peoples. The retreat of China's elephants was the result of real and transformative environmental changes that occurred across millennia, as China lost its wild forests and the creatures that called them home. Ecologically, the new anthropogenic forest biome produced by the great reforestation paled in comparison to what was lost. What Miller does want to disabuse us of, however, is the idea that these changes were synonymous with a vast loss of forest cover and, as importantly, that they somehow resulted from a centuries-long failure of environmental governance in China. Beyond his major point that the centuries between 1000 and 1600 CE saw South China reclad in plantation fir and other commercial species, Miller also argues that these centuries saw the emergence of a unique system of forest management that stands as an influential precursor to the modern forestry regimes that spread around the world in the centuries after his story ends. *Fir and Empire* not only upends our sense of Chinese history as a story of inexorable forest decline, then, but it also demonstrates that early modern China had a surprisingly innovative history of forest management.

For Miller, this story begins with a subtle but crucial change in tax policy at the beginning of the Southern Song dynasty (1127–79): the state, which to that point had only taxed agricultural land, began to tax forest lands (*shan*) as well. To do so, it surveyed and mapped these lands, and it required landowners to register their forest lands with the state. But it did not tax all of South China's forested landscape. Instead, Miller argues, the Song only taxed those areas where landowners had planted trees. Indeed, these records serve as critical proxy data in Miller's reconstruction of this new forested biome. To put it another way, this shift in taxation policy was not a process of the state coming into and regulating the forested commons. Rather, it was a story of the state recognizing that large areas planted in trees were effectively in a new kind of *agricultural* land use and should be taxed accordingly. Moreover, Miller suggests, for those who were working to regenerate South China's forests, a modest tax was a small price to pay for the state's legitimation of planted forests as a form of private property. The result of this shift was the development of a privatized and market-based forestry regime—an empire of forestry without foresters or a centralized forestry bureau—that produced a "silvicultural revolution" which quickly spread across South China. This revolution created not only a novel forest biome but also a distinctive zone of enclosure and environmental administration that sat between the agricultural lowlands and the still-unregulated highlands. So began the great reforestation.

Miller finds persistent evidence of this revolution in all sorts of other quotidian sources as well. He notes a shift during this period from the state's use of corvée labor to gather products from commons forests to its imposition of silver taxes on workers, who then had to earn wages in the private timber market to pay their taxes. This, he suggests, was clear evidence of a transition from wild forests to planted forests, a change that meant far less commons forest was open to timber and other resource gathering. He uses forest deeds and tenancy contracts in Huizhou, the epicenter of this revolution, to show how private property holdings in planted forest lands, with their long-maturing trees, evolved in complicated ways across these centuries. He demonstrates how the state managed planted forests indirectly by imposing tariffs that claimed a portion of the private timber supply coming to market as an alternative to state-led timbering operations. And he shows how the substantial demands for timber from several ambitious shipbuilding campaigns, culminating with the construction of Zheng He's famous fleet that explored the Indian Ocean and the South China Sea in the early fifteenth century, were met by relying on the private market in plantation timber, and the custom revenues it produced, rather than on a centralized forestry administration. Remarkably, Miller finds that these shipbuilding efforts produced no evidence of substantial stress on South China's timber supplies. The only construction effort that this new forested biome could not accommodate was the Ming-era building of Beijing into an imperial capital, an effort that required large old-growth timber that could only be found in the recesses of the Yangzi River gorges.

By examining these various tax, deed, and timber market records, Miller is able to skillfully render a remarkable composite sketch of a forestry regime that was at once highly productive and relatively stable across centuries, a regime that a series of Chinese empires managed remotely and largely through the mechanisms of tax policy, property law, and market regulation. Precisely because there was no centralized forestry bureau, and the sorts of archival records such bureaus tend to produce, this silvicultural revolution had remained hidden from view. Miller's signal achievement is its rediscovery.

This regime, and the estimated twenty million acres of planted forest land that it produced, came unraveled in the seventeenth, eighteenth, and nineteenth centuries, just as various European nations, Japan, and the United States were developing modern, statist forestry bureaucracies. China's nineteenth-century forest crisis was dire, and the absence of a forestry bureau to manage the problem seemed a conservation failure. Given that reality, it has been easy to assume that deforestation and weak forest regulation were timeless features of Chinese life. But it was not a crisis that had been building across a millennium in the absence of any effective state intervention. Rather, as Miller so persuasively shows, it was a recent failure of an innovative silvicultural system, indirect and market-driven, that environmental historians of China have largely missed. That system certainly had its social and ecological costs; as planted forests climbed the hills in South China after 1100 CE, they replaced natural forests and displaced native peoples who had relied on their commons resources. But those planted forests, which sprang from the tax reforms produced by the "Song wood crisis," successfully supplied the considerable timber demands of the Song, Yuan, and Ming dynasties. That was a major achievement. More than that, though, Miller helps us to see that this anthropogenic forested biome, planted and maintained by local landowners and their workers, was an unprecedented landscape transformation for a preindustrial state. By rediscovering the great reforestation of South China, and the administrative policies and practices that enabled it, Ian M. Miller has similarly transformed how we understand China's early modern environmental history.

ACKNOWLEDGMENTS

This project began its life at Harvard University under the supervision of Michael Szonyi and with advice from Peter K. Bol, Ian Jared Miller, and Paul Warde. It grew by leaps and bounds at the Yale Program in Agrarian Studies, where I was hosted by James C. Scott and K. Sivaramakrishnan, and during two visiting fellowships at the Max Planck Institute for the History of Science at the invitation of Dagmar Schäfer and Shih-Pei Chen. During its awkward adolescence, I was greatly aided by insights from Paul S. Sutter and Andrew Berzanskis at the University of Washington Press, and from two anonymous reviewers. I am astounded to find it now approaching maturity.

Over the years, I have acquired many other debts. In some ways, this book still feels like my half of a conversation with John S. Lee, one that started after Michael Szonyi's seminar on late imperial China more than ten years ago. At Harvard, Javier Cha, Sakura Christmas, Tarryn Li-Min Chun, Devon Dear, Maura Dykstra, Devin Fitzgerald, Huan Jin, Macabe Keliher, Angela Huizi Sun, Eric Schluessel, and Wen Yu were important intellectual companions. My path as an environmental historian was decisively influenced by seminars with James L. Watson and Ling Zhang. My research trips were funded by generous grants from the Fairbank Center for Chinese Studies and the Frederick Sheldon Travelling Fellowship. During my fieldwork in China, I learned a great deal from Zhang Weiran, Liang Hongsheng, and Li Pingliang. Chris Coggins was also kind enough to invite me on another research trip with him and his students. At Yale, I benefited from the insights and companionship of Anthony Acciavatti, Luke Bender, and

Sabine Cadeau. At Max Planck, I learned from conversations with Kathlene Baldanza, He Bian, Qun Che, Desmond Cheung, Gregory Scott, and especially Aurelia Campbell and Joseph Dennis. My colleagues in the St. John's University history department have been exceptionally supportive, with particular thanks to Shahla Hussain, Susie Pak, Nerina Rustomji, and my predecessor Jeffrey Kinkley. Lillian M. Li started me down the path toward Chinese history and remains a key adviser.

Several sections in this book have been particularly influenced by individual conversations. Devin Fitzgerald referred me to the rare book whose images are featured on the cover and in chapter 7. Feedback from David Bello and Micah Muscolino forced me to clarify and strengthen several major claims. The opening anecdote is based on suggestions from Jonathan Schlesinger. Comments from Peter Perdue and Valerie Hansen made me take chapter 2 back to the drawing board. Early elements of chapter 3 were influenced by He Bian; I received insight on a later draft from Dorothy Ko, Chuck Wooldridge, and Madeleine Zelin at the Columbia Modern China Seminar. Chapter 4 was heavily influenced by Maura Dykstra and Joseph McDermott. Chapter 5 was informed by conversations with Meng Zhang and revised with key feedback from Ling Zhang. Chapter 7 owes a great deal to Aurelia Campbell. I also learned a huge amount at "The Wood Age in Asia," a conference I co-organized with Bradley Camp Davis, Brian Lander, John S. Lee, and K. Sivaramakrishnan and funded by the American Council of Learned Societies and the Chiang Ching-kuo Foundation for International Scholarly Exchange. There and elsewhere I benefited from discussions with Karl Appuhn, John Elijah Bender, Tristan Brown, Yuan Chen, Fabian Drixler, David Fedman, Stevan Harrell, Kuang-chi Hung, Jung Lee, Joanna Linzer, Robert Marks, Pamela McElwee, Nancy Lee Peluso, Larissa Pitts, Holly Stephens, and Faizah Zakaria.

Finally, I must thank my family, without whom none of this would have been possible. My grandparents, Betty and Wally Miller Sr. and Bob and Vi Fogle Uretz, have been enormously supportive of my education, and this book is dedicated to them. My parents, Jane and Wally Miller, and their partners, Allan Horowitz and Christina Smith, have helped in too many ways to count. My in-laws, He Guomian and Xiao Wenjia, have provided both insight and support. My children, Rye and Kai, have been constant sources of inspiration (and distraction) and accompanied me on more than a few brainstorming "trips to the park." Most of all, I want to thank my wife,

Evelyn, for all the patience, prodding, and persistence it took to bring this to fruition.

Unless otherwise noted, all translations are my own, as are any remaining mistakes.

MAPS, FIGURES, AND TABLES

MAPS

2.1	Patterns of forest registration, early to mid-1500s	53
2.2	Forests as a percentage of taxable acreage, early to mid-1500s	54
3.1	The Huizhou and Hakka diasporas	74
7.1	The Ming and Qing logging frontiers	158

FIGURES

5.1	Night rain on Longjiang customs	108
6.1	Diagram of a flat-decked warship	136
6.2	Form for recording timber purchases	137
7.1	Lowering logs off a cliff	149
7.2	Capstan across a chasm	150
7.3	Floating logs through large rapids	151
7.4	Fatigues and harms of transport	152
7.5	Violent fires and robbery	153
7.6	Snakes and tigers run rampant	154

TABLES

5.1	Bamboo and timber taxes, 1328	106
7.1	Timber yields from imperial logging	157

A.1 Changes in forest acreage in Huizhou, by county 173
A.2 Changes in forest acreage in five southern prefectures 174
A.3 Changes in total acreage following the 1581 surveys 175

NAMING CONVENTIONS

Places have multiple names. Because this book covers a long time period, many names have changed. For clarity, I use Ming place-names throughout the text, many of which are the same as modern place-names and therefore easily recognizable. In contexts where the contemporary name was different, I indicate it in parentheses the first time it appears. For example, the primary capital of the Northern Song is given as Kaifeng (Bianjing).

People also have multiple names. Throughout the text, I choose the single name that provides the most clarity, even if this comes at the expense of consistency. This means I use temple names for Song rulers, Mongol names for Yuan rulers, and reign period names for Ming rulers. The only exception is Zhu Yuanzhang, whom I call by his personal name to avoid anachronism around the founding of the Ming dynasty. Most non-emperors are called by their personal names, but here, too, there are exceptions: I call Wang Yangming by his better-known courtesy name.

Even plants have multiple names. When naming trees in the body text, I generally provide a common name and the Chinese term but not the binomial nomenclature. In many cases this avoids both anachronism and false precision. For example the "fir" in my title translates a character (*shan* 杉) that can refer to multiple species. In South China this is often *Cunninghamia lanceolata*; in Japan, the same character is pronounced *sugi* and generally refers to *Cryptomeria japonica*; in either context, *shan/sugi* historically applied to multiple other species. Further information can be found in the glossary.

FIR AND EMPIRE

INTRODUCTION

IN 1793, RETURNING FROM GREAT BRITAIN'S FIRST DIPLOMATIC mission to China, the envoy George Macartney traveled through South China. In his diary, Macartney noted his impression of the industrious agriculture of the region. Near the border between Zhejiang and Jiangxi, the Irish earl wrote that he "did not see a spot in the whole way that was not cultivated with infinite industry," noting that "wherever the sides of hills admit of it, they are wrought into terraces, graduated with different crops" and that "the ponds and reservoirs are a public concern." Finally, Macartney observed that "the mountains are all newly planted with trees, chiefly firs, a great many thousands of acres. This is the case almost the whole way from hence to Canton."[1] Twenty-five years later, the botanist Clarke Abel accompanied another British mission to China and left even more extensive writings on its forests. He, too, noted that the hills along the Yangzi River were covered in "plantations of oaks and firs."[2] In the accounts of these two travelers, South China was dense with trees, and specifically with plantations of young firs.

Two hundred years ago, these British observers saw something that modern scholars have often overlooked: mountains full of conifers planted by human hands. No less than the ponds and farms on the lower slopes, Abel and Macartney recognized these forests as products of human cultivation. The mountains were covered with trees, not through an absence of human action, but *because people had put them there*, blanketing the upland landscape from Hangzhou to Canton. In Europe, foresters began promoting this type of conifer plantation right around the time of their travels, but in South China, forests "newly planted with trees" were not a new phenomenon. The firs that Abel and Macartney saw were the clones and offspring of trees first planted in the twelfth and thirteenth centuries. These were not just anthropogenic forests; they were forests that had been made and remade by human hands, repeatedly, for centuries.

Like any good story, the history of these fir plantations begins with a crisis. For hundreds of years, people had used and modified China's forests without calamity, encouraging the growth of useful trees through controlled burning, selective cutting, and small-scale planting. But in the eleventh century, the customary measures governing these behaviors began to fail. Wood-hungry people stripped the most densely settled regions of useful trees, and even the heavily wooded borderlands reported excessive logging. As overharvesting threatened the stability of wood supplies, government administrators also faced escalating pressures to obtain even more timber for forts, cities, dikes, and ships. In response to this climax of demands, officials and subjects alike looked for new sources of timber and new ways to conserve. They tightened regulations on community woodlots, sought out new logging frontiers, and extended the purview of state and private silviculture. Given time, any combination of these strategies might have resolved the wood crisis. But they were not given time to mature. In the late 1120s, warfare and flooding brought chaos to central China. When the dust settled, private silviculture and commerce survived, but the nascent state forestry system was gone.

Over the next five centuries Chinese landowners elaborated and spread the forms of forest management first innovated in response to the wood crisis. Planting the fast-growing China fir (*shan/sha* 杉) noted by Abel and Macartney, they supplied wood-hungry markets with a reliable stream of timber rafts. But commercial fir planting did more than solve the immediate supply crisis; it also proved astonishingly responsive to changing needs. As demand grew and prices rose, more people planted more trees, and fir plantations spread from a handful of prefectures to cover much of the upland south. In addition to fir, forest owners grew a range of other commercially valuable woody plants, including pine and camphor for timber; bamboo for poles and paper; palm for thatch and fiber; tung, lacquer, tallow tree, and camellia for oils and resins; mulberry to feed silkworms; tea to drink; and a wide variety of species for fuel, fruits, and nuts. Starting in a handful of prefectures below the Yangzi River's final southward bend, landowners replaced self-seeding woodlands with hand-planted tree farms, extending the intensive agriculture of the river valleys into an intensive silviculture in the hills. Over the following centuries, tendrils of tree plantations gradually extended as far south as Canton and as far west as the Yangzi River gorges.

Environment and institutions constrained the making of these forests across several different scales. At each level of analysis, ecology was a key piece of the puzzle: vegetative processes guided tree-growth patterns, species interactions affected community composition, and climatic conditions limited the extent of the forest biome.[3] Human actions also provided important building blocks at each of these scales: planters guided tree growth from seed to sapling to stump; they selected what trees to grow together and how to harvest them, affecting the age and species composition of each stand. Communal norms and commercial demand also informed where and when people chose to plant what trees. But if we want to explain the emergence of the regional forest biome, we must examine the keystones that held the forest assemblage together: the large-scale institutions that emerged to govern, document, and profit from commercial forests. In other words, we cannot understand China's forests without exploring the dynamics of Chinese markets and Chinese empire.[4]

FORESTS, BUREAUCRACY, AND ECONOMY

At the largest scales, silviculture was driven by the demands of states and markets and by the institutions they established to govern the wood supply. As scholars of political ecology have demonstrated, states build power over the environment by specifying what forms of knowledge matter. By surveying woodlands and counting trees, states produce information about the land in order to extract more products, making "forests" that fit their needs for timber and fuel, and ultimately their desire for control.[5] Commercial markets also transform the nature of woodlands, by turning the fruits of nature into discrete, fungible commodities. By cutting trees from their biotic communities, merchants and market regulators turn individual plants into interchangeable "timber."[6] By standardizing concepts and measurements, bureaucrats render woodlands and their products "legible" at ever-higher levels of abstraction, enabling centralized control and specialized expertise.

By abstracting trees and timber from their social-ecological dependencies, these abstractions also do violence to the interlinked communities—human and floral—from which the wood emerges.[7]

But the processes that turn wood and woodlands into abstract objects are not historically constant. Administrative forests and commodity timber did not leap, fully formed, from the minds of Kafkaesque bureaucrats. Instead, the flattened representations of woody growth on paper ledgers developed only through erratic attempts to resolve new pressures, especially growing competition for fuel and building materials. In some conceptions, these processes were specific to the early modern period, an era that German sociologist Werner Sombart called a "wooden age."[8] And China was far from the only early modern empire to face a climax of wood demand—or to undergo a revolution in forest governance—in the middle centuries of the past millennium. The conditions during China's eleventh-century wood crisis, including urbanization, military competition, and overseas expansion, were strikingly similar to those in Europe starting around 1500. In response to wood shortages, real or perceived, many European states also expanded their forest oversight, creating new forms of environmental governance and expertise in the process.[9] The European experience is, in turn, central to our modern understanding of the relationships between forestry, bureaucracy, and economy.

Because the European experience is ancestral to our contemporary understandings of forest, it is worth examining a brief history of the development of European forestry. Domestically, forest surveys were a key tool that European rulers used to transform their medieval courts into early modern states. The word *forest*, and its cousins *forst, forêt*, and *foresta*, originated as administrative terms for sylvan jurisdictions controlled by noble or urban estates, some of which were not even particularly wooded.[10] States expanded the purview of these forest jurisdictions, but only gradually. Venice was a key innovator in surveying its terra firma forests starting in the sixteenth century.[11] In most of northern and western Europe, courts only surveyed forests beyond their royal estates in the seventeenth and eighteenth centuries.[12] It was this expansion of oversight, and of forest survey in particular, that transformed the administrative term *forest* into a near synonym for the descriptive term *woodland*. *Forest*, in turn, acquired its modern ecological implications only in the nineteenth and twentieth centuries, as foresters used their newly founded professional journals and academies to develop ideas about climates, soils, and sustainability.[13] In other words, the expansive meaning of the term *forest* tracks the growing ambition of European states to control natural resources, and ultimately to measure and manage woodland ecology. But forestry did not emerge as a purely domestic affair.

As Europe's early modern forestry offices changed the administration of forests at home, their courts also sent surveyors, merchants, and botanists to traverse entire continents in search of even more materials. As they traveled, these agents sent home reports of new forests and new species in service of science, empire, and profit. Starting from the Rhine, the timber frontier moved north and east along the Baltic, then west to the Americas, and eventually south to Africa and Asia.[14] But whether they represented scientific societies, official monopolies, or private interests, European surveyors were all looking for the same thing—timber that they could substitute for more familiar domestic supplies. In the process, they classified and commodified a cascade of tree species, from Norway spruce, to Riga fir, American white pine, and Indian teak.[15] Europeans, most notably German- and French-trained foresters and Scottish surgeons and naturalists, left an indelible mark on forestry, botany, and environmental science.[16] British botanists even named South China's leading timber tree for one of their own, Scottish surgeon James Cunningham, who sent the first specimens back from Zhejiang in 1702.[17] Their terms, concepts, and principles still inform the way we understand the natural world. Yet if we strip away the past two hundred years of development, and return to Europe's forest oversight prior to 1800, China's experience looks substantially less foreign.

In China, it was a different interpenetration of bureaucracy and commerce that led to the transformation of the wooded landscape. While European states expanded their bureaucracies to oversee domestic forests and colonized abroad to expand their timber supplies, Chinese states largely did not. But the absence of bureaucratic forestry did not mean that Chinese states abandoned forest oversight entirely. Instead, administrators oversaw forests under their general-purpose supervision of taxable land, labor, and commerce. They surveyed forests in the twelfth century, five hundred years before similar surveys in Europe. They levied peasants to cut wood and ship lumber. They taxed and regulated timber shipments at the market. In the fourteenth century, they standardized *shan* 山 (literally "mountain") as the single official term for taxable forests. But instead of developing an increasingly centralized, professionalized forestry service, Chinese states minimized direct forest oversight and focused on taxing and regulating private commerce in timber. Without the development of a forestry profession, "forest" (*shan*) remained an administrative category, specifying tax rates, but carrying limited implications for land cover, let alone ecology.

China's limited, largely market-based oversight was nonetheless enough to provoke a silvicultural revolution. Despite the near-total absence of bureaucratic forest management, China's general-purpose fiscal policies enabled an astonishingly productive commerce in timber and other forest products. Through experiment and accident, administrative reforms promoted exclusive land title, standardized timber grades and prices, and eliminated menial woodcutting corvée, freeing peasants to work in the commercial labor markets. While built on very different principles and institutions, they established what European thinkers might have called a "free market"—an arena of independent timber producers competing to meet wide-ranging demand. Officials intervened in this market to fill their own needs, and occasionally perverted it with harsh rules and excessive extractions, but for the most part they kept regulation to a minimum, and gradually reduced tax rates to nominal levels. Under these conditions, timber production boomed. Between 1200 and 1600, the acreage of fir plantations and the volume of the Yangzi River timber trade increased many times over, almost entirely due to the initiative of private loggers, tree farmers, and timber merchants.

In some ways, the timber markets that emerged under this benign neglect look astonishingly modern. As Joseph McDermott has shown, forest owners developed sophisticated mechanisms for dividing risk and return, effectively a futures market in timber.[18] Officials supplied their construction projects through a fractional tariff on merchant timber and by purchasing supplies from the swelling trade in low-cost wood products. By the end of the sixteenth century, salaried workers, not corvée laborers, cut government fuel and built government ships and buildings.

Commercialization brought negative consequences as well, many of them familiar to the modern world. By maximizing the production of quantifiable commodities like timber, tree farmers caused a clear decline in unquantified ecological goods. They destroyed or degraded habitats for commercially marginal flora and fauna, especially large mammals like tigers and elephants.[19] They also reduced land cover, leading to erosion of slopes and sedimentation of rivers and wetlands.[20] By demanding exclusive ownership of forests, tree planters also dispossessed community members of their traditional claims to fuel, forage, and wild foods.[21] They displaced upland, non-Han peoples from their lands and from their long-standing roles producing forest products to trade in the lowlands.[22] All of these trends—good and ill—would emerge later in European states and their colonies.

The flip side of China's precocious commercialization was that developments in state forestry were stunted. As detailed below, there were at least three intervals when Chinese states created or expanded their forest administrations, the first in response to the eleventh-century wood crisis, the second during the imperial buildup of the early fifteenth century, and the third during the bureaucratic revival of the sixteenth century. Yet choice and happenstance repeatedly shifted policy away from centralized oversight and toward indirect, largely market-based regulation. In Europe, civil servants trained as specialized foresters and botanists to staff government bureaus and conduct colonial surveys.[23] These professions, in turn, were key to the development of forestry, biology, and environmental science.[24] By contrast, the lack of a state forest service in China meant that silviculture was largely shunned by the educated elite, who treated it as a minor branch of agriculture and confined botany to tangential aspects of medical herbology and local geography. This is why the principal timber tree of South China was named by (and for) British botanists, not Chinese ones. The productivity of China's private timber growers allowed the state to develop a very efficient, laissez-faire natural resource administration, but it also short-circuited the development of more specialized environmental expertise.

Whatever its eventual shortcomings, China's forest system was innovative enough that it was also influential abroad, most notably in Korea and Japan. In Korea, the court specifically cited Chinese precedent when it developed oversight of timber forests in the fifteenth century—also quite precocious by world standards. Korean forestry subsequently diverged substantially from the Chinese model, but it continued to reference Chinese institutions and terminology.[25] In parts of Japan, the forms of forest oversight that developed in the seventeenth and eighteenth centuries also look astonishingly like Chinese silviculture.[26] While there is not yet specific evidence of Chinese influence on Japanese tree planting, Japan adapted Chinese models for many other institutions and may have done so for forestry as well. Both Korea and Japan used the Chinese term *shan* 山 (Korean: *san*, Japanese: *san/sen/yama*) to designate their administrative forests.

Paradoxically, despite their related trajectories, Japan has often been upheld as an example of successful forest management, while China has been cited as an example of failed or absent oversight.[27] The reasons for this discrepancy probably have more to do with their histories after 1800 than their achievements to that point. When Japan modernized in the late nineteenth and early twentieth centuries, it integrated native forms of silviculture with German-derived scientific forestry, which it then exported to its colonies in Korea and Taiwan, as well as to mainland China.[28] In the same interval, China experienced decades of warfare, rebellion, and revolution that undercut most attempts to modernize and badly degraded its woodlands. As a result, Japan's modern forest transition was well ordered and well documented, while China's was disjointed and poorly understood.

Without a clear chain of documentation, the first environmental histories of China largely assumed that it did not have an effective forest system and turned to other forms of evidence to explore ecological change. Mark Elvin, in his highly influential book *The Retreat of the Elephants*, uses elephants as a proxy for the woodlands they inhabited. Extrapolating from the "retreat of the elephants," and a range of anecdotal evidence, he asserts that China's forest canopy declined in the face of Chinese expansion toward the south and west.[29] Other works, most notably Robert B. Marks's *Tigers, Rice, Silk, and Silt*, also rely on a combination of descriptive evidence and proxy data to make the case that uncontrolled growth led to catastrophic degradation, especially in the eighteenth and nineteenth centuries.[30] But is China's catastrophic nineteenth century evidence of long-term environmental dysfunction or of a functioning forest system that collapsed under novel pressures? Without an alternative framework, and despite a lack of clear evidence of degradation prior to the eighteenth and nineteenth centuries, Elvin's long-term narrative has been accepted as evidence of a millennia-long tide of deforestation.

In this study, I revise this straightforward narrative of deforestation to tell the history of China's distinct form of forest oversight. While China did not produce European-style forestry bureaus—at least not until the twentieth century—it did develop other institutions with jurisdiction over wood and woodlands. These institutions provide ample sources of evidence on social and environmental change. Government land surveys give a relatively broad view of China's forest acreage, at least of those forests registered with the state for tax payment. Forest deeds, timber tariffs, and shipyard purchases can be used to estimate the size and growth of wood markets. There are also ample records of official corvée, including the local woodcutters levied to provide fuel to government offices and the massive expeditions that logged palace-building timber in the far southwest. While imperfect, these documents allow us to replace anecdotal narratives and indirect proxies with a more synoptic view of the forests.

Instead of *deforestation*, these documents give evidence of a massive *transformation* of China's forests. Loggers did remove large swaths of the woodland canopy between 1000 and 1600, and even more thereafter. But the cutting of China's old-growth woodlands did not entail a total loss of tree cover. Instead, strong demand for timber led planters to cultivate new trees to replace those they removed, rather than leaving clearances to waste or converting them to farmland. This entailed a reduction of ecological diversity and complexity, but it was a far cry from total deforestation. It was only in the nineteenth century that China's forests began to face catastrophe, brought on by novel pressures that destabilized a formerly functional system. Despite major differences from the better-known European experience, and even the Japanese tradition, China had an effective system of forest oversight that supplied large quantities of commercial wood products and prevented catastrophic degradation, a system that provides ample evidence of institutional and environmental change across more than six centuries.

LANDS OF CAMPHOR AND FIR

The history of Chinese forest oversight is largely a regional one, a product of the South Chinese environment that transformed the nature and culture of the region itself. To understand the changes wrought by commercial silviculture, we must therefore consider its ecological and cultural precedents in the region. South China is largely defined by its northern border at the Yangzi River. North of the river is a vast sedimentary plain that was China's historical heartland. South of the river—"Jiangnan" in Chinese—is a far more variegated landscape of coastal wetlands and rice-growing plains divided by mountains above five hundred meters and peaks above one thousand. Jiangnan had a long history as a salient of Han culture, home to refugees from North China who formed cultural hybrids as they mixed with the natives of the riverine south. Further south are steep river valleys descending to the southeast coast in Zhejiang, Fujian, and Guangdong. Further west are the major rivers and seasonal lakes that feed the Yangzi River: the Gan River and Poyang Lake in Jiangxi and the Xiang River and Dongting Lake in Hunan. In these river valleys, creoles of Han culture had developed for hundreds of years, even as the highlands remained home to distinct, non-Han groups of hunters and shifting cultivators.[31] Thus, while Jiangnan's northern boundary was stable at the Yangzi River, its southern and western boundaries were unstable and fractal, with local and regional societies interpenetrating and mixing according to climate, topography, and changing institutions.

In addition to incorporating Han migrants and culture, South China had a long and distinctive political-ecological relationship with the north. North China, and especially its great plain, had been wood-poor since early history; by contrast, the south was often noted for its wealth of sylvan resources.[32] So great was this association that for centuries the principal jurisdiction on Poyang Lake was named "camphor prefecture" (*yuzhang jun*).[33] Even when different states controlled the regions north and south of the Yangzi, they were linked by trade in timber. This exchange was only strengthened when great empires unified North and South China.[34] But the south was not evenly wooded, even in early historical time. Pollen evidence suggests that large parts of Jiangnan were cleared for agriculture by the third or fourth millennium BCE.[35] The articulation of mountains throughout the region meant the south was riven with the borderlands, where highlanders traded forest products for the agricultural goods of lowland farmers. The effective boundaries of rule formed along topographical lines: while the lowlands were settled by sedentary farmers in Chinese-style states, the uplands long remained the territory of non-Sinitic peoples. In other words, the south's famous sylvan wealth was the wealth of the *upland* south.

From its first appearance in a small corner of this diverse region, silviculture transformed the landscape of South China and further warped the complex gradients between regional cultures, highlands and lowlands. The principal species of commercial timber tree, China fir (*shan*/*sha* 杉, *Cunninghamia lanceolata*) is too widespread in cultivation to determine its natal habitat, but it is certainly native to South China, and probably to Huizhou, western Zhejiang, and Jiangxi, the same region that first attested to commercial timber plantations around 1100. Institutional developments only reinforced this early advantage. The first forest surveys, first licenses for timber merchants, and first reforms to end woodcutting corvée were all products of this general region, further reinforcing the reliability, legibility, and efficiency of its timber markets.

As the commerce in timber grew, each of Jiangnan's major constituencies was involved in spreading silviculture into neighboring parts of the south. State surveyors gradually registered forests in Jiangxi and Fujian, and later in parts of Guangdong and Guangxi. Customs officials standardized timber grades and lowered tariffs throughout the extended Yangzi River market. Huizhou merchants promoted timber planting along the Yangzi River and the southeast coast. Porters from Jiangxi carried seedlings over the mountains to the far south and southwest. They collectively spread land title, commercial regulation, and silvicultural expertise together with the fir trees themselves, transforming diverse, distinctive, open-access woodlands into a blanket of privately owned timber trees. While important local and regional distinctions remained, these interconnected forest constituencies made the ecological and institutional landscapes of the south look increasingly uniform.

By extending the cultivated landscape from the river valley into the mountains, timber planters gradually shifted the boundaries between state and non-state space, and between Han and non-Han peoples. James C. Scott shows in his history of upland Southeast Asia that state actions like taxation and forced labor tend to partition the landscape between dominant ethnic groups occupying "state space" in the lowlands and other groups practicing the "art of not being governed" in the highlands.[36] In keeping with this observation, the principal name that Chinese people used for themselves until the late nineteenth century was the administrative classifier "subject" (*min*), not the ethnic classifier "Han."[37] From the state's perspective the difference between lowland "subjects" (*min*) and upland "barbarians" (*man*) was that subjects were sedentary and paid taxes through their individual households, while barbarians moved around and paid "tribute" (*gong*) through their tribal leaders. As David A. Bello demonstrates, this meant that the boundaries dividing "Hanspace" from other zones ran through ecotones, the borderlands where fixed-field agriculture gradually became too marginal to support.[38] For centuries, these lines separated taxpaying rice farmers in the lowlands from non-taxpaying swidden cultivators in the uplands. Yet even within formal compliance to the state, there was substantial room for negotiation and resistance. As Michael Szonyi demonstrates in his study of Ming military households, subjects could choose when and how to submit to the demands of the state.[39]

South China highlanders long played an outsize role in southern timber production, logging large trees that they sold into the lowland economy. Until the advent of commercial silviculture, their activities belonged to the tributary economy, not the tax economy, and they were classified as tribal peoples, not as subjects. By allowing the farm-like cultivation of the uplands, tree plantations fundamentally transformed this equation. While distinct from grain-based agriculture, silviculture was nonetheless fixed in place and productive enough to tax, allowing "state space" (or "Hanspace") to extend into the highlands. At the fractal borders between the Han lowlands and the non-Han uplands, a new region emerged, with its own distinct biome and institutions. In this Upland Jiangnan, centered on Huizhou, a new class of subjects planted trees like field crops, registered their forests to pay taxes to the state, and produced timber as a market commodity. Later, other groups of subjects emerged, most notably the Hakka (*kejia*, or "sojourner families"), who traveled out of the mountainous borderlands of Fujian, Jiangxi, and Guangdong to plant trees, tea, and other upland crops across South China.[40] These former swidden cultivators made an uneasy place for themselves on the margins, considered less barbaric than the acephalous peoples who retreated further into the mountains, but too peripatetic and culturally foreign to be fully accepted into lowland society.

In effect, the extension of human control to earlier stages of tree growth transferred the forest trades from the upland complex of logging and shifting cultivation to the lowland complex of sedentary agriculture. The newfound conformity of silviculture to the norms of taxation and property law allowed the extension of state surveillance into the uplands of South China. But forest peoples negotiated their own terms in the new administrative bargain. Some, like Huizhou merchants and landowners, became state subjects par excellence, keeping the best records in China, submitting to regular taxation, and mediating many of the state's interactions with the forest economy.[41] Some, like Hakka tree planters, accepted only provisional forms of state sovereignty. Even as they registered their households and submitted taxes, their mobility and distinctive practices enabled greater avoidance of official oversight and left them open to suspicions of heterodoxy.[42] Most of the upland south lay between Huizhou and the Hakka heartland and fell somewhere along the continuum between these two political strategies. This region represented a novel biome where human behavior toward woody plants was the primary factor promoting the growth of fir and other commercially valuable species. It also represented a novel administrative zone, a part of the empire where forests were integrated into official land oversight, and where forest peoples negotiated new terms of administrative subjecthood.

THE WOOD AGE IN CHINA

I end this introduction by suggesting that the spread of silviculture across South China forces a reconsideration not only of South China's ecology and society but also of the periodization of Chinese history itself. Traditionally, historians of China have divided the period between 1000 and 1600 according to the three major dynasties that ruled. The Song dynasty controlled most of China between 960 and 1127—a period known as the "Northern Song"—and continued to rule the south until 1279—the "Southern Song." It is known for particular achievements in trade, education, government finance, and technology. This was when printing became widespread, when the government was first staffed by examination, when China produced the world's first paper currency, and when it innovated gunpowder weapons and the mariners compass. But the Song is often considered a weak empire, constantly beset by stronger, non-Han rivals, including the Khitan-ruled Liao; the Tangut-ruled Xi Xia; the Jurchen Jin, who took North China from the Song in 1127; and the Mongols, who conquered the rest of Song territory by 1279.

The Mongol's East Asian empire, known after 1271 as the Yuan dynasty, is traditionally considered a period of harsh, foreign misrule, but also of dynamic exchange between China and other regions. Initially, the Yuan was quite powerful, defeating rival Mongol claimants, sending fleets to Japan, Vietnam, and Java, and incorporating large portions of inland Southeast Asia under its suzerainty. But it declined rapidly in the mid-1300s under a succession of weak rulers and a climax of natural disasters and unrest, culminating in the millenarian Red Turban Rebellion. In 1368, the armies of the Ming dynasty, an offshoot of the Red Turbans, forced the Mongols to retreat onto the steppe.

The Ming dynasty ruled a large empire for a long time, from 1368 until 1644, yet is often considered a weak state, especially by comparison to its successor, the Manchu-ruled Qing (1644–1911). Under its first and third emperors, the Ming had major achievements at home and abroad, creating a new tax system and law code, restoring the Grand Canal, building Beijing, and sending the famous Zheng He fleets to the Indian Ocean. But after the death of the third emperor in 1424, the court was ruled by a succession of incompetent emperors and eunuch dictators and largely retreated from engagements with the outside world. Starting in the late fifteenth century, a massive influx of silver buoyed markets, but also destabilized fiscal administration and eventually led to social unrest. In 1644, with Beijing occupied by peasant rebels, a border general opened the gates to the Manchus, who would go on to build their own dynasty that ruled an even larger empire for two and a half centuries.

This dynastic periodization, with its focus on emperors and high officials, misses great continuities in local administration of forests. There were periods when the court itself was concerned with forest administration. Between 1102 and 1120, grand councillor Cai Jing established state forest oversight in counties throughout the Song empire. In 1391, the first Ming emperor, Zhu Yuanzhang, ordered thousands of trees planted near Nanjing to provide naval stores. Between 1405 and 1424, the Yongle emperor sent enormous detachments of loggers to the west to cut timber for the Ming palaces. But these instances of direct court intervention were largely exceptional. Indeed, the two intervals when high politics had the greatest impact on the forest economy both involved the *end* of official oversight. The first was 1127, when the retreat of the Song court from North China left its nascent forestry system in disarray and cleared the board for the rise of private silviculture. The second was in 1425, when the Ming state shuttered dozens of bureaus with natural resource oversight following the death of the Yongle emperor. For the most part, it was low- and mid-level officials, not emperors and high councillors, who created the policies that most affected forest administration, and these policies largely persisted across dynastic transitions.

In addition to overlooking the persistence of local norms, the dynastic periodization misses major continuities in South China's commercial networks spanning the mid-twelfth through the sixteenth centuries. As silviculture developed, merchants and landowners built connections across the different stages of timber production, from tree planting to logging, rafting, and wholesale markets. Changes in dynasty could affect these commercial webs in various ways. When the Southern Song capital at Hangzhou fell, Huizhou merchants redirected timber from the Hangzhou market to Poyang Lake. When Zhu Yuanzhang cracked down on commerce in the 1380s and 1390s, timber markets declined.[43] But in an industry where tree-planting investments took decades to mature, stakeholders were not ready to abandon their connections overnight. Instead, commercial networks gradually expanded over time, encompassing greater territories and more tree farms. Richard von Glahn, in his recent survey of China's economic history, calls the period from 1127 to 1550 "the heyday of the Jiangnan economy."[44] More broadly, von Glahn and Paul Jakov Smith argue that the greater "Song-Yuan-Ming transition" should be treated as a unified historical interval, not a period of disruption.[45] This is certainly true when we discuss the forest economy.

Finally, due to the extended lifetimes of woody plants, there was great continuity in the landscape itself. Newly planted fir trees took at least three decades to reach commercially viable dimensions; left unmolested, they would keep growing for a century or more. Unlike an abandoned grain field, which would quickly revert to grassy waste (*huang*), an abandoned forest remained a forest. Conversely, owners generally replanted their forests after logging. Timber prices were consistently high enough that tree planting remained a worthwhile investment, especially on mountainous land where there were few viable alternatives. In the mountains of Jiangnan, generations of forest owners replanted the same plots for hundreds of years. It was only at the margins—where natural growth was plentiful or land title was insecure—that forests were logged and not replanted. Even here, norms generally shifted within one or two generations, as locals moved from permitting open access to natural woodlands to jealously guarding exclusive access to the trees they planted.

Just as Jiangnan's forest plantations emerged by replacing other forms of upland cultivation, their sustainability was eventually challenged by the arrival of a new suite of mountain crops. American sweet potatoes and maize allowed upland cultivators to vastly increase their per-acre food production.[46] Tobacco also competed with timber for slopeland plots, as did commercial crops like indigo and tea, all of which saw booming demand.[47] The descendants of the same Hakka migrants who had spread fir planting in the sixteenth century spread New World staples and commercial crops throughout the upland south in the seventeenth and eighteenth centuries. The increased productivity of mountain lands, in both calories and cash, enabled a massive population increase. Because these were annual crops, they also deprived sensitive mountain soils of cover for much of the year, leading to increased runoff that depleted the upper slopes and clogged the streams below. The nexus of land scarcity, population pressure, and ecological degradation fed a spate of conflicts between upland cultivators and their lowland neighbors.[48] These conflicts were key contributors to China's extended crisis in the nineteenth and twentieth centuries: the Taiping Rebellion and the Communist Revolution both emerged from the upland south and featured a disproportionate number of Hakka leaders.[49] In other words, we should interpret China's nineteenth-century crisis alongside its eleventh-century crisis, as bookends to a period of remarkably consistent forest oversight and comparatively stable ecology.

This book tells the story of silviculture across multiple institutions of government and economy. Chapter 1 begins with the story of the opening crisis and is called "The End of Abundance." From antiquity until at least the eighth century, I posit a period of *regulated abundance*, when simple customary regulations were generally enough to prevent people from overharvesting the "bounties of the wilds" (*shanze zhi li*). Around 750, a slate of new pressures began to emerge, peaking during the Northern Song (960–1127). In response, I argue that government and populace innovated new forms of oversight that *profited from scarcity*.

The rest of the book tells the story of the period that ensued, which can be roughly understood in two parts. First came a golden age of silviculture lasting from 1127 until 1425. Throughout this period, both state and market tapped the growing timber supply to build fleets to ply the South Seas, construct massive public works projects, and erect monumental architecture. Spanning the Southern Song, the Yuan, and the reigns of the first three Ming emperors, this was a time of both commercial and imperial growth, reinforced by an expansionary paper currency and the personalities of several powerful emperors and khans. Yet outsize ambitions ultimately destabilized this period of growth. The golden age ended with the death of the Yongle emperor, who had inflated the currency and depleted the labor supplies of his empire and caused a deep depression.

Following this expansionary period was a literal "silver age," when the forest economy recovered, buoyed by an influx of silver specie. But while commerce expanded between 1425 and the early 1600s, the Ming state went into an extended period of retrenchment and reform, ending its expansionary ambitions and learning to live within its means. A reduced state presence—coupled with an expanding economy—inevitably meant that a growing share of commercial activity fell outside the auspices of official supervision. This was a period when private landowners and merchants developed oversight with far less state intervention. It ended around 1600 with the clearance of the last major old-growth woodlands in the Yangzi River watershed, leaving the diminishing Ming state almost entirely reliant on the commercial timber supply.

The six chapters covering this extended period are structured thematically around the institutions that allowed silviculture to flourish. Chapter 2, "Boundaries, Taxes, and Property Rights," addresses how forests fit into the Chinese system of land oversight. It starts with the first surveys to record forests in government land registers in 1149, proceeds through the fourteenth-century accounting reforms that standardized *shan* as the term for taxable forests, and ends by using sixteenth-century land records to assess the spread of forest administration across South China.

Chapter 3, "Hunting Households and Sojourner Families," details how Chinese states regulated forest labor like hunting and woodcutting. It follows a major expansion in the number and variety of households registered to specific forest trades in the Yuan and early Ming, before showing how 1425 marked a turning point in labor oversight. Thereafter, reforms to the corvée system gradually rendered most specialized forestry households obsolete, leading them to enter commercial labor markets.

Chapter 4, "Deeds, Shares, and Pettifoggers," turns from the state to the commercial economy, looking at how landowners and laborers used contracts to divide the risks and rewards of timber planting. Using evidence from Huizhou, it shows how landowners modified forest deeds from simple evidence of ownership to encompass complex shareholding, and how they innovated other forms of contract to address problems specific to forest management. It then turns to private litigation manuals (*songshu*), which developed the types of specialized forest law that the dynastic codes overlooked.

The next two chapters tell the story of "Wood and Water"—the mutual reinforcement between wood markets and maritime activity. Chapter 5, "Tariff Timber," shows how the state used a fractional levy on commercial shipments to obtain a persistent supply of timber. Chapter 6, "Naval Timber," details how this timber was used to underwrite the cost of fleet construction. Both chapters show a major turning point between the proactive use of timber markets to provision expansionary states in the Southern Song, Yuan, and early Ming and the conservative focus on sustainability and cost cutting that dominated after 1425.

Chapter 7, "Beijing Palaces and the Ends of Empire," provides both thematic and chronological closure to the book. It follows the expeditions that supplied palace building in Beijing by logging in the last old-growth forests in the Yangzi River watershed. Loggers felled hundreds of thousands of giant logs between 1405 and 1425, when the palaces were completed, and projects shuttered. But when emperors revived old-growth logging in the sixteenth, seventeenth, and even eighteenth centuries, they increasingly failed to obtain meaningful yields, marking the effective closure of the Yangzi River timber frontier.

The failure of imperial logging did not end the expansion of timber markets, but it did signal another fundamental shift. From this point forward, merchants, planters, and officials took further steps to consolidate and expand the timber trade, but there were no more easy gains. The silver-buoyed markets of the eighteenth century were still enough to float thousands of timber rafts, and the wood trade continued to expand through the chaotic nineteenth century.[50] But starting around 1800, just as Macartney and Abel traveled through China, the well-ordered forest system of the previous six centuries began to exhibit the first inklings of social-environmental crisis. By the 1850s, local disorders broke into a century of warfare and disaster, leaving a lasting impression of disorder and decline. But before this collapse, South China had an extended period of order, a period when fir silviculture dominated its forests, feeding the growth of markets and the expansion of empires.

ONE

THE END OF ABUNDANCE

IN THE LATE TWELFTH CENTURY, THE SCHOLAR AND OFFICIAL YUAN Cai (c. 1140–1190) wrote his famous *Precepts for Social Life*, a manual instructing the heads of gentry families on how to run their affairs. Among many other bits of advice, Yuan noted the potential profits from planting trees. He writes, "It is really not a difficult thing to plant mulberry, fruit, bamboo, and timber trees in the spring and, after ten or twenty years, enjoy the profits [*li*]."[1] Yuan even suggested that families plant ten thousand fir trees when a daughter is born, to sell for her dowry when she reaches age.[2] He also noted that the very profitability of trees could lead to disputes, especially over the allocation of boundary trees when brothers divide the household.[3] In a section on "the suitability of clear property boundaries," he further expounds on the issue, arguing to use ridgelines (*fenshui*) as the borders of mountain forests (*shanlin*) and to avoid using trees, rocks, or mounds, all of which could be moved or faked.[4] Sprinkled among a miscellany of moral and managerial guidelines, Yuan's writings on tree planting demonstrate a remarkable development: trees had become investments. One hundred years earlier, Yuan's advice would have been impractical. One hundred years later, it would have been commonplace. But in his lifetime, the silviculture that Yuan describes was both novel and worthy of instruction.

Yuan Cai was far from the first person to try to make forests suit his needs. Intentional woodland modification started well in prehistory, when the use of controlled fire was arguably the first technology to set humans apart from other animals. People used fire to transform environments in Asia by the late Pleistocene.[5] For tens of thousands of years, this remained the principal form of anthropogenic biome modification.[6] But as human populations grew, their use of fire began to cause a crisis. Around the late second and early first millennia BCE, a wave of woodland clearance appears in the pollen, charcoal, and sediment records.[7] In the wake of this first wave of clearances, people became increasingly aware of their potential to cause lasting damage. This first wood crisis ushered in China's earliest self-conscious forms of forest oversight. China's early empires, the Qin and Han dynasties (221–207 BCE and 207 BCE–220 CE, respectively), wrote laws on wood use, established forest offices and preserves, created timber monopolies, and issued formal incentives for planting trees.[8] This system, predicated on limited management of abundant natural bounties, persisted for another thousand years.

Much as excessive burning caused a wood crisis at the advent of the historical era, excessive cutting eventually led to a second crisis, this one starting in the late first millennium CE. Like the first crisis, this was evidenced by a wave of wood clearance seen in the pollen, charcoal, and sedimentary records between the eighth and eleventh centuries.[9] Like the first crisis, it led to a sea change in how people conceptualized, institutionalized, and modified China's woodlands. Conceptually, policy makers moved from *assumptions of abundance* to *fears of scarcity*.[10] Institutionally, policy shifted from *resource management* to *property ownership*. As resources became comparatively scarce, states shifted oversight from woodcutting labor to the resource itself: registering forests as exclusive property, regulating timber as a commodity, and eventually ending the labor draft. These conceptual and legal shifts led to the greatest change in human woodland modification since the advent of anthropogenic fire: the removal of natural woodlands and their replacement by uniform tree plantations.

Silviculture allowed humans to transform woodland biomes with far greater precision than fire. People cleared the land, selected the trees to plant, limited competitive growth, and logged trees on their own schedules. This marked the point where the entire life cycle of the trees rested on human interventions, from planting and pruning to logging and planting again. Unlike negative restrictions, afforestation responded to market price dynamics. As demand grew faster than supply, high wood prices drove people to produce more trees. Finally, while forest restrictions remained local, silviculture followed the ax. After logging, planters seeded large plots with fast-growing conifers and other commercially valuable trees. At the local level, tree planting was banal, a minor activity within the household economy. But through recursion across thousands of households over hundreds of years, it created something revolutionary: a patchwork of timber and fuel trees, bamboo, tea, and fruit and oilseed trees, each cultivated on their own uniform plots, a woodland biome—or biomes—produced almost entirely by human hands.

The making of this anthropogenic forest landscape forms the central narrative of this book. But before we get there, it is necessary to consider the forms of management that preceded it, and the reasons they gave way to large-scale silviculture. I argue that the fundamental change was a shift in attitudes toward the bounties of the natural world. In wood regulations from before the eleventh century we can find nearly universal assumptions of *managed abundance*. In the commercial silviculture that ensued in the twelfth century, precepts like Yuan Cai's reflected a position of *profiting from scarcity*. This framework of scarcity, developed through the long eleventh century, would guide all the interventions discussed in the chapters to follow.

MANAGED ABUNDANCE

In the earliest Chinese written records, woods appear mostly as obstacles to be removed. As in almost all early societies, fire was the primary means of taming this wild growth.[11] But by the sixth or fifth century BCE, nascent states began to see the woods and waters as resources to manage rather than wilds to tame. Soon philosophical texts by Mozi, Mencius, and Lord Shang produced the first coherent conceptions of natural resources in the Chinese tradition. Despite major differences in political philosophies, they agreed on the basic premise of natural abundance and that this abundance could be sapped by human activity. Dozens of new seasonal regulations (*yueling*) used the same basic principles, limiting the type, frequency, and location of destructive behaviors like logging, hunting, and burning.[12] In the third century, the Qin and Han dynasties codified these rules into the first formal statutes on natural resources in the Chinese tradition.[13] They reflected a way of thinking about the environment widespread across early Eurasia.[14]

In addition to codifying wood-use regulations, the Qin and Han empires established a suite of offices to oversee them, including the imperial forester (*yu*), which gradually transitioned from an emphasis on hunting to control a broad suite of forest resources. They also established the first state monopolies, including restricted forests (*jinshan*) to supply fuel to mines and smelters, and a massive complex called Shanglin Park used both for ritual entertainment and to dominate the fuel and timber market of the imperial capital, then the biggest city in the world.[15] The Qin and Han also started the first documented tree-planting programs, principally to shade roads and dikes.[16] Yet while the imperial administration developed key capacities to manage forests, these were largely confined to the immediate hinterland of the capital. In principle, the early empires claimed exclusive oversight of all "mountain groves, ponds, and marshes" (*shanlin huze*), but in practice, they could only control limited territories. Even here, restrictions had limited application; many rulers issued edicts specifically "relaxing the restrictions on the mountains and marshes" (*chi shanze zhi jin*).[17] Rather than controlling territory, the Qin and Han usually drafted labor to harvest forest products, including prisoners forced to gather "firewood for the spirits" (*guixin*).[18] They imported most large timber from the extensive natural woodlands of the south and west.[19] Outside of a few limited times and places, the overwhelming preponderance of woodland was open-access natural growth.

Despite massive political upheaval following the collapse of the Han empire in the early third century CE, the principles of natural resource governance did not change markedly for another five hundred years. Between the third and sixth centuries, China was divided among rival polities, each of which claimed the imperial mandate but had far less capacity to control territory, enforce regulations, or draft labor. The era's short-lived courts struggled to maintain even limited controls against the claims of lesser nobles, whom they feebly attempted to prevent from "monopolizing the wilds" (*zhan shanze*).[20] During this long period of decentralization, state controls of the wilds were both impractical and largely unnecessary. This era also saw the rise of monastic Buddhism and Daoism, each of which contributed new, often paradoxical, ways of thinking about nature and natural resources. Buddhists cultivated veneration of all life, but they also developed a surprisingly strong profit motive with financial techniques brought from India. This fed rival tendencies toward both conservation and commodification of forests.[21] Religious Daoists likewise held nonhuman life in particularly high regard, but they also incorporated arcane techniques for taming dangerous and wild natures, derived in part from the non-Sinitic peoples of the south and west.[22] Religious figures in both traditions contributed to the expansion of settlements into the wooded periphery, as seen through a literature on monks battling forest demons.[23] Throughout this period, most woodland probably devolved to the control of peasants, nobles, or monks or returned to a wilder state.

Nonetheless, the proliferation of institutions with claims to woodland contributed to the spread and elaboration of forest cultivation. The period's most important manual on estate management, Jia Sixie's sixth-century *Essential Arts to Nourish the People*, describes a number of techniques for cultivating trees for commercial purposes. It includes extended sections on orchards and hedges (*yuan li*), with instructions on growing jujubes (*zao*), peaches (*tao*), crab apples (*nai*), plums and apricots (*li, mei, xing*), and various other fruit-bearing trees.[24] Jia gives instructions on cultivating mulberry (*sang*) and Chinese mulberry (*zhe*) to feed silkworms.[25] He also details methods for planting elms and poplars (*yu, baiyang*) on three- to ten-year coppicing cycles, providing the most important sources of fuel and small poles.[26] Shorter sections detail willows (*liu*), pagoda trees (*huai*), catalpas (*zi, qiu*), and bamboo (*zhu*).[27] Anecdotes from the era describe both temples and noble estates cultivating orchards, tea plantations, and fuel coppices along the lines that Jia described.[28] Yet while the scattered estates of the period bristled with orchards, woodlots, and hedges, control of human labor remained the principal mechanism for managing woodland resources. Like the imperial government, noble and monastic estates conducted their own labor drafts, dominating labor to the point of contention with the imperial government.[29] In stark contrast to its extensive coverage of other commercially valuable tree products, *Essential Arts* does not include advice on planting *timber* trees, offering only a section on logging (*famu*). This suggests that estates derived most of their timber from logging the extensive naturally seeded woodlands at the periphery.[30] As long as woods were plentiful, woodcutting levies were both parsimonious and effective. They placed the locus of woodland governance on labor that was scarce relative to the wood it cut.

In the early seventh century, the Tang dynasty (618–907) formalized this principle of managing woodlands through human labor. With the compilation of the *Tang Code* of 624, the young dynasty organized the scattered regulations of earlier centuries into a universal penal law. Two statutes in the code established specific guidelines around the use of woodlands. The first law prohibited any private entity from monopolizing the bounties of the wilds (*zhan shanye pohu li*).[31] This reflected the principle of exclusive wildland oversight seen in edicts since the Qin and Han. The second article established a fundamentally new law governing "products of the wilds with labor already invested [in them]" (*shanye wu yi jia gongli*). It defined as theft (*dao*) the taking of natural products that had already been gathered, including wood that had already been cut.[32] This meant that it was human labor that turned natural products into property. The Tang even deployed this principle to manage its own wood supply. An eighth-century contract confirms that woodcutting was a common form of labor service through the midpoint of the dynasty.[33]

Far from a unique development, the conceptualization of wildland seen in the *Tang Code* was roughly comparable to late Roman law. In translating the Chinese laws into their equivalent Latin terms, standing timber was treated as *fructus naturales*—"fruits of nature" that could not be owned. Cut timber became *fructus separati*—"fruits separated" from their conditions of production that become the property of the person who cut them. Together, these laws reflected the principle of *separatio fructuum*, or "cutting the fruit," which held that it was removing fruits of nature from their conditions of growth that rendered them property.[34] While stated most clearly in the *Tang Code*, these legal principles formalized inchoate concepts dating from before the seventh century. Later the *Tang Code* was adopted almost verbatim into the penal law of the Song dynasty with these articles unchanged.[35] Just as the Roman law would form the basis of regulations on the European continent, Tang law laid the foundations for later Chinese law. Most importantly, the articulation of a clear principle of "cutting the fruit" provided an avenue to turn rights to *use* wildland into rights to *own* wild products. This idea would eventually enable the ownership of woodland itself.

The Tang also saw further developments in silvicultural technique. The poet and essayist Liu Zongyuan (773–819) even wrote a biography of "tree planter Guo the hunchback" (*zhongshu Guo tuotuo*), a professional gardener who is also attributed a *Book of Tree Planting*.[36] Whether or not "hunchback Guo" actually wrote it, this book is notable for its extensive, intimate knowledge of tree planting. It shows that knowledgeable cultivators of the ninth century had access to a broad suite of silvicultural techniques, including planting from seeds and cuttings, transplanting, grafting, pruning, and logging. The *Book of Tree Planting* also includes the first clear instructions for planting *timber* trees, such as pine (*song*) and fir (*shan*).[37] Nonetheless, as late as the tenth century, anecdotal evidence suggests that most timber was still cut from the wild growth. Edwin H. Schafer argues, based on his survey of Tang literature, that "medieval forests must still have seemed inexhaustible" and that officials saw tree planting as a waste of time.[38]

Despite substantial changes during the first millennium CE, the fundamental premise of natural bounties prevailed. States restricted small patches of forest, peasant communities managed woodlots for fuel, monks and aristocrats planted fruit and shade trees, but the wilds were always waiting at the fringes of this cultivated tapestry. Simple regulations were still enough to promote the abundance of nature. Nonetheless, in the second half of the millennium the precepts governing woodlands began to change. While reinforcing earlier standards of open access, the *Tang Code* also laid the foundations for later concepts of property rights. While practiced only on small estates, the premodern suite of silvicultural techniques and tree species was essentially complete by the ninth century. These developments suggest that the assumptions of abundance were beginning to fail, first gradually and then with growing urgency. In the period that followed, this system entered its own crisis, a crisis only resolved through a fundamentally new conception of the natural world.

THE SONG WOOD CRISIS

Like the development of early imperial regulations, the transition to large-scale silviculture began with a crisis within the old patterns of wood use. Before this crisis, communities had maintained a reliable supply of wood products through three main mechanisms: seasonal restrictions on open-access woodlands, trade between wood-rich and wood-poor regions, and limited cultivation of forests in strategic areas. By the Song dynasty (960–1279), this system became unstable, as rising demand led to both intensified use of communal woodlots and extensive logging at the periphery. Song officials initially tried to resolve threats of wood shortage by escalating the first two mechanisms—imposing stronger logging restrictions and importing more timber—but these interventions were no longer enough. By the early twelfth century, the demand for timber was so high that people increasingly resorted to the last tool in their repertoire: tree planting. Formerly practiced in highly localized conditions, silviculture became widespread. The spread of tree planting, the most intensive mechanism for managing woodlands, was a clear indication that the other, more parsimonious forest systems had failed, and with them the assumptions that limited management was enough to secure natural abundance.

The crisis of the old system of wood oversight was the product of several overlapping shifts in the economic and geopolitical environment in the early Song. When the Song dynasty was declared in 960, it was merely the latest of six courts to control North China since the fall of the Tang in 907. But unlike their short-lived predecessors, Song emperors ruled for over three centuries, first from Kaifeng (Bianjing), where the Grand Canal joins the Yellow River (the Northern Song). After losing most of North China to a rival state in 1127, the dynasty continued until 1279, ruling from Hangzhou (Lin'an), where the southern terminus of the Grand Canal meets a large bay on the East China Sea (the Southern Song).

Smaller than the great empires that preceded it, the Song derived power more from commerce and centralization than from extensive territory. With an increasingly specialized bureaucracy, growing printing and popular literacy, a state-backed paper currency, and extensive use of bituminous coal, the Song appears in retrospect much like the states of western Europe more than five hundred years later. Some historians have considered it the beginnings of the "early modern" period in China.[39] Like these later states, the Song spent three centuries striving against the circumstances from which it emerged: military competition with powerful regional rivals, internal upheavals brought on by urbanization and an expanding commercial economy, and a wave of nearly unprecedented environmental threats.

When the Song emerged in the late tenth century, it controlled only the North China Plain. While large compared to most European states, it lacked huge territories that had formed part of the great empires of the past. While the Song was able to take possession of the south by 980, it contended against major non-Han rivals on its northern borders, including the Khitan-ruled Liao (907–1125), the Tangut-ruled Xi Xia (1038–1227), and the Jurchen-ruled Jin (1115–1234). Not only did enemy states cut off Song access to some of the richest woods on its periphery; they also posed major military threats that led all sides to escalate their wood use. In the northeast, the Song grew forests to defend its border with the Liao.[40] In the northwest, both the Song and the Xi Xia logged extensively to build forts during their mid-eleventh-century wars.[41] Both interventions removed large swaths of woodland from other use. In the meantime, iron production expanded by an order of magnitude in the eleventh century, in large part for military purposes.[42] Yet despite large investments in fort construction and weapons production, the Song could not effectively defend its borders. The Jin ultimately grew so strong that it forced the Song to retreat from its northern capital in 1127.

Ironically, this invasion was made possible, in part, by the removal of the border forest that had been planted to slow nomadic cavalry.[43] Throughout these wars, the Song military struggled to balance escalating demand for timber and fuel with limited reserves, especially in the strategic border regions of the northeast and northwest.

The Song was far more urban than its predecessors, demanding large volumes of timber for shops, houses, and government buildings and for the ships that carried their supplies. In earlier empires, urban development had focused overwhelmingly on the imperial capitals, positioned near large, state-monopolized forests in the northwest. The Northern Song capital was also large: during its peak in the late eleventh century, Kaifeng probably reached 750,000 urban residents.[44] But unlike earlier capitals that abutted on wooded mountains, Kaifeng was in the middle of the wood-poor North China Plain and had to import essentially all of its wood. In fact, the homes and workshops of the Song capital consumed so much fuel that the region could not supply enough firewood, and Kaifeng switched almost entirely to mineral coal by the end of the eleventh century.[45] Dozens of other urban centers emerged in the eleventh century as well, far more than in earlier periods.[46] All of these cities brought their own demands for timber and fuel.

To make matters worse, the Song presided over the greatest environmental crisis in a thousand years, itself both a cause and a result of woodland degradation. The Yellow River, the flood-prone lifeblood of North China, had been relatively stable since the second century CE. But for hundreds of years, sediment accumulation had gradually raised the river's banks above the surrounding countryside, threatening catastrophe when the river ran high. Extensive wood clearance only worsened the problem by exposing more soil to flow into the river and speed sedimentation. In the late tenth century, the river started to flood regularly, culminating in a massive deluge in 1048 that inundated large swaths of countryside and shifted the river's course far to the north. To manage the unruly river, Song hydrocrats ordered extensive logging for fascines to rebuild the dikes. This only worsened the regional wood shortage while further depleting nearby mountains of their soil-retaining woodlands, leading to further rounds of sedimentation and flooding. In 1128, in an attempt to slow the Jin invasion, Song troops breached the Yellow River dikes, causing another massive flood, which shifted the course of the river to the south, far past its original course. Throughout this "environmental drama," the river conservancy consumed timber on an unprecedented scale.[47]

Finally, the Song oversaw a major growth in the commercial economy, fueled in part by a major expansion in the money supply. After overseeing the greatest minting of coin in over a thousand years, the Song backed the first official printing of paper money, expanding the currency beyond the supply of copper for the first time in Chinese history.[48] With so much money in circulation, timber and fuel became market commodities, priced in cash. This transformed wood from a distinctive, locally situated product into a standardized commodity. By rendering timber, fuel, and other products fungible, commodification provided the third key mechanism for bringing wood into circulation. In the cash-rich economy, merchants multiplied the influence of the state and cities, traveling the empire looking for more wood to bring into the commercial markets.

OFFICIAL FOREST MANAGEMENT

The overlapping climaxes in military, urban, hydrological, and commercial pressures challenged the Song state's ability to find enough timber to build forts to defend its border, fleets to ply its waterways, and dikes to protect its farmland from deluge. These crises fed increasingly strident debates about the proper role of the state in taxing and regulating society and in managing the natural world. As the state realized the extent of its crisis, it doubled down on old forms of management, including restrictions on woodcutting, attempts to economize, expansion of the logging frontier, and an extension of direct forest oversight. Yet the key features of Northern Song forest policy were confusion and contention. Bureaucrats were on fundamentally new ground and disagreed about the proper course of action.

Song bureaucrats first attempted to regulate excessive wood extraction by imposing more and stricter logging bans, especially in the densely populated North China Plain. In 1049, a merchant requested a moratorium on logging in the northern portion of Dingzhou to allow its woods to recover.[49] The Dingzhou forest appears to have recovered somewhat by 1074, when its timber was cut again, resulting in another logging ban.[50] In 1080, a community in Huizhou 惠州 reported that its woods had dwindled to 12 percent of their original size and requested a total restriction on use until they recovered.[51] The growing frequency of these restrictions, especially in the densely populated North China Plain, suggests that their effectiveness declined. While scattered, these reports also evidenced a growing conflict between official demand for timber and the government's role in restricting overuse, as it was often official requisitions that led to excessive logging in the first place.

With logging restrictions proving increasingly ineffective, the most obvious means to alleviate the growing timber shortage was to expand the logging frontier. Government efforts to do so focused largely on the northwest, because it offered direct water routes to Kaifeng, and because the substantial military presence in the region offered the possibility of using soldiers as loggers. By the mid-eleventh century, the "woods that blocked out the sky" (*linmu can tian*) in the Qinglin mountains—long a preferred source of timber—had grown more scarce.[52] To replace this supply, Song officials were increasingly tempted by the further reaches of the Loess Plateau, which was relatively well forested.[53] In fact, Song officials had logged the western fringes in the early decades of the dynasty, until Tibetan (*fan*) reprisals had led Emperor Zhenzong to cancel these operations in 1017.[54] In the 1030s, the buildup of Tangut power on the Loess Plateau led to extensive logging for military construction. By 1044, the Song and the Xi Xia collectively built more than three hundred stockades.[55] Logging in the region therefore risked exposure to enemy forces on two fronts. Nonetheless, the presence of rich woodlands upstream of Kaifeng offered a tempting source of timber.

In 1068, a minor supernumerary official named Wang Shao suggested a new tack in the decades-long conflict with the Xi Xia. He argued that the Song should recruit Tibetans as clients by offering them trade goods and titles. This would solve the Song's strategic weakness while presenting the Xi Xia with enemies on multiple fronts.[56] By 1072, Song armies conquered the Xi Xia prefecture of Hezhou and incorporated it into the Song empire as Xihe Circuit, with Wang Shao appointed supreme circuit commander.[57] Xihe Circuit soon became a site of substantial institutional experimentation. Following its final pacification in 1074, more than a dozen new county- and prefecture-level towns were built to administer the region.[58] The state created official markets at the frontier to trade Sichuan tea for Tibetan horses.[59] It established markets to trade for Tibetan timber as well.[60] In 1080, the emperor appointed Li Xian, a eunuch supporter of Wang Shao, as the head administrator of these nascent timber markets.[61] Noting that Xihe was the only location in the empire with timbers large enough for imperial construction, he gave Li authority to control the timber trade from the frontier markets all the way to the capital.[62]

Over the next several years, Li Xian built the Xihe Logging and Timber Purchase Bureau (Xihe Cai Mai Muzhi Si) into a small but notable money-making operation in the northwestern borderlands. In 1081, the logging bureau was disbursed two hundred thousand strings of cash as the principal to buy timber.[63] It used profits from selling the logs downstream to finance the transport costs of grain and fodder to supply the frontier, with the principal reinvested in further timber purchase.[64] The returns on this investment were apparently significant: in 1084, Li Xian was able to borrow fifty thousand strings of cash from the logging bureau to buy stores for the military.[65] Like the larger and more famous tea and horse markets, the timber markets became an independent source of revenue and authority for a class of military and eunuch bureaucrats in the borderlands of the northwest.[66] They also increased state capacity to obtain timber in an increasingly tight Yellow River market. Yet this expansion of frontier logging was only one element in the Song's changing forest oversight.

As reports of wood shortages grew in scale and frequency, Song officials began to reconsider some of the theoretical foundations of the centuries-old wood policies inherited from the Tang. Under the patronage of Emperor Shenzong in the late 1060s and early 1070s, the reformer Wang Anshi rose to the apex of Song political power, where he began to rethink the basis of state control of the environment. Citing the *Offices of Zhou*, a classical text that had been used to justify strong forest bureaucracies in the Qin and Han, Wang argued that forest regulation was well within the ambit of the classical state.[67] He argued that "in antiquity there was not just a single tax of ten percent [on farm production] . . . there were foresters and wardens in the wilds [*shanze*], and many varieties of [other officials]."[68] Despite the wood crisis, Wang explicitly refused to tax areas used for communal fuel collection (*xide qiaocai*) or any wildlands of public benefit (*zhonghu zhili*), including mountain forests. He also forbade landlords from enclosing these lands or renting them out on false pretenses.[69] But while Wang's specific policies did not overhaul the rules governing wood use, his radical reading of the Chinese classics began to shift the underlying principles of natural resource governance. Yet this push for greater state authority was soon halted. Wang was forced to resign from office in 1076, and in 1085 his patron died. The new emperor, Zhezong, appointed Wang's archrival Sima Guang as grand councillor, whereupon Sima abolished most of Wang's policies.[70]

Despite the incomplete and short-lived nature of Wang Anshi's reforms, they laid the groundwork for more radical policies yet to come. In 1102, the young emperor Huizong, appointed another reformer, Cai Jing, as grand councillor. Cai soon revived interventionist policies modeled on Wang Anshi's administration. Using the 1070s reforms as precedent, Cai initiated a wide-reaching program to extend state oversight and generate revenue from non-agrarian land, including the restoration of monopolies on goods like tea and salt.[71] Under Wang's reforms, assistant magistrates had been key to extending additional oversight to counties with large populations.[72] Cai had a far more specific vision: he made assistant magistrates the first point of contact between the state bureaucracy and the productive landscape, enumerating new interventions that had not been part of Wang's suite of reforms. In a major policy proposal, Cai wrote: "Copper, lead, gold, silver, iron, tin, and mercury mines and smelters and timber forests should be established; woodcutting should be restricted; barren mountains should be planted, etcetera. In each county, establish an assistant magistrate to manage these affairs."[73]

Building on Wang's ideas, Cai specified a group of officials to manage state mines and forests throughout the empire. Acts from the next several decades clarified their functions. In 1105, an official in Jiangxi suggested to limit the post to counties that actually had mines and forests to manage. Following the elimination of unnecessary positions, about two-thirds of Jiangxi's counties merited the additional staff.[74] This suggests that assistant magistrates took control of preexisting woodlands, probably areas that had been common-access prior to the policy. In the absence of other directives, they were responsible for enforcing existing logging restrictions rather than any radically new policies. Nonetheless, they became the first officials with specific responsibilities for managing forests at the local level.

Like Wang's reforms, many of Cai's policies were curtailed following his retirement in 1120.[75] But state forestry projects actually grew increasingly specific and closely managed over the next several years. An act of 1123 made each assistant magistrate responsible for maintaining twenty thousand timber trees (*linmu*) in his county, with provisions to punish those who kept fewer and reward those who kept more.[76] Two years later, local officials were made responsible for including these tree counts in their regular reports on the local economy.[77] Several other undated forest regulations were probably products of this period as well.[78] One specified clear punishments for anyone cutting wood from a state forest without license.[79] Another slowed the promotion schedule of assistant magistrates who permitted the destruction of forests under their supervision and rewarded those who expanded forests with faster professional advancement.[80] Collectively, these policies shifted forest oversight from preventative to positive policies. In addition to imposing increasingly strict restrictions on logging, the state tasked county officials with surveying standing timber and rewarded them for growing the size of their forests. While these rules do not specifically mention tree planting, this would have been one way for officials to meet production targets. Regardless of whether or not officials planted trees, the new regulations shifted the emphasis on wood oversight from logging to progressively earlier stages in the growth cycle. The ultimate fate of these county forests is not clear, in part because most of Cai Jing's writings were destroyed by his critics. Indeed, his opponents were so successful in shaping the narrative that a pseudo-historical version of Cai Jing appears as a villain in the classic novel *Outlaws of the Marsh*.[81] Nonetheless, it appears that the forest policies were soon rendered defunct by the retreat of the Song court in 1127.[82]

PRIVATE FOREST MANAGEMENT

Like the Song state, private entrepreneurs developed two overarching responses to the wood crisis: logging new frontiers and intensifying forest management in the most densely populated regions. As the state focused on expanding logging into the northwest, which offered river routes to the capital and a large military presence, private merchants focused on the interconnected riverine and coastal markets of the south. While some of these regions had been logged to excess, others still had dense natural woodlands. An eleventh-century materia medica noted that "the deep mountains of the interior south" had plenty of fir in the natural growth.[83] In the early twelfth century, another text reported that the immediate hinterland of Hangzhou was "lush with lacquer, paper-mulberry, pine, and fir and frequented by merchants."[84] Even in the late twelfth century, a Song minister described portions of the Hangzhou area as "dense with old firs."[85] But as scarcities emerged in the oldest and best-known timber markets, merchants went further afield, buying timber from itinerant loggers throughout the Yangzi River basin.[86] Along the coast, cities like Ningbo (Mingzhou) and Quanzhou became particularly important centers of maritime trade in the twelfth century. As their industries developed, these ports were interlinked into an extensive trading realm that bought timber from as far afield as Guangzhou and southwestern Japan.[87] Collectively, the timber markets of the southeast coast and southern interior were probably an order of magnitude larger than the state-dominated logging regions of the north and northwest.

Meanwhile, the same pressures that led the state to intensify forest management prompted landowners to do the same. For the first time, demand was great enough that landowners began to invest in planting trees, not just for fruit and fuel, but for timber as well. Timber-planting techniques were well known before the twelfth century. As noted above, the ninth-century *Book of Tree Planting* records techniques for planting both pine and fir, the two principal timber trees of southern China. The famous poet and statesman Su Shi (1037–1101) also recorded a method of planting pines.[88] Fir planting was likewise attested for ritual and ornamental purposes. A temple near Hangzhou boasted two enormous fir trees that local tradition held had been transplanted in 893, while the firs at the "ten thousand fir" temple (*wanshan si*) in northwestern Jiangxi were planted no later than the early eleventh century.[89] In 1173, the philosopher Zhu Xi (1130–1200) planted firs on his grandmother's grave in Huizhou 徽州; sixteen of his twenty-four plantings were still alive as of 1999.[90] But while these texts demonstrate the expertise to plant pine and fir, they do not suggest that *commercial* planting was widespread.

In this respect, 1100 represents a key turning point, from limited plantings on private estates and temples to large-scale investments in timber plantations. Ye Mengde (1077–1148) spent his later years in Huzhou, in western Zhejiang, where he wrote of his plans to grow large stands of pine, fir, and tung trees on thirty-year cycles.[91] This is the first clear mention of staggering timber plantings across different plots so that the trees mature at different times. I have already quoted Yuan Cai, a native of nearby Quzhou, who wrote repeatedly of the profits from planting trees in the late twelfth century.[92] A contemporary gazetteer recorded that in Huizhou, "the hills are well suited for fir, the locals do little work in the fields, and many plant fir as their vocation."[93] Deeds from Huizhou further attest that plantations of fir seedlings (*shanmiao*) were widespread by the early thirteenth century.[94] Several agricultural manuals from the thirteenth century gave advice on how to grow fir, further documenting this expertise.[95] By then, the demand for timber was so great that it supported both a huge expansion in imports from far abroad and a fundamentally new market in purpose-grown timber in the Jiangnan interior. This marked a point of departure in biome modification—not just selective pressures on naturally seeded woodlands, but direct human intervention to plant and propagate timber.

PATHS NOT TAKEN

By the time Jiangnan landowners began planting large stands of timber trees in the twelfth century, people had been modifying China's woodland biomes for thousands of years, first through fire and then through simple rules predicated on the notion of *regulated abundance*. Despite substantial continuities in this basic framework, it persisted across a millennium of change. But eventually the growing scale of cities, ships, armies, dikes, and markets generated demands for timber and fuel that could not be fulfilled through existing mechanisms. There was no single response to this crisis. Some officials turned to the proven solutions of the past, placing logging moratoriums on depleted woodlots and establishing timber markets in newly conquered regions. Others promoted more expansive views of state oversight, extending official forest management to counties throughout the empire. In the meantime, the merchants and landlords of the south developed their own responses, extending the timber trade far upriver and overseas and supplementing natural growth with the first extensive plantings of timber trees.

Collectively, these developments offered at least three different roads out of the Song wood crisis. First, China could continue to expand its resource frontiers, with a timber monopoly in the upper Yellow River basin and private timber markets along the Yangzi River and the fringes of the East China Sea. Following these trajectories, it could have developed much like Holland, with a riverine timber frontier on one side and a maritime timber frontier on the other.[96] Second, it could develop an extensive and powerful forest bureaucracy. This would have taken China along a similar path to those later followed by Venice, Korea, France, or Prussia.[97] We might remember Cai Jing as China's Colbert, or even think of Colbert as France's Cai Jing. Third, China could follow southern landlords like Ye Mengde and Yuan Cai who pioneered commercial silviculture. Until 1127, any of these roads might have led out of the wood crisis. All this changed when a foreign army occupied the north, literally forcing the Song along a southern route. When the dust settled, the court was left ruling territory centered on the fir-planting regions of Jiangnan, having lost both the wood-poor North China Plain and the timber monopoly of the northwest. As a result, it was private merchants, not official monopolies, that would drive the timber trade, and it was private planting, not state management, that would transform China's woodland canopy.

TWO

BOUNDARIES, TAXES, AND PROPERTY RIGHTS

IN THE MID-TWELFTH CENTURY, LI CHUNNIAN (1096–1164), A VICE minister at the Song Board of Revenue, made a deceptively simple change to land survey regulations, a change that caused a revolution in the administrative landscape of South China. The 1182 *Sanshan Gazetteer* from Fuzhou describes this reform in characteristically bland terms: "In 1149, the boundary surveys were conducted. Fields were assigned [new] categories, although each county's tax was still collected according to the old quotas."[1] Later in the passage, however, the record emerges from this insipid language to note the radical outcomes of Li's policy: "Now the acreage of cultivated landholdings is nearly ten times the acreage at the beginning of the dynasty, *especially in the categories of gardens, forests, and mountain lands.*"[2] Even allowing for the poetic exaggeration typical in these accounts, the effect of the surveys was substantial. Through a seemingly minor shift in land accounting, Li's reforms brought an enormous swath of new acreage—much of it forest—under official taxation and oversight for the first time.

Li's survey methods were themselves revolutionary, substantially increasing both the quality and the content of cadastral records, but their effects went far beyond improvements in documenting the fiscal—and physical—landscape. They began the process of transforming woodlands from open, common-access landscapes into exclusive property. Over the following centuries other bureaucrats made their own seemingly pedestrian changes to the land survey regulations. In the 1310s, Yuan manager of state affairs Zhang Lü ordered tax officials in South China to standardize the categories used for land survey. Starting in the late 1360s, and culminating in the empire-wide cadastres of 1391, Ming surveyors further streamlined and extended these regulations to new regions of the south. Collectively, these shifts made forests fiscally legible to the state; in the process, they effectively rendered them a form of private property. It took centuries to realize these full effects, but the fundamental premise of private forest ownership was ingrained in Li's 1149 regulations. This shift in land oversight was the first aspect of the silvicultural revolution to be institutionalized. Li's reforms were among the greatest shifts in Chinese land policy in the past millennium. Yet, somehow, they have passed largely under the historian's radar.

Li Chunnian's land surveys responded to both the specific context of mid-twelfth-century Song politics and the more persistent characteristics of the South Chinese environment. As seen in chapter 1, eleventh-century China faced a wood crisis the likes of which had not been seen in more than a millennium. Given time to mature, a number of different policies could have led the Song into a new era of forest governance. Instead, external events interfered. In 1127, armies of the Jurchen Jin dynasty occupied the Song capital at Kaifeng and posed a very real threat to end Song rule entirely. While much of the Song bureaucracy escaped south of the Yangzi River to enthrone a new emperor at a new court in Hangzhou (Lin'an), the loss of North China prematurely ended state-centric paths of forest governance. It was in this environment that Li Chunnian proposed his boundary surveys. Having lost much of its tax base in North China, and with landlords expanding their power in the south, the Southern Song, he argued, needed to improve documentation of the landholdings that it could still tax, including the forests with nascent investments in tree planting.

This accident of history set the course for forest oversight for the next eight centuries. By the time the Southern Song fell to the Mongols in 1279, its bureaucrats had established the institutional frameworks necessary to support commercial timber plantations. When landlords began planting timber in the early twelfth century, they did so without a legal bulwark for their investments. Li's policies provided precisely this support. For the first time in Chinese history, the government surveyed, registered, and taxed forests much the same as farmland. While it took another 250 years before the state formalized the legal status of forests as exclusive property, Li's policies implicitly acknowledged forest ownership in exchange for tax revenue.

This simple act of granting land title to forest cultivators was enough to resolve the Song wood crisis. Empowered by long-term land rights, and incentivized by secular inflation in wood prices, forest owners planted timber across a broad swath of South China, replacing naturally seeded trees with human-seeded trees in both the landscape and the market. This enabled Chinese states to meet their strategic timber needs without active participation in territorial forest management. But while registration was key to forest proprietors, forest taxes were only a small piece of the state's revenue puzzle, never more than a single-digit percentage of the land tax. Facing few wood shortages, and receiving little direct tax revenue, China's administrators worked to streamline forest management rather than expanding it. The result of this equation was a forest system that combined minimal state documentation with widely distributed ownership. This basic arrangement lasted until land reform in the 1950s.

While forest title was the product of compromises forged during Li Chunnian's lifetime, it also responded to more general conditions that prevailed in South China in the long term. Unlike North China, much of which is an astonishingly flat, sedimented plain, South China is reticulated with hills, mountains, rivers, and lakes and the resulting diversity of biomes. Warmer and wetter than the north, South China boasts a wide variety of subtropical trees and bamboos. The region is also endowed with extensive waterways, both natural and man-made. In stark contrast to northern rivers, which are prone to both sedimentation and flooding, these southern rivers are almost ideal for floating timber rafts. These were ideal conditions for the emergence of commercial silviculture.

South China also featured a distinct institutional legacy, the outgrowth of its highly varied environment and long history of independent regimes. In contrast to the predominantly yeoman society of the north, South China had long featured a complex suite of landholding practices and multiple strata of landlords and tenants. When bureaucrats first allowed the private circulation of farmland in the eighth century, they were responding specifically to the irregularity of landholding in South China. When the Song court moved south in the twelfth century, it allowed the enclosure of the south's other domesticated biomes, including forests, orchards, ponds, and fishing grounds. As later bureaucrats elaborated these policies over the next several centuries, they remained a unique feature of South China. North of the Yangzi and west of the river's famous gorges, the state generally did not bother to register or tax forests or ponds.

Even after the reforms, not all woodland was taxable forest, nor were all forests planted with timber trees. Few landowners chose to register woodlands of low commercial value, including those at high elevation or distant from navigable waterways that would permit timber rafting. Large swaths of woodland therefore remained outside of official purview except when they came under dispute. There were also other uses for taxpaying forests (*shan*), including growing bamboo, fuel, fiber crops, oil seeds, tea, and dyestuffs and housing graves. Nonetheless, in the core provinces of the south, most timber forests were registered with the state, and most registered forests were planted with timber.[3] I therefore use the forest registration as a convenient—if incomplete—proxy for the spread of timber planting itself. To trace the spread of forest registration, I have compiled tax records from local gazetteers (*difang zhi*), a distinct genre of Chinese text that lies between local history and geography.[4] The data in these gazetteers are highly problematic, often copying earlier figures verbatim or with extensive simplifications and outright falsehoods.[5] They also reproduce problems inherent in the surveys themselves.[6] Yet despite their flaws, these data present a remarkable picture of forest registration, showing the spread of a fundamentally new form of forest management and, by extension, a fundamentally new form of forest biome. From its nascence in the mid-twelfth century, forest registration—and, by extension, tree planting—spread across much of South China, stopping only at physical or climatic barriers to the growth of the principal tree species.

BOUNDARY SURVEYS

To understand the significance of the forest surveys, it is important to grasp the distinct features of the Chinese property system. What we understand as landownership is not a single right; it represents a bundling of several distinct claims, including the rights to access, to use or harvest products of the land, and to sell land or transfer it to heirs; it also includes responsibilities for rents and tax payments. The modern bundle of claims assigns most of these rights and responsibilities to a single entity. But historically, states recognized very different bundles of claims.

Until the mid-eighth century, Chinese peasant households only claimed the *use* of their farmland, which was parceled out in equal plots. With the exception of small plots of mulberry land (*sangtian*), their farms were not heritable or transferable. Instead, the state claimed long-term ownership; once a peasant passed out of working age, the government reclaimed his land and transferred it to another worker.[7] Gradually this system became untenable, as nobles and monasteries acquired large swaths of land tax-free and as peasants in the south wrote private deeds to buy and sell land against the wishes of the government. To shore up its finances in the wake of a major rebellion, the Tang dynasty recognized this state of affairs, changing the bundle of rights by allowing land to circulate on the private market. Officials instituted surveys to document landownership, taxing each household on its actual acreage rather than an assumed equitable distribution of farmland.[8] Over the next several centuries, the Tang and its successors gradually acknowledged private deeds as evidence of landownership as well.[9] Under this compromise, the state's cadastres functioned as a central record of land title, backing the private, registered contracts that allowed more flexible circulation of ownership and tenancy rights, creating a system that persisted until the twentieth century.

Even as farmland circulated on private land markets, woodlands, wetlands, and other non-agrarian landscapes were initially kept separate from the system of private ownership. Instead, the state retained the underlying claims to all of the "mountains and marshes" (*shanze*), permitting *use*, but forbidding individuals from *owning* the land. Because woodlands and wetlands were open-access, there was no need to survey them, although woodlots in heavily populated areas did have informal boundaries. Even under Wang Anshi's land reforms in the mid-eleventh century, official policy reinforced the principle that woodlands were open-access, communal areas and could not be enclosed, rented, or sold.[10] This changed only with the retreat of the Song court to the south in 1127, which took it into the epicenter of the area that was just then undergoing a silvicultural revolution.

As forest users began planting trees for profit, they prompted a complete rethinking of the relationship between land, value, and ownership. When timber was cut from natural growth, the wood-use rights ingrained in Song law were sufficient. But laws that based ownership on the *felling* of timber did little to protect upfront investments in *planting* trees. As Jiangnan landowners began to plant trees commercially, they began to shift these norms, recognizing that the upfront investment of labor granted logging rights to the people who planted them. This was a logical extension of the principle that work established ownership of natural goods. But regardless of local practice, claims to own standing timber were not backed by formal regulations. This changed with Li Chunnian's surveys, which created a central ledger of forests for the first time.

The Southern Song's land surveys began shortly after the Treaty of Shaoxing stabilized the Song-Jin border in 1141, allowing Song officials to move from reactive infighting toward building proactive policy. In 1142, Li Chunnian, then a local official in Zhejiang, noted that many land registers had been lost during the Song-Jin war, allowing widespread tax avoidance. He suggested that new land surveys were necessary to any tax reform, both to rebuild the fiscal basis of the state and to equalize the tax burden. Li's survey methods made several substantial methodological advances, creating the first centralized records of plot boundaries. They were also the first surveys to include forests and other non-agrarian landholdings. Like most attempts to redistribute the tax burden, Li's policies faced significant opposition. Some opponents wanted to rely on landowners' self-reported acreage rather than sending out official survey teams; others sought to tank the reforms entirely. But the results of test surveys in 1142 were successful enough that Li was elevated to a ministerial post in the Board of Works. Despite substantial opposition, Emperor Gaozong ordered Li's surveys to be carried out empire-wide in 1149.[11]

Li Chunnian's surveys offered an implicit bargain to landowners: they had to pay taxes, but registering their plots would give them substantial advantages in case of dispute. Previous registers had recorded only the owner, grade, and acreage for each plot of farmland, relying on in situ markers and local memory to resolve boundary disputes. In the flat north, this parsimonious system had saved official labor by recording only the information needed for tax collection, but it was far less effective at marking boundaries of irregularly shaped plots in the hills and watercourses that threaded the south. Unlike in these earlier surveys, Li recorded the boundaries of each plot (*jingjie*) in books of aerial plot diagrams (*dianji bu*). This centralized record keeping also extended up the administrative hierarchy: one set of registers was maintained at the county, to be updated every time land was sold or leased; copies were sent to the prefecture every three years; and the transport commissioners in charge of forwarding taxes to the capital held a final set of registers.[12]

This system of record keeping gave the government both a carrot to entice landlords to register their properties and a stick to punish them if they did not. As a carrot, the centralized record of land title offered landholders an incentive to register their plots as proof of ownership. Legal cases from the early thirteenth century confirm that tax registration gave owners substantial advantages in court.[13] As a stick, the government reserved the right to confiscate any cultivated land that was not entered in the registers; the heads of local self-defense organizations (*baozheng*) were responsible for inspecting the plots and attesting to the accuracy of their diagrams.[14] This provided a uniform and authoritative record of land title that merged the fiscal needs of the state with the evidentiary needs of southern property owners.

Li's registers were also the first time that woodlands and wetlands were surveyed in a systematic way. Unlike earlier rules that specifically excluded non-agrarian land from surveyed acreage, new regulations held that mountains and wildlands (*shanye*), wetlands, and other "lands of popular benefit" (*li yu zhongong*) should have their boundaries clearly noted in the registers (*mingli jiezhi zhu ji*).[15] This marked a major shift in the understanding of the non-agrarian landscape. Instead of unbounded, open-access wilds, forests could now have clear borders and internal divisions. Nominally the regulations reserved "lands of popular benefit" as commons, forbidding their sale. Yet demarcating the boundaries of woodlands made it possible for people to lay claim to all the produce within the declared limits. This implicitly allowed landowners to claim all the wood on their plots instead of only the logs they cut, effectively granting them exclusive title to the land they planted with trees.

Furthering the institutionalization of forest ownership, officials soon began to ignore the nominal policy of maintaining woodlands as open-access plots, treating them as de facto private property. In 1160, Huang Yingnan, a minor official in Jiangxi, attempted to rent out more than twenty-eight hundred *qing* of state-owned land (about eighteen thousand hectares, or forty-five thousand acres), principally "fallow fields, mountain forests, pools and marshes" (*huangtian, shanlin, poze*).[16] This enormous acreage—representing either the remnants of Cai Jing's defunct county forests or lands seized from owners who failed to report them to surveyors—constituted more than 5 percent of all landholdings in the prefecture.[17] By renting them out, Huang effectively treated "mountain forests, pools and marshes" as private property. By the 1190s, Yuan Cai noted that it was common practice to sell or rent forests through contracts.[18] While the law still theoretically held that forest plots were common land, both officials and landlords effectively treated them as *bounded*, if not fully *private* property.

By surveying and leasing state-owned forests, the government was merely catching up to a preexisting market for private forest plots.

While ecclesiastical and noble estates had pressed claims to forests for hundreds of years, Li Chunnian's surveys marked a categorical expansion of forest ownership. Between 1149 and 1156, surveys were conducted throughout East and West Zhejiang, East and West Jiangnan, Hunan, and Guangxi and in most of Sichuan, Guangdong, and Fujian. They were never carried out along most of the northern border (in Huainan, Jingdong, or Hubei) due to its proximity to an enemy state, and most outlying islands and tribal areas were allowed to submit taxes under their former assessments.[19] Finance officials continued to improve the surveys through the late twelfth century, updating boundary records. Finally, in 1189–90, officials in southern Fujian (Tingzhou and Zhangzhou) compiled their own registers, incorporating regions where rebellion had previously made surveys impossible.[20]

Throughout these regions there was a clear pent-up demand for centralized records of land title. While scattered and incomplete, the limited records extant from the late twelfth and early thirteenth centuries all show huge increases in taxable acreage following the surveys, largely in categories like forests (*shan*), "orchards and groves" (*yuanlin*), and mountain land (*shandi*). In the 1175 *Xin'an Gazetteer* from Huizhou, recorded acreage increased more than 90 percent over earlier figures, with the greatest increase probably coming in the new category of forests (*shan*).[21] Other areas reported similar trends toward the enclosure of forested land. In Fuzhou 福州, the surveys incorporated significant amounts of new land, principally "orchards and groves, mountain land, ponds, and reservoirs" (*yuanlin, shandi, chitang, poba*).[22] In Taizhou, Li Chunnian's surveys yielded two new volumes of boundary records in three main categories—paddy fields (*tian*), dry fields (*di*), and forests (*shan*).[23] The sudden and substantial increase in the registered acreage of forests suggests that these plots had already been claimed as de facto private property before the boundary surveys. The records do not state exactly how these plots came to be registered, but the logic of the situation is clear: people took advantage of the surveys to shore up claims to land they had previously planted with trees, by recording their plots in centralized registers. This marked the first time that woodlands were officially surveyed and recorded as bounded, private properties, a shift representing the culmination of changes in the woodland tapestry that had been under way since the eleventh century. Regardless of their earlier history, government records now existed to support land title to forests.

TAX ACCOUNTING

The boundary maps produced in the mid- to late twelfth century formed a durable basis of forest ownership for the next hundred years of Song rule. When the Mongol Yuan dynasty conquered South China in 1279, it largely left Song tax institutions in place. Yet by 1290, when the Yuan conducted its first household surveys in the south, the tax system was in a state of confusion. Part of the problem was that there were major differences between North China, which had been ruled by the Jin dynasty for one hundred years prior to Mongol rule, and South China, which had been ruled by the Song. But on top of the understandable differences between the territories conquered from two different states, there were profound discrepancies within local jurisdictions as well. In the south, the forests and wetlands added to the tax books since 1149 had yet to be compiled into any semblance of order. To make matters worse, many local officials had created and modified tax categories as an expedient way to generate revenue. The result was an overwhelming assortment of unclear and highly circumstance-specific taxes. As one administrator wrote in the early 1300s: "There are tax categories that did not exist in the past but do now, and others that existed historically but do not anymore; none of these meet their original purposes. Some plots have fallen to ruin, while others were seized by the state; some taxes were eliminated, while others had temporary shortfalls or increases. Based on recent reports from the counties and prefectures, administration is extremely problematic."[24] In response to this disordered state, Yuan officials eventually enacted a series of reforms, including a complete overhaul of the system of land tax accounting.[25]

In 1314, recognizing that inequities in landholding were a key source of social problems, Manager of State Affairs Zhang Lü ordered a thorough reorganization of land records.[26] Zhang personally proceeded to Jiangzhe—the Yuan jurisdiction including portions of Jiangnan and Zhejiang—where he had previously headed the branch secretariat (*xingshu sheng*); other officials were sent to Jiangxi and Henan. Zhang required owners to report their own landholdings or face punishments or even seizure of their property, but many rich families simply bribed clerks to falsify the records. The court issued partial tax breaks on self-reported landholdings to further incentivize owners to register them, but it still took until the late 1320s before substantial new acreage was added to the records.[27] Even these updates did little to curtail the growth of magnate power, and the reorganization of 1314 is generally considered a failure, falling far short of Zhang Lü's professed goals.[28]

Despite failing to stem growing inequities, Zhang Lü's reforms did succeed in overhauling the system of land tax accounting, creating a standard format that was used throughout Jiangnan. Under Zhang's direction, the Jiangzhe Finance Commission (Caifu Fu) ordered subordinate jurisdictions to record acreage in cadastral charts (*bantu*) according to six standard categories: paddy fields (*tian*), dry fields (*di*), forests (*shan*), pools (*dang*), ponds (*tangchi*), and miscellaneous property (*zachan*).[29] The reforms were immediately apparent in Zhenjiang and Huizhou, where landholdings were reported in the standard categories in 1315.[30] Total reported acreage in Huizhou in 1315 was 15 percent above twelfth-century figures, suggesting that some new properties had been registered.[31] Elsewhere it took longer for reforms to proceed. Nonetheless, registers were updated in Nanjing and Ningbo no later than 1344.[32] Categories for reclaimed wetlands continued to vary by jurisdiction, but the six main categories of farmland, forests, and ponds were now consistent throughout the region.[33]

In a striking continuation of earlier trends, this overhaul of land tax accounting was only effective on a regional basis, emerging from Jiangnan, where a combination of punishments for avoidance and tax breaks for self-reporting helped incentivize landowners to update their registration. Even here, Zhang's reforms did not represent a fundamental shift in policy. They were accompanied by a small increase in general acreage, nothing like the sudden increase in forest registration that had accompanied Li Chunnian's surveys in 1149. Their more important effect was to standardize land accounting, allowing officials at the branch secretariat to sum revenues across six uniform categories of landholding used throughout the region.[34]

In further retrospect, Zhang Lü's reforms were products of a short-lived interim of effective government, soon undercut by infighting at the Yuan court and unrest in the provinces. Starting in 1351, the Yuan faced a spate of overlapping disasters, including the outbreak of the Red Turban Rebellion—a major uprising of believers in the millenarian Maitreya Buddha. Despite effective initial responses, much of the empire fell out of court control by 1355.[35] In 1368, one of the Red Turban generals declared victory over his rivals, including other rebel leaders and the rump of the Yuan state. Zhu Yuanzhang and his Ming dynasty imposed a radical vision for reforming society, including a renewed desire to order the countryside.

The consolidation of Ming authority in the 1360s and 1370s marked a return to effective centralized rule after decades of unrest and enabled the further consolidation of land records. Even before founding the Ming, Zhu Yuanzhang made moves to reestablish an organized tax base by conducting a new set of land surveys of the region of Jiangnan he controlled. Starting in 1368, the official beginning of Zhu's reign as the Hongwu emperor, some localities around his capital at Nanjing compiled registers to enable collection of the land tax.[36] Two years later, edicts ordered officials to compile receipts (*hutie*) recording the members and property of each household. Gradually these piecemeal acts gave way to a more comprehensive land policy, as surveys were conducted throughout the empire by 1391.

The Hongwu surveys produced the most comprehensive landholding records in centuries, yet these data were nonetheless flawed. The acreage figures were an administrative fiction that allowed finance officials to readily combine figures from vastly different areas. Rather than imposing a uniform aerial *mu* (about one-seventh of an acre), localities reported *fiscal mu* that varied from one aerial *mu* to as many ten.[37] Other highly localized measuring standards continued to persist well into the sixteenth century.[38] Nor were the surveys carried out with uniform attention in all localities. In the most densely populated regions of the south, officials were able to conduct surveys quickly and generally produced records of high quality.[39] But further afield the survey process was far more onerous, only gradually producing records that were often of questionable veracity.

In the densely populated prefectures of Jiangnan, a long tradition of property registration contributed to both the speed and the quality of surveys in the region, now split between the Ming's Southern Metropolitan Region and parts of Jiangxi. In Huizhou, local self-defense organizations had compiled their own land registers during the interregnum of the 1350s and 1360s to ensure continued enforcement of land title.[40] As a result, officials had to do little more than update the existing figures, a task they were able to complete by 1369. Yet in three of six counties, *less* land was recorded in the early Ming than in the Yuan—two lost all records of forests—and the remaining three saw essentially no change in registered acreage.[41] In other words, the Hongwu surveys may have actually been *less* effective at registering land than the less famous efforts of the Southern Song and Yuan. Neighboring parts of Zhejiang and Jiangxi were likewise able to complete new registers within a few years of the Ming founding, also by copying and updating existing cadastres.⁴² They were further aided both by familiarity with the process and by substantial local resources. For example, in 1386 more than a thousand National University students were sent to help with the land surveys in Zhejiang Province.⁴³ Similar patterns were likely observed in other regions with good records from the Yuan.⁴⁴

This was in stark contrast to regions where record keeping had lapsed in the Yuan, where officials took decades to complete the new land surveys. In these jurisdictions, the Hongwu cadastres were the first updated registers in over a century and may have been the first time that landholdings had ever been surveyed. In Jiangxi, the more peripheral southern and western prefectures took more than three times as long to survey than the more metropolitan northeastern regions.⁴⁵ It was only in 1391 that acreage figures were available from all of Jiangxi's prefectures.⁴⁶ Southeastern Zhejiang likewise took far longer to complete its surveys than its more prosperous northern and western prefectures.⁴⁷ Land records were even worse in the southeastern province of Fujian, and the new surveys were both more arduous and more productive. As of 1381, recorded acreage in Fuzhou 福州 increased more than five times over the nominal figures in the Yuan cadastres.⁴⁸ In Quanzhou, officials had to compile the new registers based on 200-year-old records from the late Song.⁴⁹ In these regions, the Hongwu surveys appear to have had a fairly large effect, bringing central Jiangxi, southern Zhejiang, and coastal Fujian into the more normative cadastral regime of Jiangnan.

Still further afield, the Hongwu surveys may have been the first time that landholdings were ever recorded by the central government, but the records were also of correspondingly lower quality. In Guangdong, Song and Yuan officials had had almost no success in registering land. Eight separate attempts to survey the region had all failed to account for its landholdings, and even these limited records had quickly fallen into disuse. The Hongwu surveys added acreage to official cadastres, yet progress remained uneven. As late as 1531, five counties in Guangzhou and Chaozhou still had minimal records of landholding.⁵⁰ In Huguang, in the Yangzi River interior, the Hongwu surveys were little more than an administrative fiction. Figures reported in the early Ming cadastres were largely estimates of the amount of land available to reclaim rather than reports of actual landownership.⁵¹ In the far southwest, in Guangxi and Guizhou, most land fell outside the cadastral regime entirely. Ming statutes allowed these "vulgar border places ruled by chieftains" to record land in their own ways, or not at all.⁵²

In the parts of Jiangnan where they were most effective, the Hongwu surveys reaffirmed the accounting categories used in the mid-Yuan, making forest (*shan*) the standard category applying to all taxable forests. The 1397 *Great Ming Code* further formalized this by designating forests a category of landed property (*tianzhai*), a development explored further in chapter 4. By the late 1400s, "paddy fields, dry fields, forests, and ponds" (*tian, di, shan, tang*) became a fixed expression, designating the four main categories of taxable land (and discarding the other two categories used in the mid-Yuan). Yet the use of these accounting categories did not result from a clear act of policy. Indeed, none of the hundreds of surviving edicts from the Hongwu period specifically mention either this system of land classification or a desire to register and tax forests. While high-level bureaucrats now used the term *forest* in official documents, the surveys and registers that governed them remained specific to South China. The Ming's taxable forests were a continuation of Song and Yuan policies rather than the product of novel ambition on the part of Zhu Yuanzhang.

If the Hongwu surveys did little to overhaul land tax accounting, they were nonetheless critical to Zhu Yuanzhang's program to centralize the tax system. In 1391, he ordered these data compiled into a new form of register that gathered together each household's property under a single heading.[53] The new tables of household property supplemented the spatially organized registers already in use. They responded to the problem of accounting for families with landholdings dispersed across multiple jurisdictions, making it easier for county bureaucrats to calculate the total tax responsibilities of each family. Their offices now maintained two sets of cadastres: the spatially organized books of "fish-scale registers" (*yulin ce*), named after the resemblance of cadastral maps to fish scales, and the new tables of household property, called "yellow registers" (*huang ce*) for their yellow covers.[54] These two sets of registers formed the "warp and woof" of tax oversight: the fish-scale diagrams innovated by Li Chunnian made it easy to locate properties in the landscape; the Hongwu yellow registers functioned as a general reference on household wealth.[55]

The yellow registers were the first complete set of tax books since the eleventh century and allowed far more fiscal oversight of landholdings than the limited and broken systems of the late Song and the Yuan. Yet any potential for fiscal centralization was undercut by Zhu Yuanzhang's personal philosophies and proclivities. Zhu was highly suspicious of finance, both state and private, and sought to impose a radical vision of self-sufficiency. He was also suspicious—perhaps paranoid—of threats to his power and eliminated nearly all of the top positions in the central bureaucracy to elevate the emperor as the sole seat of judgment. This meant that while Ming landholding records were potentially far superior to those of the Song and Yuan, the Ming court had no administrators with authority to set new fiscal policy. Instead, it was largely local officials—generalists, rather than tax specialists—who used the registers to set quotas within their local jurisdictions.[56] Rather than attempting to maximize revenue, they used these quotas to anticipate local expenditures across a wide range of highly specific products.

Despite the paradoxes of the Ming tax system, the local quotas generated based on the yellow registers made it easy for officials to make substitutions. Almost immediately after the yellow registers were completed in 1391, policies allowed taxpayers in some southern provinces to submit cash instead of grain.[57] Officials could also use the standard categories of landholding to fine-tune taxes based on different forms of land use. In many counties, forests were not only taxed at a different *rate* than farmland; they were also taxed in different *goods*, often paying cash rather than grain or cloth. Household-based landholding records also made it easy to determine the most prosperous families in a village or district, a standard used to designate the intermediaries responsible for ensuring collection of the land tax.[58] Nonetheless, tax accounting standards soon declined in the face of contradictions intrinsic to the tax system and widespread tax avoidance. As chapter 3 details, local and regional officials eventually worked to change the tax system to bring property owners' incentives more in line with state needs. Yet property registration depended as much on the initiative of the property owner as on the state.

While flawed and limited by modern standards, the land surveys of the Southern Song, Yuan, and early Ming were nonetheless transformative. They established a distinctly southern form of taxable property, a category that now encompassed forests. In core timber-producing prefectures like Huizhou, the forest plots depicted in these cadastres formed a continuous chain of documentation stretching across hundreds of years. Elsewhere forest records were more erratic, reflecting a more tenuous investment in timber production and limited state interest or capacity to conduct surveys. But where it worked well, official registration was the cornerstone of a productive forest economy. For landowners, centralized title records allowed them to invest in planting trees with confidence that they or their heirs would still hold the rights to harvest the timber thirty years later. For the state, the surveys gradually integrated forests into the fiscal regime at ever-higher levels of administration: Li Chunnian's revolutionary "fish-scale" diagrams in an ad hoc and highly localized way, Zhang Lü's standardized account books at the provincial level, and the Hongwu cadastres throughout the south and nominally across the entire empire. This gave officials more and more license to treat forests as a generic form of property. But because forests generated little tax revenue, standardization also gave officials license to ignore the ground-level complications of silvicultural management.

THE SPREAD OF FOREST REGISTRATION

After 1391, there was little further change in the regulations that established forests as bounded, exclusive, alienable property. Yet over the course of the next two and a half centuries, far more woodlands were integrated into the official regime, largely as landowners registered their own plots. Forest registration, and by extension forest planting, spread in two ways. First, silviculture moved uphill, as landowners registered and planted ever-higher slopes. Second, silviculture followed the ax to new frontiers. After loggers cut the primary woodlands in the south and west, locals gradually replanted the areas with trees, registering their plots to ensure ownership of the timber harvest. In this way, forest registration moved from its nursery in western Jiangnan and Zhejiang into Jiangxi and Fujian, and eventually into Guangdong, Guangxi, and Hunan. Throughout these two processes, forest registration spread almost entirely through private initiative, not state action. Finally, in 1581, Grand Secretary Zhang Juzheng carried out another major land survey, the first in nearly two centuries. The effects of this survey varied widely: in some regions, registered acreage increased by 30–40 percent; in one prefecture, it tripled; but in others acreage remained about the same. Overall, surveyors added perhaps 25 percent more land to the tax books, most of it newly claimed from lakeshores and mountain slopes.[59] Yet total tax returns did not increase, suggesting that landowners were offered lower tax rates as an incentive to report their properties to the state.[60] The surveys may have had the effect of registering commercial forests in new regions, especially in the south and west; the data are too coarse to be sure.

If summary tax figures are inconclusive, local sources provide a more demonstrative record of changes in forest registration. Cadastral maps from

Huizhou show the expansion of farms at the expense of forests in densely settled areas and of forests at the expense of unclaimed land in more peripheral places. In relatively dense, long-settled areas, many maps show ladder-like terraces of paddies extending up a col, bounded by steeper slopes on both sides. Yet even as clearance and terracing removed some forests from timber production, landowners enclosed new forests at the margins of settled areas. Maps of more peripheral areas in Huizhou depict large forest plots with incomplete boundaries, often partly defined by mountain ridges. For private forests to have extended into this rugged landscape, more accessible areas must have already been claimed.

In addition to the spread of forest enclosure to the peripheries of old timber-producing prefectures, forests were also registered in new parts of the empire. By the late fifteenth and sixteenth centuries, the incorporation of woodlands into the land regime can be seen through the patterns of forest registration. In Zhejiang, Jiangxi, and the Southern Metropolitan Region, forests were uniformly incorporated into the cadastral regime. Other distinct patterns of forest registration document the spread of timber planting to regions further south (map 2.1). In coastal Fujian, mid-Ming land records retained a distinctive array of land types including categories like "grove" (*lin*) and "garden/orchard" (*yuan*) in addition to the standard term for forests (*shan*).[61] These nonstandard accounting categories were artifacts of the initial wave of forest surveys in the 1140s; their persistence into the Ming shows that Fujian fell outside of regular administration during the Yuan, when land categories were standardized. Proceeding further down the southeast coast, a second region stretches from western Fujian to northeastern Guangdong and a single prefecture in Guangxi. In the mid-Ming, these regions had erratic patterns of forest registration, generally only in the most metropolitan counties in each prefecture. Nonetheless, given the sorry state of land registration in Guangdong and western Fujian prior to the Ming, these few forests must have been newly registered property.

In parts of Jiangxi and Zhejiang, more detailed landholding figures allow us to track the relative importance of forests to the taxpaying landscape. Across the Yangzi River highlands—the belt of prefectures stretching from Raozhou and Guangxin to Shaoxing and Ningbo—forests were reported in every county and accounted for at least 20 percent of fiscal acreage (map 2.2).[62] Not only does this region include the uplands closest to the cities of Jiangnan, but it also corresponds with the administrative regions with the longest histories of forest registration. This zone of extensive forest

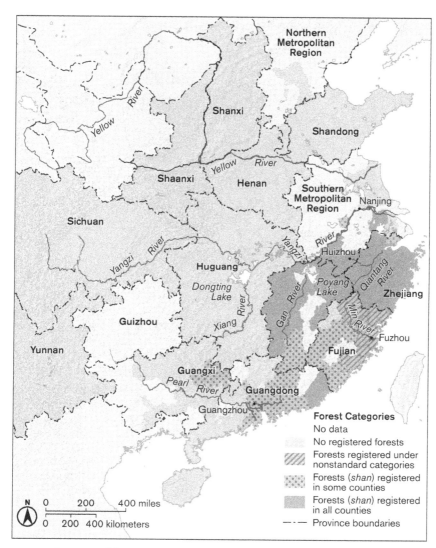

MAP 2.1 Patterns of forest registration, early to mid-1500s. Data from prefecture and province-level gazetteers. Map layers from China Historical GIS version 6.

registration traces the administrative boundaries of the Jiangnan forest belt—a unique biome of anthropogenic forests that emerged as the product of similar climate and topography, similar market access, and a shared institutional history. The data also show forest registration spread westward, crossing Poyang Lake and extending into central and western Jiangxi, where

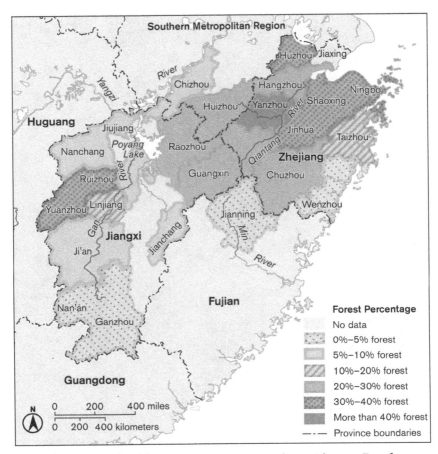

MAP 2.2 Forests as a percentage of taxable acreage, early to mid-1500s. Data from prefecture and province-level gazetteers. Map layers from China Historical GIS version 6.

forests made up a smaller proportion of registered acreage than in the Jiangnan core. In Jiangxi's southernmost prefectures, forest holdings were reported in only a handful of counties, representing a very small fraction of total acreage.

Other anecdotes from across the south give life to the contours painted by the administrative data and demonstrate the further spread of tree planting. By the mid-Ming, scattered records document extensive timber production in western Jiangxi. In Pingxiang County, there was a stony marsh (*shize*) where loggers "cut tall trees during the dry season and left them to await the rain; when the rains ended, they would float the logs out."[63]

Yuanzhou also had a booming tung and tea oil industry, probably based in trees planted on purpose-driven plantations.[64] Further south in Taihe County, several lineages pioneered the local planting of fir trees in the fifteenth century, by which time there was already "long established planting of pine, camphor, and three species of oak used for fuel and building materials."[65] By the early seventeenth century, Jiangxi's southernmost prefecture, Ganzhou, exported timber cut from the natural growth as well as purpose-grown on fir plantations.[66]

Planting practices soon began to spread out of Jiangxi into neighboring regions. In the sixteenth century, officials in Guangdong promoted plantation forestry to support local livelihoods. They recommended that locals grow pines, specifically referencing Su Shi's planting techniques from the eleventh century and suggesting tenancy contracts of ten to twenty years.[67] Within a century, firs began to cross the Nanling Mountains into Guangdong. *New Comments on Guangdong*, from 1678, describes the process by which fir planting spread: "There is not much fir in Guangdong. The saplings come mostly from Jiangxi, and the majority of those buying them are landowners who have clear-cut their plantations and are planting replacements. They therefore take a number of seedlings that equals the number of stumps. Guangdong and Guangxi have plenty of timber trees and only forty or fifty percent use fir. For this reason the species is not often planted."[68]

This passage makes quite clear that trees were only planted *where forests had been clear-cut*. In the late seventeenth century, there were still plentiful natural woodlands south of the Nanling, and more than half of the region's timber was cut from the wild growth. Plantation forestry was specifically associated with nonnative fir, imported as saplings from north of the Nanling Mountains.

Planting spread west from Jiangxi as well, probably reaching Hunan in the early eighteenth century. By the mid-eighteenth century, elders in Hengyang County in central Hunan claimed that fir had been planted there "for generations" and that plantations, formerly few in number, now spread across the landscape.[69] Further west, in Qiyang County, the transition was still under way. While landlords planted some timber in the early 1700s, locals did not respect property boundaries and felled so many trees that landlords stopped planting them. There was even a local saying that "stealing trees was not theft" (*tou shumu bu wei dao*), reflecting the persistent understanding of timber as a natural product available to whomever cut it. It was only with firmer enforcement of property rights that fir planting spread across the landscape, "turning every district green with fir" by the 1760s.[70] These anecdotes further demonstrate the importance of land title. Without adequate demand, the right trees, knowledge of planting techniques, *and* the right legal regime, the novel community of pines and firs would fail to spread, die off, or be destroyed by rampant logging. When people tried to force the spread of ideas or practices without meeting other conditions, their attempts invariably failed.

The timber species of South China's tree-planting revolution are now grown across the region. A recent survey of China's tree species shows *Cunninghamia lanceolata* (China fir) and *Pinus massoniana* (horsetail pine) extending from the Yangzi River to the southern slopes of the Nanling Mountains and from the seacoast to the Yun-Gui Plateau.[71] Connecting the dots, the snapshot of mid-Ming forest registration shown on maps 2.1 and 2.2 marked a midpoint in the spread of timber planting. First developed in Jiangnan in the eleventh and twelfth centuries, this array of practices spread throughout the subtropical highlands of South China by the late eighteenth century.

FORESTRY AND ADMINISTRATION

By nearly any measure, the institutional and ecological shifts in South China's forest system were both early and extensive. Li Chunnian compiled South China's first systematic land registers—including forest maps—in 1149. Chosŏn Korea, another comparative prodigy, did not conduct its first major forest surveys until 1448.[72] Systematic forest cadastres were not seen in most of Europe or Japan until at least the seventeenth century.[73] Jiangnan landowners began to invest in timber plantations in the twelfth and thirteenth centuries; the practice was widespread in South China by 1600. Korea was also an early adopter of artificial plantations; relying in part on Chinese precedent, the Chosŏn court introduced and elaborated a pine-planting regime in the fifteenth century.[74] Japan and Europe were again comparative latecomers. In Japan, conifer plantations were largely a product of the eighteenth century.[75] And while Nuremberg planted firs and pines as early as the fourteenth century, artificial plantations only became widespread in Europe in the early 1800s.[76]

Yet to the Chinese state, forests were simply another category of landholding: officials surveyed, registered, and taxed forests the same way they surveyed, registered, and taxed farms. Because tree plantations generated little tax revenue, forest oversight was simply not a major official concern. Yet without the state conducting surveys, centralizing record keeping, and formalizing the laws of property, landowners would have had limited incentive to plant trees on a commercial scale. Despite the almost total disinterest of the Southern Song, Yuan, and Ming states in territorial forestry, their subtle changes in law and procedure formed the basis of forest ownership, which was key to landowners' confidence in planting trees. With title records in place, landowners gradually spread intensive timber planting across much of four provinces by 1600. By rough estimate, perhaps twenty million acres that had been natural woodlands in 1100 were planted with fir and pine five centuries later. Between 1600 and 1800, this figure may have doubled. Without the state, there would still have been tree planting in South China, but landowners would not have been enabled to transform biomes on such a scale.

Unlike in Europe—or in neighboring countries like Korea and Japan—South China's forest surveys did not come from a specialized forestry bureau, nor did they lead to the creation of one. Instead of an official forest bureaucracy, South China's system of forest registration promoted an extensive private stratum of forest owners. This meant that silvicultural expertise, and the proximate behaviors that promoted the growth and spread of timber trees, was the product of private groups and not the state. As long as their land title was secure, forest owners had no reason to demand greater regulation; as long as wood supplies were sufficient, officials had no reason to force it upon them. In contrast to Europe and Northeast Asia, where forest surveys reinforced trends toward centralization, in China they produced precisely the opposite tendency. To better understand this divergence between the centralization of forest registration and the decentralization of forest management, we must understand the non-state groups most responsible for managing forests on the ground. The following two chapters therefore turn from the rules governing forest land to those governing forest labor.

THREE

HUNTING HOUSEHOLDS AND SOJOURNER FAMILIES

AS SILVICULTURE LED TO A TRANSFORMATION OF PROPERTY RIGHTS, it also changed the state's fundamental relationship with its subjects' labor. Chinese states had long imposed direct levies on their subjects to provide labor for state projects and to collect a wide range of non-agrarian products. While the land tax (*tianfu*) and commercial tariffs (*shangshui*) produced far more income, these household-level imposts were just as significant for the functioning of the government. While large, fungible streams of grain, cloth, and cash were key to funding the court and the military, the labor service (or corvée, *yaoyi*) kept the gears of government turning by providing part-time workers for a range of tasks. Other miscellaneous levies (*zachai*) supplied government bureaus with a wide range of products not provided by the major revenue streams. Villagers sent paper, ink, and wax to their county magistrates; supplied game, honey, and other local delicacies to princely courts; and provided their local garrisons with shoes, padded jackets, and even the feathers and fish glue for fletching arrows. They also produced a miscellany of products used by court offices: tung oil to polish the emperor's chairs, bird plumes for officials' caps, and dye goods and medicines for the licensed trade in textiles and pharmaceuticals. Most significant of all, village levies were the primary source of fuel for government offices.

The factor unifying all these household levies was the command of labor. Under the *Tang Code* and its successors, it was human work that turned natural bounties into property. If peasants could claim firewood through the labor of cutting it, officials could claim firewood by mobilizing peasants to cut it on their behalf. The same logic applied to fish, game, honey, or drugs: the state obtained these wildland products by drafting people to catch, kill, gather, or glean. This principle is clear in the very language used for these levies. As a verb, *chai* means "to conscript" or "to dispatch"; as a noun, it includes "levies" of labor or of *the goods gathered by that labor*.[1] If we were to map these labor-based exactions, they would draw the negative image of the regular taxable landscape. The state used the land tax to derive standardized commodities from domesticated fields; it used labor levies to derive locally specific goods from a range of highly varied, wild woodlands, swamps, mountains, and lakes.

Miscellaneous levies were more than just a way to bring non-agrarian *goods* into the state metabolism; they were also a way to bring non-agrarian *households* under government oversight. At the margins of agricultural life, certain households were designated to supply the state with woodland, wetland, or mine products in place of grain and cloth. The most significant (and well researched) of these were the tea, smelter, and saltern households that supplied their respective monopolies.[2] But there were dozens of other categories of households distributed in smaller numbers: hunting households to provide game, fishing households to catch marine products, and even specialized households to pilot the massive timber rafts destined for imperial construction.[3] Many of these groups did not farm enough to pay the standard land tax. Instead, the state taxed them according to their primary livelihoods as hunters, loggers, miners, and fisherfolk.

While goods levies depended on the command of labor, human work was not a sufficient condition to produce the natural products they demanded. When officials taxed firewood by drafting woodcutters, they assumed there were branches available for them to cut; they likewise assumed there were fish for fishing households to catch, game for hunting households to hunt, and a whole suite of other wildland products available to gather. Through the first millennium CE, the availability of non-agrarian goods had been assured by the ban on monopolizing the wilds. But starting in 1149, the state allowed landowners to claim forests as exclusive property, effectively abrogating the principle that reserved woodland as open-access commons. Legally, forest owners might grant usufruct rights to their fellow villagers, but they were certainly not inclined to grant the state similar rights—to do so would amount to allowing their property to be taxed twice, once as a landholding and again under the labor levy. Ecologically, the spread of tree plantations left less habitat for wild flora and fauna.

Landowners responded to the decline of open-access woodlands by cultivating forest products on plantations. In addition to timber and fuel, they grew bamboos and palms; fiber, dye, and drug crops; and oil-producing trees like tung, tallow, camphor, and lacquer. But some biota—especially carnivores, large game, and many woodland plants—responded poorly to cultivation and depended on the persistence of wild environments. These plants and animals retreated as their habitats were cleared and retreated again as hunters and pickers targeted the limited remaining natural woodlands for intensified extraction. The expansion of cultivated landscapes—even cultivated *woodland* landscapes—necessarily entailed a retreat of wild landscapes.

With wild lands in decline, state exactions of their flora and fauna could no longer be sustained. To avoid exacerbating local shortages, officials gradually stopped collecting goods in kind, replacing direct levies with a silver tax surcharge used to buy cultivated substitutes. Eventually, in recognition that land had replaced labor as the limiting factor in production, they rolled this silver fee into the land tax, producing a single line item assessed on each cultivated acre called the "single whip method" (*yitiaobian fa*). As others have noted, the single whip was a response to the influx of silver in the sixteenth century, which allowed far more of the economy to be taxed in currency.[4] But it was also a response to a crisis in the management of wildland resources through labor conscription.

The twilight of household levies and the switch to silver budgets was a mixed bag for the state, allowing more flexible accounting but leaving government offices susceptible to price inflation. For the households directly targeted by wildland levies, the impact was even greater. As the state removed itself from labor oversight, it left a major vacuum in the sectors of the landscape that had been most heavily taxed by the household levies, especially the woods. Since a large and growing swath of woodlands was now privately owned, the management of forest labor now fell to landowners. In the meantime, the households formerly responsible for hunting and logging had to earn silver to pay their new tax surcharges. To do so they turned to the market, selling their labor as well as the forest products they had long produced. By the late sixteenth century, two discrete strata of forest specialists entered into this commercial arena. Landowners from Huizhou and other regions with long-standing traditions of timber planting were the capital. They hired workers to cultivate their own forests and traveled abroad to trade in timber, bringing managerial expertise to regions that had just begun to invest in commercial timber plantations. Hill people from Fujian, Jiangxi, and Guangdong were the labor. These hunters, loggers, and swidden cultivators traveled throughout the south to work on the commercial tree plantations—and tea, indigo, and tobacco plantations—that replaced wild woodlands. Around this time, some documents begin to name these highlanders "Hakkas" (*kejia*), a term often translated as "guest families," but also carrying implications of both "client" and "sojourner." In other words, these forest specialists were named according to their role in the silver economy—as China's first major itinerant labor force.

The story of forest labor told here overlaps temporally with the transformations of forest land. By the Song, the state had already begun to expand its oversight of non-agrarian trades by taxing tea producers and saltern households. This was followed by a significant enlistment of hunting, fishing, and logging households in the Yuan and early Ming. For two or three centuries, states extended *both* land-based taxes and labor levies into the woodlands, registering forest households and forest land simultaneously. But woodland levies could not expand indefinitely. By the late fifteenth century, the spread of tree plantations had substantially reduced the availability of open-access woodlands and caused difficulties for households dependent on the wilds. The state responded by replacing in-kind levies with a silver tax used to buy woodland products on the market, promoting the commercialization of markets for forest labor. This shift from labor dues to cash taxes, coming about four hundred years after the first wave of forest enclosure, marked the second major policy change in response to the silvicultural revolution.

HOUSEHOLDS AT THE MARGINS

Long before the Song, Chinese states had created monopolies as a way to tax non-agrarian goods like salt and tea. Like the decision to allow land to circulate on the private market, this policy emerged in part from tax shortfalls. In the late Tang, these monopolies—especially on salt—made up a major component in state finance.[5] By the Song, tea households (*chahu*), smelter households (*yehu*), and saltern households (*zaohu*) all supplied the state directly with their respective products, albeit in highly varied and regionally dependent ways.[6] Activist ministers like Wang Anshi and Cai Jing expanded the tea and salt monopolies even further. In some regions, these monopolies could be key to the extension of state power to non-agrarian populations.[7] In addition to taxing these specialized households, the Song also imposed labor service on its commoner population, including a regular corvée to cut firewood, and more erratic levies to log large timber.[8] In addition to their recognized importance in state finances, these household levies were a way for the Song to derive both control and revenue from non-agrarian environments.

The spread of household registration to non-agrarian peoples took on an entirely new character under nomadic rulers. Innovations began under the Khitan-ruled Liao dynasty, contemporaries of the Northern Song. In order to tax the steppe and forest peoples of the north as well as the agrarian population of the south, the Khitan created a dual administration, imposing a head tax on the northern groups and land taxes on the sedentary farmers.[9] This dual system was highly influential. The Jurchen Jin dynasty adopted it when it conquered the Liao in the early 1100s, and the Mongols adopted it when they conquered the Jin, in part under the tutelage of a Khitan noble named Yelü Chucai.[10] In these early stages, the dual system focused on incorporating sedentary farmers into nomadic states. Yet as they integrated North China into their empire, the Mongols went far beyond their Liao and Jin predecessors. Within the sedentary population, they oversaw a proliferation of increasingly specific household categories, including separate classifications for artisans (*jiang*), Chinese military households (*junhu*), and a wide range of other smaller professional groups including Confucian scholars (*ru*), physicians (*yi*), musicians (*yueren*), and diviners (*yinyang*).[11] The Mongols also retained the smelter and saltern households clustered around mines and salt marshes.[12] Tax extraction remained capricious until well into the reign of Kublai Khan (1260–94).[13] Nonetheless, the basic outlines of this complex household system were in place by the time the Mongols conquered South China from the Song in 1279.

As they incorporated the former Song territories, the Mongol household system shifted again, this time to incorporate the distinctive non-agrarian groups of South China. Reorganization of the former Song territories began with the imposition of existing categories, starting around the time of the first provisional census in 1290.[14] But it also involved the creation of new household groupings to incorporate hunting, fishing, and mining groups.

By 1294, an island jurisdiction near Ningbo created new categories for tea households, boat households (*chuanhu*) taxed in shark skins, and hunting households (*buhu*) taxed in fox pelts.[15] By the early 1300s, one county near Nanjing (Jinling) had more than eight hundred gold-panning households (*taojin hu*), including the ancestors of the Ming founder Zhu Yuanzhang.[16] These specialized tax categories appear quite similar to the better-documented system used by the Qing for taxing hunters, pearl divers, and mushroom pickers in the north, a system that probably developed from the Mongol legacy.[17]

By the 1300s, some sources began to organize the new household groups into superordinate categories like North Chinese (Hanren) and Southerners (Nanren), categories that many historians have viewed as a racial hierarchy with Mongols at the top and their sedentary subjects at the bottom.[18] But while the Mongols may have had both implicit and explicit bias against their Chinese subjects, this was only loosely systematized.[19] Throughout the late thirteenth and early fourteenth centuries, household categories were principally organized for tax purposes, and in an erratic and highly localized fashion.[20] Far from a uniform or ideological imposition of racial hierarchies, they emerged through a process of trying to tax disparate, complex, and mobile populations. Like the Song's tea and saltern households—and the hunting groups later organized by the Qing—the Yuan's hunting and fishing families represented an attempt to incorporate new peoples and new environments into the state's fiscal regime.

VILLAGES AND THEIR DISCONTENTS

Mongol rule in China declined starting in the 1350s, before giving way to the radical vision of Zhu Yuanzhang and his Ming dynasty in 1368. Perhaps due to his personal history at the margins, and certainly in reaction to the excessive extractions of the Mongols, Zhu attempted to create a system of self-sufficient villages. When the Ming compiled a census and land surveys, the goal was not to maximize revenue; they were intermediate steps toward the reorganization of the population into administrative villages (*lijia*) starting in 1381 and culminating with the yellow registers a decade later.[21] This village system represented the centerpiece of Zhu's policies, used for both organizing revenue and social engineering. Nominally, each village was created as a group of 110 households that oversaw tax collection, labor service, policing, and dispute resolution. The ten wealthiest households took turns serving as village head (*lizhang*), each taking on responsibilities for ensuring the village's tax payments for one year in the ten-year rotation. The hundred ordinary households were split into ten "tithing" groups (*jia*) and performed the more menial duties, also on a decennial basis.[22] Villages were further grouped into a spatial hierarchy of wards (*tu*), townships (*du*), and cantons (*xiang*) within each county.[23] Officials used these village hierarchies to make the government self-sufficient. Each office set quotas for the goods needed to maintain itself, including a wide range of items like fuel, paper, and wax for government offices; arrows and uniforms for military garrisons; and even game for official banquets.[24] Officials then divided these quotas among subordinate jurisdictions: between the counties in each prefecture and province, and between the townships and villages within each county. While based on earlier systems of mutual surveillance, the early Ming villages represented a new high-water mark of the penetration of governmental oversight beyond the limits of the formal state.[25] In areas that had only been marginally integrated into the Song and Yuan, village administration also marked the beginnings of a widespread documentary culture and fixed social units in relation to the state instead of purely by family or tribe.[26]

Yet while Zhu Yuanzhang reintegrated many of the Yuan's professional household categories into uniform administrative villages, he retained several important distinctions between status groups, including the main division between commoners (*min*), artisans (*jiang*), and military (*jun*), as well as the more locally specific categories for saltern and tea households.[27] Zhu even extended and amplified some of the marginal household categories that counted groups engaged in woodland and wetland economies. In 1382, the year following village registration, Zhu also required boat people to register as fishing households (*yuhu*) at river mooring stations (*hebo suo*) throughout the empire.[28] In addition to subjecting them to mutual surveillance, this registration held fishing households responsible for annual payments of marine goods. While based in "boat" or "fishing households" of the Yuan, the mooring stations centralized taxation of a peripatetic population and extended it to regions of the southeast coast largely untouched by earlier states.[29] In other areas, the Ming retained hunting households (*liehu* or *buhu*) that had been established in the Yuan, gradually expanding the program in the fifteenth century.[30] The Ming even created a separate category for three thousand households near Nanjing who were specifically required to cut reed fuel for the capital.[31] Elsewhere, the Ming worked to collect the major products of each local environment: game, hides, and feathers from Fujian; tung oil and lacquer from Jiangxi; timber and bamboo from Zhejiang; and, most importantly, fuel.[32] While Zhu Yuanzhang imagined an empire of uniform villages, this vision gave way to a more pragmatic administration that aimed to incorporate and tax non-agrarian peoples and non-agrarian landscapes as well. In the end, this was a less radical departure from the Mongols than it appeared.

The village system also brought a new slate of fiscal problems, including many related to the goods quotas, which were too inflexible to respond to changes in local environments or governmental needs. While village standardization allowed for easier budgeting, the household system was also rife with regional irregularities. Because taxes were based on official demand, levies were not distributed uniformly or according to local productivity. Border regions, transit corridors, and the hinterlands of the capital were taxed especially highly to meet the needs of nearby government offices. Paradoxically, these policies also opened the door to a radical departure from the ideals behind them, as the greater state penetration into local economies enabled a massive expansion of state levies.

In 1398, the Ming founder died and was succeeded by a grandson, whose reign had barely begun before he was deposed by his uncle, who seized the throne to rule as the Yongle emperor. While Yongle governed with his father's autocratic style, he showed no commitment to the principles of self-sufficiency behind the tax quotas and village system. Instead, he oversaw a massive expansion of the physical infrastructure of the state—building his personal estate at Beijing into a massive new capital, dredging the Grand Canal to supply Beijing, and launching expeditions to the Indian Ocean, the steppe, and Vietnam. The Yongle reign effectively marked the Ming's second founding. It left two long-term legacies: dual capitals—Nanjing on the Yangzi and Beijing in the north—and the social and environmental consequences of a massive expansion of the command economy.

Leaving the specifics of building ships and palaces to later chapters, it is worth emphasizing the sheer scale of labor service requisitions to supply them. Between 1406 and 1420, perhaps a million laborers were conscripted throughout the empire to construct the imperial palaces in Beijing.[33] By very rough estimate, more than a million large trees were cut from the frontiers to supply this construction, requiring another labor force of a million or more loggers.[34] Between 1411 and 1415, another 165,000 laborers were conscripted to dredge the Grand Canal and build embankments.[35] The dikes were constructed from wooden fascines, which probably required a comparable force of corvée laborers to cut timber and bamboo. While these laborers were drawn from all parts of the empire, the burden fell especially hard on artisan households and on the regions neighboring the projects themselves. To pay for his large projects, Yongle printed large quantities of paper money. By 1425, government-issued paper currency circulated as low as 2 percent of its face value and was effectively abandoned.[36] Collectively, these efforts strained both forced labor drafts and cash economies to their breaking points.

When the Yongle emperor died in 1424, the empire must have heaved a collective sigh of exhaustion and relief. By then, the Beijing palaces and Grand Canal were largely completed. The court launched one final fleet under Zheng He's command in 1433 before canceling the missions entirely. The culmination of these large-scale projects greatly reduced the demand for labor, yet it is clear that imperial policy also shifted away from such outsize demands on labor and material. Under pressure to decrease the massive and irregular corvée burdens imposed by Yongle, his successors the Hongxi and Xuande emperors sought to return to policies of self-sufficiency. They canceled many projects outright. In 1425, Hongxi issued an edict that "wherever the government had placed restrictions [jin] on mountain workshops, gardens, forests, lakes, wetlands, kilns and foundries, fruit trees and beehives, all [was] to be returned to the common people."[37] Further edicts under the Xuande emperor clarified and broadened this rule.[38] The state also faced the unintended consequences of Yongle-era monetary expansionism. Following the collapse of the paper money supply, rich households hoarded silver and copper cash, plunging markets into currency famines and depression.

The excessive levies of the Yongle era also led to widespread tax evasion and even emigration from the most heavily taxed areas. To avoid reporting for corvée, some households fled their registration entirely, either absconding to the frontier or becoming subservient to larger households. Others falsified their registration status, hiding wealth and workers, and even changing household category to avoid the more onerous forms of labor service. By the mid-1400s, the official census had little correspondence with the actual population and entire villages were filled with ghost households. This only increased the burden on those families whose registration remained current.[39] Due to the collapse of the currency and retrenchment from large projects, the trend toward tax evasion occurred at a time when the bureaucracy was both overextended and resource-poor. For more than half a century, the household census and land registers contained little more than empty figures, often copied from the previous decennial surveys.[40] Population and landholding figures are almost entirely missing for the years between 1421 and 1491, and sometimes even later.[41]

SILVER ACCOUNTING

In the mid-fifteenth century, officials began to innovate new ways to function within the constraints imposed by their predecessors without resorting to the same extractive tendencies that led to the near collapse of the early Ming system. Through local experimentation, officials in the interior south gradually began to resolve the worst problems with the corvée system. In several Jiangxi counties in the 1430s, Ke Xian introduced an "equalized corvée method" (*junyao fa*) that merged corvée under four main headings called "four levies" (*sichai*). The four headings included administrative village duties (*lijia*), which were mostly related to tax collection; "equalized corvée" (*junyao*), which grouped together most of the miscellaneous goods levies; and more self-evident categories for postal service (*yizhuan*) and militia (*minbing*). In the 1440s and 1450s, the next generation of officials brought this reform to higher-level jurisdictions: Han Yong and Xia Shi to the rest of Jiangxi, and Zhu Ying to Fujian, Guangdong, and Shaanxi.[42] Much like the mid-Yuan tax reforms that consolidated land tax categories, Ke's equalized corvée made little change to the levies themselves; but by classifying them into standard categories, he made it easier to redistribute the burden among households and villages. This provided temporary relief for the communities most damaged by earlier extractions, but it also failed to resolve the fundamental inequities that led to tax flight.

The second major shift in household levies came on the heels of the equalized corvée reforms, when an influx of silver allowed officials to convert household impositions to cash payments. As officials rebalanced corvée assessments, they also began to substitute silver surcharges for some of the in-kind levies of goods and labor. This began in the 1450s, when the local magistrate Han Yong converted some county-level levies for ritual goods into payments called "public expense silver" (*gongfei yin*).[43] Over the next eighty years, other officials in Jiangxi and western Fujian expanded this conversion to encompass most household levies. Conveniently, the equalized corvée reforms had already compiled these levies into neat and consistent categories, making substitutions easier; in some places they were even called "equalized silver" (*junping yin*).[44] Yet whether assessed directly or commuted to silver, the quotas became uneven over time, leading inevitably to tax evasion.[45] As long as levies were assessed on the household, families continued to flee or falsify their status to avoid extractions.

By the mid-1500s, local officials again reported widespread tax flight across the regions of the south most responsible for levies of forest products. In southern Jiangxi, the magistrate Hai Rui reported, "[Whereas] prior to 1551, [this county] had forty-four villages, today it has only thirty-four . . . [and] there are many half villages, or even villages with only one, two, or three parts in ten."[46] In a nearby county, the magistrate Qian Qi wrote, "One village often takes on many villages' levies, [and] one household often takes on several households' corvée. Requisitions are excessive, and goods and labor are insufficient."[47] Xu Jie, another local official, summed up the situation in Jiangxi, where he said, "[People] are not troubled by the land tax, they are troubled by corvée."[48]

In the mid-1500s, officials finally resolved the paradox of corvée: instead of applying fixed quotas to mobile and changing populations, they imposed them on immovable assets. The first generation of reforms, started by Ge Gaiyi in 1522, followed the previous strategy of commuting levies to silver and redistributing them. But instead of redistributing this silver quota by village, he divided each county's corvée quota by its total tax assessment and imposed it as a surcharge on each picul of tax grain. He called this "village equalization" (*lijia junping*).[49] Around this time, the leading scholar Gui E submitted a similar proposal to the Board of Revenue, intending to carry it out empire-wide, but received no response.[50] In the 1550s and 1560s, a second generation of reformers took up the idea again, dividing the total corvée duty in each county by its total acreage, ignoring the problematic census, and creating a single line-item tax. Replacing "single line reform" (*yitiao bianfa* 一條變法) with a more poetic homophone, they called this the "single whip method" (*yitiaobian fa* 一條鞭法). For two decades, province-level officials including Wang Zongmu, Cai Kejian, and Zhou Rudou attempted to convert and redistribute corvée throughout Jiangxi. In the face of opposition from princes with estates in the province, the measure repeatedly failed. Finally, in 1572, a third generation of officials led by Liu Guangji promulgated the policy province-wide.[51] Meanwhile, Wang Zongmu and Hai Rui, both of whom had experience with the single whip at low-level posts in Jiangxi, spread the new accounting method to Shandong and the Southern Metropolitan Region, while Pang Shangpeng implemented similar policies in Zhejiang.⁵² Finally, in 1580, Grand Secretary Zhang Juzheng promulgated the single whip empire-wide.⁵³

The shift to silver accounting in the late fifteenth and the sixteenth centuries came from the grass roots, as local officials learned hard truths about the changing fiscal landscape. They realized that the land tax was harder to avoid than labor levies, if only because the land was fixed and workers could move. People continually gave birth, died, and moved, rendering population data quickly obsolete, but land remained in place. This meant that once land had been registered, officials needed only to update information on its ownership. Proprietors were also generally inclined to keep the state abreast of land transactions: buyers had incentives to register property to have an official record of ownership in case of a title contest, and sellers had incentives to change the registration to decrease their tax liabilities. Placing the silver surcharge on acreage therefore made it far harder to evade than the earlier levies based on household composition. Yet despite its advantages over earlier reforms, the single whip method was essentially an accounting trick that redistributed the existing tax quota. To reform Jiangxi's taxes in 1570, Liu Guangji did not send agents into the countryside to survey landholdings or count households; he locked seven leading officials and a tax expert in the examination hall to perform calculations.⁵⁴

Despite the lack of administrative outreach, the single whip reforms totally transformed the Ming state's position in the economy, replacing direct levies of goods and labor with a silver budget. In fifteenth-century Chizhou, villages rotated responsibility to send 104 woodcutters to cut fuel for county, prefecture, and Nanjing offices; in the sixteenth century, the prefecture *hired* 104 workers, each paid twelve taels of silver out of the land tax surcharge.⁵⁵ Many levies of woodland products were also replaced with goods bought with tax silver. Prior to the single whip reforms, Jiangxi collected just over two thousand catties of tung oil (around one thousand kilograms), most of which was sent directly to the warehouse that supplied court workshops; following the reforms, tung-producing areas split a tax surcharge of sixty silver taels, which they forwarded to court to *purchase* oil.⁵⁶ Almost all woodland levies likewise shifted to line items in a silver budget.

The conversion of thousands of discrete revenue items into their cash equivalents made little overall difference in state budgets. Using the best available figures from seventeenth-century Jiangxi, non-agrarian, non-textile goods accounted for only 2 percent of the value of the autumn tax and essentially none of the summer tax.[57] But the effect on laborers was profound, effectively transforming a forced labor economy into a cash economy. In heavily wooded areas, forest products were often the only goods to sell to earn the cash needed for tax payments. The 1632 gazetteer from Kaihua County, in western Zhejiang, noted the importance of timber exports in meeting this new expense: "In Kaihua County there is little farmland and the people plant fir for their livelihood. They log every thirty to forty years; this is called 'clearing the forest.' In this county fir is the best local product, followed by ginger and lacquer, and then charcoal. The profits from ginger, lacquer, and charcoal are only one-fifth those of timber. If you ask the elders, they will say that the profits from fir are not less than ten thousand [taels] per year. For this reason few households flee the land tax."[58] Kaihua was just one of dozens of counties where local livelihoods relied overwhelmingly on forest products and that now needed to sell them to raise cash. Even in Liaoning, in the far northeast, households previously responsible for cutting fuel and fir timber for the state now owed silver payments instead.[59]

As forest communities were exposed to the market, they found that each product brought its own commercial strengths and weaknesses. Timber, especially fir, was the most valuable, but it required risky multi-decade investments. Other products offered shorter harvest cycles but lower profits. These included bamboo, both structural poles and edible shoots; firewood and charcoal; dyestuffs like indigo; fiber crops like hemp, ramie, mulberry bark, and palm fronds; and drugs and spices like ginger. Other goods could be harvested repeatedly once trees matured. These included resins like lacquer and pine tar (*songzhi*); oleiferous fruits like tung, tree tallow (*wujiu youzhi*), and camellia seed oil (*chayin you*); and a wide range of edible fruits and nuts. Like Kaihua, most communities diversified their options by planting a variety of forest crops. There were clear regional specializations: tallow trees (*wujiu*) near the mouth of the Yangzi, tung in Yuanzhou, indigo in Ji'an, drugs in Linjiang, paper mulberry in Guangxin and central Hunan, tea in Zhejiang and northern Fujian, and citrus and lychees in Quanzhou. Some forest production fed substantial industrial development, including pulp for Yanshan's papermakers and fuel for Jingdezhen's porcelain kilns. The runaway growth of these commercial-industrial towns (*zhen*) in the sixteenth and seventeenth centuries stymied attempts to fit them into the normative hierarchy of administrative cities.[60] But fir was king, probably accounting for more than half of forest acreage across broad swaths of South

China. Throughout this forest belt, the state removed itself from controlling production or transport of most of these goods. Instead, the market was made by two major diasporas working in concert with the forest owners: timber merchants, who were principally from Huizhou, at the center of the Jiangnan forest belt, and forest workers, who were overwhelmingly from the Wuyi Mountains at the corner of Fujian, Jiangxi, and Guangdong.

TRANSPLANTS AND MIGRANTS

Of the two groups of sojourners involved in spreading commercial forestry, Huizhou merchants had the longer documented history in the trade. Traveling abroad from their mountainous prefecture in the middle of Jiangnan, Huizhou merchants dominated markets throughout South China by the mid- to late Ming.[61] The rise of this remote and mountainous region to commercial preeminence was a direct outgrowth of its role in wood markets. In the twelfth century, Huizhou was at the epicenter of the revolution in tree planting. Huizhou also had a direct river route to the Song capital at Hangzhou and received special treatment under the tariff regulations of the twelfth century.[62] This gave Huizhou a key advantage in the nascent market in commercially planted timber. As more timber entered the cash economy, gradually in the fourteenth and fifteenth centuries, and in a great rush in the sixteenth and seventeenth centuries, Huizhou merchants dominated the sale of other regions' timber as well. The Kaihua gazetteer quoted above cites the special role played by Huizhou merchants in this market. While noting that timber enabled Kaihua landowners to meet their tax burdens, it added the caveat that "they must let men from Huizhou clear the surplus [timber] and transport these goods to Jiangnan without obstruction."[63] Similar anecdotes confirmed the position of Huizhou merchants throughout the Yangzi River basin and down the southeastern coast. Through their market advantage established in the Southern Song, Huizhou traders developed the connections, the capital, and the expertise to emerge as the preeminent timber wholesalers in the Ming.

Huizhou's importance in wood markets was further cemented by the growth of nearby Jingdezhen as a porcelain production center. A market town just south of Huizhou, Jingdezhen developed as its kilns were tapped to supply porcelain to the Yuan court in the thirteenth century and to the Ming court in the fifteenth century.[64] In the sixteenth and seventeenth centuries, the state removed most monopolistic strictures on porcelain production, and Jingdezhen became the preeminent maker of blue-and-white ware, not just for the court, but for the world market.[65] Throughout the growth of Jingdezhen into a major industrial center, Huizhou was its main fuel supplier, again via direct water routes, and Huizhou merchants were involved in shipping ceramics out of Jingdezhen.[66] Huizhou moneylenders also became Jingdezhen's main source of working capital to bridge potters from production to sale.[67] Once again, their early position in the market allowed them to dominate.

From their advantageous position in Hangzhou's officially regulated timber markets, Huizhou merchants expanded horizontally to become the most important middlemen in the timber trade. Building on their positional advantage in Jingdezhen's fuel markets, Huizhou merchants expanded vertically to dominate trade and finance in the world's greatest porcelain industry. By the late Ming, they were by far the most important timber traders across the south—not only in neighboring regions like Jingdezhen and Kaihua, but throughout the Yangzi River networks; in Fujian, Guangdong, and Guangxi; and along the Grand Canal (see map 3.1).[68] As they traveled across the south, buying and selling timber, fuel, and a plethora of other goods, Huizhou merchants were also a key vector for the transmission of expertise on forest management, financing, and market conditions.

As Huizhou merchants took pole position in the trade in wood products, tree planting became especially associated with another diaspora: peoples from the Wuyi Mountains in Fujian. Until the sixteenth century, this region was populated by a heterogeneous and shifting group of tax refugees from the lowlands and non-Sinitic upland peoples.[69] These groups interfaced with the Chinese state indirectly, in part by submitting tribute in tea, timber, or mine or animal products. This changed with the twilight of direct levies in the sixteenth century, a policy shift that made these marginal highlanders choose a side: either fuller integration into the growing commerce in forest products or retreat from participation in lowland society. A sixteenth-century account notes this bifurcation:

> In Fujian there are wandering people that grow tea, mainly of the three surnames Pan, Lan, and Lü. They used to share a single ancestor but have since divided.[70] Those who do not enter their names into household registration wander the cliffs and abandoned lands, living there by farming and hunting to feed themselves, but not paying land tax or

corvée. They wear their hair bound into buns and go barefoot. Each is subject to a chief, who they call elders, and who wear kerchiefs and long robes. [Others] travel abroad to various places, never staying for long: from Tingzhou they go to various prefectures in Jiangxi, where they produce fir to export via the mouth of the Ben River [a tributary of the Yangzi]; to Huizhou, where they produce firs to export via the mouth of the Rao River [a tributary of Poyang Lake]; and to Zhangzhou, where they produce fir that is sent to eastern Zhejiang by sea.[71]

This passage neatly summarizes how the fissiparous mountain societies of southwestern Fujian split into two discrete groups. The first group—those who did not register their households or pay taxes—retained their identity as non-state peoples. They came to be known as She, perhaps a term for the shifting cultivation they practiced. The second group traveled abroad from their Wuyi homeland, entering lowland society as forest laborers. They came to be known as Hakka (*kejia* or *kehu*), often translated as "guest families" but perhaps better understood as "sojourners."[72] While the sixteenth-century emergence of the Hakka was driven by multiple factors, the shifts in forest corvée are the missing piece of this puzzle. Previous scholarship has focused on the role of Hakka migrants as miners—especially in Guangdong—and in growing cash crops like hemp, ramie, and tobacco.[73] But as this anecdote shows, they were also heavily involved in the forest economy, planting timber on plantations from coastal Fujian to Huizhou and Jiangxi (map 3.1). The pull of growing markets for forest products allowed the Hakka a place at the fringes of the Chinese state as forest and mining specialists. But unlike in previous periods, their role in the forest economy was demarcated through private arrangements rather than officially designated household categories.

VILLAGERS AND SOJOURNERS

For hundreds of years, China's household registration system was predicated on keeping families in place. The state wanted people to stay in their villages so they could be surveilled, and, more importantly, so they could be taxed. By fits and starts, the Song, Yuan, and early Ming states extended the household system from the main tax base of farmers to tea growers, salt producers, miners, fisherfolk, hunters, and dozens of other non-agrarian

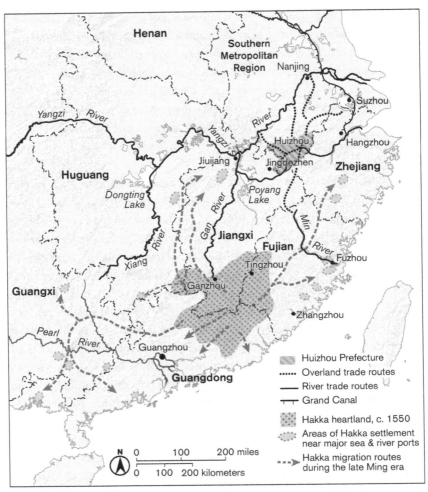

MAP 3.1 The Huizhou and Hakka diasporas. Adapted from Du, *Order of Places*, map 1.1, and Leong, *Migration and Ethnicity*, map 2.1 (original created by G. William Skinner).

peoples; in the process, they assigned these peoples to specialized households in an attempt to fix them in administrative space. Conversely, when Chinese states wanted people to be mobile, they placed them in groups that allowed—or enforced—mobility, especially craft (*jiang*) and military (*jun*) households. Arguably, this predilection toward enforced localization persists in modern China's household (*hukou*) system. Yet the assumption of fixed residence was a poor model of behavior, even for farmers, who fled and falsified their household registration to avoid excessive corvée. It was even less accurate for the shifting vocations of fisherfolk, placer miners, hunters, swidden cultivators, loggers, and the other peripatetic peoples of the non-agrarian fringe.

To make the thankless job of meeting quotas still more difficult, tax collectors had to deal with changes in the land as well as the movement of people. Landowners gradually converted much of the diverse natural woodland of South China into artificial forest plantations. They greatly increased production of a handful of tree species—especially pine, fir, and bamboo—at the cost of substantially reduced habitats for a much wider array of woodland plants and animals. A small number of forest owners curtailed the rights of a much larger number of others, who lost their freedom to hunt, gather, pasture animals, cultivate crops, and cut wood in what had long been open-access areas. Like the assumptions of fixed residence, static tax quotas also worked poorly in a changing fiscal landscape. Even grain and fiber-crop yields could fluctuate with the weather and decline as soils were depleted. The premise of meeting fixed targets of wild goods like furs and mushrooms was even less sustainable, as Jonathan Schlesinger shows in his study of Qing levies in Manchuria and Mongolia.[74]

As officials struggled to reallocate quotas and rebalance the corvée system, the commercial economy offered another solution. For centuries, rural entrepreneurs had invested in planting timber trees and other forest crops. Starting in the late 1400s, these commercial forest economies were buoyed by an influx of silver. By fits and starts, county magistrates began to take advantage of the growing money supply by converting their local levies from the command economy to the cash economy. Not coincidentally, these reforms emerged from the hotbeds of commercial silviculture in the middle south, especially Jiangxi and Fujian. Eventually, generations of gradual policy change came together in the revolutionary single whip reform, an accounting method that reduced the plethora of labor and wild goods extractions into a single surcharge assessed on fixed, cultivated land. In the 1560s and 1570s, provincial administrators promulgated the single whip across their jurisdictions; in 1580, Zhang Juzheng took the method empire-wide. Now, instead of taxing wax and timber directly, officials bought them out of a silver budget, and instead of providing fuel or game to the state as a condition of their registration, many households now looked for similar work on the market.

In addition to centralizing accounting, the single whip reforms meant that the state intervened far less in local relationships between land and labor. As these reforms did away with the direct pressures of labor service, they also created a new imperative to earn cash to pay taxes. The shifts in forest markets and goods levies created both new pressures and new opportunities for households on the wooded fringes of agrarian society. Some, like the Huizhou merchants, leaned hard into the silver economy, registering their property and their commerce with the state. Some, like the She, stayed on the margins as shifting cultivators and non-state peoples. And some, like the Hakka, found themselves in a rather unhappy middle ground. The end of corvée did not spell an end to coercion; it simply left relations between land and labor to be worked out between individual households.[75] If anything, the end of official labor drafts led to a proliferation of new forms of private, contractual subordination, including shifts in bond servitude, or subordinate relations to others' households, and changes in tenancy, or subordinate relations to others' landholdings.[76] In chapter 4, I explore the implications of this contractual market for the management of commercial forest plantations.

FOUR

DEEDS, SHARES, AND PETTIFOGGERS

IN 1520, TAN JING SOLD HIS OWNERSHIP INTEREST IN A FOREST TO his uncle Tan Yongxian. This seemingly minor transaction is one of thousands documented in forest deeds preserved in Huizhou, the prefecture at the epicenter of the revolutionary changes in South China's forests. Individually, most of these deeds are too short and too formulaic to tell us much, but collectively the Huizhou archive paints a striking picture of how the forest economy worked and, more importantly, how it changed.[1] Just as significantly, these documents record the simple, repetitive acts that produced the forest landscape: property registration, subdivision of labor and capital investments, selection and planting of trees, negotiation of management responsibilities, and valuation of timber. With the exception of property registration, most of these processes were opaque to the state; Tan Jing's deed records nearly all of them. I therefore start by considering the terms of this single document before turning to the broader corpus of similar negotiations.

Tan Jing's deed begins by documenting the location and status of his forest. It notes that Tan Jing "previously contributed to the collective purchase of Hu Yuanqing's cadastral registration [*jingli mingmu*]."[2] As was general practice, it gives both the local name for the village containing the forest—"east spring" (*dongyuan*)—and its location in the local administrative hierarchy—"*bao* 5." This allowed officials to readily locate the plot in both the physical landscape and the county's land registers. The purchase of the cadastral registration also meant that the sale was recorded at the county seat and the land title was secured against rival claims.

Next, the deed notes how rights to the land and the trees were subdivided into shares. Because Tan Jing contributed to the purchase of the plot, he owned a share in the land itself. In addition, he and his uncles Yongxian and Yongfang "bought a number of sections [on this plot] planted with fir by Tan Gong and his cousin Hongjing." Tan Jing accrued other shares when he "collaborated with Tan Qi to plant another section with fir and worked with a group to plant another forest section with seedlings."[3] These clauses reveal that the forest was actually split into two types of shares—*capital shares* held by those who contributed to the purchase of the land and *labor shares* held by those who planted sections with fir. Any of these could be bought and sold. Tan Jing acquired capital shares from the original land purchase; he acquired labor shares through his own work planting seedlings and by buying them from Tan Gong and Tan Hongjing. When Tan Jing sold his ownership interest, the sale explicitly included "the above forest plot and the other items held under his name, including all shares of fir seedlings that he planted or purchased."[4] In other words, he sold his capital shares, shares acquired through his own labor, and all the labor shares that he had purchased.

These clauses also record the ways the Tans modified the forest on their new plot. For several years after purchase, various Tan men planted sections of the forest with fir, the preferred timber tree. The Tans also determined its age composition by cultivating the various sections (*kuai*) sequentially. Each section probably contained trees of uniform age that would mature simultaneously, allowing them to be clear-cut and replanted. By planting multiple sections at different times, the Tans could log and replant them on a rolling basis, to spread out the risks, profits, and labor over multiple years.

After detailing the shareholding arrangements, the deed previews the future arrangements for managing the forest. It specifies that all of Tan Jing's holdings were "included with this deed and sold to be placed under his uncle Yongxian's name," noting that this would "consolidate [ownership] for easier management."[5] As the majority owner, Tan Yongxian could more easily determine when to cut and sell the timber. Over time, other mechanisms developed to make this type of management decision possible even if ownership remained divided among a large number of shareholders.

Finally, the deed specifies a price, noting that "the parties met face-to-face and agreed on a current value of 1.7 taels of silver."[6] The value of the land itself was probably fairly low. This means that this price largely reflected payment for Tan Jing's past labor, an approximation of the current value of the standing trees, or an estimate of the expected future value of the timber. In a theoretical, frictionless market, these three quantities would converge. In actuality, the price probably reflected elements of each of these valuations, as well as complicating factors like family obligations among the Tans.

The Tans registered their forest and paid annual taxes on that basis, but all other aspects of their management diverged from official norms. They separated claims to forest *ownership* from claims to forest *production*, and they further subdivided each of these claims into multiple shares. The state formally opposed this sort of unbundling of land rights, yet magistrates were generally willing to enforce claims as long as they were clearly documented and taxes were paid. Because official regulations made few provisions for forest management, the rules and procedures for planting, protecting, and harvesting timber developed as local norms. Deeds, contracts, and low-level litigation recorded the valuation and subdivision of forest land, labor, and products and the rules for preventing and responding to theft and fire. Here, too, officials were willing to enforce contracts, as long as they did not grossly violate the basic tenets of penal law. This chapter tells the history of these arrangements, negotiations that were critical to the forest economy but left outside the purview of state administration.

TAX AND TITLE

Chinese officials were basically agnostic to the specifics of land use as long as plots were registered and paid tax. But planters like the Tans were far from indifferent to the state. Prior to the twentieth century, China did not develop anything precisely resembling Western civil or contractual law. Indeed, the notions of "contract," "property," and "rights" are all imperfect fits to the Chinese legal context.[7] Property rights cannot be traced to any specific legal precedent; instead, ownership claims were enforceable due to a general agreement between the state and landowners on the form and content of documentation.[8] To the individual stakeholders, the documents themselves were often less important than the acts they recorded, especially the face-to-face negotiations and the ritual act of signing the contract.[9] This meant that regardless of other context, the first function of forest deeds was to provide evidence of a claim to ownership. For this reason, essentially every land deed opened with an abbreviated chain of title, noting the names of the sellers, the sources of their claims to the land, the property's location and boundaries, and generally its tax rates. Implicit in these first clauses was the de facto agreement that lay behind the functioning of the land system: state enforcement of landholder claims in return for registration and tax payment.

While many deeds survive without substantial context, one extensive set of materials allows us to follow the complete history of a wooded property in Quanzhou, Fujian. Above all else, these documents demonstrate the importance that registration held for landowners. The first set of documents records the process of selling this wooded estate in 1265, when Quanzhou was held by the Southern Song. First, the owners posted a notice (*zhangmu*) to invite potential buyers of a large property consisting of "a garden plot, a forest [*shan*], a pagoda, a one-room building, and all the flowers, fruit, and other trees [*huaguo deng mu*] contained within."[10] This notice reflected the practice of giving kin and neighbors the opportunity to buy the property before it was offered to outsiders, often known as first right of refusal. Second, following the sale, the sellers wrote a receipt to inform the government and update the registration (*gaoguan jimai zhan*). This provides the most detailed evidence of land title, recording the history of ownership, boundaries, and the tax assessment on the property. It also notes that village elders reviewed the sale, attesting to the veracity of the title and ensuring that there were no liens on the property (*bie wu wei'ai*). A final clause notes that the buyer would pay future taxes. The third document is a deed of sale, to be retained by the buyers. It contains similar clauses to the tax receipt.[11]

A similar set of four documents records the process of selling this estate again, this time in 1366–67, when Quanzhou was controlled by the Yuan dynasty, but about to fall to the Ming. By this point, the original forest and fruit plantation had been split into two plots, the first planted principally with camphor trees (*zhangshu*) and the second with lychee (*lizhi*). Again, the sellers first posed a formal sale offer and checked for rival title claims. Once the sale was completed, they reported it to the state to update the tax registration and transferred the two plots to their respective buyers through deeds of sale.[12] This tantalizing set of records shows that sales under two different dynasties and separated by a century followed essentially identical documents and procedures. The sale process required the input of kin, neighbors, and village elders and produced records for both the local government and the private owners.

Materials from Huizhou further demonstrate the lengths to which owners went to maintain title records, even when the state was absent. As Yuan rule disintegrated during the millenarian Red Turban Rebellion, Huizhou was controlled by Han Lin'er, the nominal head of the northern Red Turban movement after the death of his father, Han Shantong, in 1351. In 1355, Han Lin'er formally established a state, nominally a restoration of the Song dynasty, and built the outlines of a central government close to Huizhou.[13] Soon thereafter, Huizhou landowners began to give formal recognition to Han's regime by using his official reign period on their deeds, presumably in the hope that Han's court would enforce their ownership claims.[14] A hastily compiled land register from Qimen County also bears a reign date from Han's regime.[15] Yet by 1363, the course of warfare turned against Han Lin'er. After living as a prisoner of Zhu Yuanzhang—the eventual Ming dynasty founder—Han was drowned in 1366.[16] During the brief period between Han's demise and Zhu's victory, Huizhou was again plunged into statelessness. Landowners scrambled to find ways to ensure their transactions and back up their title claims. In 1367, at least one deed used Yuan reign periods despite the total lack of Yuan presence in the prefecture. In fact, the deed notes that the *baojia* self-defense organization—not the Yuan state—was responsible for recording the plot and resolving any disputes.[17] Almost as soon as Zhu Yuanzhang declared victory in 1368, Huizhou deeds switched to his Hongwu reign period, and locals hastened to register their land with the Ming. Huizhou was one of the first prefectures to produce land registers.[18] Like Quanzhou landowners in the transition from Song to Yuan rule, Huizhou landlords during the Yuan-Ming interregnum registered their deeds with any reasonable authority. In the absence of a functional state, they relied on other institutions like the *baojia* to keep records and enforce contracts. But once the Ming restored a centralized, hierarchical order, they quickly moved to register any new sales with capped officials.

The effective institutions of the early Ming did not last. The decennial surveys to update land and population registers became dysfunctional by the 1430s. This lack of state oversight was reflected on the ground where many forest deeds from the late 1420s through the 1440s left plot numbers, boundaries, and acreage blank, presumably because they lacked adequate points of reference.¹⁹ Tax flight also left many orphaned properties, which the state awarded to village heads to apportion as they saw fit, as long as they continued to pay taxes.²⁰ Transactions from the 1430s reflected the cash-poor state of the post-Yongle economy: land sales were often transacted in cloth or grain rather than cash.²¹ When the economy recovered in the 1440s, the overwhelming majority were denominated in silver, not in copper coins or paper notes. Yet throughout the mid-century depression, Huizhou forest owners continued to record their land sales, even if the details were lacking. When the economy and bureaucracy began to recover in the 1450s and 1460s, locals helped restore the registers to the well-kept state of the early Ming. Deeds often left acreage figures blank, but they now noted that this information was no longer missing; it was omitted because it was available in the local land registers.²²

Nonetheless, new complications emerged during the commercial expansion of the late 1400s and the 1500s. According to Ming regulations, households were only allowed to own land in their home townships.²³ In spite of that, some families acquired plots across township boundaries and even in other counties. To manage this situation, the buyers of these properties paid taxes under the names of previous owners, who remained on the books as a sort of pass-through tax account. Deeds recorded this curious manipulation of the tax law to ensure that the plots paid taxes under the state's regulations, but also met the management needs of the new owners.²⁴ Other deeds specifically noted the buyers' responsibilities to transfer tax payments into their names during the next decennial land surveys.²⁵ Once again, owners took steps to ensure smooth transfer of title, even when official records failed to keep pace with the private land market. After the single whip reforms were implemented in Huizhou around 1570, deeds made explicit that their assessments included both the base tax and the corvée-replacement surcharge.²⁶ After Zhang Juzheng's surveys of 1581, many noted that they reflected the "clarified measurements in the new cadastres" (*qingzhang xince*).²⁷ Throughout multiple shifts in land oversight across more than three centuries, landowners took steps to ensure that they held a clear title claim.

SHAREHOLDING

After ensuring that their title was secured against rival claims, many forest owners proceeded to disaggregate ownership through shareholding and partnerships. Shares enabled forest owners to subdivide the risks associated with the decades it took for timber to mature; they provided a mechanism for remunerating forest laborers for the work of transplanting seedlings in advance of the timber harvest; and they made it possible for both owners and planters to spread their investments between forests that matured at different times. Yet these features emerged not through design, but through experimentation and the recursive planting, inheritance, and sale of forests.

In the thirteenth and fourteenth centuries, most forests in Huizhou were large, single-owner properties. Partible inheritance, sale, and partnerships gradually led to the subdivision of forest rights. By the fifteenth century, the overwhelming majority of forests were jointly managed through shareholding arrangements.[28] This tendency toward subdivision peaked in the sixteenth century, when new processes emerged that promoted consolidation of ownership through the reaggregation of partible claims into portfolios of shares in multiple properties. Eventually, consolidation took another form, as lineage corporations emerged to combine forest management under a single institutional umbrella.[29] By the nineteenth and twentieth centuries, the overwhelming majority of forests were corporate properties endowed to lineage graves and shrines. But in the Ming, these corporate entities were still in their infancy.[30] In the fifteenth and sixteenth centuries, the overwhelming majority of forests in Huizhou were neither single-owner plots nor trust properties; they were partitioned through shareholding.

Shareholding emerged as a solution to the problem of dividing ownership of large, spatially irregular plots whose real value was in their living trees. Under partible inheritance, it was standard for land to be parceled out to each of the sons upon the death of their father, but forests were far harder to divide fairly than farmland, a fact noted by Yuan Cai as early as the twelfth century.[31] By the Ming, it was rare for inheritance documents to specify physical partitions of forest land.[32] It was also theoretically possible to divide plots by counting the trees and dividing them among the parties.[33] Sample forms for selling forests included clauses that allowed the seller to include or exclude specific trees from the sale.[34] But in practice, sellers principally used these clauses to enumerate high-value fruit or oilseed trees, not timber trees.[35] Like physical partition, tree counting was the exception rather than the rule. Far more often, each heir received an equal share in the entire plot.[36] These shares included partible rights to any standing timber, bamboo, and fuelwood and anything else on the plot, including annual crops like chestnuts and even bond servant houses (and, by extension, bond servant labor).[37]

Shareholding appeared through another dynamic as well—the advance sale of stakes in the timber harvest. Unlike farmland, which produced annual crops to meet the regular needs of their owners, forests only yielded a timber harvest once every two to three decades or longer. If owners needed cash in the meantime, they had to sell a portion of their shares. An active market allowed owners to cash out early on the expected future value of their holdings rather than waiting for the timber to mature.[38] Some sold out of immediate need, others for convenience of management.[39]

In addition to partible inheritance and advance sale, there was also a third mechanism to divide forests into shares: partnerships. By the fifteenth century, it was common for forest owners to lease land to tenant planters, or to form partnerships to divide the expense and labor of sowing seedlings. Forest tenants contracted to manage forests for long-term periods, generally the twenty-five to thirty years from planting to logging; in exchange, they received rights to a fraction of the timber profits as well as to any annual crops interplanted with the young trees for the first few years. This bundle of rights and responsibilities was known as "forest skin" (*shanpi*). Under these rental contracts, forest owners retained the remaining portion of both timber profits and crop harvests; they also retained long-term ownership of the land and any accompanying tax responsibilities. Their bundle of rights and liabilities was known as "forest bones" (*shangu*).[40] Perhaps the clearest description of a forest partnership comes from a 1493 deed by which Fang Bangben and Fang Bo arranged to plant their large forest property. The Fangs had previously bought a forest plot of more than twenty-nine *mu* (about five acres) from two other urban landlords. They then contracted with Kang Xinzu and Wang Ningzong to plant the property with fir seedlings, agreeing to divide the future profits five ways: each of the two tenants received one share; Fang Bo, who owned one-third of the "forest bones," received one share; and Fang Bangben, who owned two-thirds of the "bones," received the remaining two shares.[41]

The designation of "landlord" and "tenant" shares mapped only imperfectly onto the social class of their owners. As seen in the Tan deed that opened this chapter, members of a single kin group frequently held both types of shares. In the fifteenth and early sixteenth centuries, most timber *merchants* were also planters, selling timber from both their own plots and those planted by others. In Chen Keyun's study of the Li family timber business, nine of the thirty-nine men named in the account books were both tenant planters and timber wholesalers.[42] As Joseph McDermott argues, these arrangements were far more like long-term investment partnerships than agricultural tenancies.[43] Indeed, some contracts were even titled "forest partnership agreements" (*huoshan hetong*), although "forest rental contract" (*zushan qi*) remained the more common term.[44] By the mid-1500s, contracts even began to use terms that more closely tracked how forest rights actually functioned: ownership shares (*zhufen*) and labor shares (*lifen*).[45]

Despite the effective transformation of timber production into shareholding partnerships, the relationship between owners and tenants remained unequal. While ownership and labor claimed roughly equal proportions of the timber harvest, owners were free to buy and sell their stakes, but laborers were generally not allowed to transfer their shares without the landlord's consent.[46] Owners also retained the underlying rights to the forest plot, entitling them and their heirs to a proportion of timber yields in perpetuity, while laborers only received stakes in the trees they planted. Over time, the distinctions between these contractual positions led to a growing gulf between two classes: those who held *any* ownership shares and those who held *only* labor shares. The terminology of "owner" and "tenant" also mattered in court. Under laws that presumed property to be farmland, adherence to conservative forms of contract remained the best means of assuring that agreements would hold up under official scrutiny and that penalties for violations would be those specified in the penal code. In this context, tenants could be punished more harshly for cheating their landlords than landlords for cheating their tenants. Thus, ownership shares remained "land deeds" and labor shares remained "tenancy contracts."

By the late fifteenth century, the processes of household division, advance sale, and partnership compounded on each other, leading to the recursive subdivision of forests. As each share came to represent a declining proportion of the timber yield, it became common for owners to parcel together shares in multiple forests. For example, a single deed from 1428 involved the sale of twenty forest plots, five of which were split into two shares and fifteen of which were split into twelve shares, suggesting that they were the results of two large partnerships.[47] In 1463, two brothers sold shares in six plots with at least four different shareholding agreements, including three different share divisions from their inheritance and two plots purchased from outside the family.[48] By 1500, parcellation had reached extremes, with individual plots split into 240 shares, 696 shares, 348 shares, and 540 shares.[49] Many deeds simply specified that they sold "all the shares held by this household" without going into this kind of detail.[50] By grouping together shares in multiple properties, deeds came to function less as proof of landownership and more as investment portfolios. Yet even if the parceling of shares simplified financial record keeping, it led to new complications for the management of the shared plots. Once a plot had dozens of owners, it became unwieldy for them all to participate in its day-to-day management.

By the mid-1500s, forest managers created new forms of record keeping to address the complications of highly divided plot ownership. Some ownership groups compiled inventory lists (*qingdan*) of all the subdivisions of each section in a forest. They produced these central directories of shareholding in direct response to the increased prevalence of ownership disputes. As repeated subdivision rendered ownership unclear, inventory lists centralized shareholding information in a single location to review before sales.[51] The compilation of these lists also reflected the fact that official records of land title were neither detailed enough nor updated with enough frequency to track changes in shareholding.

The emergence of portfolio deeds and inventory lists reflected increasing distance between the nominal responsibilities of a small number of "landlords" and the more abstract financial commitments of a larger shareholder group. Shares that began as commitments to actively managing forests started to function as freestanding investments, often purchased by urban investors who had little personal business in the management of their properties. Rather than owning large shares in a small number of forests, absentee shareholders often owned small stakes in many discrete plots in multiple forests and even multiple districts. This was more than incidental accrual of shares over time; it reflected intentional hedging against the risks of losing an entire plot of timber to fire, theft, or disease. Diversification also allowed owners to spread their investments between forests that matured at different times to provide a more regular stream of income.

Starting in the late 1570s and the 1580s, a final shift reflected the near-complete transformation of forest partnerships into abstract investments: the shift from fractional to decimal accounting. Decimals were initially created from fractional shares in order to ease the calculation of silver tax surcharges after the single whip reforms.[52] A deed from 1578 shows this process from start to finish: it gives the acreage of the entire plot (2.3 *mu*), specifies the fractional share (one-seventh), and finally calculates the decimal acreage equivalent to this share to use for tax assessment (0.33 *mu*).[53] Decimal accounting also made it easier to calculate the total value of shares of different sizes from different plots, as demonstrated by another deed from 1586. Rather than finding a common denominator for multiple different fractions, one owner converted each of the shares into a decimal, summed them to a 0.01995 stake in the plot, and carved off a 0.0015 share to sell.[54] While initially based in tax calculations, the shift to decimal notation also made the valuation of complex portfolios much easier. It may have also reflected the simplification of computation as the abacus became more prevalent in the sixteenth century.[55] Regardless of its origins, decimal notation completed the abstraction of forest shares as financial holdings rather than proportions of land and labor. While fractional division followed clear processes of household division and partnership, decimal notation eliminated any traces of this ownership history. We might conceive of a one-eighth role in planting trees, but a 0.0015 share is only sensible as an abstract financial stake, not as any concrete share of trees, time, or labor. Decimal shares completed the transformation of forest deeds from rights to physical land and trees into abstract securities fully removed the material realm they represented.

SHIFTS IN LAND AND LABOR RELATIONS

As deeds came to function as investment portfolios, new contractual forms emerged to fulfill their original functions: documenting ownership and labor responsibilities. As early as the 1430s, some ownership groups began drafting forest shareholding agreements (*fenshan hetong*) to specify how to manage the properties that underlay their increasingly abstract investments.[56] With ownership divided among dozens of stakeholders, it was no longer clear who was responsible for supervision, especially during the period between planting and felling. For five-year-old "mature stands" (*chenglin*) of fir to grow to marketable size took at least twenty years and sometimes as many as fifty. These were decades when the forest required little labor but presented growing risks of fire and theft. The most common solution was to make tenants or bond servants responsible for patrol and firefighting. Many agreements imposed fines of up to ten times the market value of timber to punish theft or negligence among forest workers.[57] Most villages resolved minor cases of wood theft internally, but in more brazen cases of timber poaching, the entire community was alerted to help apprehend the perpetrators, who were then turned over to state authorities.[58]

Theft from within the ownership group was more complicated than policing outsiders. Given the large number of stakeholders, there was a substantial moral hazard that one "owner" would seek to claim more than his share of the timber harvest. Shareholders could also be tempted to harvest wood to meet their own immediate needs without consulting the rest of the ownership group. Self-policing was therefore a major concern. Many associations began to impose fines on their members for violations. McDermott notes one association that created a particularly clever system of mutual surveillance. The community of eight lineages distributed numbered carry poles. To cut timber or fuel, members had to approve their harvest with the head of their administrative village (*li*) and to verify their ownership stake in that specific property. Illicit loggers could easily be identified by their numbered carry poles, which would be obvious if they tried to sell the wood anywhere within the district.[59]

As tenants became the main parties responsible for planting forests, labor practices also shifted. Most tenancy contracts were nominally established for the entire multi-decade maturation period, but labor was overwhelmingly concentrated in the first few years, when planters burned away weeds, planted seedlings, and intercropped grains and fiber crops. But after three to five years, when owners customarily inspected plots to ensure that trees were maturing, the labor needs dropped off precipitously, as did the sideline income from cover crops. If the planters were bond servants or restrained by strict contracts, they had little choice but to stay on the land. To deal with their limited income after the initial planting, most worked multiple plots; in theory, they could rotate between plots on short cycles until their first plot came to maturity. Yet few planters could afford to wait that long to receive a cash return on their labor. Therefore, many tenants sold their shares back to the landlord around the time of the initial inspection; others sold them illicitly or used them as collateral on loans.[60] Some contracts reflected the short-term nature of planting and were only written for three years.[61] More often the landlord retained the prerogative to call on tenants for the entire thirty years, or to buy back their shares, presumably at a rather steep discount.

For most of the fifteenth and sixteenth centuries, the groups of "tenants" and "owners" overlapped substantially. Yet the bifurcated markets in land and labor created a ratcheting effect, making it easy for landlords to acquire labor shares but difficult for laborers to acquire ownership. Many tenancy contracts specifically noted that land remained the exclusive property of the owners and placed the onus of growing timber exclusively on the tenants. In the seventeenth century, new barriers were raised to forest laborers who wished to use their labor to acquire long-term stakes in future timber profits. As of 1611, some landlords required laborers looking to acquire long-term shares in the timber harvest to pay an extra fee.[62] While some forests were still worked by communities of owner-planters acting in concert, many were now owned by a class of absentee shareholders and planted by an itinerant rural proletariat.

With planters no longer on-site for the duration of trees' maturation, other aspects of the forestry labor market were also transformed. Following the initial three-year planting stage, forests entered a decadelong period of maturation with few labor requirements. Aside from occasional thinning and patrols to prevent theft and fires, forests could largely be left alone. The second major period of forest labor came at the end of the maturation period, when the trees were felled. In the seventeenth century, it became increasingly common to draw up clearance contracts (*pinyue*), often arranged through an urban merchant who acted as a middleman between forest owners and logging teams.[63] Loggers were typically paid by the pole and were responsible for all their own expenses, including sacrifices to the local spirits. They could also be fined for cutting trees aside from those they were hired to clear.[64] Gradually the specific labor needs of forestry—heavy during planting, light during maturation, and heavy again during clearance—led to the emergence of a tripartite division between planters, guards, and loggers. Instead of members of a self-contained and overlapping community of foresters, forest guards were reduced to servile status, dependent on the benefice of their landlords, while planters and loggers were generally itinerant laborers, often Hakka migrants from the Wuyi Mountains.

WOOD LAW

Unlike in early modern Europe, Korea, or Japan, there was little specialized wood law in China, leaving forest owners, tenants, and laborers to work out their own terms. Formal oversight of forests was minimal, amounting to little more than basic land surveys and tax collection. While official land surveys demarcated forests as discrete properties, the state specified next to nothing about their management. Even basic ownership rights remained a legal gray area for more than two hundred years after the first forest surveys were conducted in 1149. It was only in 1397 that the *Great Ming Code* formally granted forest owners exclusive, heritable, alienable rights by classifying forests as real estate (*tianzhai*), opening forests to a wide range of general-purpose property law. By this point, the few laws specific to wood rights were largely dead letters. Aside from the laws governing imperial parks, none of the *Ming Code*'s laws on forests generated any substantial precedent for the next two and a half centuries.[65] Without productive wood laws, legal innovation to account for the complexities of forest management came almost exclusively from below, through contract and litigation.

While its wood laws produced very little jurisprudence, the *Great Ming Code* nonetheless reflected a major change in wood regulation, formalizing the long-standing de facto status of forests as exclusive property. The *Ming Code* nominally used the *Tang Code* as a model.[66] In theory, this should have returned to the centuries-old principle that kept woodlands as open-access commons; in practice, the centuries of intervening precedent were more significant. The *Ming Code* did include provisions against monopolizing woodland, but it changed the tenor of the law markedly. Instead of giving wildland regulations their own statute as in the *Tang Code*, the *Ming Code* downgraded them to a subsection of the law "Fraudulently Selling Fields and Houses" (Daomai tianzhai). While the Tang and Song penal codes stated that "mountains, wilderness, ponds, and embankments" (*shanye hupo*) were "held in common with the public" (*yu zhong gong*), the Ming law referred to forest workshops (*shanchang*) and other non-agrarian sites as "state or private" (*guan min*) property.[67] This turned on its head the clause that had previously defended wildlands against the very principle of ownership, now used as a defense of exclusive state or private landholdings against unlawful occupation.

Ming compilers copied other regulations on wood use from the *Tang Code*, and likewise downgraded them in importance. The provision against stealing timber, a statute in its own right in the *Tang Code*, became a subsection of the *Ming Code*'s "Stealing Wheat and Rice from Fields" (Dao tianye gumai).[68] The Ming article "Discarding or Destroying Things Such as Utensils and Crops" also includes provisions against destroying timber copied almost directly from the *Tang Code*.[69] In a productive historical contrast, Chosŏn administrators used the Ming law as precedent for a substantial forest administration in Korea.[70] But in China, these laws generated essentially no further jurisprudence on wood rights. With little fanfare, these few articles in the *Ming Code* completed the legal process begun in the Song, transforming forests into a subcategory of landholding little different from farmland in the eyes of the law.

Yet forests were not farms; their management was complicated by partnerships and securitization, multi-decade growth periods, and substantial risks of fire and theft. As much as possible, forest owners hashed out these complexities in the types of contracts seen above. But when contracts were violated or unclear, they turned to litigation. It is in this genre of lawsuit, principally preserved in private litigators' manuals (*songshu*), that we can find the best evidence of the hazards particular to forest management and of the legal innovations that helped diminish or overcome these risks.

Litigation by third parties was technically illegal under Chinese dynastic law. Nonetheless, private litigation masters (*songshi*) were noted as early as the eleventh century and proliferated in the Southern Song. These pettifoggers were colloquially known as "brush-pen hatpins" (*erbi*) in reference to the manner in which they advertised their trade. From the Song through the Ming, Jiangxi and Huizhou were particularly notorious hotbeds of litigation, with manuals and even private schools that offered legal training.[71] Despite attempts to stamp out litigators and to destroy these manuals, they continued to circulate, primarily in manuscript form. The earliest extant litigators' manual is from the Ming, *A Brush-Pen Hatpin's Critical Points* (Erbi kenqing; c. 1500–1569), written under the colorful pseudonym "the falsehood-revealing hermit of a small utopia" (*xiao taoyuan juefei shanren*).[72]

Where dynastic law left forest as a generic placeholder, the "falsehood-revealing hermit" is rather specific on the finer points of forest ownership. His text focuses principally on the petty yet complicated matters (*xishi*) related to property and household affairs.[73] The section on households (*hu*) contains a subsection specifically on "mountain plots and grave land" (*shantian mudi*), a guide to forest law not found in official texts. *Critical Points* avoids including multiple versions of similar suits.[74] Instead, each case is presented to demonstrate how to argue a particular type of dispute, including several specific genres of forest conflict. It reveals that landholders and pettifoggers developed their own standards for how to litigate forest ownership, shareholding, and illicit logging, transforming an official category that specified little more than a tax grade into the locus of substantial grassroots legal innovation.

The first clear example of the standards for litigating wood disputes comes from a simple case of contested ownership. In the comments on the case, *Critical Points* notes the importance of maintaining forest registration to prevent timber theft: "There are only two methods for contesting forests. Forests that have been purchased require clear deeds and satisfactory [evidence of] transferring tax responsibilities. Inherited, shared forests without deeds [as evidence] require consulting the *bao* registers and large and small contracts [between owners and tenants]. The forest's neighbors can verify management of the property."[75]

Statutory law does not mention a clear difference between purchased and inherited property, yet land deeds are careful to note this distinction. This commentary tells us why: the two situations produced different types of evidence. If a deed existed, it provided the most up-to-date information about ownership. But without a recent deed, inherited property required consulting the cadastres, which would identify the claimant (or his ancestor) as the owner of the property.

A second sample case in *Critical Points* demonstrates another complexity in forest litigation: demonstrating the ownership of both land and trees. In this suit, the plaintiff was careful to present deeds and tax receipts to prove that he had purchased the property. But because the plot had been abandoned, he also had to demonstrate that the timber was the product of his own labor. To do so, the anonymous plaintiff specifically claims that he "went to the forest to set up boundaries and plant seedlings," prior to fleeing during a period of banditry.[76] Through the evidence of purchase and planting, the plaintiff thus established claims to own both the plot and the timber that had grown on it.

Forest title could also be contested through false evidence, often through duplicate deeds, which are specifically addressed in *Critical Points*. In one sample suit, the plaintiff had purchased a property, registered it to his household, and planted it with trees. To contest his claim to the timber, another party bribed the original seller to create a second, fake deed with an earlier sale date. This type of falsified evidence was common in all types of land transactions, but forest owners were especially susceptible to title contests just before the timber matured. The commentary notes that in cases like this, both the seller and the rival claimant could be accused of the crime of falsifying claims to the forest.[77] In cases like these, tax registration was the best way for owners to prove their claims and recoup their losses.

The complexities of shareholding, and the increased divisions between owners, planters, guards, and loggers, provided another avenue for theft and disputes to emerge. One sample case in *Critical Points* presents the example of a neighbor who bought a half share to a forest and used it as a pretext to log the entire property.[78] Another suit involves a buyer accused of forcing a shareholder to sell shares he did not own.[79] In another sample case, parties with no shares simply fabricated them in order to claim a portion of the profits.[80] Like simpler cases of timber theft, all three conflicts emerged at or near the time of the timber harvest. As in simpler forms of land title dispute, *Critical Points* shows that shareholding conflicts were best resolved by having third-party documentation of ownership, especially by writing shareholding arrangements into the tax registration documents. Despite its complexities, shareholding did not upset the basic framework of forest litigation. Partial owners were able to use deeds as evidence, and clever litigators fit shareholding situations into the basic laws on real estate, in part by referring to these cases as generic thefts of "property" (*ye*). To teach others how to resolve these increasingly complex disputes, litigation masters circulated notes in specialized manuals like *Critical Points*.

Shareholding was not the only legal wrinkle posed by commercial forests. With the removal of ownership groups from day-to-day management, they increasingly relied on forest wardens (*shoushan*), generally bond servants who were given houses and fields to till in exchange for this thankless and dangerous job. Yet Ming law lacked provisions specific to the contracts between workers and their employers, especially when the workers were not easily classified as "tenants." *Critical Points* simply lists cases involving wardens under the more general heading of "theft and robbery" (*daozei*). In some cases, wardens were injured or killed in defense of their employers' property. In *Critical Points*, the author's commentary provides the specific statutory punishments to demand in court in such a case, noting that the use of an ax in committing a robbery aggravated the penalty for assault on the warden by one degree.[81] But in other cases, wardens and owners found themselves on opposite sides of a dispute. Generally poor and isolated, wardens had substantial opportunities to steal the timber they were tasked with guarding. In one such case, tenants recruited to guard a forest took advantage of their isolation to steal from the forest that the owners had "expended considerable labor and capital to plant with fir, pine, bamboo, and other timber." While litigated under the more general statute on theft, the sample plaint argues that "harming one's master is worse than robbing outsiders" (*shang zhu shenyu wai zei*), which would have aggravated the punishment by one or more degrees.[82] Once again, clever litigators were able to repurpose general precepts of Ming law to fill a vacuum in formal jurisprudence—in this case arguing for a specific legal standard for wardens stealing from the forests they were hired to protect.

PLANTING AND THE FOREST BIOME

By the fifteenth century, Huizhou's forests had been planted and replanted for hundreds of years, yet tenancy contracts are almost the only records of the process. These scattered documents show hints of the acts that went in to cultivating timber. Planters dug out the weeds (*chumao*), burned away the grasses (*shaohuang*), and planted seedlings or slips (*miao, cha*). According to figures given in forest deeds, one *mu* generally held between two hundred and six hundred trees (approximately twelve hundred to three thousand trees per acre), with the bottom end of the range being more typical.[83] During the first several years, tenants also planted millet, hemp, or other dry-field crops, which served both to protect the young seedlings and to provide for the tenants subsistence.[84] While many plots were clear-cut prior to planting, others retained mature trees, sometimes multiple kinds of trees.[85] Despite some variety in specific circumstances, these contracts clearly describe cyclical planting and clearing of uniform-age plantations, not the lumbering of old-growth or mature secondary woodland nor the selective felling of trees in a mixed-age forest.

The processes described in these contracts were essentially the same planting methods reaching back to the twelfth century, and perhaps as early as the ninth.[86] Transplanting of fir slips and pine seedlings; interplanting with dry-field crops; periodic thinning to encourage tall, straight trunks; and twenty-four- to thirty-year harvest cycles for timber are also described in Xu Guangqi's seminal work, *Complete Book of Agricultural Administration* (Nongzheng quanshu; c. 1630), where he considers this forestry as typical of western Jiangnan, including Huizhou as well as neighboring Xuancheng, Chizhou, and Raozhou.[87] Essentially the same methods were reported in the 1960s by the Oxford-trained forester S. D. Richardson, and again by a team of Chinese and American foresters in the 1990s.[88] While individual partnerships rose and fell, many of the same forests were planted and replanted with the same species and the same methods for nearly eight hundred years.

While it remained densely wooded, the southern landscape was overwhelmingly the product of human intervention; the majority of its forest areas were plantations of fir, pine, and bamboo. Based on Chen Keyun's figures, we can estimate that approximately two-thirds of registered forest land in Huizhou was under timber, with about 3 percent set aside specifically for growing seedlings (*miaomu*); the remaining third was split between graves, fruit orchards, and bamboo and tea farms.[89] Anecdotally, these approximate proportions probably held in other heavily forested parts of the south.[90] While the topic is complex, it is clear that community compacts and official restrictions protected other wooded areas from development, especially near graves, lineage temples, and critical watersheds. But by 1600, the majority of Huizhou's woodlands were monocultural stands of timber trees, reflecting a landscape transformation that was largely completed in the twelfth and thirteenth centuries. While Huizhou was at the far end of the continuum of silvicultural practices, similar conditions probably prevailed in much of Zhejiang, Jiangxi, and the Southern Metropolitan Region and in northern and coastal Fujian.

The transformation of South China's diverse woodlands into patchy monocultures brought substantial new hazards. By simplifying the forest ecosystem, planters increased the risk posed by fires, livestock, and soil depletion. Pine and fir are both substantially more susceptible to forest fire than most subtropical broad-leaved trees, and young trees pose greater fire risks than more established stands.[91] Once forest fires grow large, often in their preferred environment of young conifers, they become far less selective of fuel and can easily spread to more mature trees, field crops, and broad-leaved or mixed forest.[92] In other words, uniform plantations of young conifers provided a nearly ideal fuel environment for wildfire ignition. Grazing animals also presented a greater hazard to a uniform plantation of young trees than to a mixed forest. Even if they did not graze on the trees themselves, livestock could trample an entire plot of seedlings in a matter of hours.[93] Pure stands of fast-growing conifers also have a pronounced tendency to deplete the soil, with effects often visible as early as the second round of planting.[94] Without the intrinsic risk-reducing diversity of mixed-age, mixed-species communities, plantation forests were particularly susceptible to these hazards. By parceling each plot among multiple owners, and by giving owners stakes in multiple plots, shareholding represented a financial mechanism for mitigating these risks, but did little to stem the ecological damage.

In addition to greater environmental hazards, forest plantations created greater moral hazards than the mixed forests they replaced. Woodlands had long been used as common reserves of fuel, food, and other goods by the entire community. Woods were a particularly important resource to the poor, an eco-social buffer enabling those with limited resources to maintain subsistence by gathering wood and wild foods. When forests were enclosed, nonowners lost their access rights, abrogating this informal safety net. In most cases, community members did retain some rights to gather fuel, even on private property, and some woodlands were specifically protected as commons.[95] Nonetheless, when individuals enclosed forests, they did so at the expense of the rest of the community. This left the landless poor with few options but to steal wood from their wealthier neighbors. Here, too, shareholding provided a mechanism for reducing the impact of losing common-access land. By allowing forest laborers to acquire stakes in the timber they planted, shareholding encouraged the entire community to buy into collective management. But despite the incorporation of wealth-sharing mechanisms, private timber plantations brought a major loss of security for large swaths of the community. For wealthy landlords, plantations offered regular, predictable profits. For poor laborers, the ability to acquire shares in a distant timber harvest did little to mitigate the loss of the woodland safety net.

The emergence of contractual forms of risk management and profit sharing marked the twilight of the eco-social support system. Mixed forests persisted at the margins of settlements and continued to provide fuel, fodder, and famine foods to the broader community, especially its poorest members. These natural woodlands were also less prone to fire, flood, and erosion and provided richer habitats for a more diverse array of flora and fauna. But by the sixteenth century, the landscape was dominated by uniform stands of fir and other commercial species. Even the remaining old-growth woodlands existed only on inaccessible slopes or through another human intervention—designating woodlands around graves, temples, and sensitive watersheds as sacred *fengshui* forests.[96] Woodland, like farmland, was now almost entirely the product of human action.

FIVE

WOOD AND WATER, PART I

Tariff Timber

THE WOOD CRISIS OF ELEVENTH-CENTURY CHINA ENDED, NOT WITH an escalation of official forest oversight, but with an attitude of benign neglect, in large part because the initiative of private landowners substantially reduced the need for officials to intervene. Thanks to a salutary climate, fast-growing tree species, and sophisticated business practices, South China produced forest products in large quantities. It was also densely veined with navigable waterways, which made it easy to get timber to market. This nexus of sylvan and riverine endowments made it largely unnecessary for officials to regulate trees in the forest. Yet it would be going too far to suggest that China had no wood bureaucracy. Instead, Chinese states made up what they lacked in *forest* oversight with a sophisticated suite of offices to manage the *timber* supply. Chinese officials worked in several ways to harness the steady stream of wood already on the water. This chapter focuses on their primary tool to manage the wood supply: a fractional tariff that claimed a portion of each log raft that arrived at market for official use. In chapter 6, I turn to the most significant source of wood demand: the official shipyards, which worked together with the tariff offices to standardize and regulate commercial timber.

South China's wood-water nexus was far from a novel feature. Long before the development of timber plantations, Chinese empires shipped timber from the wood-rich south to the wood-poor North China Plain. Some of this shipping was in official hands, but much of it was conducted by private timber merchants. By the 960s, and perhaps long before, officials developed a tariff system to take advantage of this traffic in wood products. Leaving the difficult and dangerous work of lumbering and log rafting to specialists, the state set up customs stations specifically to tax bamboo and timber rafts. The tariff "drew a portion" (*choufen*) of these bulky materials at the very sites where they were most needed for shipbuilding and construction: at major river confluences and near large cities. With minimal official intervention, timber merchants sent regular flotillas of log rafts from the forests to the cities, resource streams that literally flowed toward sites of administration. As long as the state could draw off a fraction of these materials, it had no reason to invest in producing them itself. But the functionality of these tariffs depended on large, well-watered, wooded hinterlands, without which commercial taxes could not have provided timber in sufficient quantity to meet official needs.

Compared to China's broad woodlands and networked watercourses, the forests of Europe and Northeast Asia were highly fragmented. Atlantic powers like Spain, France, Holland, and England competed over a succession of logging frontiers from the Baltic to the North Atlantic and Caribbean and eventually the Indian Ocean.[1] Knowing that their overseas supplies could be cut off by blockade, these states worked to cultivate domestic timber and obtain logging colonies.[2] In central Europe, smaller states like Venice and the German principalities had even less purview to expand abroad, and they worked all the harder to maximize their limited forest resources.[3] In northern and eastern Europe, timber exports were a rare profit center that governments worked to monopolize.[4] Elsewhere, the Ottoman Empire, Korea, and Japan controlled unified territorial entities with rivers that diverged into different seas—different conditions leading to a similar fragmentation of timber oversight.[5] Only Holland, with its position astride both the Rhine and the North Sea, controlled converging shipping lanes like those in eastern China.[6] And indeed, Holland's leaders pursued a similar market-based solution to their timber supply problem. Yet even Holland's timber markets were a fraction of the territories controlled by Chinese empires.[7] With its large, forested territory and expansive shipping lanes, it is no wonder that

China followed a different tack in managing its timber supply than its smaller and more fragmented contemporaries.

Even as the specifics of the timber supply shifted repeatedly, with market cycles, changes of dynasty, and secular changes in forest oversight, the points of contact between producers and consumers remained relatively fixed, at a handful of depots at the major transshipment centers. At these customs stations, small staffs of bureaucrats issued licenses, calculated yields, and disbursed supplies to their respective bureaus. Working together with the shipyards and building offices, tariff officials standardized grades for lumber, roundwood timber, fuel, and other materials, gradually developing the types of specialized expertise that eluded their peers in the territorial bureaucracy. While the Song, Yuan, and Ming courts still conducted occasional logging operations to supplement the tariff, the interface between the customs stations and the plantation economy was so effective that they had almost no need for ongoing forestry offices. Market-based oversight, not territorial control, was the principal state intervention into the changing forest landscape.

EARLY DEVELOPMENTS

While it eventually developed a profound symbiosis with the plantation economy, the tariff system long predated the development of commercial tree planting. Its early history is somewhat murky, but the timber tariff probably developed from commercial taxes on wood products developed in the late eighth century. A major rebellion in 755–63 forced the Tang dynasty to cede control over large portions of the countryside to semi-independent military governors. To make up lost revenue, the post-rebellion Tang state imposed a number of new commercial taxes and monopolies, most notably on salt.[8] In 780, Tang officials also instituted a tax on forest products: "a ten percent tax on all bamboo, timber, tea, and lacquer in the empire, to be paid in normalized copper cash."[9] It is not clear how this tax was originally collected, but by the founding of the Song in 960, the bamboo and timber portion was assessed as an in-kind tariff on wholesale shipments. This tariff, called the "drawn portion" or "drawn disbursement" (*choufen, choujie*), mirrored both the name and the function of several other commercial taxes, including an assessment on certain mines and the tariff on foreign luxury goods imported via Guangzhou.[10]

The tariff depots of the early Song demonstrate the working of a system that was already fairly mature, and probably inherited from earlier regimes. Depots to collect and store bamboo and timber (*zhumu chang*) were located in the western suburbs of the capital, Kaifeng, as were yards collecting other bulk goods, including two coal depots (*tan chang*) and one for bamboo slats (*choushui bo chang*).[11] Each of these depots tapped a slightly different supply chain: bamboo slats came from a tax on merchant shipments (*choushui*); coal came from annual labor service quotas (*nian'e*); and the bamboo and timber depots collected timber cut by military and civilian corvée, bought by licensed merchants and eunuch compradors, and derived from tariffs on all commercial shipments throughout the capital region.[12] The receiving depots had counterparts charged with preparing timber for state use: a lumber-working yard (*shicai chang*) to measure and cut timber for construction and a lumber recovery yard (*tuicai chang*) to repurpose substandard timber as scrap wood, poles, or fuel. The lumberyards also had close relationships with the shipyards, and officials and laborers from one site were occasionally dispatched to assist at the others.[13] While the evidence is most extensive for Kaifeng, anecdotes suggest that similar yards were present in major cities throughout the empire.[14]

From the late tenth century onward, the state increased oversight of the supplies collected in its depots, especially in Kaifeng. In 993, the State Finance Commission (Sansi) ordered the capital customs station to establish standard grades of lumber.[15] Annals from the next few decades report figures for wood and timber tax receipts that were presumably collected in this way: 280,000 bundles of firewood and 500,000 loads (*cheng*) of coal in 997, and 3.6 million planks of wood and bamboo and 30 million *jin* (approximately 15 million kilograms) of charcoal, firewood, and reed fuel in 1021.[16] The latter report also includes government expenditures.[17] These comprehensive figures allowed leaders to plan and set policy. In 1010, the emperor ordered that a two-year supply of timber be retained for the repair of dikes and dams and the rest sold.[18] Two years later, he asked the Finance Commission to make a comprehensive analysis of official timber needs and cancel any unnecessary lumbering operations.[19] Starting in 1023, building projects had to be submitted to the State Finance Commission *before* being supplied with government materials (*guanwu*).[20] Gradually the information compiled at the tariff bureaus gave high officials greater leeway to plan for future expenditures.

While the bamboo and timber depots obtained supplies from multiple places, their most consistent source was a tax collected on log rafts as they were landed for wholesale. This tariff provided a ready supply of materials and also gave the state a way to manipulate the wood markets. By "drawing and disbursing" (*choujie*) wood from existing shipments, the state obtained fuel and lumber in the cities without having to undergo the expense of logging and rafting itself. The tariff also gave the state a mechanism to drive prices on the wood market. To encourage imports, officials could reduce or eliminate wood taxes to give merchants incentives to increase imports and lower prices. Examples of these interventions are scattered throughout Northern Song records.[21]

Nonetheless, the tariff was not without its faults. When tax rates were too high—up to 30 percent in the Northern Song—they provided a strong disincentive to imports and increased the price of timber. High duties also provided opportunities for official graft, as bribes were often far cheaper than the cost of the timber taken by the state. Anecdotal evidence points to a relatively large corruption problem: in 980, an astonishing number of high officials and imperial kin were implicated in a plot to import timber from the northwest without paying tariffs; in 1017, the State Finance Commission reported that the tax exemption on official timber imports had become a source of widespread graft; in 1080, prefectural officials were punished for skimming profits from the tax itself.[22] The concentration of oversight at urban markets also meant that the state had limited knowledge about conditions in regional woodlands. But despite these drawbacks, the bulk goods tariff was a net positive to the state, at the center of a highly functional system that generated timber for state needs without the central bureaucracy needing to concern itself with logging in the provinces.

REGULATING THE PLANTING ECONOMY

As detailed elsewhere herein, an invasion by the Jurchen Jin forced the Song court to retreat from Kaifeng in 1127, eventually decamping to the southern city of Hangzhou (Lin'an). Paradoxically, losing access to North China's forests enabled Song officials to greatly simplify the state's timber supply. Like Kaifeng, the new capital was located at a commercial nexus. But unlike Kaifeng, Hangzhou had direct access to the rich woodlands of South China, importing timber via the Qiantang River, Grand Canal, Yangzi River, and coastal shipping routes. The layout of the city reflected these two sources of forest products: there were bamboo and timber depots in both the northern suburbs with access to the Grand Canal and Yangzi River and the southern suburbs on the Qiantang River.[23] Most other Southern Song cities had direct water access to at least one of the major timber trade routes.[24] The Hangzhou court also benefited from other regional development. For centuries, locals had constructed polders, seawalls, and canals throughout the Yangzi River estuary, leaving twelfth-century Jiangnan riddled with waterways enabling the easy transport of bulk materials, including timber.[25] The broad flow of resources was further enabled by expansion of the money supply through a paper currency called *huizi*, issued on a small scale in 1161, on larger scales in 1170, and during fiscal crises in 1205–8 and 1211. While condemned by both contemporaries and historians, increases in the money supply enabled the broader circulation of goods, including a large-scale flow of copper coins to Japan in exchange for timber, sulfur, and gold.[26]

Through its superior resource endowments, the Hangzhou court was able to increase the availability of timber without recourse to the command economy. After the retreat to the south in 1127, there are almost no records of logging projects directly overseen by the Song state.[27] Instead, a virtuous cycle of trade brought ever more wood into the cities. More timber enabled the construction of more canals, warehouses, and especially more ships, which furthered future imports. By manipulating the timber tariff rates, the Southern Song state was generally able to maintain the wood reserves it needed for state purposes, achieve a steady source of general-purpose income, and stimulate the timber market in response to occasional crises. When additional wood was needed, the state dispatched officials to purchase it from wholesalers—either at urban markets or in timber-exporting regions—largely using paper money. In doing so, it increased both the volume of cash and the volume of timber in circulation.

During the opening decades of the southern court, rebuilding dominated policy and the court lifted tariffs across the board. As the Song armies continued to fight north of the Yangzi, the court reduced wood taxes to aid in rebuilding northern cities in 1128 and again in 1130.[28] While these measures did little to reverse the destruction of the north, the Southern Song court continued to use tax holidays to promote rebuilding. The court suspended taxes on transport materials for a year to aid the settlement of refugees in the south after the Jin wars.[29] When fires burned parts of Hangzhou in 1133 and 1140, the state excused building materials from commercial taxes.[30] According to informal recollections, enterprising merchants took advantage of the tax holidays to import timber into the capital, alleviating the wood shortage and making huge profits.[31] The state likewise forgave taxes on wood imports to rebuild after fires or warfare in Yangzhou in 1135, Zhenjiang in 1150, Guangnan (Guangdong and Guangxi) in 1166, and Huainan in 1207 and 1209 and to alleviate other local shortages in 1203, 1231, and 1233.[32]

While officials used occasional tax relief to encourage wood imports, they otherwise preferred to keep the tariffs in place to supply government construction. In 1128, riverine jurisdictions in the middle Yangzi were ordered to construct nearly three thousand grain transport ships to supply the capital. When construction was delayed, the court redirected the timber tariff to provide the primary source of shipbuilding materials.[33] Tariff timber was also used to rebuild dikes in Hubei in 1153, to build housing for refugees in Huainan in 1162, and to build barracks and stables for soldiers in Chizhou and Jiangzhou in 1161.[34]

The Southern Song also addressed the corruption that flourished around the tariff. When an 1129 investigation revealed that some tax officials collected illegal surcharges on top of the regular tariff, all officials were required to report excessive fees or be held accountable for the same crime as those collecting illegal taxes.[35] In 1156, Hangzhou prefect Rong Ni discovered that tax officials and clerks were using official requisitions to force merchants to sell goods at discount. He ruled that henceforth any official purchase order should be refused and reported.[36] These reforms did not eliminate the abuse of official privilege—another investigation in 1178 revealed officials who forced merchants to sell below market price.[37] Nonetheless, it was now more difficult to use official position to force merchants to sell at or below cost.

Having targeted abuses among tax officials, court reformers turned to address corruption among official timber purchasers. A new 1160 regulation required that official timber buyers—previously tax free—pay the same commercial taxes as private merchants; abuses of rank to avoid taxes would be punished as a "violation of imperial command" (*weizhi*).[38] In 1162, the court extended the 1160 ruling to the military as well. In 1166, a cavalry officer dispatched to buy twenty thousand poles of timber requested that the wood be excused from taxes and tariffs. Superior officials refused his request on the basis of the 1162 order.[39] Two years later, another garrison requested a tax release on the timber to expand its barracks and stables. The court also denied this request, referencing the 1166 request as precedent.[40]

As it reformed the tariff system, the state tried to balance the need for revenue with the need to prevent graft and to keep high transaction costs from halting the flow of wood. By the early 1150s, the desire to hasten imports from the timber-rich areas led to a new policy to license merchants. In the fir-planting regions of Huizhou and Yanzhou, tax officials issued affidavits to timber wholesalers, allowing them to avoid all taxes en route, paying a single tax of 30 percent upon arriving at the capital at Hangzhou.[41] The elimination of repeated tariffs represented major savings for merchants trading at the capital. In 1173, one observer reported that timber bought in Huizhou for one hundred copper cash sold for two thousand at Hangzhou.[42] While this is almost surely an exaggeration, the establishment of a single tariff of 30 percent allowed merchants to charge a smaller markup and still make a substantial profit. By the thirteenth century, timber licenses were even used to regulate emergency tax forgiveness. In 1204, when yet another fire in Hangzhou led to an urgent need for construction materials, the Zhejiang Fiscal Commission granted timber merchants temporary licenses excusing one-third of the commercial taxes en route and the entire tax assessed at Hangzhou.[43] A similar, temporary permit was issued on shipments of building materials to Hangzhou in 1220.[44] These targeted, licensed tax breaks replaced the wholesale tax holidays used earlier in the dynasty.

Over the course of a century, gradual, directed reforms made it significantly more difficult for officials to profit from loopholes in the tax and tariff system. While the tariff added to the cost of individual official timber requisitions, regulations stabilized the timber market in ways that benefited producers and consumers alike. By 1200, most bamboo and timber depots now collected the tariff in cash rather than in kind.[45] This suggests that the price of timber was stable enough that the state preferred to replace a guaranteed supply of building materials with general-purpose revenue. In some ways, the Southern Song benefited from the reduced size of its empire. Tariff reforms proceeded overwhelmingly by local initiative at Hangzhou and in a handful of prefectures upstream. The Qiantang River connecting Huizhou to Hangzhou developed as a particularly well-licensed marketplace for timber.

Outside of the Qiantang River system, records are less complete, but there are indications that tariff reforms proceeded as well. An 1158 order simplified the wood markets of Jianzhou, Fujian, by imposing a single category of commercial tax on all timber.[46] In 1196, an edict prohibited ethnic Chinese (Hanren) from entering the forests in southern Sichuan; instead, they were instructed to "wait for the 'barbarians' [*man*] to bring planks and timber to the river and ship them to the waterways below Xuzhou to trade."[47] As the result of an investigation on excessive taxation, local administrations in border regions were required to publicly post rates for all categories of taxable goods, including timber.[48] As in Hangzhou, these reforms were largely undertaken on a local basis, but without the power of the court behind them they did not achieve the same levels of sophistication. Unlike the preceding Kaifeng court, which had to balance the oversight of several highly diverse streams of timber, the Hangzhou court focused overwhelmingly on regulating a single river valley, resulting in a far more coherent system of wood markets.

INTEGRATING EMPIRES, MERGING MARKETS

If the Southern Song was better able to regulate its smaller empire following the loss of the north, the Yuan faced precisely the opposite challenge: reintegrating northern and southern timber markets. For more than a century, North China had been rocked by warfare and emigration, first during the Jin invasion in the early twelfth century and again by the Mongol invasion in the early thirteenth century. During these periods of upheaval, officials resorted to the command economy to replace the materials previously acquired through commercial tariffs. Yet with the restoration of peace following the completion of the Mongol conquest of North China in 1234, they gradually returned to a more indirect system of taxation and oversight. While the section of the *Yuan History* on timber taxes is lost, the management of timber economies in Mongol North China can be at least partially reconstructed by reference to the bamboo monopolies. These monopolies worked in various ways: sometimes the state controlled production directly; in other cases, it had exclusive right to buy bamboo from private producers (monopsony). The state then sold bamboo to the public according to three categories with set prices. In 1267–68, the monopoly was reorganized as a system of licenses sold to private merchants; it was abolished entirely in 1285, shortly following the conquest of South China. The tenants of former state monopolies now paid a cash rent (*zu*) on state-owned bamboo forests instead of supplying bamboo, while private producers paid a cash tax (*shui*) rather than being forced to sell their production to the state.[49]

In South China, the Yuan benefited from far more continuities with the tariff oversight of the Southern Song. In the absence of centralized accounts, these continuities can be reconstructed through local records. In Huizhou, Yuan administrators inherited and modified rates at a main prefectural tariff station—first converting to a cash tariff in 1278, then fixing its quota in 1284. In 1311, as Huizhou's primary wood markets along the Qiantang River diminished in importance, local officials closed the station. Yet they continued to operate smaller depots that taxed Huizhou's secondary wood market: the south-flowing rivers that supplied fuel to the Jingdezhen kilns.[50] The Zhenjiang tariff depot presents another case of continuity across the Song-Yuan transition. Collection of the tariff appears to have lapsed during periods of heavy fighting in the 1270s, but it was restored almost immediately and reorganized several times between 1287 and 1324. Revenues at Zhenjiang declined by about 10 percent in the early Yuan and then rebounded to more than twice their Southern Song peak.[51] Yuan officials also operated a long-standing tariff depot in Suzhou, about which details are not forthcoming.[52] Throughout Jiangnan, local officials were quite flexible in shifting tariff administration in accordance with local markets, with changes in the central administration having little impact on the functioning of county- and prefecture-level wood depots.

By the early 1300s, the Yuan state integrated the distinct northern and southern timber taxes into an empire-wide revenue stream.[53] In 1328—the only year with central records—taxes on lumber and bamboo were collected in parts of both the north and the south, but the figures reveal a hodgepodge of different policies (table 5.1).[54] The revenues collected in the north were quotas, probably based in forest rents, while the revenues collected in the south and at Beijing had no quotas and were probably from tariffs that varied depending on the volume of trade. This was the Yuan empire's broader legacy: the reincorporation of thriving regional wood markets into a single empire-wide revenue system.

TABLE 5.1. Bamboo and timber taxes, 1328

	QUOTA WOOD	QUOTA BAMBOO	NONQUOTA WOOD AND BAMBOO
Capital region	676 poles	2 poles	9,428 poles (73 wood; 9,355 bamboo)
Henan	58,600 planks	269,695 poles	1,748 poles
Jiangzhe	—	—	9,355 poles
Jiangxi	—	—	590 poles

Source: Schurmann, Economic Structure of the Yüan Dynasty, 160–62.

In the 1350s and 1360s, much of China was again plunged into chaos, as the millenarian Red Turbans revolted against Yuan rule. When Zhu Yuanzhang emerged victorious from the Red Turban wars in 1368, his young Ming dynasty depended on the continuation of Yuan tariffs. Until 1380, the Ming revived, retained, and expanded the cluster of timber depots in Jiangnan to benefit from the regional economy. In Suzhou, Ming officials added five new customs stations to the prefecture between 1367 and the early 1370s. With six customs in a single prefecture, this was clearly an epicenter of the timber trade. In 1377, the six bureaus reported total receipts of more than 62,000 poles of timber; 922,000 poles of bamboo; 215,000 *jin* of large firewood (approximately 100,000 kilograms); 158,000 *jin* of charcoal (80,000 kilograms); and nearly 8,000 bundles of smaller fuel, reeds, and hay.[55] Many other local and regional tariff stations, including those in Huizhou and Hangzhou, continued to operate after the disruptions of the wars died down.

FROM AUTARCHY TO INFLATION

If the first decade of Ming rule saw a revival of both the timber trade and the timber tariff, Ming monarchs soon put their unique stamps on the system. Once government was firmly established at Nanjing in the 1370s, Zhu Yuanzhang made clear his ideals for local self-sufficiency and ended the short-lived continuity with Yuan tariff institutions. His vision was not just to make local governments self-sufficient; Zhu intended for even larger projects to be supplied directly from local resources. Zhu wanted Nanjing's fuel supply provided locally and levied labor service on two nearby counties to provide the three thousand laborers necessary to cut and transport reed fuel from islets in the Yangzi River to the capital.[56] He conscripted transport ships from private households along the rivers or constructed them through irregular levies of timber and labor.[57] Even for large and concentrated needs, Zhu preferred to obtain supplies locally and through direct levies.

Having established the principles of self-sufficiency for his government, Zhu Yuanzhang even tried to eliminate the tariff system entirely. In 1380, he issued an edict closing all customs stations in the empire.[58] It is highly doubtful that this order was ever carried out universally as stated. Nonetheless, Zhu's other policies greatly disturbed the thriving markets in the lower Yangzi region, so there was less commerce to tax anyway.[59] But despite Zhu's best efforts to make his capital self-sufficient in resources, it proved impractical to run an empire under self-imposed autarchy. In 1393, he changed the tariff system again, probably as the oversimplified supply lines established in the previous two decades failed to provide enough materials. Perhaps recognizing either the need or the opportunity to tax the extensive Yangzi River timber trade, he established tariff stations at two locations near Nanjing, one at Longjiang (figure 5.1) and one at Dashenggang.[60] Yet even as Zhu reestablished customs stations, he portrayed them as part of a continued drive toward self-sufficiency. The same year he established Longjiang as a tariff station, Zhu designated it as the primary site for building transport ships for the Yangzi River.[61] Regulations required that Longjiang shipwrights rely almost exclusively on materials obtained through the tariffs.[62] Hangzhou also established a customs station specifically to collect timber for building transport ships for the lower section of the Grand Canal.[63] As a further indication of their intended purpose, these new customs were overseen not by revenue officials, or by the Bureaus of Construction or Transport, but by the Bureau of Military Farms (Tuntian Qingli Si), an office otherwise tasked with making the military self-sufficient.[64]

FIG 5.1 Night rain on Longjiang customs. Detail from a woodcut depicting a large flotilla of logs moving along a river. The original caption reads, in part, "Southwest of the city walls, outside the Yifeng Gate, is a fort and customs station to tax timber from Hunan and Sichuan for use in building official ships." Image from *Nanjing Illustrated* (Jinling tuyong; 1624). Courtesy of the Library of Congress, Chinese Rare Book Digital Collection

Like their Northern Song and Yuan precursors, and unlike the specialized customs stations of the Southern Song, Ming tariff offices collected materials from a variety of sources, including direct goods levies as well as the bamboo and timber tariff. The tariff was the most important source of timber and other building materials, but its fuel receipts were supplemented by a specialized reed tax (*luke*) on households living along the Yangzi River.[65] As in the Song, inferior building timber was also repurposed as fuel. These combustibles were distributed to the imperial household, government offices, and state workshops according to fixed grades and quotas.[66] In 1391, the Ming court established official plantations in the hinterlands of Nanjing to provide a direct supply of ancillary shipbuilding materials like tung oil, palm fiber, and lacquer.[67] These goods were also shipped to the two main customs depots, which issued reports on stock and inflow every ten days and disbursed materials to various government workshops based on these figures.[68] Accounts were summarized monthly and forwarded to the Board of Works annually.[69] Only in case of shortfalls in the tariff materials could additional supplies be requisitioned, either by purchase or by state-supervised logging (*caiban*).[70]

Despite their ostensible role in promoting a self-sufficient, planned economy, the tariff stations sat astride extremely active wood markets. Nanjing tariff regulations list a total of thirty-two different categories of goods, including six varieties of roundwood timber, two of cut boards, five of bamboo, and four of fuel. In contrast to contemporary northern markets, the Nanjing timber market was dominated by just two types of tree: fir and, to a lesser degree, pine. The river customs also favored fir with a preferential tariff rate. While most timber and semifinished wood products were taxed at 20 percent, the highest-value fir timber and several kinds of cane and bamboo were taxed at the lowest rate of one-thirtieth (3.3 percent), the going rate on most commercial products.[71] This 3.3 percent tax on fir was only one-tenth the rate assessed at Hangzhou in the twelfth century, yet Nanjing still appears to have been able to meet most of its timber needs through this tariff. This suggests that the Jiangnan timber market had grown substantially since the Song.[72] Despite Zhu Yuanzhang's initiatives to promote a planned and self-sufficient agrarian economy, timber markets continued to flourish. Building on the foundations established in the Song, plantation-grown conifers were the dominant species on the market.

As detailed elsewhere herein, Zhu Yuanzhang's chosen successor was soon deposed by a junior son, Zhu Di, who reigned as the Yongle emperor.

As Yongle moved the capital to his seat at Beijing, he set up timber yards to supply it. In 1407, five bamboo and timber depots were built in a ring around the city, each taxing a discrete transport route. The most important of these stations was at Tongzhou, where canal traffic from the south was offloaded.[73] In 1413, the state set tax rates for the Beijing depots, naming fifty-one different categories of bulk goods, including eight types of timber, four of cut boards, and twelve of fuel. As at Nanjing, the overwhelming majority of goods—including most timber and fuel—were taxed at 20 percent. Lime, mineral coal (*shitan*), fir timber, and several other goods were taxed at the lower rate of two-thirtieths (6.7 percent).[74] Beijing's market catchment incorporated a far greater range of timber species than Nanjing's: conifers such as pine and cedar imported from the north and northwest, hardwoods (especially fruitwoods) cut in the Central Plains region, and shipments of southern species like China fir. The Beijing fuel market was even more complex, including several types of crop wastes; two grades of mineral coal (*shitan* and *meizha*, the latter referring to coal fragments); several grades of fuelwood; and wood charcoal.[75] Even as fir dominated southern timber markets, northern supplies of fuel and timber remained complex, provided by multiple biomes, species, and institutions.

While Zhu Yuanzhang had failed to end tariffs by fiat in the 1380s, the system regressed significantly as a less-intended consequence of state policy in the 1420s and 1430s. Following the death of the Yongle emperor in 1424, his successors ended many of the extractive policies of the early Ming, while other institutions failed during the economic decline that followed. In Shaoxing alone, fourteen customs stations were closed in 1425. At least four of these had been run expressly for the purpose of collecting timber and bamboo.[76] Between the Xuande reign (1426–35) and the 1460s, Huguang, Jiangxi, and Zhejiang Provinces built their own transport ships to avoid the cost of sending materials to the main yards in Nanjing.[77] This suggests that customs stations were shuttered in these provinces or were independent of central oversight. The one exception to this general trend was a new customs depot established at Zhending in 1436 to supply logs directly from the Western Hills to Beijing.[78] Otherwise, there is a near total lack of customs records for the next two to three decades, an absence that parallels administrative retrenchment across the board in the mid-1400s.[79] In 1497, a Board of Works official was unable to identify *any* staff dispatched to the Hangzhou branch office prior to 1466.[80] Jiujiang, another particularly well-documented customs station, has no records of the period from 1429 to 1449.[81] While absence of evidence must be addressed carefully, there are strong circumstantial reasons to believe that the second quarter of the fifteenth century saw the near-total devolution of market oversight south of the Yangzi. With deeply depressed markets, there was little timber trade to tax and little reason for the state to staff its river customs. The shuttering of customs stations was a de facto acknowledgment of these autarkic conditions.

With the gradual recovery of markets in the 1450s and 1460s, customs stations began to reappear. In 1449, a eunuch was sent to oversee the Jiujiang station in an attempt to generate revenue for the privy purse from the booming middle Yangzi trade.[82] In 1457, a censor sent to Hunan to deal with a tribal rebellion revived tariff collection there as well, establishing a customs station at a princely estate as an expedient measure to raise timber to build warships.[83] After a period without central state management, the Board of Works resumed oversight of the Hangzhou customs station in 1466.[84] In 1471, the state reestablished customs stations at the major transshipment points in the south, including Wuhu, Huzhou, Jingzhou, and Taiping, and formalized oversight at the Hangzhou and Jiujiang stations.[85] The following year, a garrison commander named Wang Li, probably an official at the military shipyards in Nanjing, suggested distributing new grades for bamboo and timber to these stations, and the Board of Works dispatched officials to oversee them.[86]

In the late 1400s, the economic situation shifted markedly as silver flooded the markets, and the price of timber rose rapidly. Having previously switched to collecting silver, some depots switched back to collecting timber in kind to offset inflation in the cost of timber.[87] At Hangzhou, officials collected timber and bamboo for use on-site, but also began to sell overflow, taking advantage of rising timber prices to fund other projects.[88] By collecting timber in kind, the value of the tariff grew with inflation and with the growing scale of the timber trade. By the mid-1500s, the timber collected at the Hangzhou customs had a face value two and a half times greater than in the 1400s.[89] Part of this increase was due to inflation in timber prices. Figures from the official shipyards at Nanjing suggest that the price of timber increased by more than 70 percent between the 1490s and 1545.[90] Yet even accounting for inflation, the tariff offices collected more materials. By rough estimate, the volume of timber traded at Hangzhou doubled in the first half of the 1500s.[91]

Nonetheless, the return to in-kind tariffs was probably both localized and temporary. By the sixteenth century, government expenditures were all on the rise, and the promise of general-purpose silver revenue was too much to pass up. Records from Jiujiang, a major station taxing the middle Yangzi, give a rough sense of how the tariff worked at high-volume customs stations of the mid-Ming. For large timber rafts, officials calculated the linear size by summing their length, width, and depth.[92] Merchants paid a rate of 4.862 taels of silver per linear *zhang* (approximately three meters, or ten feet).[93] Smaller shipments were taxed by the log: 0.003 taels per pole under one *chi* in circumference (approximately one-third meter, or one foot); 0.007 taels per pole between one and two *chi*; and 0.04 taels per pole larger than two *chi*. For bamboo rafts, officials established a standard depth of one *chi*—considered equal to three poles of bamboo—and a standard length of two *zhang*. Then they counted the width in poles and estimated the total number of poles based on the standard length and depth. Each pole was then taxed at a rate of 0.002 taels. The tariff office charged the same per-pole rate on smaller bundles of bamboo.[94] This system allowed rapid calculation of the silver tax on the large rafts of wholesalers, while also permitting greater precision in taxing the smaller shipments of lesser merchants.

Officials in emerging timber markets in the south and west also established new customs stations. Because the same ships that carried salt upstream often returned with shipments of forest products, many of these new stations were initially founded to oversee the government salt monopoly before expanding to tax timber as an ancillary source of income. The locus classicus of this salt-timber nexus was a pair of customs stations established in southern Jiangxi, a major timber frontier in the Ming. In 1510, Wang Zhi, a low-level military official, proposed to establish customs offices in southern Jiangxi in order to finance the regional military garrison. Two stations were set up, one in the military-administrative region of Nan'an and another in the civil prefecture of Ganzhou. While Wang Zhi's career is otherwise lost to history, a far more famous figure soon arrived. Wang Yangming (also known as Wang Shouren) would later rise to fame as the most important Neo-Confucian philosopher of the Ming. But in 1516, he was a pacification commissioner (*xunfu*) dispatched to deal with poor governance and revolts in the Ganzhou region. Wang Yangming's inspection revealed that the tax stations were badly mismanaged: individual shipments were often taxed twice, once at Nan'an and again at Ganzhou, and officials often accepted bribes. Wang instituted better oversight, and considered closing the Nan'an station entirely, touching off a decades-long debate. Ultimately, customs were too important as a source of revenue in this otherwise poor and unruly region, and both stations were maintained through the rest of the dynasty.[95] By 1620, the local economy had grown to such an extent that even the Ganzhou station collected its timber tariff in silver rather than in kind. Pooled with other commercial taxes, regional officials used this silver to meet the full range of expenses, including the *purchase* of timber for construction and shipbuilding.[96]

The records of the Ganzhou customs also fill in the picture of expanding timber markets. By the seventeenth century, even Ganzhou produced plantation-grown fir in smaller sizes—generally under a two-foot circumference. By this point, Ganzhou timber producers had the facilities to process fir logs into square-cut (*fang*) and board-cut lumber (*ban*), but the prefecture also taxed "free-floated" timber (*qingshui liu*) of far greater size than the plantation-grown fir. These larger logs were probably cut from old-growth woodlands and then floated downstream piecemeal, unlike the timber shipped in rafts from tree farms. Other types of trees were also sold in up to four-foot circumference. Alongside the evidence in chapters 2 and 3, this further demonstrates the spread and elaboration of timber planting and processing across the interior south. By 1620, Ganzhou—an unruly frontier a century earlier—was increasingly well integrated into the Yangzi River timber markets. While loggers still cut from the natural growth, plantation-grown fir now made up a growing proportion of timber exports.

A MILLENNIUM OF MARKET OVERSIGHT

Bulk goods tariffs were the focal point of interventions into wood markets under the Song, Yuan, and Ming dynasties, yet even this six-century span understates the continuities of timber market oversight. The basic tariff institutions were innovated as early as 780 and continued along similar lines for another two and a half centuries of Qing rule.[97] While specifics varied, the basic continuities across more than a millennium are truly astounding. Tariffs enabled state offices to ensure their own wood supplies, and to shift the price of wood for private consumers, all without requiring direct oversight of the diverse and changing forests of their empires. By collecting and taxing the trade in timber and fuel, tariff depots both responded to existing conditions and created new markets. Timber depots were consistently placed at natural confluences along major shipping routes, with the most important offices in the suburbs of the capitals: Kaifeng, Hangzhou, Nanjing, and Beijing. The state's high demands for timber and fuel made each of these cities the most important wood markets in their respective empires and the centers of state oversight.

Tariff policies changed in response to both politics and market conditions. In periods with well-functioning markets, the tariff was used to collect timber and fuel for state use. When the economy was especially cash-rich—as in the late Song, mid-Yuan, and mid- to late Ming—tariff officials generally taxed rafts in cash or silver instead of collecting timber directly. This allowed them to use tariff receipts for more general budgetary needs, although runaway inflation occasionally led administrators to return to collecting timber in kind. In periods of conflict or autarchy, including the Song-Yuan wars of the 1270s, the late Yuan wars of the 1350s and 1360s, and the post-Yongle depression of the 1420s and 1430s, wood markets collapsed, and tariffs were suspended. Rulers and administrators could also use timber tariffs to change the terms of the economy. Song officials used tax holidays and licenses to encourage wood imports and lower prices for urban consumers. Yuan magistrates continually adjusted their tax collection to reflect market conditions and maximize revenue. In the early Ming, Zhu Yuanzhang imposed a policy of self-sufficiency and closed customs stations for ideological reasons. Officials in the mid-Ming revived contracts and licenses as pragmatic means to manage suppliers in a vibrant and fast-changing marketplace.

The functions played by bulk goods depots also depended on the regional arrays of institutions involved in provisioning the state with timber, fuel, and other materials. In the Northern Song, Kaifeng's depot stacked together timber logged by military supernumeraries in the northwest, civilian corvée in the north, merchant lumber teams in the south, and tributary chieftains in the southwest. By contrast, Hangzhou's two main depots in the Southern Song relied overwhelmingly on merchant-supplied timber. This pattern of northern command economies and southern merchant capital was repeated in the Ming. Nanjing, which functioned as the seat of government for South China, was supplied largely, but not exclusively, by taxing merchant timber. Meanwhile, Beijing, in the north, assembled a wide variety of corvée-, merchant-, and military-logged materials, with each of its five bulk goods depots facing a different regional supply.

Finally, timber tariffs changed the use of regional forests and responded to changes in supply. In the early Song, the Kaifeng timber depot brought together a huge variety of tree species, including pine and cedar from the northwest and fir and an astonishing variety of subtropical broad-leaved trees from the south. By the early Ming, Nanjing's Longjiang depot focused overwhelmingly on grading and taxing just two types of southern conifers—fir and pine. By marking fir as the premium timber species, tariff regulations recognized that it was both desirable and widely available; by granting a preferred tax status, bureaucrats only encouraged the further development of fir plantations. Yet while the state's oversight of wood markets helped transform China's regional forests, this effect was largely indirect, in the form of standards for size, species, and grades of timber and fuel that were largely provided by other parties.

While the tariff bureaus were not principally responsible for the growth of the market for timber, they clearly benefited when the supply of wood and timber grew. What is more, tariff data provide some of the best insights into this market. While there are no continuous series of tariff data (at least not until the mid-Qing), scattered anecdotes and figures allow some very rough estimates of its growth. Based on the fluidity of Southern Song tariff collections, the timber supply may have doubled during the twelfth and thirteenth centuries. The very limited Yuan data suggest that timber production in Jiangnan grew by another 50 percent during the early fourteenth century. Ming Nanjing's wood market may have been five to ten times the size of Southern Song Hangzhou's. After a substantial downturn in the second quarter of the fifteenth century, the timber market matched or exceeded its previous peak by the late 1400s, and probably doubled again in the early 1500s. While very approximate, these estimates correspond with the greatly expanded territory put toward timber production documented in chapter 2. It was this unprecedented expansion in China's forest economy that allowed Huizhou's merchants to go from regional timber producers in 1150 to empire-spanning financiers in 1600. Indeed, the booming timber trade in sixteenth-century China is almost reminiscent of nineteenth-century commodities markets in the Atlantic world—the economy that produced many of Europe's and North America's modern business practices.

As timber markets expanded, the tariff system became more and more significant to state revenues and almost the only locus of official wood oversight. Chinese states did continue to dispatch logging teams, principally to provision the naval shipyards and the Imperial Construction Bureau. The strategic importance of warships, and the symbolic importance of palaces, meant that high officials supervised these projects long after deciding that official logging was obsolete for other purposes. But as the fir growers of South China became more effective at producing high-grade timber, as merchants developed standards in collaboration with shipyard and construction officials, and as the frontier of old-growth trees receded, the state gradually abandoned these logging projects as well. By the end of the sixteenth century, even the naval shipyards and the Imperial Construction Bureau got their timber primarily on the market, not in the forest.

SIX

WOOD AND WATER, PART II

Naval Timber

HISTORIANS HAVE OFTEN NOTED THE IMPORTANCE OF NAVAL TIMBER to empire building, especially to the growing rivalries of the early modern period. Starting around 1500, gunpowder weapons, new shipbuilding techniques, and overseas colonization fed a naval race among the Mediterranean and Atlantic powers. Within the next two centuries, navies transformed from glorified troop transports into specialized forces for fighting at sea.[1] As Robert Greenhalgh Albion shows in his classic study of the British navy, timber became a key constraint in the construction of a specialized fleet. It should be no surprise that the supply of naval timber was a constant focus of early modern European statecraft.[2] While the literature on Asia is in a more nascent stage, it is clear that similar considerations affected empires from the Red Sea to the Yellow.[3] Shipbuilding timber was a baseline cost of empire, but it was also a strategic good, key to both the circulation of necessities and the projection of power.

In some ways, naval developments in China between about 1100 and 1430 are a striking preview of the European fleet races of later centuries. In the 1100s and 1200s, intense warfare between the Song, Jurchen Jin, and Mongol Yuan states spurred rapid innovation, including the use of gunpowder weapons, large-scale construction of specialized warships, and the development of an independent naval administration. Following the Yuan unification of China, Mongol fleets looked further abroad to take territory, secure loyalty, and monopolize trade from Japan to Java. The breakup of the Yuan empire in the 1350s and 1360s brought another wave of naval competition, including the battle of Poyang Lake, one of the largest inland naval conflicts in history. After the Ming dynasty reunified China, it, too, launched fleets abroad. Between 1405 and 1433, the famous Ming armadas under Zheng He sailed as far as India and East Africa. Technologies like the mariner's compass and gunpowder weapons developed during the Song maritime expansion and spread to Europe, influencing the naval race on the Atlantic. When Europeans challenged China for maritime dominance in the nineteenth century, they used cannons and navigational tools that ultimately derived from Chinese inventions.[4] Yet in other ways, the European and Chinese experiences are not comparable, as the Chinese faced very different resource geographies, strategic considerations, and political constraints than their European contemporaries. For example, it is positively misleading to compare the Zheng He expeditions—often the only mention of Ming China in world history textbooks—to the European "age of discovery."

Instead of abstract comparison, this chapter seeks to build a more grounded understanding of Chinese maritime exploits by embedding them in their material and institutional constraints. While ships could be abstracted as pawns in a grand strategy or lines on a bureaucrat's ledger, they ultimately began their life as timber. The structural characteristics of woody plants indelibly shaped the ships built from their materials. Shipwrights selected different types of lumber for underwater hulls than for masts or deck planks, and Yangzi fir performed differently than Korean pine or Fujianese camphor, let alone European oak. Ships were also built to serve different ends on different waters. Purpose-built "sea hawks" handled very differently than grain barges or fishing sampans. Finally, ship construction depended on the large-scale dynamics of the timber supply. Emperors could issue orders for as many ships as they wanted, but shipyards could only fulfill them if they had enough supplies. In China, these three constraints—on wood, water, and institutions—largely overlapped, reinforcing a division of the maritime realm into three main regions.

Of China's three naval fronts, the Yangzi River was by far the most important. Without command of the great river, a southern state could not secure itself from attack, and a northern state could not hope to dominate the south.[5] For centuries, the Yangzi was the site of major naval battles and developed a distinct military culture around fast, oared warships, a tradition that continues to the present as the Dragon Boat Festival (Duanwu Jie).[6] Yangzi River fleets also employed paddle ships (*chechuan*) to sail against the current and tower ships (*louchuan*) to lay siege to riverside fortresses. Working in the fir heartland, Yangzi River shipwrights used this single, fast-growing, durable, and straight timber for almost every component, from masts to planking.[7] The Yangzi was also the epicenter of the timber trade, boasting substantial revenues from the timber tariff and thousands of log rafts for purchase. This made it an ideal place to build ships for comparatively little expense. It was on the Yangzi that the Song built East Asia's first substantial navy, the Mongols built much of the fleet for the invasion of Japan, and the Ming built the treasure ships that sailed to the Indian Ocean.

The second major area of fleet operations was the South China Sea, which, while less strategically important than the Yangzi, was at least as significant commercially. The South China Sea linked China into the great monsoon trading networks extending as far west as Arabia and East Africa. Until the eleventh century, these long-distance routes were dominated by sojourning Arabs, Persians, and Indians. But following a major liberalization of trading restrictions in 1070, merchants from Fujian and Guangdong began to supersede foreigners in the South Seas trade.[8] For the next several centuries, Chinese states worked to dominate the South China Sea to control this trade. South Sea ships were built for different purposes than Yangzi River ships, generally with V-shaped hulls for blue-ocean stability rather than the U-shaped hulls needed to traverse sandy shoals. Due to the distinct environmental endowments of the southeast coast and its connections to Southeast Asia, Fujianese shipwrights built with camphor and teak as well as fir, incorporating techniques from the Indian Ocean and the Malay world.[9] The relationship between shipyards and the state was also quite different on the southeast coast, where officials were as apt to press merchant ships into service as they were to build their own.

The third distinct naval region was the Yellow Sea, between Korea and North China. Maritime routes from the Yangzi River to Beijing and Liaodong ran through the Yellow Sea, as did the sea routes to Korea. This was frequently a zone of naval conflict during periods when the north and south were controlled by different states and a key transport route when the Grand Canal was inoperable. Compared to the South China Sea, tides and winds in the Yellow Sea were very unpredictable. To staff their Yellow Sea navies, both China and Korea recruited "pirate" navies from the fishing and smuggling communities of the islands and peninsulas. Yellow Sea ships were also of different design than either the Yangzi River ships or the great trading junks of the South Seas. In Korea and Liaodong, they were built principally of pine.[10] Unlike in South China, Yellow Sea shipyards in both China and Korea tended to draft corvée loggers to supply their timber rather than taxing it from merchants.

To unify China, an aspiring empire had to unify these three maritime realms and dominate the zone where they overlapped in the East China Sea. This entailed strategic mastery of distinct patterns of wind and tide; it also required domination of the multiple forest ecologies and institutions that brought wood to the water. In the early stages of empire building, the Song, Jin, Yuan, and Ming dynasties each assembled irregular flotillas of fishing boats, merchant vessels, and hastily built craft of questionable seaworthiness; when possible, they also seized warships from their predecessors and rivals. This smash-and-grab approach to naval construction sometimes worked in the short run, but it was not the basis for long-term maritime power. More mature empires faced a very different challenge: how to make their navies sustainable. The forests of the southern interior were already afloat. In theory, naval officials merely had to transform flotillas of fir logs into fleets of fir-beamed warships. Yet in practice, the material and institutional transformation of trees into timber into ships was anything but straightforward.

THE JIN WARS AND THE TRANSFORMATION OF THE SONG NAVY

In its founding decades, the Song developed a powerful fleet during its wars to conquer the south from 960 to 979. In doing so, it built on a wave of developments in shipbuilding, harbor construction, and canal dredging over the previous two centuries.[11] But once the conquest was complete, the Song greatly reduced the fleet. For the most part, naval units were little more than small detachments attached to provincial garrisons.[12] These small fleets served important purposes in patrol, bandit suppression, and naval training.[13] Nonetheless, the Song navy lost much of its importance after the conquest of the south. Through much of the eleventh century, the only specialized military fleets were the elite "tiger wings" (*huyi*) of the imperial guard and the southeast sea patrol fleet in Guangdong. While each of these was responsible for early innovations, including the development of rockets, bombs, and new types of seagoing warships, naval development was not a Northern Song priority.[14]

For the next century and more, the Song built ships in places where it could command labor or where there were extensive woodlands, or ideally both. Yangzi River garrisons built warships for the rivers, while seagoing ships were built at Guangzhou.[15] Military units in heavily wooded Zhejiang logged (*caikan*) and operated lumberyards (*shanchang*) to supply the shipyards.[16] Circuit-level transport bureaus built their own barges to transport the grain tax.[17] Their shipyards were concentrated along the Yangzi River and the Grand Canal, especially in tree-rich Jiangxi and Hunan.[18] For the first century of the Northern Song, shipbuilding was largely treated as a corollary to the command of any large pool of labor.[19]

Starting in the early twelfth century, policies began to shift toward more judicious use of timber. In 1114, the state ordered the Ningbo shipyards to stop cutting living timber unless they received specific written permission and to use tariff materials instead.[20] New deadlines and budgetary limits were also imposed on the shipyards.[21] To save on materials, the court even ordered reductions in the size of transport ships, from 300 to 250 units of grain.[22] With growing fleets, and perhaps growing pressures on the forest resources, we see the first attempts to economize.

This all changed in 1127, when Jurchen armies invaded North China and the Song court fled southward across the Yangzi River. After a short-lived attempt to regroup in the north, the court settled in Hangzhou, finding itself defending a northern frontier largely defined by the Huai and Yangzi Rivers.[23] Almost immediately, the Song officiate began an unprecedented naval buildup to defend this great moat. During the retreat, Li Gang, a vice president in the Department of State Affairs, reactivated all naval units and reorganized them into two main navies, one for the Yangzi River and one for the seacoast.[24] These nascent fleets included a confusing array of ships assembled from dozens of different garrisons, including paddle wheelers, galleys, scout ships, and flat-bottomed "sand ships" (*shachuan*).[25] To create a more unified fleet, Li Gang ordered shipyards to focus on building a single style of ship, the high-capacity, low-cost "mullet ships" (*daoyu chuan*) used by Jiangnan merchants.[26] The court also ordered the Suzhou (Pingjiang) shipyards to construct two additional types of ships: eight-oared galleys and smaller four-oared "sea hawks" (*haigu chuan*).[27] To cover this substantial expense, the state levied a tax on all seagoing vessels (*haichuan shui*) to use for military finance. Between central and local officials and transport costs, this tariff drew off seven parts in fifteen (46.67 percent) of merchants' trade goods, an astoundingly high rate that led to a correspondingly high rate of tax evasion.[28]

In late 1129 and early 1130, Jin armies gave the Song fleets their first real test, crossing the Yangzi, capturing Nanjing (Jiankang) and Hangzhou (Lin'an), and pursuing the Song emperor to sea. A much larger Song navy soon arrived to defeat the Jin fleet, forcing the Jin army to retreat across the Yangzi.[29] Nonetheless, the danger of a second Jin invasion led the Song to a second wave of naval buildup. In 1131, Zhejiang shipyards disassembled ferries to repurpose as large warships.[30] In 1132, the court ordered another 980 warships built across five circuits.[31] The fleet buildup culminated in the 1132 establishment of the Office of Coastal Control (Yanhai Zhizhi Shisi), which brought the coastal defense fleet under the imperial guard. Specialized naval officials were now given ranks equivalent to their counterparts in the Fiscal Commission.[32] While the Song-Jin war continued for another decade, this powerful Song navy prevented any further invasions across the Yangzi.[33]

Following its retreat, the Song court also faced banditry throughout much of the south.[34] In 1130, a local sectarian leader on Dongting Lake established the breakaway kingdom of Chu. While the leader was soon captured and executed, his lieutenant Yang Yao continued the resistance on Dongting, the large lake that feeds into the Yangzi in Hunan. Leading perhaps four hundred thousand rebels, Yang seized warships from the Song fleet and logged the region to build their own paddle-wheeled tower ships (*che lou dachuan*).[35] To counter the Chu threat, the Song built hundreds of its own river warships. In 1133, the four river circuits constructed a total of 480 warships, most of which were probably small sampans.[36] Between 1132 and 1135, when Yang was finally defeated, officials submitted multiple paddle-wheel designs to the court, including small four-wheeled interceptors and ships with five, nine, and even thirteen wheels.[37] The emperor ordered shipyards in the region to build a total of fifty-six paddle wheelers.[38] Much of the expense of shipbuilding was underwritten by the timber tariff.[39] Just as the Jin invasion led to the buildup of the coastal fleet, the Chu rebellion forced the Song to expand its presence on the middle Yangzi.

After two decades of relative peace, warfare returned to the Song in the late 1150s with the rise of the Jin Prince of Hailing. In 1150, conspirators assassinated the Jin emperor and placed Hailing on the throne. He soon raised taxes and labor service to extreme levels to fund his imperial ambitions, including a greatly expanded fleet.[40] In 1159, Hailing recruited shipwrights from South China, set up shipyards in Tongzhou, and impressed thirty thousand sailors.[41] The Tongzhou shipyards relied heavily on corvée labor, sending four hundred thousand conscripts to log nearby and thousands more to dredge a canal to float warships to the sea.[42] With word of the invasion plans, the Song's long-dormant shipbuilding program also returned in force. The Song court ordered Fujian to build ten mullet ships and six larger oceangoing vessels and Jiangnan shipyards to build two hundred warships and one hundred transports.[43] As Li Gang had done in 1127, officials sought to establish a uniform standard for their warships to ensure that fleets could sail together as units.[44]

If the Song navy played a key role in defending the Yangzi in 1131, it was even more critical during the Song-Jin war of 1161. In November, a Song fleet defeated the main Jin force of six hundred ships off the coast of Shandong. In addition to a better-constructed and better-sailed fleet, the Song ships also used new military technologies, including catapult-hurled gunpowder bombs and incendiaries.[45] While the Jin army was able to seize Hezhou, on the Yangzi's north bank the defeat of the main Jin navy left it using grain barges as troop transports and building ships with timbers torn from houses. Outnumbered Song defenders held off the invasion long enough for a large fleet of paddle wheelers and seagoing "whales" (*haiyu*) to arrive, defeating repeated Jin attempts to cross the river.[46] Ultimately, the second Song-Jin war was not decided on the battlefield. In 1161, the Prince of Hailing was murdered in his tent by members of his own entourage.[47] Nonetheless, the Song victories off Shandong and on the Yangzi demonstrated clear naval superiority based on a larger, better-built, and better-sailed fleet of specialized warships.

While the Song court briefly canceled ship construction in 1164, fleet construction soon resumed and reached new levels.[48] Between 1165 and 1189, the Song expanded its five existing naval squadrons and established ten new ones. Figures are incomplete, but by conservative estimate the Song navy in 1190 was three to five times larger than it had been in 1160.[49] It continued to expand in the early 1200s, establishing another five squadrons and further expanding existing ones. The largest squadron guarding the mouth of the Yangzi reached 11,500 men. Estimating from troop sizes, it probably maintained at least fifty large warships and hundreds of smaller craft.[50] Most other squadrons were about one-third to one-half this size. Meanwhile, innovations continued, with warships growing ever larger, including galleys with forty-two oars and "sea hawks" (*haigu*) up to four times the size of earlier vessels.[51]

In addition to the ships built at naval shipyards, the Southern Song relied on merchant vessels bought, borrowed, or commissioned for government use. Immediately following the southward retreat of the Song court in 1127, it commandeered more than six hundred ships from merchants in Fujian and Guangdong and divided them into three six-month terms of service.[52] In 1132, all ships over 1.2 *zhang* in the beam (approximately 4 meters wide) were registered for patrol duty.[53] In the lead-up to the war of 1161, overseas merchants contributed a total of 436 vessels to the Song navy.[54] Both merchant patrols and contributions to the navy continued through the end of the Song.[55] Given the extent of private trade, this was an efficient way to staff the navy. By 1259, nearly 4,000 ships larger than 1 *zhang* (3 meters) in the beam were registered in the three ports of Ningbo, Wenzhou, and Taizhou alone.[56] The Song also relied on private shipyards to construct official naval vessels. Quanzhou, which lacked an official shipyard, received commissions to construct naval vessels throughout the twelfth century.[57] State commissions probably also went to both state and private shipyards in Ningbo, another shipbuilding hub.[58] Taking advantage of the flourishing trade from Ningbo to Guangzhou, the Song outsourced much of its coastal defense to private merchants and contracted much of its shipbuilding to private shipyards.

Throughout the buildup of the Southern Song navy from 1127 through the end of the twelfth century, its superiority rested on the strength of trade. In contrast to Northern Song shipyards, which relied on military loggers to supply lumber, the Southern Song made almost no use of forced labor. In official sources, there is only one clear mention of corvée, an edict from 1164 when the Song court specifically canceled an emergency measure from the war of 1161.[59] Prior to the 1160s, the court simply disbursed money to buy timber, assuming it was available on local markets. After 1161, as naval bases were built in strategic locations that lacked timber, the court sent officials with specific instructions on where and how to buy supplies.[60] Along the Yangzi, shipbuilding was largely financed and supplied through timber tariffs. Along the seacoast, fleets were a mixture of merchant ships pressed into service and warships financed by tariffs on overseas trade. But throughout the Southern Song, the power of the navy was an extension of commercial wealth, and of timber markets in particular.

THE MONGOLS GO TO SEA

The Mongol empire is generally thought of as a land empire, deriving its military superiority from its highly mobile cavalry and effective use of siege weapons. Yet at its peak in the mid-1280s, the Mongol-ruled Yuan dynasty also boasted the largest navy East Asia had seen to that point in its history. Like most of the empire, the Yuan navy was built by grafting its conquests—the Jin, Koryŏ, and Song fleets—onto the trunk of the Mongol imperial project. The thirty-year peak of naval expansion under Kublai Khan (r. 1260–94) revealed the capacities of a large and diverse empire to deploy multiple labor forces and draw on a continent's worth of forests to build a large fleet quickly, but it also showed the limitations of a roughly grafted assemblage of regional timber economies without a coherent or sustainable system to integrate them.

During the Mongols' initial conquests, they had little need for a navy. They only began to build significant waterborne forces in 1259, following an unsuccessful attack on the Song dynasty's Yangzi River fortress city of Xiangyang. Realizing he would need a navy to cross the Yangzi and defeat the Song, Kublai Khan began extensive preparations for an amphibious assault. In 1265, he ordered ships built at the Mongol capital of Dadu (Beijing), at Kaifeng, at Dengzhou on the Shandong Peninsula, and at Guanghua just upriver of Xiangyang. He appointed Zhang Xi, a longtime naval officer from coastal Shandong, as director of the navy (*shuijun zongguan*). While it failed in its initial assault on Xiangyang, this small Mongol fleet repulsed two attempts by the Song navy to break the siege in 1269 and 1270. This was enough to convince the khan of its importance, and he gave orders to expand the fleet by an astounding five thousand warships and seventy thousand men. Xiangyang held out for another three years, until March 1273, before finally falling to Yuan forces. In the meantime, the Yuan navy had grown to nearly four times its previous size.[61]

After capturing Xiangyang, the Yuan continued to build up their navy to further press its advantage. In 1273, they built another two thousand warships, half at newly captured Xiangyang and half at Kaifeng. The following year, Kaifeng built another eight hundred ships, probably bringing the fleet to around six thousand craft.[62] Over the winter of 1274–75, the expanded Yuan navy proceeded down the Han River, twice outflanking Song fleets, burning more than three thousand ships, and gaining the south bank of the

Yangzi near Wuhan.[63] In March 1275, they defeated another force of five thousand vessels near the point where the Grand Canal crosses the Yangzi, capturing two thousand Song ships and rendezvousing with the Kaifeng-built wings of the fleet.[64] In July, the combined Yuan navy faced the Song's coastal defense fleet, defeating several larger warships of the "yellow goose" (*huanggu*) and "white falcon" (*baiyao*) classes. These engagements broke the back of the Song's river defense fleets. By the end of the summer, the Yuan fleet advanced to the delta and was in full command of the Yangzi.[65]

Having defeated the Song's riverine navy by copying its ship designs, the Yuan proceeded to build a blue-ocean navy using the same model. They took control of nearly eight hundred sea ships from the Song coastal defense fleet and used an undamaged white falcon–class warship as a model for building a hundred more, staffed with a combination of North Chinese and former Song sailors. Yuan envoys also recruited the pirate chiefs Zhu Qing and Zhang Xuan, who brought five hundred large ships and thousands of experienced sailors. When the fleet set sail at the end of 1275, it boasted forty-one wings, perhaps ten times the size of the Mongol navy in 1268.[66] The Song officially capitulated in 1276, while the Yuan fleet continued to pursue the rump of the court down the southeast coast, finally defeating it in Guangdong in 1279.[67]

Even as Kublai's first fleet was fighting on the Yangzi, he forced the king of Koryŏ to build him a second fleet in Korea. In 1258, Kublai's brother Möngke had subdued Korea, taking members of the ruling family hostage to ensure their loyalty. Following the deaths of both Möngke and the Koryŏ king in 1259, Kublai sent one of these former hostages to rule Korea as King Wŏnjong. Almost immediately upon assuming the throne, Wŏnjong began building ships to support the invasion of the Southern Song. While these efforts were initially delayed by an attempted coup, shipbuilding eventually continued.[68] In 1266, the khan instructed the king to build one thousand ships for the invasions of the Song and Japan. Once again, Korean compliance was delayed by anti-Mongol resistance, this time by holdouts on Cheju Island, off the southwest coast of the peninsula.[69] Yet preparations for the invasion of Japan commenced elsewhere in Korea. In the winter of 1273–74, loggers cleared the hills in the southwestern province of Chŏlla, supplying timber to a force of more than thirty thousand shipwrights commanded by the Korean general Kim Panggyong. The khan's leading shipwright, Ji Gongzhi, traveled between Shandong, Chŏlla, and Xiangyang to oversee the construction of multiple fleets.[70] After a delay caused by the death of King

Wŏnjong, the invasion of Japan launched in November 1274 with twenty thousand to thirty thousand Mongol, North Chinese, and Korean soldiers; seven thousand Korean sailors; and seven hundred to nine hundred ships.[71] After successful forays onto the islands of Tsushima and southwestern Kyushu, the invasion fleet was forced back to sea by inclement weather in late November.[72]

Despite the limited success of the first invasion, Kublai Khan was enthusiastic about a second foray into Japan. He granted a temporary respite from shipbuilding while completing the conquests of South China and Cheju Island. But as soon as the final Song holdouts were defeated in 1279, Kublai ordered the shipyards to resume preparation. He ordered six hundred ships built in the former Song prefectures of Yangzhou, Changsha, and Quanzhou; transferred riverine units to the coast to allow coastal detachments to deploy to Japan; assigned the last Song holdouts to oversee coastal shipbuilding; and transferred the remnants of the Song fleet for repair and redeployment. Kublai also sent a Mongol officer to the Korean court to oversee the construction of nine hundred ships, plus another three thousand built in Koryŏ shipyards with timber from recently subdued Cheju Island.[73] Logging was probably overseen by the region's newly established myriarchies (Mongolian: *tumen*, Korean: *manhobu*, Chinese: *wanhufu*).[74] By the end of the year, the southern fleet had one hundred thousand soldiers ready for invasion—largely former Song subjects, deserters, and pirates. The Koryŏ king personally led the eastern fleet.[75] The two fleets combined to number around four thousand ships.[76]

The eastern fleet departed for Japan in May 1281, engaging Japanese forces but finding them better prepared than in 1274. The southern fleet did not arrive until early July, when it was also attacked by Japanese forces. The two fleets joined only in mid-August, whereupon they were almost immediately beset by a typhoon—the famous "wind of the gods" (*kamikaze*) credited with saving Japan. Many ships sank, especially from the southern fleet, whose ships and sailors handled poorly outside their home waters. By contrast, most of the eastern fleet managed to retreat to Korea.[77]

This was far from the end of Yuan shipbuilding. In 1282, Kublai ordered 4,000 ships built in Liaodong, Hebei, Cheju, Chŏlla, Yangzhou, Nanchang, and Quanzhou. The Koryŏ king promised another 150 ships, while 3,000 typhoon-damaged ships recovered were sent for repair. In 1283, the khan dispatched master shipwright Ji Gongzhi to South China with orders for 1,000 more ships. Meanwhile, forests near the Yellow Sea shipyards were under heavy pressure to provide adequate timber. The Pingluan yards in Hebei sent two detachments of nine thousand soldiers to log the Tushan and Qianshan ranges and another eight thousand soldiers and civilians to float logs to the shipyards. In one season of lumbering, they reportedly cut 186,000 logs. Elsewhere, Kublai's soldiers seized private timber stocks and even tore down houses, while coastal and riverine populations were pressed with massive labor service duties. Revolts broke out across South China, leading Kublai to furlough the soldier-lumberjacks and suspend shipbuilding. But soon the detention of the khan's ambassadors in Champa (now central Vietnam) provoked a further change of plans. Rather than sending the fleets east to Japan, he sent them south. As in Japan, the Yuan navy floundered.[78] In 1285, Kublai again made concrete plans for the invasion of Japan, but once again sent his forces south rather than east, this time to Annam (northern Vietnam). It was only in 1286 that Kublai formally ended planning for the invasions of Japan, whereupon the people of Zhejiang were reportedly "so glad that their cheers sounded like thunder."[79] Yet naval expeditions continued. In 1293, Kublai sent fleets south to Java, and he continued to entertain plans for a third invasion of Japan until his death in 1294.[80]

Kublai's navy was not simply one great mass of ships, but rather the gradual accretion of boats captured or converted from different fleets, with thousands of others purpose-built in shipyards from Chŏlla to Quanzhou. The Yuan naval buildup showed its military-industrial machine at peak capacity, even as the processes of building the fleet changed over its thirty-year history. For its first decade, the fleet was essentially a wing of the Yuan's North China army (Hanjun). The khan's major shipwrights were almost all military officers with prior service to the Jin. In the 1260s, the Koryŏ king also began to contribute ships and men from his own household budget. Starting in the 1270s, the Yuan built thousands of ships in southern ports captured from the Song and hundreds more in southwestern Korea. Throughout Korea and North China, Mongol myriarchs oversaw massive deployments of forced labor. By contrast, while South Chinese shipyards were heavily taxed, there are no reports of logging corvée south of the Yangzi. Instead, the southern fleet was presumably built with timber purchased or requisitioned on the market. Despite its rapid successes, the irregular nature of this fleet revealed itself during the invasions of Japan and Southeast Asia, as hastily built ships and impressed sailors performed poorly outside of their home waters.

DAOIST IMMORTALS AND TREASURE FLEETS

By the mid-1300s, the Yuan navy was a shadow of its former self. Due to sedimentation of the Grand Canal, the Yuan were forced to ship grain to Beijing by sea, where they were repeatedly defeated by the pirate commander Fang Guozhen. With little other recourse, the Yuan offered Fang favorable terms for "surrendering" to the court in 1349, and again in 1353 and 1356. During Fang's final "capitulation," the Yuan navy revealed its full weakness by granting Fang command of a sea transport battalion (*qianhu*). By 1356, it was Fang's thousand-ship fleet—not the regular Yuan navy—that controlled most of coastal Zhejiang.[81] The rot in the Yuan navy soon spread to the rest of the state. In 1351, the court sent an army to deal with scattered rebels in northern and central China; in response, the rebels merged into two main armies, known as the Red Turbans (Hongjin) for the colored head scarves and banners they used to identify themselves. In 1352, the Red Turbans seized control of much of the Yangzi River valley and large parts of North China, before being driven back by Yuan forces in 1353. As on the seas, the court empowered a motley array of local bandits, self-defense forces, and breakaway commanders to push back the millenarian rebels.[82] Through several further years of warfare, these acephalous armies further coalesced into several self-declared states, including Zhang Shicheng's "Wu kingdom" in Jiangnan; the "Great Han" state of Chen Youliang in the middle Yangzi; and Han Lin'er's "Song dynasty" in southern Anhui, effectively controlled by his nominal subordinate Zhu Yuanzhang.[83]

As these rival regimes sought to extend their control, the Yangzi River became a major axis of naval conflict. Zhang, Chen, and Zhu each built up fleets from a motley array of fishing vessels, merchant ships, and purpose-built warships, for which they presumably logged the surrounding regions.[84] In 1363, the buildup of the previous decade culminated in the battle of Poyang Lake in Jiangxi, where the navies of Chen Youliang and Zhu Yuanzhang each sought to gain control of the key outlet to the Yangzi River. At the height of the battle, Zhu's fleet was said to number one thousand ships and at least one hundred thousand men, facing Chen's force of perhaps twice the size and including large tower ships.[85] After a lengthy siege at the riverside fortress at Nanchang, the battle broke when Zhu loaded dozens of vessels with gunpowder and used them to break Chen's line of battle. Fearing further fire attacks, Chen's remaining captains divided their fleets, allowing Zhu's more maneuverable navy to defeat them one at a time. The battle ended when Chen Youliang was shot in the eye during a last-ditch attempt to break out of the lake.[86] As Hok-lam Chan reveals, the records of this battle are full of unbelievable occurrences, including the intercession of Daoist immortals to warn Zhu of sea demons and foretell Chen's death.[87] Nonetheless, the battle of Poyang Lake was inarguably one of the largest inland naval conflicts in history and perhaps the first time that cannons were used from the decks of ships.[88] Once Zhu defeated Chen's navy, he was able to dominate the Yangzi River and easily defeated Zhang Shicheng, his last major rival in the region. In 1367, Fang Guozhen surrendered to Zhu on favorable terms, bringing with him the oceangoing fleet that enabled Zhu's conquest of the southeast coast.[89]

Having defeated his rivals through naval might, Zhu Yuanzhang recognized the importance of shipbuilding, but faced the new challenge of making it sustainable. Shortly after the declaration of the Ming dynasty, he established a shipyard at Longjiang in Nanjing to build both military and transport ships.[90] Each of the capital battalions (*jing suo*) was also assigned responsibility for building its own ships.[91] In 1391, Nanjing officials planted over five hundred thousand tung, lacquer, and palm trees to supply ancillary materials to these shipyards.[92] Starting with the establishment of the Longjiang customs in 1393, much of the shipbuilding previously done in the provinces was moved to the Longjiang shipyards to take advantage of tariff materials. Regulations required that these shipyards use materials from the timber tariff whenever possible.[93] These regulations set an enduring precedent, although perhaps not the one the Ming founder intended.

Following Zhu Yuanzhang's death and a brief succession struggle, the Yongle emperor took command and reoriented shipbuilding toward his northern capital at Beijing and expanded the overall scale of the Ming navy. To ship supplies north, Yongle built two new shipyards, one on the Yangzi at Qingjiang to build river transports and another at Weihe in Shandong to build sea transports.[94] Provincial tariff stations forwarded materials to provision these shipyards: timber from Jiangxi, Huguang, and Sichuan; cash from Zhejiang and the Southern Metropolitan Region; and iron and tung oil from Fujian.[95] Labor was provided by a levy on nearby populations, 70 percent borne by commoners and 30 percent by military households.[96] But Yongle's greater legacy was a massive buildup in seagoing vessels for his various expeditions, including the famous Indian Ocean armada and a fleet used for the invasion of Annam. In 1403, his first year on the throne, Yongle issued orders for a total of 561 ships, almost all of them built on the Yangzi

River or the southeast coast.⁹⁷ In 1404, the capital garrisons in Nanjing built another 50 ships, and Fujian constructed the first 5 ships built specifically for the expedition to the Indian Ocean.⁹⁸ In 1405, a single edict commissioned an astounding 1,180 ships, again principally from South China.⁹⁹ In total, the *Veritable Records* contain orders for 2,339 ships issued by the end of 1407 and 2,868 ships by the end of the Yongle reign in 1424.¹⁰⁰ During these three decades, the Ming's oceangoing navy may have exceeded 3,000 ships.¹⁰¹

To build all the ships demanded by the emperor, the Longjiang shipyards doubled in size, largely through the addition of specialized yards to build the "treasure ships" (*baochuan*) for the expeditions to South and Southeast Asia and East Africa led by Zheng He.¹⁰² According to the official biography of Zheng He, these treasure ships measured 44 *zhang* in length and 18 *zhang* in the beam.¹⁰³ There is some controversy over how to interpret these measures, but some scholars argue that they may have been between 385 and 440 feet long (117–34 meters), which would make them the largest wooden ships ever built.¹⁰⁴ For comparison, Christopher Columbus's flagship was 86 feet long, and European ships only reached lengths of 200 feet during the Napoleonic Wars.¹⁰⁵ Zheng He's armada ultimately made six expeditions under Yongle, and a seventh under the Xuande emperor, each with a complement of around 250 ships, 40 of which were the massive treasure ships.¹⁰⁶ At least 150 orders for treasure ship construction are attested in the historical record.¹⁰⁷

The Yongle boom in shipbuilding, especially the construction of the Zheng He fleets, is often treated as fundamentally unprecedented. A widely circulated image shows a treasure ship towering over Columbus's flagship the *Santa Maria*.¹⁰⁸ Jack A. Goldstone's influential metaphor compares the scale of the Zheng He expeditions to the Apollo moon missions.¹⁰⁹ Yet there are several controversies associated with these interpretations. On the one hand, there are serious questions regarding the size and number of ships used on the missions. Details on the number and size of ships derive from rather dubious sources, including a fantasy novel and histories written centuries after the expeditions.¹¹⁰ Stelae from the 1430s missions suggest that both the number and the size of the ships may have been substantially smaller.¹¹¹ Scholars have also used naval architectural analysis and archeology of the treasure shipyards to question the plausibility of building ships over 400 feet long.¹¹² On the other hand, there was a clear precedent for very large armadas of massive ships. As we saw above, Kublai's fleets had as many as 4,000 ships, and the biggest ships of his era reached 20 *zhang* (200 feet). The treasure ships followed the trajectory of naval developments over the previous three centuries toward ever-larger fleets of ever-larger ships.

Regardless of the exact size of Zheng He's fleets, they were clearly enormous projects. But did they pose economic or environmental ruin? Edward Dreyer argues that in absolute terms the costs of the expeditions were not too large to be borne by the Ming fisc.[113] I would add that the demands of timber and labor did not greatly exceed the capacity of Jiangnan shipyards. As seen above, Yangzi River shipwrights had repeatedly fulfilled orders for hundreds and even thousands of ships per year in the twelfth and thirteenth centuries. While loggers were sent to the upper reaches of the Yangzi in Sichuan and the Min River in Fujian, probably to cut mast timber, contemporary accounts otherwise give no mention of logging expeditions.[114] This suggests that the demand for timber was a large but manageable burden. While the fleets were a significant expense, they probably did not significantly deplete forest resources.[115] If anything, the main effect of the Yongle projects was probably to shift much of South China's forest production from private construction to state projects.

While they may not have deforested the empire, the Yongle projects caused an acute fiscal and political crisis. The decade following the Yongle emperor's death in 1424 saw widespread retrenchment across almost all state institutions; shipbuilding was no exception. The court substantially reduced quotas for the Longjiang shipyards in 1428.[116] In 1435, the Nanjing garrisons and the Board of Works brokered a compromise attempted to stabilize the operations at Longjiang by splitting the cost of materials 40–60.[117] To pay its end, the board rented out state-owned farmland near the Longjiang yards, collecting rents in goods like tung oil and hemp (*huangma*) that were used to make naval stores.[118] The court made similar provisions to save costs at the Qingjiang shipyards as well. Between the Xuande reign (1426–35) and the 1460s, the Yangzi River provinces built their own transport ships to avoid the expense of forwarding materials to Nanjing. For three decades, the Qingjiang yards only built grain ships for the Southern Metropolitan Region.[119] During the Zhengtong reign (1436–50), the court reduced the annual quota of seagoing transports at Weihe by 70 percent.[120] Overall, the middle decades of the fifteenth century saw a massive drawdown in the size of the navy to half or less of its former strength.[121] By the early sixteenth century, the Ming navy—like the Yuan navy before it—struggled even in engagements with pirate fleets.[122]

SHIPYARDS IN THE LONG SIXTEENTH CENTURY

While the post-Yongle decline of the Ming navy was pronounced, the Ming shipyards ultimately accomplished something that had not been done since the Southern Song—they made shipbuilding sustainable. The renaissance at the shipyards began in the 1460s, as an influx of silver began to revive the economy, allowing officials to expand production again. Customs stations began to reopen in the 1460s and 1470s, often for the express purpose of providing shipbuilding funds.[123] Starting in 1462, the court once again designated the Qingjiang yards to build all the grain ships for the south. Instead of constructing their own transports, the southern provinces now forwarded silver tariff receipts to Qingjiang, which bought materials on the open market. The court also revived the Weihe yards as the principal shipyards for oceangoing transports.[124] The availability of silver made it far easier to supply these shipyards with currency rather than going through the difficulty of shipping materials. Yet even as the growing money supply simplified logistics, it subjected the shipyards to a new problem: inflation, especially in the price of timber.

Inflation was a fundamentally new problem for the shipyards, one that the Ming fiscal system was especially ill equipped to address due to its reliance on fixed tax quotas. Between 1462 and the 1480s, the cost of each ship built at Qingjiang doubled, largely due to increases in timber prices. To make up the difference, the state diverted additional funds from the customs stations at Hangzhou, Wuhu, and Huai'an and pressed the military households of the Nanjing garrisons with tax surcharges. Officials even returned to collecting timber tariffs in kind in an attempt to stock the shipyards while avoiding the growing burden of timber price inflation.[125] By the early sixteenth century, inflation was felt at the Longjiang yards as well. In 1503, Longjiang had to request additional funds from every prefecture in the Southern Metropolitan Region. By 1516, Longjiang's fast warships (*kuaichuan*), formerly built for 100 taels, now cost 130 taels each, although the shipyards brought the cost down by 10 taels by reusing materials stripped from decommissioned ships. By 1521, fast warships cost 150 taels apiece, and costs continued to increase. Throughout this period, worker salaries were held constant, so the rising expenses came entirely due to increases in timber prices.[126]

Account books submitted to Qingjiang by the merchant Chen Xu allow us to follow timber price inflation into the 1530s and 1540s. According to

Chen, the cost of materials for grain ships increased from 52.5 taels per ship in 1524 to 60 taels each in 1545.[127] The smaller shipyards attached to each garrison also felt the rising cost of materials. By the 1540s, shipbuilding costs at the Nanjing garrisons were so unsustainable that the heads of supernumerary household groups (*bangjia*) were reduced to selling family members to raise the money they needed to pay their tax surcharges. Others committed suicide.[128] While we cannot read too much into these sparse accounts, they suggest that timber price inflation averaged around 3.5 percent annually in the late 1400s and around 2.5 percent per year in the early 1500s, before falling below 1 percent in the 1530s and 1540s.[129] While this would be fairly modest inflation by modern standards, even a small increase in the cost of timber wreaked havoc on Ming institutions with fixed budgets.

Despite the problems caused by inflation, the conversion to silver budgets allowed shipyard officials to compile better records and standardize prices. In 1501, officials at Qingjiang compiled *Treatise on Transport Ships* (Caochuan zhi), containing an institutional history of the shipyards and a list of standard prices for materials.[130] In 1503, the Longjiang shipyards posted a clear list of salaries for shipwrights.[131] In 1518, Longjiang regulations took advantage of better market information to peg the price of materials to the going price of timber.[132] In 1523, the Weihe shipyards were closed, concentrating transport shipbuilding entirely at Qingjiang, near the other main yards at Longjiang and the capital garrisons.[133] Finally, in 1529, the state appointed specialized managers to the Longjiang shipyards, which had previously been managed by the same officials overseeing the Longjiang customs.[134] The concentration of management at the Nanjing-area shipyards, and especially at Longjiang, soon allowed officials to consolidate the reforms of the previous two decades.

Starting in 1529, the new Longjiang managers developed regulations for reporting materials requisitions. The shipyards now submitted material requests in duplicate, sending one copy to the Nanjing Board of Works and one to the Longjiang customs. Shipyard and tariff officials worked together to assess timber stocks, set a date for construction, disburse materials from the tariff depots, and purchase any additional timber needed. When construction was completed, the shipyards produced reports in duplicate, one for the board and one for the construction office.[135] The 1540s brought further reforms across all three shipyards. In 1541, the Nanjing Board of Works required that the Longjiang customs record exact length and circumference for each pole of timber, rather than grading them according to rough sizes. Before forwarding materials to the shipyards, customs officials checked each item against their records to ensure that workers did not substitute inferior materials during transport.[136] In 1542, officials at the Nanjing Board of War compiled price lists for ships constructed at Nanjing garrisons, explicitly based on the standard prices set for the Qingjiang yards. Both shipyards now paid the same fixed prices for *nanmu* (*Phoebe nanmu*) and fir logs based on their circumference in Chinese feet (*chi*).[137] In 1543, officials established a standard dimension for timber planking as well, at one *zhang* by one *chi* by one *cun* (roughly ten feet by one foot by one inch).[138]

In 1545 and 1546, negotiations between the shipyards and leading timber merchants led to a second raft of systematic reforms. The court established the Imperial Timber Pavilion (Huangmu Ting) to oversee the shipping routes along the Yangzi and prevent log rafts from blocking the rivers, either by accident or by merchants intentionally trying to monopolize (*longduan*) the timber market.[139] The garrison shipyards also communicated with Longjiang to create standardized one-foot measures to use at the two regional tariff depots, all three shipyards, and the Board of Works office.[140] Using these standard measures, officials at the tariff depots now branded each log to indicate its size, one character (*zi*) for each foot of circumference. The shipyards now referred to timber as four-, five-, and six-character poles. The military even negotiated an agreement with leading merchants to supply a package of the large timbers needed for each ship, including one six-character log, three five-character logs, and three four-character logs of fir or *nanmu*.[141] Starting in 1546, the Longjiang shipyards used the same standard prices as the Board of War, which was itself based on the price lists first produced at Qingjiang around 1500.[142] The shipyards also established standard discounts for subgrade timber, including hollow, rotten, bent, or warped logs. They enumerated punishments for shipyard workers or merchants who defrauded the state. Finally, they published diagrams depicting the components of each type of ship (figure 6.1) and a standard form for purchasing officials to list the size, grade, and production location of each timber; the name of the vendor, inspector, and accountant; and the price based on the standard lists, after accounting for any flaws (figure 6.2). They forwarded this form to the bureau responsible for finances and to the officials overseeing sawyers to ensure the timber purchases were received intact.[143] Shipyard officials also produced several sets of records for future

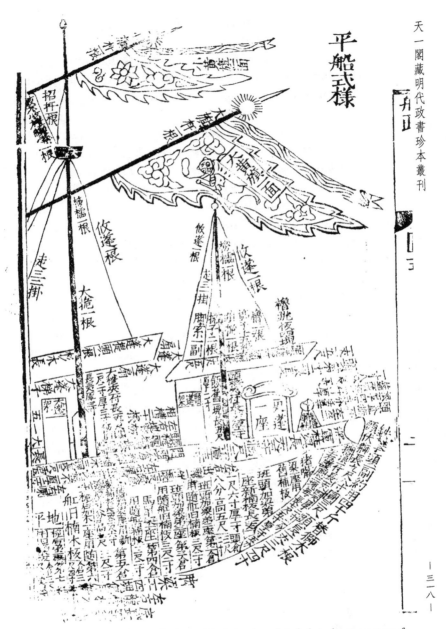

FIG 6.1 Diagram of a flat-decked warship (*pingchuan*). Labels indicate names of individual components, sometimes their dimensions. Elsewhere, the text provides standard prices and other specifications for each part. Image from *Shipyard Administration* (Chuanzheng; 1546), reprinted in *Tianyige cang Mingdai zhengshu zhenben congkan*. Courtesy of the C. V. Starr East Asian Library, Columbia University.

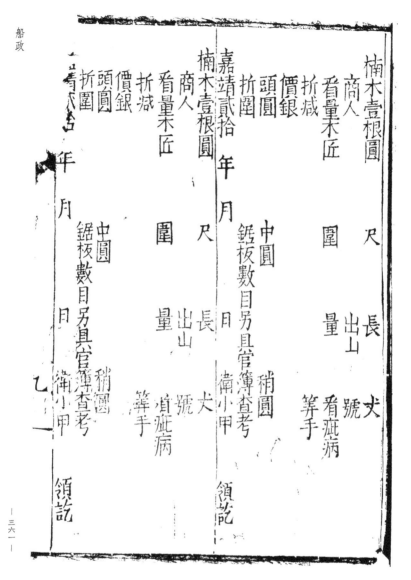

FIG 6.2 Form for recording timber purchases. This page and the following page (not pictured) include four identical forms, which could be printed from a woodblock as needed. A note reads, "Consult the official registers for the number of boards to saw." This form is for purchases of *nanmu* (*Phoebe nanmu*). A note later in the text indicates that the form should be modified for the purchase of fir or other types of wood. Image from *Shipyard Administration* (Chuanzheng; 1546), reprinted in *Tianyige cang Mingdai zhengshu zhenben congkan*. Courtesy of the C. V. Starr East Asian Library, Columbia University.

administrators, including a new edition of *Treatise on Transport Ships* (1545), *Shipyard Administration* (Chuanzheng; 1546), and *Treatise on the Longjiang Shipyards* (Longjiang chuanchang zhi; 1552).

Half a century after the reforms of the 1540s, another shipyard official, Ni Dong, recorded further improvements in shipyard operations in *New Treatise on Shipyard Administration* (Chuanzheng xin shu; c. 1590). The addition of fifty years of experience allowed further improvements to scheduling, budgeting, and oversight. Top officials now laid out schedules for new ship construction; large, medium, and small repairs; and teardowns of defunct vessels. They checked their timber stocks every fall to plan for timber purchases the following spring and estimated a budget while allowing actual prices to shift in accord with market conditions. To prevent theft or improper handling, lower-level officers now kept monthly records and marked each log with the names of the workers and overseers responsible for its storage and processing.[144]

After a century of erratic timber procurement in the 1400s, the Ming state gradually outsourced much of the labor to merchants. The shipyards commodified timber through forms that specified standards for size, type, and price but that also accounted for the subjective nature of individual logs by branding them with the names of those responsible for purchase, storage, and finishing. These same standards allowed board officials to budget for shipbuilding from a general-purpose treasury and shipwrights to build ships without worrying about how to requisition the materials. By the 1590s, the compilation of more than seventy years of records allowed officials to anticipate and track changes in the price of timber, avoiding the budgeting problems experienced in the early years of the century. This was arguably the peak of Ming timber management, a system built atop the markets, customs depots, and shipyards that processed logs into lumber and lumber into ships.

FORESTS AND CHINESE SEA POWER

Chinese sea power rested on different principles and faced different rivalries than those of the later European powers. The Song navy was mostly defensive and built for warfare on the lakes and rivers as much as on the sea. The Yuan invasions of Japan were amphibious assaults, not protracted naval warfare. Yuan and Ming expeditions to Southeast Asia were largely intended to open sea-lanes for commerce and diplomacy, not to explore and conquer.

Like the European navies in Robert Greenhalgh Albion's seminal exploration in *Forests and Sea Power*, the Chinese fleets of the twelfth through sixteenth centuries demanded a large and high-quality supply of timber. But unlike in Europe, China's fleets were built by a shipyard administration without an accompanying forest bureaucracy. Finance and labor were major concerns at the peaks of Song, Yuan, and Ming shipbuilding, but only rarely did bureaucrats worry about finding adequate sources of timber. While forced laborers supplied the fleets of the Northern Song, Jin, and Yuan, in the Southern Song and Ming the overwhelming majority of naval timber was supplied by private merchants, through either tariffs or licensed sales. Timber depots in Song Hangzhou and Ming Nanjing developed sophisticated lumber operations built around the standard sizing, grading, and pricing of timber; a paper trail to track materials from point of collection to point of use; and clear penalties for violations of market guidelines. With limited (but important) exceptions, Chinese states concentrated their timber oversight at the customs office, not in the forest.

The navy was, in turn, largely a reflection of the forests—and markets—that undergirded it. In the Northern Song, this meant a diffuse and varied array of ships built by provincial garrisons and transport commissions. Under the Southern Song, the navy resembled its two main timber sources: a Yangzi River fleet built in official shipyards with the fir timbers of Jiangnan and an oceangoing fleet built by the trading communities of the southeast coast. The navy yielded by the larger, more heterogeneous Yuan empire was a similar hodgepodge of pine ships from Korea, fir riverboats from Jiangnan, and a camphor-hulled fleet from Fujian. In the early Ming, the massive Zheng He fleets were largely constructed at Nanjing using fir timbers, reflecting the emerging dominance of Jiangnan's tree plantations. The growing size of the fleet reflected the growing capacity of timber markets to supply the shipyards. Yet while officials at the shipyards recorded their reforms in specialized treatises, developments in merchant operations are harder to probe. We likewise know very little about the shipwrights and carpenters at the other end of the commodity chain. Nonetheless, it is clear from the cameo appearances of merchants and woodworkers that they provided extensive input into price dynamics and standard measures. Much like the development of forests as property, the emergence of timber as a commodity depended on the willing participation of a range of actors, not the exclusive fiat of the bureaucratic state.

SEVEN

BEIJING PALACES AND THE ENDS OF EMPIRE

IN 1533, A MID-LEVEL OFFICIAL NAMED GONG HUI PUBLISHED THE volume *Essays on Timber Rafting in the Western Regions*, based on his experiences overseeing logging at the Ming dynasty's southwestern frontier. In this remarkable book, Gong describes the substantial ingenuity developed by Ming logging teams to cut and transport huge trees in difficult terrain, including the use of slip roads, "flying bridges," and massive capstans to tow logs up slopes. He also reveals the substantial perils of the mountainous region, including malaria, widespread starvation, and attacks by tribes and wild animals. But why was a Ming official cutting trees in such a distant and dangerous frontier in the first place? As this chapter explores, the southwestern frontier was one of the *only* places where Ming officials oversaw logging at all. Elsewhere, private plantations and timber markets were far more effective sources of wood. But the deep gorges of the southwest were among the only places in the empire with trees large enough for imperial construction.

If shipbuilding was a major impetus leading European empires to expand their grasp on forest resources, in China the greatest pressures on the logging frontier came from monumental architecture. The reasons for this divergence depended largely on both material and cultural difference between the two contexts. South China's tree plantations produced more than enough timber to supply the navy. But unlike in Europe, where monumental buildings were often built of stone, China's imperial architecture was almost singularly dependent on a supply of exceptionally large trees. In the classical form of East Asian building, the entire mass of the upper stories rests on a framework of beams and pillars (*liangzhu*), an architectural style that literally places great weight on its structural timbers. Because timber frames set the fundamental dimensions of each building, monumental structures required monumental pillars, and monumental pillars required monumental trees.[1] The spread of plantations that supplied timber to the shipyards came at the expense of old-growth woodlands with trees large enough for palace building. Paradoxically, this meant that the same trends that enabled a laissez-faire approach to general-purpose forestry also demanded that the state take a more direct hand in obtaining timber for the imperial palaces. It was the construction of Beijing, and its repeated reconstruction, that led to the last and greatest official logging operations in South China, projects that spelled the final decline of old-growth woodlands in the greater Yangzi River watershed.

Southwest China had long been a source of timber for imperial construction, but the early Ming logging projects in the region were unprecedented, some of the largest forced labor operations in history. Between 1406 and 1421, the Yongle emperor built Beijing into an imperial capital on an exceptional scale. State construction teams conscripted an estimated one million workers from throughout the empire to work on the palaces.[2] This was mirrored by a comparable effort in the gorges of the upper Yangzi River, where officials ordered hundreds of thousands of loggers to cut enormous trees and tow them to the waterways.[3] The state levied thousands of other workers to navigate the log rafts along the difficult route down the Yangzi River and up the Grand Canal to Beijing.[4] This fifteen-year effort represented the apex of the Ming command economy.

Aside from dispatching logging teams from the Han interior, the Ming emperors demanded timber from the native rulers of the southwest. During their conquest of the region, the Yuan had enrolled non-Han tribes into native offices (*tusi*). Rather than regular taxes, these groups submitted tribute (*gong*) through their hereditary rulers. The Ming inherited and modified this system, granting nominal bureaucratic rank and regalia to tribal leaders and standardizing the forms of tribute and suzerainty.[5] In the upper Yangzi, the standard tribute included enormous trunks of palace-grade fir and *nanmu*. This created a rather curious exchange of symbolic materials: the Ming state sent Chinese textiles that native officials wore as proof of their rank, while native officials sent giant timbers that Chinese emperors used to construct their edifices of power.

Through a massive escalation of forced labor and tributary extractions, the Yongle palaces set a standard that future emperors struggled to match. While no record survives to document the full extent of the logging program, 380,000 timbers remained in storage in 1441, twenty years after the completion of the original construction.[6] This astounding figure suggests that millions of trees were logged under Yongle's command. But later, when temples and palaces needed repair, officials struggled to find timber of adequate size and quality to replace the massive originals; the best and most-accessible woods had already been logged. Just as significantly, later courts simply could not command labor on the scale of the Yongle emperor.

Eventually, the Ming court did revive frontier logging, its hand forced by a series of fires that damaged the most important buildings in the imperial palace. But when sixteenth-century emperors ordered new timber requisitions, their officials struggled to supply their work teams, an enterprise rendered all the more difficult as they were forced to press deeper into the mountains to find worthwhile timber. Native officials faced similar problems and repeatedly went to war over the few remaining areas of old-growth woodland. In the face of growing costs and scarcities, official logging became largely defunct in the late sixteenth century. While the early Qing emperors revived palace logging in the late 1600s and early 1700s, they had even less success. By 1700, even the deep gorges of Sichuan and Guizhou had been cleared of accessible old growth. As Aurelia Campbell shows, the depletion of old-growth woodlands even forced changes in imperial architecture, with buildings made more ornate to make up for losses in the scale and natural beauty of the structural timbers.[7] These imperial logging operations marked the twilight of natural woodlands along the Yangzi River. While humans could increase the supply of smaller commodity timber, they could do nothing to speed the growth of the massive trees demanded for palace frameworks.

TIMBER, TRIBUTE, AND FORCED LABOR

For centuries, Chinese capitals in the north and east had imported giant timbers from the southwest. The Han government had a specialized timber office (*muguan*) in Sichuan.⁸ The Tang cut a canal specifically to ship timber and bamboo from the southwest.⁹ The Song was no exception to this pattern: northern Sichuan was heavily logged during the eleventh-century wood crisis.¹⁰ Later that century, the dynasty accepted timber as tribute from southwestern tribes.¹¹ Throughout this millennium, southwestern logging policies reinforced an ethnic and ecological barrier between Han merchants in the lowlands and non-Han loggers in the mountains. In fifth- and sixth-century South China, tales circulated of exchanges between Han merchants and "timber visitors" (*muke*), mysterious humanoids who could "cut fir from the high mountains" and would "trade it with men, exchanging timber for knives and axes."¹² Over time, this relationship was gradually formalized. For example, in 1196, the Southern Song court prohibited ethnic Chinese (Hanren) from entering the mountains in southeastern Sichuan to cut timber themselves, instructing them to "wait for the 'barbarians' [*man*] to bring planks and timber to the main river course to trade."¹³ While the ethno-ecological logging frontier shifted over time, the basic pattern of exchange was astonishingly persistent. Ming sources suggest that until the 1400s, "[Han] axes could not enter" the rich forests along the tributaries of the upper Yangzi.¹⁴

In the first decades of the Ming, logging continued to follow the dynamics of earlier periods. On several occasions, the court sent officials to oversee non-Han tribes in harvesting this timber for imperial construction in Nanjing. According to a stone inscription from northeastern Yunnan, in 1375 an official from Yibin County led 180 indigenous laborers to cut 140 trunks of fragrant *nanmu* for palace construction.¹⁵ This timber probably went to the major expansion of the inner court that started in 1378.¹⁶ The court designated another site in northeastern Yunnan as a state forest (*guanlin*) and had its best trees branded with the mark "imperial timber" (*huangmu*) to reserve them for court use.¹⁷ Yet Zhu Yuanzhang soon curtailed the construction projects as part of his broader drive toward self-sufficiency. In 1379, he even closed the primary timber yard in Nanjing, apparently intending to end construction entirely.¹⁸ In 1390, Zhu Chun, Zhu Yuanzhang's eleventh son, took control of the frontier markets in Sichuan and reduced tributary requirements to a nominal amount.¹⁹ Following the opening of the Longjiang customs station at Nanjing in 1393, the court specified that all future building projects should rely exclusively on tariff timber and the building offices should not conduct any unnecessary logging.²⁰ Yet despite nominal attempts to restrict it, tribal logging continued. In 1387, Minde, the native prefect of Mahu, sent a shipment of fragrant *nanmu* timber to Nanjing.[21] Zhu Chun also used logs from Sichuan to build his own estates at Chengdu.[22] Despite Zhu Yuanzhang's attempts to reduce the footprint of the state, the early Ming regime continued the trend to demand timber tribute from the southwestern gorges.

After a succession struggle following Zhu Yuanzhang's death in 1398, power transferred to the Yongle emperor, who moved the court to his estate at Beijing in 1403 and conducted a series of massive building projects to expand the city into an imperial capital on a new scale.[23] While Beijing had served as the Yuan capital Dadu, large portions had fallen to ruin in the late fourteenth century. Between 1403 and 1420, Yongle had Beijing's walls and palaces rebuilt and expanded.[24] For his monumental buildings, Yongle turned to the same forests as his father, his brother, and even earlier rulers: the great fir and *nanmu* trees of the upper Yangzi River gorges. In 1406, in preparation for the first wave of building projects, he sent high officials from the Board of Works to find the largest and most beautiful tree specimens in Sichuan, Jiangxi, Huguang, Zhejiang, and Shanxi.[25] While the court would ultimately take timber from all of these places, supernatural influences revealed Sichuan as the prime site for imperial logging. Song Li reported that one night during his visit, several large trees fell into the river and floated downstream of their own accord. The emperor considered this a sign from the spirits and named this site Sacred Tree Mountain (Shenmu Shan).[26] Whether as a continuation of historical precedent or through divine intervention, this region became the focus of the most intensive timber extraction under Yongle. In the course of building Beijing, Song Li visited Sichuan four more times. The court also sent inspecting censor Gu Zuo to provide high-level oversight, while the eunuch official Xie An spent twenty years on-site.[27]

Even with giant trees located, the labor for these logging projects remained a significant issue, with officials left with a devil's choice between dispatching Han laborers at great expense or using local non-Han populations at the risk of revolt. Stone stelae scattered through the region provide snippets of information on the scale of the effort. An inscription at Yibin County in southern Sichuan documents an effort from early 1406:

> Eight hundred workers came to this place
> Of steep mountain streams and treacherous roads.
> Officials carefully applied their minds and we applied our strength,
> [Our quota of] four hundred poles of timber was quickly fulfilled.[28]

The wording of this poem suggests that these laborers may have traveled to the site from the Chinese interior. In other instances, it is clear that the workers were drawn from non-Han populations. Another inscription from 1406 records that a nearby logging project was supervised by a native official, who led 110 of his subjects to tow logs to the rivers.[29] Another stela from northeastern Sichuan also documents logging orders received in the fall of 1406. In this case a village head was dispatched to oversee the cutting and transport of ten rafts of timber (approximately eighty poles), apparently through the use of village labor.[30] These inscriptions mark a scattered record of the massive mobilization brought on by the palace construction, which probably entailed thousands of similar logging projects throughout the west and southwest.

Logging in the upper Yangzi gorges was only the beginning of the work of transporting the logs to the capital. Even after work teams floated individual timbers out of the mountain streams and bound them into rafts, these logs still had to travel hundreds of miles to Beijing. To guide log rafts to the capital, counties along the river system designated special "imperial timber transport households" (*huangmu jie hu*)—rafting specialists charged with floating timber in place of other corvée.[31] Once they reached the capital, workers piled the logs at the specially designated Sacred Timber Depot (Shenmu Chang), part of the larger transshipment complex established at Tongzhou in 1407.[32] A bus station in Tongzhou is still named Imperial Timber Depot (Huangmu Chang), carrying a record of this legacy.

Within a few years, reports began to circulate of the difficulties experienced by loggers. In 1413, the court soundly critiqued the official overseeing logging in Shanxi for overworking the commoners and soldiers under his command.[33] The Board of Revenue reported that logging communities were so heavily taxed that any additional demands would make them resort to selling property, wives, and children.[34] In 1414, military loggers in Sichuan's tribal regions reported food shortages.[35] In 1416, another group of military lumberjacks was attacked by followers of a Daoist cult in Shanxi.[36] But despite these difficulties, the projects continued until Yongle's death in 1424.

THE RETURN TO THE GORGES

The passing of the Yongle emperor had a huge impact on all the extractive economies of the empire, and imperial logging was no exception. The year after Yongle's death, his successor issued an edict announcing his pity for the soldiers and corvée laborers who transported the logs—but making no mention of the tribal laborers who cut much of the timber—and ordered an end to the project. All remaining logs were stacked for future use.[37] This was part of a broader drawdown in state extractions in the late 1420s and the 1430s that culminated in the closure of most official logging and mining projects throughout the empire.[38] With the completion of Beijing and the closure of the Sichuan timber yards in 1424, the Ming largely refrained from large-scale logging operations for more than a century. When officials were dispatched to Huguang to collect large timber for a Nanjing palace in 1426, they soon ran into difficulties, leading the court to cancel logging and issue orders to make do with existing supplies.[39] In 1441, the Beijing court started another round of construction to rebuild the Three Halls in the central aisle of the Forbidden City, which had burned down in 1420 and never been fully repaired.[40] Yet there was still enough timber left over from the Yongle reign to complete these projects using materials on hand.[41] While no complete statistical account of timber procurement exists for the early fifteenth-century operations, these retrospective accounts suggest that their scale was enormous. For much of the fifteenth century, officials preferred to economize by using existing supplies and limiting logging operations in the southwest.

Eventually, the Yongle-era supplies did run out, and the state conducted logging on and off for much of the late fifteenth century. Detailed records are not forthcoming, but we do know that there were some logging projects in the southwest, if only because they were canceled by the Hongzhi emperor (r. 1487–1505). In 1511, the Zhengde emperor sent Assistant Secretary Liu Bing to Sichuan, Huguang, and Guizhou to oversee logging, but soon canceled operations when Liu's materials were found to be poor quality. In 1521, the Jiajing emperor went so far as to end the dispatch of soldiers to guard the Sacred Timber Depot in Beijing, suggesting that it no longer held any meaningful supplies.[42] In 1528, a new policy required that any further repairs be approved and budgeted by the Board of Works before dispatching logging teams.[43]

While state-overseen logging was minimal and erratic for much of the late fifteenth and early sixteenth centuries, the native officials of Sichuan and Guizhou continued to send shipments of timber according to standardized tributary mechanisms. They presented these timbers—generally the largest and highest-quality *nanmu*—to the Ming court in exchange for ceremonial gifts, titles, and even money. In 1484, She Lu, the female ruler of Yongning, presented a shipment of large timbers to the court and was "rewarded according to regulations."[44] The rulers of nearby Youyang sent twenty poles of timber in 1512, and again in 1524.[45] Peng Shiqi, the native official of Yongshun, sent thirty large logs and two hundred smaller ones in 1514, "personally supervising their transport to the capital" so he could present his son and heir to the court. Three years later, Shiqi sent another 470 poles of *nanmu* and his son also sent a shipment of unspecified quantity. After the second present, the court advanced Shiqi to a higher rank with the gift of a four-clawed serpent robe and made his son a supernumerary official.[46] These examples, while scattered, show that there were regularized mechanisms for native officials to exchange pillar-sized logs for official titles and regalia. While these ranks were essentially nominal with regard to their placement within the official hierarchy, they clearly carried substantial symbolic power for the non-Han rulers of the southwest, as evidenced by the extreme lengths to which they went to submit timbers to the court.

The situation changed again in the mid-sixteenth century, when a series of fires damaged some of the greatest structures in the court. In 1540, lightning struck the Ming ancestral temple and it had to be rebuilt.[47] In 1556, the Three Halls burned down again, requiring thousands of large timbers for the repairs needed to retain the scale of the original Yongle construction.[48] The Three Halls burned yet again in 1584 and required large-scale repair.[49] A mere two decades after ending official logging, seemingly for good, the Jiajing emperor resumed it in response to the 1540 fires, sending two high-level Board of Works officials, Pan Jian and Dai Jin, to Huguang and Sichuan to reopen logging.[50] Repeated damage to imperial architecture in the following decades meant that Pan and Dai were followed until at least 1606 by a near-constant rotation of officials drawn from the upper ranks of the Censorate and the Board of Works.

The logging bureaucracy in the mid- to late sixteenth century was both large and complex. The highest-ranking official of each detachment was given the title "timber supervisor" (*dumu*) and corresponding oversight of other officials.[51] The obituary of one such timber supervisor, vice censor-in-chief Li Xianqing, reveals the extent of this timber bureaucracy. In the 1540s, Li had command of at least twenty-two mid- and low-level officials supervising more than forty-five logging sites in Sichuan, Huguang, and Guizhou (see map 7.1).[52] In 1556, the projects grew even larger. The court dispatched a board secretary and two assistant secretaries to oversee logging of large timber in the three southwestern provinces; two assistant secretaries to supervise logging of smaller timbers, one in the north and one in the lower Yangzi region; a board-level official and a bureau-level subordinate to supervise stone quarrying for building slip roads; and four censors to oversee the provisions and salaries for these substantial detachments. Two years later, the court added another board secretary, two vice secretaries, and two high-level eunuch supervisors to the timber administration, along with new regulations limiting their ability to draw salary.[53] The number of lower-level officials and laborers presumably increased by similar proportions.

Overseeing large labor teams in a remote and dangerous frontier was enormously expensive, with frequent cost overruns. In 1556, the court required the Boards of Revenue, War, and Works to produce 300,000 taels of silver for logging expenses.[54] That same year, Guizhou was responsible for 4,709 poles of fir and *nanmu* at a cost of 720,000 taels of silver, but the provincial treasury held just under 15,000 taels, or about 2 percent of what was required. Additional funds had to be disbursed from other provincial treasuries: 100,000 from Guangdong; 140,000 from Yunnan; and 90,000 from Jiangxi.[55] Logging costs in neighboring Huguang eventually exceeded 3 million taels.[56] The court stripped rank from a number of regional officials for failing to meet deadlines and quotas.[57] Expenses were even worse during the 1584 reconstruction. Despite a much smaller order for 1,132 poles, Guizhou again faced the prospect of cost overruns: the treasury only had 20,000 taels, one-sixth of the estimated 100,000 required.[58] Total expenses for the project exceeded 9 million taels.[59]

Facing the culmination of declining stocks of old-growth timber and growing costs of supplying workers, the logging operations of the sixteenth century could not rival the productivity of the Yongle projects. The mid-century timber supervisor Li Xianqing noted that the best remaining trees were increasingly confined to woodlands far within the gorges and could only be transported to navigable waterways at great difficulty and expense.[60] The trees were so massive and the terrain so remote that it took five hundred workers to tow each log over mountain passes (figure 7.1). Dozens of specialized metal-, wood-, and stoneworkers were needed on-site to make tools and cables and build slip roads.[61] They built "flying bridges" (*feiqiao*) and capstans (*tianche*) to transport the logs across thousand-foot defiles and enormous hawsers to tow them up slopes (figure 7.2). Even after these efforts, many trees were unsuitable for use; perhaps 80 percent were discarded because they were hollow, and others were damaged or lost during accidents along the way. Dragging the timber to the waterways was only half the job. Even once the trees reached the rivers, log drivers had to float

FIG 7.1 Lowering logs off a cliff. Detail of a woodcut from *Essays on Timber Rafting in the Western Regions* (Xi cha huicao; 1533). Courtesy of the Library of Congress, Chinese Rare Book Digital Collection.

them through dangerous rapids (figure 7.3). Upon reaching calmer water, workers tied them into rafts of 604 poles, joined with large quantities of bamboo to make them more buoyant. A team of forty men towed each raft until they reached deeper currents (figure 7.4), whereupon twenty or thirty

FIG 7.2 Capstan across a chasm. Detail of a woodcut from *Essays on Timber Rafting in the Western Regions* (Xi cha huicao; 1533). Courtesy of the Library of Congress, Chinese Rare Book Digital Collection.

such log rafts were launched together for the three-year, 10,000-*li* (approximately 3,000-kilometer) journey to Beijing.[62]

These were far from the only difficulties facing loggers in a distant and dangerous frontier. In his *Essays on Timber Rafting in the Western Regions*,

FIGURE 7.3 Floating logs through large rapids. Detail of a woodcut from *Essays on Timber Rafting in the Western Regions* (Xi cha huicao; 1533). Courtesy of the Library of Congress, Chinese Rare Book Digital Collection.

Gong Hui depicts violent robberies (figure 7.5) and snake and tiger attacks (figure 7.6) among the many dangers of the region.⁶³ Working in a sparsely populated mountain area also meant that labor teams had to carry their own food. Gong's illustrations also depict workers weak from malaria (*yanzhang*) or starving to the point of eating bark and grass and others captured while running away. He sums up the difficulties with a parallel phrase: "The labor force numbers in the thousands; the days number in the hundreds; the supply costs number in the tens of thousands each year."⁶⁴ According to another Sichuan saying, "A thousand enter the mountains, but only five hundred leave" (*Ru shan yiqian chu shan wubai*).⁶⁵ In addition to hard labor, loggers in the mountainous western frontier faced dozens of environmental hazards. The sixteenth-century timber supervisor Li Xianqing expressed his doubts that palace-building timber had ever been obtained in quantity, even during the Yongle reign.⁶⁶

Official logging teams were not the only ones facing increased difficulties obtaining timber in the sixteenth century. Non-Han rulers continued to

FIG 7.4 Fatigues and harms of transport. Woodcut from *Essays on Timber Rafting in the Western Regions* (Xi cha huicao; 1533). Courtesy of the Library of Congress, Chinese Rare Book Digital Collection.

supply the court with giant timber in exchange for titles and gifts. But these native officials logged in the same regions as their peers dispatched from Beijing, and they faced the same difficulties finding suitable trees. In 1541, the year after lightning struck the Ming ancestral temple, Guizhou circuit inspector Lu Jie reported that the tributary polities of Youyang, Yongshun, and Baoqing were fighting over timber to supply the reconstruction project. The court ordered officials to prevent the conflict from spreading through the region.[67] The absence of further records suggests that the conflict was suppressed. Yet these expedient measures did not eliminate the roots of the problem—growing demand for a shrinking supply of old-growth trees—and the next round of timber requisitions led to further escalations.

The second documented timber war started in the mid-1580s, at the height of western logging to supply the Wanli-era reconstruction of the Three Halls. In 1585 or 1586, Yang Yinglong, the hereditary pacification commissioner of Bozhou, presented seventy especially beautiful timbers to the

FIG 7.5 Violent fires and robbery. Detail of a woodcut from *Essays on Timber Rafting in the Western Regions* (Xi cha huicao; 1533). Courtesy of the Library of Congress, Chinese Rare Book Digital Collection.

emperor and was gifted a flying fish robe, the mark of a second-rank official.[68] An Guoheng, the ruler of the native office of Shuixi, became jealous of Yang's growing status and also requested to send timber to the Ming court. But Guoheng's shipment did not arrive at court. Furious, the emperor threatened to strip Guoheng of his rank unless he made up the promised tribute.[69] Three years later, Zaiweibing, the head of the Youyang native office, sent twenty timbers valued at over thirty thousand taels and was granted the robes

FIG 7.6 Snakes and tigers run rampant. Detail of a woodcut from *Essays on Timber Rafting in the Western Regions* (Xi cha huicao; 1533). Courtesy of the Library of Congress, Chinese Rare Book Digital Collection.

of a third-rank official.[70] By 1589, the logging competition among native officials, doubtless further inflamed by other rivalries, devolved into open warfare. Yang Yinglong infuriated the court even further when he reneged on a commitment to send troops to fight Hideyoshi in Korea, one of the requirements of native chiefs. Eventually, Yang united several groups in an all-out rebellion that spread through large parts of the southwest. Sentenced to beheading, Yang was allowed to ransom himself in 1593 for forty thousand taels, an astronomical fee slated for contribution toward the logging effort.[71] But Yang reneged on this commitment, and the rebellion continued. By 1598, Yang reportedly had 140,000 troops in arms, forcing the Ming court to dispatch an even larger army to put down the rebels. Yang eventually committed suicide, his family was executed, and the Bozhou native office was eliminated, its territory integrated into nearby counties.[72] In many ways, his death signaled the end of the timber tribute system. While Yang Yinglong's rebellion was not just about timber, the competition to log the last and best trees was a major contributor to conflicts between native officials.

By the sixteenth century, the western old growth was in such decline that the Ming court had to supplement its timber with materials bought from southern merchants. Li Xianqing writes that officials of the 1540s oversaw *logging itself* in Sichuan and parts of western Hunan (*du* [place-name] *zhi mu*), but oversaw the *purchase of timber* (*gou mu*) in the rest of Huguang.[73] Reliance on merchants increased in the late 1500s due to cost overruns. In the 1580s, two Guizhou officials, Shu Yinglong and Mao Zai, cited the recurrent nature of lumbering expenses (*caimu gongfei xun zhi xing*) and the tendency toward cost overruns to argue that it was impractical to resort to temporary solutions like forwarding bullion from other jurisdictions. They suggested asking merchants to quote market prices for standardized grades of timber, a practice that was by then standard in the shipyard administration.[74] Because prices were best in Guizhou but the province had little local tax base, Shu and Mao argued that funds from other provinces should continue to be directed there to purchase timber on the market and that officials be stationed there to oversee the merchants and loggers.[75] The reliance on timber merchants only increased thereafter.[76]

Despite the declining yields of the late Ming, early Qing monarchs again dispatched loggers to the gorges. In 1667, almost immediately after the pacification of Sichuan, the Kangxi emperor ordered cutting in the region. While his officials reported that there were still large trees in the mountains, they failed to supply enough fir and *nanmu* for palace construction, and the court substituted pine from Manchuria. In 1683, Kangxi ordered another southwestern logging operation but halted it after surveys revealed the difficulty of the task. Most timber was purchased from southern merchants instead. The Yongzheng and Qianlong emperors sent further logging expeditions in 1726 and 1750, but quickly canceled them in the face of declining yields. As in the Ming, the Qing court ordered timber to be purchased at market rates; this became the main source of imperial timber in the 1680s and the exclusive source after 1750.[77]

PEAK TIMBER

Despite the repeated failures to provide sufficient quantities of timber, the surveys and logging operations of the 1540s, 1580s, 1660s, 1680s, and 1720s were substantial projects that demonstrated the capacities of the Ming and Qing states. Dozens of officials were dispatched to distant frontiers to oversee large labor teams. They noted in official registers (*ce*) the size and grade of any fir or *nanmu* poles and the distance between the trees and the nearest river. These surveys were forwarded to higher-level officials for planning purposes. Over the course of the sixteenth and seventeenth centuries, successive rounds of surveys gave later generations of officials a panoptic view of the western forests that allowed them to make necessary changes to the logging administration, in particular the switch to purchasing timber on the market.[78]

Did the large-scale logging of the three-province frontier result in deforestation and environmental degradation?[79] The evidence for deforestation is mixed. From the early 1500s onward, officials repeatedly noted that near the main rivers the hills were bare (*tongshan*), a result of overcutting, and wrote that lumber teams had to push deeper into the mountains to find poles of sufficient size. The removal of old-growth fir and *nanmu* is further apparent when we compare the lumber yields (table 7.1). In 1441, 380,000 poles were *left over* from the Yongle-era logging (1406–24). Yields were substantially lower in the sixteenth century. In 1557, the Sichuan-Guizhou region yielded 15,007 poles. Logging teams cut a reported 24,601 poles in 1606. In the 1680s, they cut 4,500 poles of *nanmu* and a similar amount of fir in Sichuan and Guizhou; officials remarked that this was only one-third of the earlier yield and that only one-tenth of the *nanmu* and one-fifth of the fir were considered adequate for use. The 1727 requisitions obtained only 1,044 suitable poles of *nanmu*. A low was reached in 1750, when the yield of the logging bottomed out at a mere 144 poles.[80] According to these figures, the best yields of late Ming logging approached only 1–2 percent of early Ming operations, and mid-Qing logging obtained no more than 5 percent of the already-diminished late Ming yields.

TABLE 7.1. Timber yields from imperial logging

YEAR(S)	POLES CUT IN THE SOUTHWEST	POLES REACHING BEIJING
1406–1424	*760,000–1,500,000 or more	380,000 remaining as of 1441
1557	15,007	—
1606	24,601	—
1685	8,559	1,830 suitable for use
1727	*5,220	1,044 suitable for use
1750	*720	144 suitable for use

Sources: "Timber Administration," *Yongzheng Sichuan tongzhi* 16; "Timber Administration," *Daoguang Zunyi fuzhi* 18; Lan, "Ming Qing shiqi de huangmu caiban."
* Indicates an estimate based on the number of poles reaching Beijing.

Yet declining timber yields were not the same as total deforestation. Official reports made clear that there were still large woodlands in Sichuan in the late sixteenth century, and even in the seventeenth and eighteenth centuries. Total clearance was limited to valleys with good water access; in the deeper mountains, there were still large stands of old growth. Instead, declining timber yields reflect a fundamental shift in the nature of imperial logging. In the late 1300s and early 1400s, sparse records suggest that logging concentrated on a small region in southern Sichuan and neighboring parts of Yunnan and Guizhou. By the 1540s, officials were sent to oversee timber extraction across a much larger frontier covering Sichuan, Guizhou, and Huguang (Hunan and Hubei). Except for a few sites in central Huguang, all of these forests were logged by corvée or tribal laborers overseen by Ming officials. But by the 1680s, conscript lumbering concentrated once again on southern Sichuan, roughly the same region targeted in the early Ming (map 7.1). This suggests two progressive adaptations: in the 1500s, timber supervisors responded to shortages of large trees in southern Sichuan by expanding the logging frontier to new regions; in the late 1600s and early 1700s, their successors concentrated imperial logging where extreme topography limited commercial operations. Paradoxically, this returned them to the same sites targeted in the early Ming: the deep mountains of southern Sichuan.

While imperial logging ceased in most of the western frontier by the end of the Ming, commercial logging continued under the oversight of private landowners, private logging teams, and private merchants. In Hunan and

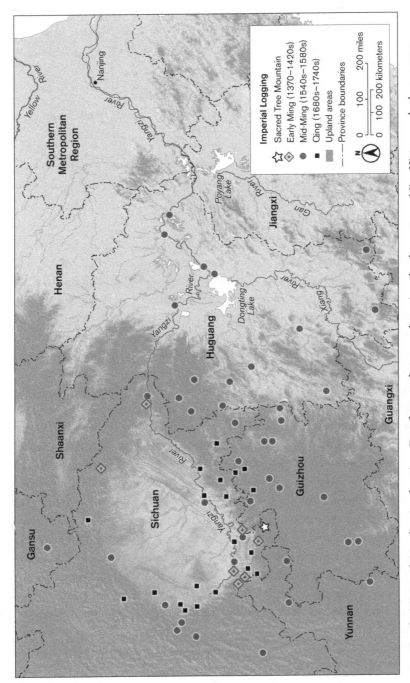

MAP 7.1 The Ming and Qing logging frontiers. Data from prefecture and province-level gazetteers, *Ming History*, and other sources. Georeferenced using TGAZ. Map layers from China Historical GIS version 6.

Hubei and along the east-flowing rivers in eastern Guizhou, the state switched to taxing the timber harvest at the market rather than in the forest. As Meng Zhang shows, the Qing reinterpreted the timber tribute as a system of licenses for wood merchants to procure materials on behalf of the state. Eastern Guizhou later became a major site for the expansion of commercial silviculture.[81] These markets produced more than enough ordinary-size timber for most building projects without the need for direct oversight of loggers. Imperial cutting continued in the Sichuan gorges, but only to obtain timber bigger than commercial forests could provide. The decline of imperial timber yields was therefore tied to the last major period of logging in the natural growth. While some old-growth woods remained, largely in inaccessible valleys and at high altitudes, the riverward slopes of mountains were logged clear of their best timber.

The three booms in imperial logging—in the early 1400s, mid- to late 1500s, and late 1600s—were the dying gasps of the old forest system, one predicated on bountiful nature harvested by forced labor. Once the deep valleys of the far west were cleared of accessible old growth, commercial plantations were the only remaining sources of timber in the Yangzi River watershed. Outside of remote mountains and sacred groves, anthropogenic forests also accounted for the overwhelming majority of tree cover in the region. From its beginnings in western Jiangnan and Zhejiang around 1100, the revolution in forest ownership, forest oversight, and forest composition had spread west and south along the Yangzi River and its tributaries. By 1700, this transformation reached its political and environmental limits in the mountains of Sichuan and Guizhou.

CONCLUSION

IN THE SIX CENTURIES AT THE CORE OF THE STUDY, SOUTH CHINA underwent a radical environmental shift. This shift encompassed the widespread removal of tree cover, a depletion of woodland that was often both locally acute and regionally apparent. Yet rather than the *deforestation* of South China, this shift broadly resulted in the *creation* of a new type of forest across the region. While some woodland was permanently cleared as farmland or left as waste, the more common transformation was a shift from naturally seeded, mixed woodland to human-planted conifer plantations. This transformation was so widespread and so dependent on human behaviors that it can only be described as the creation of a new forest biome—a pattern of woody vegetation conditioned by the subtropical climate of South China, but overwhelmingly created, spread, and governed by human action.

The easiest aspect of this transition to trace is the development of a bureaucratic category to enumerate and administer economically productive *forests* and differentiate them from more diffusely conceptualized *woodland*. For centuries, laws and norms reinforced conditions of managed abundance, maintaining woodlands as open-access, tax-free lands whose bounties could be freely harvested according to simple regulations. These rules and attitudes all shifted in the eleventh century, when fears of wood shortages replaced assumptions of abundance. Soon, both state and private stakeholders moved to prevent and even profit from scarcity. Gradually, the managerial category *forest* (*shan*) became the primary nexus between state and private claims, largely replacing the more diffuse concepts of the wilds (*shanze* or *shanye*). By 1200, the state surveyed and registered forests across the south. By 1400, law established forests as exclusive property. By 1600, accounting reforms eliminated most woodcutting corvée. Landownership replaced access rights; market-based oversight replaced forced labor; formal contracts and cadastres replaced informal rules of use.

To establish forests as both anthropogenic biomes and administrative sites—and to ensure that they persisted—silviculture had to meet two conditions. First, people had to clear the existing vegetation and replace it with planted trees. Second, they had to document their claims to the territory. It was only through the combination of these two transformations, one physical, one administrative, that diffuse, open *woodlands* became bounded, exclusive *forests*. In the absence of either of these conditions, the land generally reverted to the nonadministrative landscape and to different forms of use and patterns of vegetation as well. The spread of the administrative category *forest* is therefore a useful proxy for the environmental transformation that started in the mountains of Jiangnan and Zhejiang in the 1100s and expanded into Jiangxi and Fujian by the 1500s and into Hunan and parts of Guangdong, Guangxi, and Guizhou by the late 1700s.

Because surveys were themselves a part of the forest revolution, it is difficult, if not impossible, to say precisely what South China's woodlands looked like before this transition. But we can say with some confidence how these physical and administrative acts transformed them. Throughout the south, planters cleared old growth and spread blankets of fir, pine, and bamboo across the middle slopes of mountains. Locally, they planted stands of other commercially valuable woody plants like camphor, tung, and tea and nonwoody plants like hemp, ramie, and indigo. Zooming out, a broad swath of territory from the Yangzi River in the north to the West River in the south, from the South China Sea in the east to the Yun-Gui Plateau in the west, was defined by the interpenetration of two biomes: a planted grassland in the lower elevations and a planted woodland in the higher ones. This eco-administrative transformation of woodlands accompanied an eco-social transformation of woodland peoples. Much as taxpaying farmers had long dominated the lowlands, taxpaying foresters now dominated the uplands. Only the most inaccessible highlands and swamps remained as refugia for other communities, whether of woody plants or of humans.

LOST MODERNITIES

The development of forest oversight provides an important case study of Chinese administrative knowledge. When compared to the European and Northeast Asian experiences, China's forest administration appears both precocious and strange, a sort of "lost modernity," to borrow Alexander Woodside's turn of phrase. As Woodside argues, China's early bureaucratization left it with an advanced experience of both the benefits and the pitfalls of administrative formalism.[1] Similar patterns can be seen in the administration of landscapes as well. As early as 780, and with some maturity by the late twelfth century, the tariff system gave Chinese states a direct line of oversight over wood as a commodity. Cadastral forms treating forests as landed properties developed in 1149 and were essentially mature by the 1390s, while forest labor contracts reached a peak of complexity in the early 1600s. These all proved highly efficient ways of managing forests for revenue purposes, but at the cost of an increased bureaucratic distance between officials and the environment.

The positive side of the balance sheet was not trivial. So great was the productivity of the Yangzi River timber market—and the tariffs that drew upon it—that it underwrote a massive naval expansion without the need to substantially change the forest administration. While the *expense* of shipbuilding was a constant complaint during the East Asian naval race of the twelfth to fifteenth centuries, only occasionally did this translate into pressures on the woods themselves. Indirect, market-based management was so effective that it largely preempted the Chinese state from more direct impingements on its forests. There were still periods of intense state interest: Li Xian conducted major logging projects in the 1070s, as did the Prince of Hailing in the 1160s, Kublai Khan in the 1270s, and the Yongle emperor in the early 1400s. Cai Jing developed incentives for tree planting in the early 1100s, and Zhu Yuanzhang ordered extensive forest cultivation in the 1390s. South China's forest administration could have developed around these more direct interventions, much as forestry did in parts of Europe and Northeast Asia.

These "paths not taken" make for provocative counterfactuals that should force careful reflection. If not for the Jin invasions in the 1120s, it is quite possible that Cai Jing would be remembered as the father of state forestry—China's Colbert—instead of as the villain in a kung fu novel. If not for the Mongol conquests of the 1270s, South China might have anticipated Venice's or Holland's development around merchant capital rather than being reintegrated into the command economies of a continental empire. If Yongle had not usurped the throne in 1402, Zhu Yuanzhang's quest for self-sufficient economies might have led to forestry focused on sustainable yield rather than to a forced labor assault on the gorges. These path dependencies should serve as a warning against both cultural and environmental determinism. The Yangzi River forest system was not the simple product of the regional environment, nor was it the necessary outcome of an abstract "Chinese" culture.

Nonetheless, the early emergence of bureaucracy in China repeatedly tipped key policies away from direct environmental interventions and toward general-purpose administrative forms. Instead of official ordinances or specialized wood courts, the most lasting changes in Chinese forest oversight were incidental to broad reforms in land surveys, tax accounting, and property law. Indeed, the most astonishing feature of Chinese imperial bureaucracies was their capaciousness to encompass a vast range of environments and a plethora of different institutions to manage them. Chinese bureaucrats were able to manage this portfolio of productive environments across major shifts in both high politics and local ecology. The transitions documented in the preceding chapters were remarkably continuous across bloody metamorphoses between regional and multiregional empires; a massive shift in woodland composition, from mixed natural growth to conifer plantations; and a complete transformation in woodland management, from informal logging restrictions to written contract and cadastre. In terms of state policy, these pivotal developments in politics, ecology, and regulation resulted in little more than the transfer of wood revenue from the state's fiscal oversight of labor (corvée) to its fiscal oversight of land (the land tax). In the meantime, the imperium repeatedly created and eliminated specialized institutions from the Xihe Logging Bureau to the Longjiang shipyards without causing major changes in the basic dynamics of the timber supply.

Yet for all their efficiencies, administrative forms are imperfect proxies for the things they are supposed to record—a hard-learned lesson that modern bureaucrats have only begun to rediscover. As James C. Scott argues in *Seeing Like a State*, schematic visions of the environment do violence to the complex interdependencies they presume to replace. Or to borrow a phrase from business management, "What gets measured gets done." In China's forest system, this inevitably meant that bureaucrats gave administrative priority to measurable quantities like acreage, log dimensions, and prices, especially when compared to fuzzy "ecosystem services" like soil retention, climate stabilization, and wildlife habitat. These created growing discrepancies between the engrained lives of woodland communities and the abstracted formalisms of wood on paper. Woodlands that had functioned as complex webs of flora and fauna were replaced by forests that mostly served to produce timber and fuel.

Even within the human species, the prioritization of commodity production came at the expense of less fungible goods like fuel, famine foods, and hunting and grazing land. The woodland as eco-social safety net for the community gave way to private property that served only a small number of owners. As seen in contexts from South and Southeast Asia to the Americas, a second-order consequence of forest enclosure was to deprive thousands of woodland communities of their traditional roles and endowments.[2] But as this study shows, the enclosure of woods and deprivation of woodland communities was not strictly an outcome of European imperialism. These trends emerged in China long before Europeans colonized abroad, largely as forest owners adopted the forms of property rights used by lowland farmers and extended them into the hills. Title enforcement was the carrot tempting landlords into the system of cadastral oversight, while the monetization of taxes was the stick driving forest laborers into the contractual labor market.

Throughout this process, the very mechanisms that gave the state and forest owners oversight blinded them to community impoverishment, except to the extent that these declines impinged on timber production, tax payments, or contract fulfillment. Nonetheless, the simplification of complex environments inevitably led not only to the loss of fuzzy goods like "ecological services" but also to declines in the very wood yields measured by administrators. As shipyard supervisors and logging officials both discovered, the supply of timber depended on many factors that they did not measure. In a prescient foreshadowing of the modern world, sixteenth-century bureaucrats responded to declining wood yields by adding more boxes to their forms. But no number of formal categories could fully account for continental shifts in the supply and demand for timber, the influx of foreign silver, the erosion of hillside soils, or the displacement of woodland peoples to the frontiers and the contractual labor market. This precocious modernity anticipated the pitfalls of scientific forestry as it developed in Europe.

It is nonetheless misleading to treat Chinese forestry as an immature version of the European experience. For one thing, there was no single "European" forestry, with substantial differences even between the oft-conflated French and German schools.[3] For another, the development of forestry, and of related disciplines like botany, cannot be separated from broader intellectual and political dynamics. In Europe, this included a plethora of competing states that allowed rival schools to flourish, compete, and learn from each other. By contrast, in China the civil service curriculum was dominant, and learning was highly conditioned by the forms of knowledge valued by the imperium. In this schema, forestry was treated as a minor branch of agriculture, and botany was left to the several miscellaneous traditions of textual commentary, local geography, and medical herbology. Finally, it mattered that forestry developed later in Europe, where it benefited from additional centuries of development in cameralism, survey techniques, and worldwide botanical exploration.[4] There are indications that China may have been headed in a convergent direction in the eighteenth century, when some texts began to specify greater gradations between tree species, officials began to promote "best practices" in upland land use, and landowners began to note the environmental degradation wrought by slope clearance.[5] Yet before these developments had a chance to mature into an independent trajectory of forestry, botany, or environmental science, as they began to do in Europe around that time, China entered a major period of crisis. As European empires expanded, the Chinese empire fell apart, and it was European forestry, not Chinese, that influenced most of the modern world.

THE MIGRANT CRISIS

Forest history also helps to understand the very crises that led to China's decline in the nineteenth century, crises that had a lot to do with the movement of people in the upland south.[6] Since Herold J. Wiens's 1954 work *China's March toward the Tropics*, historians have been preoccupied with the southward expansion of Chinese states at the expense of non-Han peoples. Much like Frederick Jackson Turner's ideas about the American West, scholars of China have ascribed significant importance to the declining availability of land to absorb migrants, especially after 1800. In *The Retreat of the Elephants*, Mark Elvin reframes this civilizational narrative in environmental terms, with the advance of the Chinese state mirrored by the retreat, not only of non-Sinitic peoples, but of elephants and the woodlands that sheltered them. In *The Great Divergence*, Kenneth Pomeranz lists the relative poverty of China's frontiers—as compared to European colonies in the Americas—as a key factor in the divergence between continued European development and Chinese stagnation. Some versions of the narrative take a more straightforward Malthusian line, where an absolute shortage of land relative to the growing population doomed Chinese patterns of development.[7] Others give a more nuanced telling of events, showing that the "closure" of the frontier was a complex process that encompassed changes in both land use and land rights that precipitated environmental degradation and community impoverishment.[8]

At China's southern frontiers, upland settlement played a key role in the emergence of a new form of eco-social conflict. In particular, the numbers of Hakkas and "shack people" (*pengmin*) dependent on uplands multiplied just as South China began to run out of unclaimed hill land suitable for exploitation. Upland settlers brought a cascade of conflicts—between mountain landlords and the new class of tenants and squatters, between short-term cultivation and long-term depletion, between upland cash cropping and runoff downstream. The introduction of New World crops was another precipitating factor in the highland population expansion: the shack people often cleared land to cultivate maize and sweet potatoes for subsistence, although they also mined and planted annual commercial crops like indigo, tobacco, and tea.[9]

The migrants of the eighteenth and nineteenth centuries arrived in an upland environment that was already intensively exploited. By the time the shack people arrived, the most accessible and productive slopes in South China were already covered in forest plantations. This left them either to eke out a living in the few marginal niches ignored by timber and tea planters or to compete with forest owners for land. Because sweet potatoes and other annual crops leave the ground bare for long periods and consume soil nutrients at high rates, they led to further depletion of sensitive upland soils and the well-documented problems with erosion. Because Hakkas and shack people competed with timber farmers for land, their arrival led to well-documented social conflicts.

Fights over land rights, whether between highlanders and lowlanders or between tenants and landlords, were not new to the nineteenth century. Nonetheless, the growing conflicts of the mid- to late Qing both reflected and precipitated the emergence of new forms of social organization in the highlands, tied to the Hakka diaspora in particular. As David Ownby shows, marginalized men created secret societies—including the "triads" of kung fu cinema—and became increasingly heterodox in the face of suppression. These societies spread throughout southeastern China along with the movement of landless men, many of whom were laborers in upland industries including timber planting and cash cropping.[10] Later, the Communists brought another novel form of social organization to the highlands.[11] Mary S. Erbaugh and Sow-Theng Leong document the particular connection between Hakkas and the rebellions and revolutionary movements emerging from South China between 1850 and 1949: Taiping leader Hong Xiuquan was a Hakka, and so were major Communist revolutionaries like Zhu De and Deng Xiaoping.[12] This connection may be a bit too facile; despite the preponderance of Hakka revolutionaries, Stephen C. Averill shows that ethnic identity did not map directly onto political affiliation.[13] Nonetheless, changes in land use and wood rights were a red thread connecting revolts and rebellions across South China for generations. The nineteenth and twentieth centuries merely brought more dispossessed people with new forms of organization to an environment increasingly crowded with rival claimants and depleted of resources.

My point here is not that the Taiping Rebellion and the Communist Revolution were fundamentally ecological conflicts. Ecology cannot be abstracted from human actions on the land and its biota, nor can human culture be extricated from its interactions with nonhuman life. Instead, my argument is that these uprisings were not the simple consequences of population pressure, ethnic conflict, or the displacements of capitalism. They were specifically conditioned by eight centuries of developments that pushed people into the hills and hill people into the markets, even as mountain land became less available as it was enclosed for fir plantations. This was not a case of a growing population and a static supply of land *in general*—it was a case of a growing hill population and a shrinking supply of woodland *in particular*. The ensuing conflicts had valences across lines of ethnicity, religious orthodoxy, and state-subject and landlord-tenant relations. But a fundamental condition of these conflicts was the end of upland cultivation as a tenable subsistence strategy, in the face of both long-term trends toward forest enclosure and an unprecedented short-term growth in the population attempting to live on the hillsides. Similar dynamics collapsed the balance between mountain forests and lowland farms in nineteenth-century Korea and central Europe and conditioned a century of revolts from the French revolutions to the Tonghak Rebellion.[14]

PATHS OUT OF THE FOREST

Where does China's forest history go from here? When I started this project, I thought I was writing a preface to the intertwined social and environmental crises of nineteenth-century China. A decade later I can only speculate on the eco-social dynamics of those rebellions. Instead, I hope that this book presents a convincing articulation of the frameworks that conditioned state oversight in the forests and wood markets that preceded them. In this conclusion, I have used these frameworks to postulate about the trajectory of Chinese empire, both in comparison with European empires and through the crises that ended the imperial state. The first set of conjectures concerns the interplay between administration and expertise and ultimately speaks to the origins of environmental science and environmentalism. The second concerns the nineteenth-century crisis in the preceding systems of resource governance. In both cases, I have made an implicit comparison between China, which supposedly failed to produce a "modern" solution, and western Europe, which veered unsteadily toward modernity—whether this is construed as an intellectual, material, or technological advance. I hope that the foregoing chapters have demonstrated the contingencies in these developments. At various times China demonstrated what appeared to be convergent evolution toward forms of expertise, economy, and ideology that paralleled (or anticipated) developments in Europe. Yet its history remained distinct. For more than six centuries, China thrived while following a path that minimized state interventions in the forest. Thus far, this is a far longer history of success than the ongoing worldwide experiment with scientific forestry. This suggests that we must question the inevitability and superiority of the forest institutions we now take for granted.

By answering one set of questions about forests and empire, I have uncovered a slew of others, referenced obliquely in this text. I allude to wood rights and wood disputes in several chapters, especially as they relate to land use and labor migration. These are complex issues, especially in China, where wood rights were often tied to the further complications around graves and *fengshui*.[15] Treatment of wood disputes also presents an avenue to introduce individuals to the story, including oft-silenced ones like women, children, and illiterate peasants. Wood fuels, such as firewood and charcoal, deserve their own study, especially as they relate to the use of coal and to the energy transitions of the nineteenth and twentieth centuries. Changes in other uses of wood as well, whether for carpentry, furniture, or medicine, have their own rich history to explore, as do poetic and literary imaginations of woodlands. These are all important and complex questions for further research. I will now use these final few paragraphs to return to the larger story about ecological and institutional change.

China's landscape is neither entirely new nor entirely old. Between about 1000 and 1600, the woodlands of South China transitioned from one human-encompassing biome—a mixed forest modified by fire, swidden, hunting, and selective logging—toward another biome with even greater human influence, a landscape dominated by fir plantations. There were further continuities through the mid-eighteenth century. After that, it is clear that South China's woodlands underwent another radical shift between about 1750 and 1980, one largely but not entirely conditioned by the predations of warfare and radical social policy. Paradoxically, despite important new developments, the picture of landscape change since 1980 has been more of a return to pre-eighteenth-century form than a continuation of nineteenth- and twentieth-century trends. This suggests that China has not fully exited the age of forests that it entered in the Song.

More importantly, the continued importance of millennium-old forms of wood use suggests that we must reconsider the terms in which we understand forests and forestry. Forests are not mere containers or conditions for human action; while they change slowly, they do change. But nor are forests exclusively the products of human behavior; trees have their own complex behaviors and interactions. While planting, pruning, and logging remain the most important human behaviors promoting a biome dominated by young conifers, these trees produce their own constraints and potentials. Neither forests nor forestry could exist without one another. Even terms like *forest* and *timber* represent administrative attempts to both reflect and modify patterns of biotic growth. Given the depth and intensity with which human habitation has had an impact on the Chinese environment, biomes, even supposedly wild ones, are conditioned by human rules, norms, and behaviors. Given the continued material importance of the products of forestry and agriculture, even supposedly human institutions are closely intertwined with the biota from which they are built.

Like the ship of Theseus, institutions are constantly rebuilt as rotten planks are replaced with new ones, yet these structures show surprising persistence well beyond the lifetime of any of their components. New timbers are grown, selected, and worked to fit into place. New workers are trained by the retirees they replace. Written records and unspoken norms specify the rules and sequences of operations. The long-term growth of the trees themselves provides its own form of continuity. In the face of malignant fiat and benign neglect, these patterns, the cumulative product of years of secondary growth, are strikingly hard to change. From one perspective, Chinese administrators tacitly recognized these constraints, imposing bureaucratic forms at an intermediate level of specificity and leaving individual communities to follow their own internal dynamics. From another perspective, administrators remained distant from the communities they governed because abstract authority was unable to shift deeply ingrained local patterns. Ultimately, the institutions that emerged were not inevitable, nor were they the simple products of high-level decisions; they were compromises, conditioned by the communities they governed and the repeated attempts of rulers to graft and prune these local forms into a coherent whole.

APPENDIX A

Forests in Tax Data

There have been a number of important studies of Ming dynasty tax data, most notably Ping-ti Ho's *Studies on the Population of China*, Ray Huang's *Taxation and Governmental Finance in Sixteenth-Century Ming China*, and the career work of Liang Fangzhong. These studies have shown the highly unreliable nature of land registration data as a direct index of actual acreage under cultivation. Instead, it is clear that these data are at best indexes of *fiscal* acreage—that is, the number and the size of tax accounts. Yet while these figures are not especially useful to account for absolute territorial shifts, they are nonetheless quite useful as rough indicators of the number of fields and forests brought under state accounting and oversight. Furthermore, while the summary accounts given in high-level sources like the *Ming shi* and *Da Ming huidian* sum together figures of widely varying provenance, the use of local and regional data from gazetteers makes it possible to develop a higher-degree spatial and temporal specificity. Sometimes it is even possible to parse land and populations by category—including the subdivisions of acreage into paddy (*tian*), dry fields (*di*), forests (*shan*), and ponds (*tang*).

The compilation of landholding figures was itself a historically contingent process. The physical landscapes represented by acreage figures changed markedly in 1149, and in smaller ways in 1315, 1391, and 1581 (to choose four major points of divergence). Nonetheless, these figures are useful to roughly gauge the degree of land registration, especially if we compare data within a given jurisdiction across time to minimize the difficulties presented by locally variant units of measurement. Furthermore, while provincial and empire-wide units of account changed markedly, the jurisdictions governed by prefectures and counties were relatively stable—especially in the southern interior. This appendix presents some of the specific data used in the preceding chapters to index the spread of forest registration, starting with Huizhou Prefecture, the single-best longitudinal data set, and proceeding to more scattered data from Jiangxi and a single prefecture in Fujian.

CHANGES IN FOREST ACREAGE IN HUIZHOU PREFECTURE

Huizhou Prefecture offers the best single time-series cadastral data for Song, Yuan, and Ming South China, broken down by county and (after 1315) by landholding type (table A.1). While these data are peculiar to Huizhou, a prefecture at the epicenter of the shifts in forest registration practices, they nonetheless allow the most consistent source base for tracking change over the *longue durée*. On top of the anecdotal accounts cited in chapter 2, these data provide the clearest evidence of changes in land registration following the 1149 surveys. Except in Wuyuan, acreages jumped by at least 60 percent in every other county and tripled in three of the more peripheral ones. These three counties—Qimen, Yi, and Jixi—were also the three counties with the highest proportions of forest acreage in 1315 (boldfaced in table A.1). This suggests that the substantial increase in registered acreage in 1149 can largely be attributed to the addition of forests to the tax books.

Registered acreage increased far more modestly in the long thirteenth century, and principally in two other counties, Xiuning and Wuyuan, that had shown the most modest increases in the twelfth century. It is unclear whether this was the result of gradual accretion of self-reporting or a sudden burst during the Yanyou Reorganization. Then between 1315 and 1391, recorded acreage actually fell, driven largely by the disappearance of forests from the books in Wuyuan and Qimen (italicized in table A.1). This was due to tax breaks granted by a short-lived regional regime in the 1350s (not, as Joseph McDermott has suggested, by Zhu Yuanzhang). Modest increases in recorded acreage were seen through the rest of the Ming, driven largely by the gradual reporting of forests in these two counties, although forest acreage in Wuyuan and Qimen never again reached the level reported for 1315. It is also worth noting that gradual self-reporting during the thirteenth and fifteenth centuries was at least as successful in accounting for new acreage as were the more strident attempts to expand registration under Hongwu (1368–91) and Zhang Juzheng (1581). Overall acreage for the prefecture increased 15 percent through self-reporting in the late Song and early Yuan;

TABLE A.1. Changes in forest acreage in Huizhou, by county

	SHE	XIUNING	WUYUAN	QIMEN	YI	JIXI	HUIZHOU TOTAL
			% Change in total acreage				
Early twelfth century to 1175	81.00	63.00	17.00	**260.00**	**263.00**	**196.00**	93.00
1175–1315	2.00	53.00	20.00	2.00	7.00	4.00	15.00
1315–1391	0.40	0.00	−62.50	−82.60	−7.30	0.10	−38.10
1391–1491	17.00	29.00	55.00	71.00	5.00	6.00	26.00
1491–1611	10.00	−5.00	12.00	140.00	0.00	3.00	16.00
			% Forest				
1315	19.00	15.00	46.00	**69.00**	55.00	51.00	45.00
1369	19.00	15.00	*0.00*	*0.00*	55.00	51.00	26.00
1391	19.00	15.00	*0.00*	*0.00*	60.00	51.00	25.00
1491	16.00	15.00	19.00	14.00	57.00	48.00	26.00
1611	17.00	13.00	19.00	58.00	56.00	46.00	25.00

Sources: Chunxi Xin'an zhi; Hongzhi Huizhou fuzhi.
Notes: Boldfaced figures indicate the three counties with the greatest increase in acreage in the twelfth century and their large percentage of forested acreage in 1315. Italicized figures indicate the two counties whose forests were removed from the cadastres in the 1350s or 1360s.

remained flat in the late Yuan and early Ming (setting aside the disappearance of forest acreage in Qimen and Wuyuan); increased 26 percent in the fifteenth century, with similar increases in both forest and non-forest acreage; and showed only a modest increase in the long sixteenth century.

CHANGES IN ACREAGE ELSEWHERE IN THE SOUTH

No other single prefecture boasts a data series comparable to Huizhou, but for several regions in Jiangxi and Fujian, scattered figures allow us to trace some changes in forest registration in the Ming (table A.2). In areas near Huizhou, patterns of land registration probably looked quite similar. Raozhou, just south of Huizhou, presents the closest comparable case. There registered farmland acreage increased by about 10 percent in the early sixteenth century, while forest acreage increased by little more than a rounding error. In 1581, Zhang Juzheng's surveys added nearly a quarter more farmland, much of it coming at the expense of forest, which decreased by

TABLE A.2. Changes in forest acreage in five southern prefectures

	% Change 1315–1391		% Change 1391–c. 1511*		% Change c. 1511–1611	
	NON-FOREST	FOREST	NON-FOREST	FOREST	NON-FOREST	FOREST
Nan'an*	—	—	−22.67	−3.23	—	—
Raozhou	—	—	7.97	0.37	24.77	−13.61
Ruizhou	—	—	—	—	6.51	0.26
Jianning	—	—	−0.40	1.73	—	—
Huizhou*	−19.20	−65.52	26.49	25.85	10.70	3.64

Sources: Jiajing Nan'an fuzhi; Zhengde Raozhou fuzhi; Zhengde Ruizhou fuzhi; Jiajing Jianning fuzhi; Hongzhi Huizhou fuzhi; Jiangxi sheng fuyi quanshu.
* These two prefectures do not have data for 1511. Nan'an's closest available data are from 1531. Huizhou's closest available data are from 1491.

more than 13 percent. This probably reflected Zhang's surveys reregistering forests that had been converted to farmland into the proper tax brackets. While no comparable longitudinal data are available for these areas, it is likely that the entire belt of prefectures from Lake Poyang to Hangzhou Bay looked relatively similar to Huizhou and Raozhou, with a huge spike in forest registration in the twelfth century followed by relatively gradual increases thereafter.

Jianning, Fujian; Ruizhou; and Nan'an, a militarized post in southern Jiangxi, show a range of other possibilities. In Nan'an, registered acreage decreased markedly in both farmland and the very small amount of forest (less than 0.5 percent of registered acreage) in the sixteenth century, probably due to tax flight. In Jianning, acreage remained fairly stable, showing a small decrease in non-forest acreage and a small increase in forest. In Ruizhou, another prosperous prefecture in central Jiangxi, we know only that non-forest acreage increased modestly following the 1581 surveys, probably through the reclamation of wetlands. While these data are from just a handful of locations, they give a sense of the range of developments.

A final bit of evidence of landscape change, albeit indirect, comes from the comprehensive acreage figures available for parts of Jiangxi before and after 1581 (table A.3). The 1581 surveys conducted under Zhang Juzheng have generally been considered failures. However, if we look at the prefectural-level data, this picture changes somewhat—in some regions the surveys were markedly successful at increasing taxable acreage, some of which

TABLE A.3. Changes in total acreage following the 1581 surveys

	BEST FIGURE 1501–1541	1597	% CHANGE
Raozhou	63,728	70,547	10.7
Guangxin	49,238	48,113	−2.3
Jiujiang	9,659	12,485	29.3
Nanchang	49,987	70,461	41.0
Linjiang	27,307	34,038	24.6
Ruizhou	36,293	37,723	3.9
Jianchang	14,251	17,017	19.4
Yuanzhou	16,528	22,397	35.5
Ganzhou	10,861	33,528	208.7
Total	277,852	346,309	24.6

Sources: *Zhengde Raozhou fuzhi*; *Jiajing Guangxin fuzhi*; *Jiajing Jiujiang fuzhi*; *Wanli xinxiu Nanchang fuzhi*; *Longqing Linjiang fuzhi*; *Zhengde Ruizhou fuzhi*; *Zhengde Jianchang fuzhi*; *Zhengde Yuanzhou fuzhi*; *Tianqi Ganzhou fuzhi*; *Jiangxi sheng dazhi*.

probably came from registering new forests. Looking at nine prefectures that have extant land registration figures from both before and after the surveys, the picture varies substantially. I propose that we are seeing at least four somewhat different trends.

Northeastern Jiangxi—Guangxin and Raozhou—was the most developed part of the province, with very high rates of forest registration dating from the Song, when they were part of East Jiangnan alongside nearby Huizhou. Here the amount of registered acreage changed only modestly. Yet as noted above, this probably hides a relatively significant transfer of taxable acreage from forest to non-forest, at least in Raozhou. As in neighboring Huizhou, much of the original forest acreage in this region was gradually being converted into farmland.

In most of the rest of the province, registered acreage increased by 20–40 percent. I suggest that this was actually two distinct processes—wetland reclamation near Poyang Lake and forest registration in the mountainous Jiangxi borderlands. In the three prefectures nearest Poyang Lake—Nanchang, Jiujiang, and Linjiang—acreage uniformly increased by 24–40 percent. In nearby Ruizhou, it increased more modestly. This almost certainly reflected the belated registration of land reclaimed from the lakeshore over the course of the previous century.

In mountainous Yuanzhou in the west and Jianchang in the east, acreage increased by a similar amount, but probably for a different reason. Neither of these prefectures had much wetland to reclaim, but both probably had substantial unclaimed woodlands. Yuanzhou in particular had a well-developed forest sector in the mid-Ming, with forests accounting for more than 30 percent of taxable acreage prior to the 1581 surveys. Detailed figures for Jianchang are missing from most of my data series, but by the mid-Qing it also had an active forest industry. I suggest that these regions may have undergone a wave of forest enclosure in 1581, perhaps comparable to the developments seen further east in 1149, but probably of lesser significance.

Finally, in southern Jiangxi, Ganzhou *tripled* its recorded acreage during the 1581 surveys. Ganzhou was an unruly frontier in the early 1500s, but boasted a maturing timber business by the early 1600s. This massive wave of land registration during the 1581 surveys reflected the multivalent process of incorporating Ganzhou more fully into state authority. As part of the broader Hakka heartland, the registration of Ganzhou land was part of the trend by which they emerged as a taxpaying population. Given the importance of forest products to both the Ganzhou region and the Hakka population, some of the newly taxable acreage was almost certainly forest.

While incomplete, these data suggest a range of scenarios. At one end of the spectrum, places like Raozhou—and indeed the entire belt of prefectures from Poyang Lake to Hangzhou Bay—probably saw only modest change in taxable forest acreage after 1149. If anything, much of this region probably saw forests transformed into farmland, with the registration category changed during the 1581 surveys. At the other extreme, places like Ganzhou and Nan'an had difficulty maintaining tax records until the late Ming. But once they developed commercial forestry, they saw a huge boom in land registration after 1581. In between these poles, many prefectures in central Jiangxi (and similar regions) simply did not have large forest economies. But those that did—like Yuanzhou and perhaps Jianchang—went through a wave of forest registration and development in the mid-Ming.

APPENDIX B
Note on Sources

Without digital methods and online repositories, this book would probably have taken an entire career to research. With these tools and sources, I was able to complete it in a decade. To avoid further confusing an already dense and sometimes meandering narrative, I have largely elided discussion of research methods from the body text. Nonetheless, these deserve some degree of explanation.

By far the most significant tool used in this research—one that underlies most recent historical work but is generally not acknowledged—was full-text search. By using full-text search for keywords like "fir" (*shan* 杉)—in both specialized databases of Chinese sources and more general search tools like Google and Baidu—I was able to range across an enormous body of highly varied sources. In this way, I discovered entire genres of text, some of which I did not previously know existed. This is how I found several treatises on shipyard administration (*chuanzheng*), most of them freestanding texts; it is also how I found treatises on logging administration (*muzheng*), most of them hidden in the later chapters of gazetteers. In addition to identifying highly topical treatises, full-text search also allowed me to find anecdotes scattered widely in otherwise generalist accounts. For example, the *Xu zizhi tongjian changbian* is a general account of Song history and government with no specialized sections on forests or timber trade. By using full-text search, I identified dozens of small instances of changing policy—anecdotes that collectively allowed me to paint a broad picture of Song forest interventions.

Just as significantly, full-text search allowed me to identify other search terms. Slowly, I built a mental map (and a Google spreadsheet) of the linkages between keywords like "bamboo and timber" (*zhumu*), "proportional tariff" (*choufen*), "logging requisition" (*caiban*), and dozens of others that collectively made up the bureaucratic mechanisms for managing forests and woodland. Because the premodern Chinese state did not have a single, centralized forestry bureau, it was especially important to be able to track interventions across multiple institutions and their preferred interventions.

There are trade-offs to this approach. What keyword search gains in breadth, it tends to lose in context. The choice of keywords is also very significant—some are too specific and yield few results, some are too general and return a lot of extraneous information. The best are keywords that map closely onto clear ontologies in the source texts. But even when these ontologies are clear, keywords structure the inquiry in less expected ways. This text is guided, in part, by the vocabulary underlying Chinese botany, tax accounting, and construction administration. Indeed, I can easily recall the keywords used to develop a line of inquiry for each of the chapters. Finally, in order to use full-text search, I relied almost entirely on digital repositories, with a strong preference for those without paywalls or other access restrictions. The bibliographic information supplied by these repositories is not always complete. In some cases, it is difficult to identify the physical edition underlying the digital one, adding a degree of uncertainty to the chain of documentation.

In addition to keyword search, I also used regular expressions (regex) as a way to access large volumes of data, including most of the data used in chapter 2 and appendix A. I worked with researchers at the Max Planck Institute for the History of Science, and their Local Gazetteer Research Tools, to develop regular expressions to tag known keywords and to identify related data based on its structure in the gazetteers. For example, knowledge of the vocabulary of tax accounting allowed me to tag and extract large volumes of tax data through a semi-automated process, quadrupling the scale of my data set in a matter of a few weeks. Like keyword search more broadly, regular expressions also builds upon the underlying semantic and structural content of historical texts.

All histories are a function of their sources, shaped by the archives they use, and the reading biases of their authors. This book is no exception. Yet it is worth being aware that in this case the "archive" is not a set of boxes in a physical repository, or even a genre of texts, but a loose array of disparate sources, many of them digital. And the "reading" process depends in part on computationally assisted methods like full-text search and regular expression tagging, as well as on my own human perceptual and cognitive capacities.

GLOSSARY

PEOPLE

Cai Jing 蔡京 (1047–1126)
Cai Kelian 蔡克廉 (active 1560s)
Chen Xu 陳旭 (active c. 1524–45)
Cheng Changyu 程昌寓 (active c. 1130)

Dai Jin 戴金 (active c. 1541)

Fan Chengda 范成大 (1125–1193)
Fang La 方腊 (?–1121)

Ge Gaiyi 曷改益 (active c. 1522)
Gong Hui 龔輝 (active c. 1540)
Gu Zuo 顧佐 (?–1446)
Gui E 桂萼 (?–1541)
Guoheng 國亨 (active c. 1587)

Hai Rui 海瑞 (1514–1587)
Han Lin'er 韓林兒 (1340–1366)
Han Tongshan 韓山童 (?–1351)
Han Yong 韩雍 (1422–1478)
Huang Yingnan 黃應南 (active c. 1160)

Ji Gongzhi 棊公直 (active c. 1270s and 1280s)

Ke Xian 柯暹 (1389–1457)
Kim Panggyong 金方慶 (1212–1300)

Li Chunnian 李椿年 (1096–1164)
Li Gang 李綱 (1083–1140)
Li Xian 李憲 (active c. 1073)
Liu Bing 劉丙 (?–1518)
Liu Guangji 劉光濟 (active 1544–78)
Lu Jie 陸杰 (1488–1554)

Mao Zai 毛在 (1544–?)
Minde 銀德 (active c. 1387)

Ni Dong 倪涷 (active 1570–90)

Pan Jian 潘鑒 (1482–1544)
Pang Shangpeng 龐尚鵬 (1524–1580)
Peng Shiqi 彭世麒 (active c. 1514)

Rong Ni 榮薿 (active 1141–58)

She Lu 奢祿 (active c. 1484)
Shen Kuo 沈括 (1030–1095)
Shu Yinglong 舒應龍 (active c. 1580)
Song Li 宋禮 (1358–1422)
Su Shi 蘇軾 (1037–1101)

Wang Anshi 王安石 (1021–1086)
Wang Li 汪禮 (active 1453–72)
Wang Yangming 王阳明 aka Wang Shouren 王守仁 (1472–1528)
Wang Zongmu 王宗沐 (1524–1592)

Xia Shi 夏時 (1395–1464)
Xie An 謝安 (active 1406–40)

Yang Yao 楊幺 (1108–1135)
Yang Yinglong 楊應龍 (1551–1600)
Ye Mengde 葉蒙得 (1077–1148)
Yuan Cai 袁采 (c. 1140–1190)

Zaiweibing 再維屏 (active c. 1589)
Zhang Juzheng 張居正 (1525–1582)
Zhang Lü 章閭 sometimes written 張閭 or 張驢 (active 1306–14)
Zhang Rongshi 張榮實 (active 1234–77)
Zhang Xi 張禧 (active 1260–76)
Zhang Xuan 張瑄 (active c. 1275)
Zhou Rudou 周如斗 (active 1547–77)

Zhu Chun 朱椿 (1371–1423)
Zhu Qing 朱清 (active c. 1275)
Zhu Xi 朱熹 (1130–1200)
Zhu Ying 朱英 (1417–1485)

TREES

bai/bo 柏 cedar, cypress (*Cupressaceae* family with scaly, rather than needlelike, leaves, principally in the *Cupressoideae* subfamily)
baiyang 白楊 poplar (*Populus sp.*)

chu 楮 paper mulberry (*Broussonetia papyrifera* aka *Morus papyrifera*)

gui 桂 cassia, osmanthus (certain *Cinnamomum sp.* especially *Cinnamomum cassia*, as well as certain *Osmanthus sp.* especially *Osmanthus fragrans*; note that in Chinese, the genera *Cinnamomum* is split roughly in half, with some species called *zhang* and others called *gui*)

huai 槐 pagoda tree, sophora (*Styphnolobium japonicum*, formerly *Sophora japonicum*)

jiu 桕 or wujiu 烏桕 tallow tree (*Saporum sebiferum*)

li 栗 chestnut (*Castanea sp.*)
li 梨 pear (*Pyrus sp.*, principally *Pyrus pyrifolia*)
li 李 plum, Chinese/Japanese plum (*Prunus salicina*)
liu 柳 willow (*Salix sp.*)
lizhi 荔枝 lychee (*Litchi chinensis*)

mei 梅 plum, green plum, ume (*Prunus mume*)

nai 柰 apple, crab apple (*Malus sp.*)

qi 漆 lacquer tree, Japanese sumac, varnish tree (*Toxicodendron vernicifluum*)
qiu 楸 zelkova, Manchurian catalpa (*Catalpa bungei*)

sang 桑 mulberry (*Morus sp.*, principally *Morus alba*)
shan/sha 杉 fir (refers to several species of conifer that are morphologically similar to true firs, *Abies*, generally with short needles and straight boles; the evolving classification of these species generally involves multiple different genera now grouped within the *Cupressaceae* family: in South China, *shan/sha* does not refer to true firs but instead most often refers to *Cunninghamia lanceolata* [China fir] or *Cryptomeria japonica* [Japanese cedar], and it may also include *Taxodiacia* [bald cypress], *Metasequoia glyptostroboides* [dawn redwood], and *Tsuga*

[hemlock]; in North China, especially the far northeast, *shan* often does refer to true firs, *Abies*, or to certain species of larch, *Larix*)
shi 柿 persimmon (*Diospyros kaki*)
song 松 pine (*Pinus sp.*); the major commercial pine species in South China is Masson's pine / horsetail pine: mawei song 馬尾松 (*Pinus massoniana*)

tao 桃 peach (*Prunus persica*)
tong 桐 tung (*Vernicia fordii*)

xing 杏 apricot (*Prunus armeniaca*)

yu 榆 elm (*Ulmus sp.*)

zao 棗 jujube, Chinese date, red date (*Ziziphus jujuba*)
zhang 樟 camphor (certain *Cinnamomum sp.*, especially *Cinnamomum camphora*; note that in Chinese, the genera *Cinnamomum* is split roughly in half, with some species called *zhang* and others called *gui*)
zhe 柘 Chinese mulberry (*Maclura tricuspidata*)
zhu 竹 bamboo (subfamily *Bambosoideae*)
zi 梓 catalpa (*Catalpa sp.*)

OTHER TERMS

baiyao 白鷂 white falcon, a class of seagoing warship
ban 板 boards, board-cut lumber
bangjia 幫甲 head of supernumerary households at military garrisons
bantu 版圖 cadastral charts
baochuan 寶船 treasure ships
baojia 保甲 local self-defense and mutual responsibility group
baozheng 保正 head of a local self-defense group (*baojia*).
buhu 捕戶 hunting household

Caifu Fu 財賦府 Finance Commission
caikan 採砍 logging
cha 插 tree slip or cutting, or to plant from a slip or cutting
chahu 茶戶 tea household
chayuan 茶園 tea plantation
chi shanze zhi jin 馳山澤之禁 relax the restriction on the mountains and marshes
choufen 抽分 or **choujie** 抽解 drawn portion, the tariff on bamboo, timber, and bulk goods
chuanhu 船戶 boat household
chumao 鋤茅 dig weeds
chupi 楮皮 paper mulberry bark

dang 蕩 pools
dao 盜 theft
dao tianye gumai 盜田野穀麥 stealing wheat and rice from fields
daomai tianzhai 盜賣田宅 fraudulently selling fields and houses
daoyu chuan 魛魚船 mullet ship, a style common in the lower Yangzi
di 地 dry field
dian ji bu 坫基簿 cadastres of areal plot diagrams
dumu 督木 timber supervisor

erbi 珥筆 brush-pen hatpins, a colloquial name for litigation masters (*songshi*)

fan 蕃 Tibetan or Central Asian
fang 枋 square-cut lumber
feiqiao 飛橋 flying bridge
fenshan hetong 分山合同 forest shareholding agreement

gong 貢 tribute
gongfei yin 工費銀 public expense silver, a mid-1400s tax reform
guanlin 官林 state forest
guanmin 官民 state or private [property]
gui xin 鬼薪 [cutting] firewood for the spirits, a Qin/Han punishment

haigu chuan 海鶻船 sea hawk ship, a four-oared galley
haiyu 海鰌 whale, a large seagoing warship
hebo suo 河泊所 river mooring station
hu yi 虎翼 tiger wings, elite naval units of the Song imperial guard
huanggu 黃鵠 yellow goose, a class of seagoing warship
huangma 黃麻 hemp
huangmu 皇木 imperial timber
huangmu jie hu 皇木解戶 imperial timber transport household
huoshan hetong 伙山合同 forest partnership agreement
hutie 戶貼 household receipt

jin yin tong tie ye 金銀銅鐵冶 gold, silver, copper, and iron smelters
jingjie 境界 plot boundaries
jinshan 禁山 restricted forest
junping yin 均平銀 equalized silver, a late 1400s tax reform
junyao 均徭 equalized corvée, a mid-1400s tax reform

kejia 客家 Hakka, literally "guest families" or (better) "sojourner" or "tenant families"
kuaichuan 快船 fast warships

li yu zhonggong 利於眾共 of public benefit
liehu 獵戶 hunting household
lifen 力分 labor share
lijia 里甲 administrative village or village-tithing group
lijia junping 里甲均平 village equalization, an early 1500s tax reform
lin 林 grove, woodland
linmu 林木 timber trees
linmu can tian 林木參天 woods that block out the sky
longduan 壟斷 monopolize
ludang 蘆蕩 reed pools

man 蠻 "barbarians," especially non-Han peoples of the interior south
meizha 煤渣 coal fragments
miao 苗 seedling
minbing 民兵 militia
muguan 木官 timber office

pinyue 拚約 clearance contract

qingdan 清單 inventory list
qingzhang xince 清丈新冊 clarified measurements in the new cadastres, i.e., acreage based on the 1581 surveys

ru 儒 Confucian scholar

shanchang 山場 forest workshop, lumberyard
shantian mudi 山田墓地 mountain plots and grave land
shanye 山野 or **shanye hupo** 山野陂湖 mountains, wilds, ponds, and embankments, a variant of *shanze*
shanye wu yi jia gongli 山野物已加功力 products of the wild with labor already invested in them
shanze 山澤 or **shanlin huze** 山林湖澤 mountains and marshes or mountains, groves, ponds, and marshes wilds; open-access lands
shanze zhi li 山澤之利 bounties of the mountains and marshes
shanze zhi rao 山澤之饒 products gathered from the wilds
shaohuang 燒荒 burn the grasses
She 畲 an ethnic group of the Wuyi Mountains, perhaps related to their practice of swidden agriculture, or a transliteration of the term for "person" in their language
Shenmu Chang 神木廠 Sacred Timber Depot
Shenmu Shan 神木山 Sacred Tree Mountain
shicai chang 事材場 lumber-working yard
shitan 石炭 mineral coal
shuijun zongguan 水軍總管 director of the navy

sichai 四差 four levies, a mid-1400s tax reform
songshi 訟師 litigation master
songshu 訟書 litigation manual

tang 塘 or **tangchi** 塘池 pond
taojin hu 淘金戶 gold-panning household
tian 田 paddy field
tianche 天車 winch, crane, or capstan
tianfu 田賦 land tax
tongshan 童山 bare mountain
tuicai chang 退材場 lumber recovery yard

wanhufu 萬戶府 myriarchy, command of 1,000 troops; Mongolian: *tümen*, Korean: *manhobu*

xide qiaocai 觿得樵採 common-access fuel collection
Xihe Cai Mai Muzhi Si 熙河採買木植司 Xihe Logging and Timber Purchase Bureau

yanzhang 煙瘴 miasmatic vapors, probably malaria
yaoyi 徭役 corvée, labor service
yehu 冶戶 smelter households
yu 虞 hunter, forester
yuan 園 garden or orchard
yuan li 園籬 orchards and hedges
yuanlin 園林 orchards and woodlands
yue ling 月令 seasonal regulations
yuhu 漁戶 fishing household

zachan 雜產 miscellaneous property
zaohu 灶戶 saltern household
zhonghu zhili 眾戶殖利 public benefit
zhuanyun si 轉運司 transport bureau
zhufen 主分 ownership share
zhumu chang 竹木場 bamboo and timber depot
zushan qi 租山契 forest rental contract

NOTES

INTRODUCTION

1 Barrow and Macartney, *Earl of Macartney*, 2:356-57.
2 Abel, *Narrative of a Journey*, 167.
3 These frameworks are best analyzed through ecological processes rather than assuming a hierarchy of scales. See Allen and Hoekstra, *Toward a Unified Ecology*.
4 While I have largely avoided the associated jargon, this framework is heavily influenced by Manuel DeLanda's "assemblage theory," which seeks to explain how complex systems emerged from autonomous entities and processes. DeLanda, *Thousand Years of Nonlinear History*; DeLanda, *New Philosophy of Society*.
5 Scott, *Seeing Like a State*; Sivaramakrishnan, *Modern Forests*; McElwee, *Forests Are Gold*; Peluso and Vandergeest, "Genealogies of the Political Forest."
6 Cronon, *Nature's Metropolis*. For further theorization, in particular the concept of metabolic rift, see Foster, "Marx's Theory of Metabolic Rift"; Moore, "Transcending the Metabolic Rift."
7 This general thesis is expressed most clearly in Scott, *Seeing Like a State*.
8 Radkau, *Wood*, 25-27, 156-58.
9 For surveys and responses to the idea of a European wood crisis, see Radkau, *Wood*, chaps. 2-3; Warde, "Fear of Wood Shortage."
10 Jørgensen, "Roots of the English Royal Forest"; Rackham, *History of the Countryside*, 129-39, 146-51; Radkau, *Wood*, 57-70; Warde, *Invention of Sustainability*, 60-61.
11 Appuhn, *Forest on the Sea*.
12 Kain and Baigent, *Cadastral Map*, 331-34; Matteson, *Forests in Revolutionary France*; Oosthoek and Hölzl, *Managing Northern Europe's Forests*; Radkau,

Wood, chaps. 2–3; Warde, *Ecology, Economy and State Formation*; Warde, *Invention of Sustainability*, 177–82, 188–92, 198–200; Wing, *Roots of Empire*.

13 Grove, *Green Imperialism*, esp. chaps. 7–8; Lowood, "Calculating Forester"; Radkau, *Wood*, 172–204; Scott, *Seeing Like a State*, chap. 1; Warde, *Invention of Sustainability*, 201–27.

14 Albion, *Forests and Sea Power*; Funes Monzote, *From Rainforest to Cane Field*, chaps. 2–3; Grove, *Green Imperialism*; Moore, "'Amsterdam Is Standing on Norway,' Part I," and "Part II"; Wing, *Roots of Empire*, chap. 2.

15 See esp. Albion, *Forests and Sea Power*, chap. 1.

16 See esp. Grove, *Green Imperialism*.

17 It is actually named for both James Cunningham and Allan Cunningham, another British botanist, who never visited China. Brown, *Miscellaneous Botanical Works*, 1:461n1.

18 McDermott, *New Rural Order*, vol. 1, chap. 6.

19 Coggins, *Tiger and the Pangolin*; Elvin, *Retreat of the Elephants*, esp. chaps. 1–3; Marks, *Tigers, Rice, Silk, and Silt*.

20 Marks, *Tigers, Rice, Silk, and Silt*; Osborne, "Highlands and Lowlands."

21 Menzies, *Forest and Land Management*, chap. 5. This issue is a major topic of concern in European forest history (e.g., Matteson, *Forests in Revolutionary France*; Radkau, *Wood*; Warde, *Ecology, Economy and State Formation*) but is inadequately addressed in Chinese history.

22 Marks, *China*, chap. 5.

23 Grove, *Green Imperialism*, 133–45, 257–58, 271–73, 282–91, 346, and chap. 8; McElwee, *Forests Are Gold*, chap. 1; Peluso, *Rich Forests, Poor People*, chaps. 2–3; Sivaramakrishnan, *Modern Forests*, esp. chap. 4; Warde, *Invention of Sustainability*, 212–27.

24 See esp. Grove, *Green Imperialism*; Warde, *Invention of Sustainability*.

25 Lee, "Forests and the State."

26 Totman, *Green Archipelago*, chaps. 5–6; Totman, *Lumber Industry in Early Modern Japan*.

27 See, e.g., Richards, *Unending Frontier*, chap. 4; Williams, *Deforesting the Earth*, 216–20; Radkau, *Nature and Power*, 112–15 and passim.

28 Hung, "When the Green Archipelago Encountered Formosa"; and personal communication. Curiously, Japan's modern forest administration replaced *shan/san/yama* with the other common character for woodland, *lin* (Japanese: *rin* or *hayashi*, Korean: *lim* or *im*). This means that we can trace the approximate contours of the transition from premodern, Chinese-derived to modern German-Japanese-derived forest oversight through the shift from *shan/san* to *lin/rin/lim*.

29 Elvin, *Retreat of the Elephants*, esp. chaps. 1–3. This builds on more than a decade of Elvin's work, starting with the short research program in Elvin, "Environmental History of China." Most of Elvin's major theories of war, water control, and environmental change were first developed in Elvin, "Three Thousand Years of Unsustainable Growth" and "Environmental Legacy of Imperial China."

30 Marks, *Tigers, Rice, Silk, and Silt*. See also Averill, "Shed People"; Osborne, "Local Politics of Land Reclamation"; Vermeer, "Mountain Frontier." In Elvin and Liu, *Sediments of Time*, see Kuo-tung Ch'en, "Nonreclamation Deforestation"; Ts'ui-jung Liu, "Han Migration"; Osborne, "Highlands and Lowlands"; Vermeer, "Population and Ecology."
31 Anderson and Whitmore, "Introduction: 'The Fiery Frontier'"; Churchman, "Where to Draw the Line?"; Chittick, "Dragon Boats and Serpent Prows"; Kim, "Sinicization and Barbarization"; Clark, *Sinitic Encounter in Southeast China*.
32 See, e.g., "Tribute of Yu" [Yu gong], *Shang shu*; Sima Qian, "Biographies of Wealthy Merchants" [Huozhi liezhuan], *Shiji* 129.
33 "Yuzhang jun" is listed in the geographic treatises of Ban Gu, *Han shu* 28a; Fan Ye, *Hou Han shu* 112; Fang Xuanling, *Jin shu* 15; Shen Yue, *Song shu* 36; Liu Xu, *Jiu Tang shu* 40.
34 See Lu Jia, "Natural Endowments" [Zizhi], *Xinyu* 7; Huan Kuan, "The Basic Argument" [Benyi], *Yantie lun* 1; Wang Fu, "On Excessive Luxury" [Fuyi], *Qian fu lun* 3.
35 Xiaoqiang Li et al., "Population and Expansion of Rice Agriculture"; Dodson et al., "Vegetation and Environment History."
36 Scott, *Art of Not Being Governed*.
37 On the transformations of the meaning of "Han," see Elliott, "*Hushuo*," Giersch, "From Subjects to Han," and other essays in Mullaney et al., *Critical Han Studies*; Harrell, *Ways of Being Ethnic*, chap. 14; Tackett, *Origins of the Chinese Nation*.
38 Bello, *Across Forest, Steppe, and Mountain*, esp. chaps. 1 and 4.
39 Szonyi, *Art of Being Governed*.
40 Leong, *Migration and Ethnicity*.
41 Due to their extensive records, the scholarship on Huizhou is substantial. Key English-language works include Du, *Order of Places*; McDermott, *New Rural Order*, vol. 1; Zurndorfer, *Chinese Local History*.
42 Leong, *Migration and Ethnicity*; Ownby, *Brotherhoods and Secret Societies*.
43 The extent and significance of this crackdown has been debated, but it certainly damaged the commercial prosperity of Jiangnan. See von Glahn, "Towns and Temples"; von Glahn, "Ming Taizu *Ex Nihilo*?"; Schneewind, "Ming Taizu *Ex Machina*."
44 Von Glahn, *Economic History of China*, chap. 7.
45 Paul Jakov Smith, "Introduction: Problematizing the Song-Yuan-Ming Transition"; von Glahn, "Imagining Pre-modern China."
46 Ho, "Introduction of American Food Plants"; Mann, *1493*, chap. 5; Mazumdar, "New World Food Crops"; Leong, *Migration and Ethnicity*, 119–22 and passim; Osborne, "Local Politics of Land Reclamation."
47 Benedict, *Golden-Silk Smoke*, chaps. 1–2; Gardella, *Harvesting Mountains*; Leong, *Migration and Ethnicity*, chap. 1.
48 Averill, "Shed People"; Marks, *Tigers, Rice, Silk, and Silt*; Leong, *Migration and Ethnicity*, chaps. 3, 7, and 8; Osborne, "Local Politics of Land Reclamation"; Osborne, "Highlands and Lowlands."

49 Erbaugh, "Secret History of the Hakkas"; Leong, *Migration and Ethnicity*, chaps. 3–4.
50 An excellent study of this period is provided in Meng Zhang, "Timber Trade along the Yangzi River"; the same project is the basis of Zhang's forthcoming book, *Sustaining the Market*.

CHAPTER ONE: THE END OF ABUNDANCE

1 Yuan Cai, "Timely Planting of Mulberry and Timber" [Sangmu yinshi zhongzhi], *Yuanshi shifan* 3.
2 Yuan Cai, "Advance Planning" [Zaolü], *Yuanshi shifan* 2.
3 Yuan Cai, "Timely Planting of Mulberry and Timber," *Yuanshi shifan* 3.
4 Yuan Cai, "Suitability of Clear Property Boundaries" [Tianchan jiezhi yi fenming], *Yuanshi shifan* 3.
5 Bruce D. Smith, "Ultimate Ecosystem Engineers"; Bond and Keeley, "Fire as a Global 'Herbivore.'"
6 For example, the first Chinese written records—"oracle bone" inscriptions (*jiagu wen*) documenting divination at the Shang court (c. 1700–1027 BCE)—provide clear evidence of anthropogenic fire used for hunting and to clear land. See Fiskesjö, "Rising from Blood-Stained Fields."
7 Changes in vegetation included the proliferation of pines and weeds that prefer cleared areas at the expense of broad-leaved species like oaks (terrestrial woodlands) and alders (in wetlands) and the sudden appearance of layers of charcoal, suggesting widespread burning. Sun and Chen, "Palynological Records," 537, 540–41; Liu and Qiu, "Pollen Records of Vegetational Changes," 395; Ren, "Mid- to Late Holocene Forests"; Dodson et al., "Vegetation and Environment History." Around the same time, methane levels diverged from their downward trend, probably also due to clearance and the proliferation of rice agriculture. Xiaoqiang Li et al., "Population and Expansion of Rice Agriculture," 42, 48.
8 Elvin, "Three Thousand Years of Unsustainable Growth," 7–10; Miller, "Forestry and the Politics of Sustainability"; Sanft, "Environment and Law"; Schafer, "Hunting Parks and Animal Enclosures."
9 There is physical evidence of these clearances in pollen, charcoal, and sediment records. Sun and Chen, "Palynological Records," 537, 540–41; Zhao, "Vegetation and Climate Reconstructions," 381; Mostern, "Sediment and State in Imperial China," 128; Wenying Jiang et al., "Natural and Anthropogenic Forest Fires."
10 On the difference between the fear and reality of wood scarcity, see Warde, "Fear of Wood Shortage."
11 See, e.g., Pyne, *Fire*.
12 Elvin, "Three Thousand Years of Unsustainable Growth," 17–19; Miller, "Forestry and the Politics of Sustainability," 601–5.
13 Sanft, "Environment and Law."
14 Compare to Gadgil and Guha, *This Fissured Land*, 20–27; Teplyakov, *Russian Forestry and Its Leaders*, v, 1–2.

15 Schafer, "Hunting Parks and Animal Enclosures," 332–33; Lewis, *Sanctioned Violence in Early China*, chap. 4. One source claims that Shanglin Park contained "more than three thousand kinds of famous fruits and strange trees," but lists only ninety-eight distinct varieties in the text. Zhou Weiquan, *Zhongguo gudian yuanlin shi*, 50–51. On the use of Shanglin Park to dominate the regional wood market, see Miller, "Forestry and the Politics of Sustainability," 607–9.
16 Elvin, "Three Thousand Years of Unsustainable Growth," 18–21; Marks, *China*, 83–86; Miller, "Forestry in Early China," 605–9.
17 For example, Sima Qian credited Han Wendi with this act. Sima Qian, "Biographies of Important Merchants," *Shiji* 129.
18 Miller, "Forestry and the Politics of Sustainability," 606; Sanft, "Environment and Law"; Hulsewe, *Remnants of Ch'in Law*, 15; Lau and Staack, *Legal Practice*, 27–28; Barbieri-Low, *Artisans in Early Imperial China*, 132 and chap. 6 generally.
19 References to this trade appear widely in Warring States, Qin, and Han texts. See, e.g., "Tribute of Yu," *Shang shu*; Sima Qian, "Biographies of Wealthy Merchants," *Shiji* 129; Lu Jia, "Natural Endowments," *Xinyu* 7; Huan Kuan, "The Basic Argument," *Yantie lun* 1; Wang Fu, "On Excessive Luxury," *Qian fu lun* 3.
20 Elvin, "Three Thousand Years of Unsustainable Growth," 25; "Miscellaneous Levies—Mountains, Marshes, Fords, and Ferries" [Za zhengxian—shanze jindu], Ma Duanlin, *Wenxian tongkao* 19.
21 Gernet, *Buddhism in Chinese Society*, 116–29 and chap. 3; Marks, *China*, 138–41; Schafer, "Conservation of Nature," 282–84; Walsh, *Sacred Economies*, chaps. 4–5.
22 See, e.g., "The Commandments of Lord Lao" [Taishang Lao jun jinglü], trans. Kristofer Schipper, in De Bary and Bloom, *Sources of Chinese Tradition*, 1:395; Girardot, Miller, and Liu, *Daoism and Ecology*; Clark, *Sinitic Encounter in Southeast China*, 33–36.
23 Lewis, *China between Empires*, 216–20.
24 Jia Sixie, *Qimin yaoshu* 4.
25 Jia Sixie, "Growing Mulberry and Chinese Mulberry" [Zong sang zhe], *Qimin yaoshu* 5.45.
26 Jia Sixie, "Growing Elm and Poplar" [Zhong yu baiyang], *Qimin yaoshu* 5.46.
27 Jia Sixie, *Qimin yaoshu* 5.47–51.
28 Examples of estate forests are referenced in Lewis, *China's Cosmopolitan Empire*, 25–26, 126; Elvin, *Pattern of the Chinese Past*, 80–82. On Buddhist temple forests, see Gernet, *Buddhism in Chinese Society*, 116–29; Walsh, *Sacred Economies*, chaps. 4–5; Marks, *China*, 138–41; Menzies, *Forest and Land Management*, chap. 4; Schafer, "Conservation of Nature," 282–84, 288.
29 See Twitchett, *Financial Administration under the T'ang*.
30 Jia Sixie, "Cutting Timber" [Fa mu], *Qimin yaoshu* 5.55.
31 *Tang lü shuyi*, Article 405. The law is translated more literally as "Monopolizing Profit from Mountains, Wilderness Areas, Shores, and Lakes" in Johnson, *T'ang Code*, 2:469.

32 *Tang lü shuyi*, Article 291.
33 That woodcutting was a form of labor service is attested indirectly, in a contract for the substitution of a man's corvée duties while he was away on business. Quoted in Hansen, *Negotiating Daily Life in Traditional China*, 69.
34 Adolf Berger, *Encyclopedic Dictionary of Roman Law*, s.vv. "fructus," "fructus separati," "separatio fructuum."
35 *Song xingtong*, Articles 291 and 405.
36 Liu Zongyuan, "Biography of Tree Planter Guo the Hunchback" [Zhongshu Guo tuotuo zhuan], *Liuzhou wenchao* 5.
37 Guo Tuotuo, *Zhongshu shu* 1-3.
38 Schafer, "Conservation of Nature," 299-300.
39 For a review of this scholarship, see von Glahn, "Imagining Pre-modern China."
40 Yuan Julian Chen, "Frontier, Fortification, and Forestation."
41 Mostern, "Sediment and State in Imperial China."
42 This somewhat controversial estimate appears in Hartwell, "Cycle of Economic Change," 104-6. See also Hartwell, "Revolution in the Iron and Coal Industries"; Hartwell, "Markets, Technology, and the Structure of Enterprise." Hartwell's estimate has been critiqued, notably in Wagner, "Administration of the Iron Industry." Wagner argues that Hartwell's means of calculation are based in overly simple extrapolation of tax data, and he probably overestimates Song production and underestimates subsequent production. For other judgments on Hartwell's estimation, see Golas, *Mining*, 169-70n495; von Glahn, *Economic History of China*, 245n87; Wright, "Economic Cycle in Imperial China?" All accept Hartwell's qualitative conclusion that iron production increased substantially in the eleventh century but question his quantitative projections.
43 Yuan Julian Chen, "'Frontier, Fortification, and Forestation."
44 Von Glahn, *Economic History of China*, 245.
45 The locus classicus description of mineral coal in Song China is Shen Kuo, *Mengxi bitan* 24. Several scholars have argued for the growing use of coal in the eleventh century, especially in the Central Plains region. See Hartwell, "Markets, Technology, and the Structure of Enterprise," 160-61; Golas, *Mining*, 186-96; McDermott and Yoshinobu, "Economic Change in China," 375.
46 In the eleventh century, twenty-seven cities had commercial tax revenues of at least one-tenth those of the Song capital at Kaifeng, suggesting they were roughly an order of magnitude smaller than the capital. Von Glahn, *Economic History of China*, 249-50.
47 This remarkable story is told in Ling Zhang, *The River, the Plain, and the State*. On the role of clearance in the northwest in Yellow River flooding, see Mostern, "Sediment and State in Imperial China."
48 Von Glahn, *Fountain of Fortune*, 48-51.
49 SHY *xingfa* 2.29.
50 CB 258.90.

51 SHY *bing* 4.9.
52 SHY *xingfa* 2.124.
53 "Gao Fang," *Song shi* 270, quoted in Qi and Qiao, *Zhongguo jing ji tong shi*, 249–50. CB 44.
54 Early Song logging operations in Tibetan territory, Qinzhou, and Longzhou: CB 21.47, 21.51, 21.61, 28.11, 71.95, 73.83, 77.17, 78.55, 82.90, 82.99–100, 83.98, 83.114, 86.56. Cancellation of logging projects in the northwest: CB 88.33, 88.39, 90.57.
55 Mostern, "Sediment and State in Imperial China," 134.
56 Paul Jakov Smith, "Irredentism as Political Capital," 84–87; "Wang Shao," *Song shi* 328.
57 CB 239.37.
58 Mostern, "Sediment and State in Imperial China," 134; Mostern, *"Dividing the Realm,"* 195–202.
59 Paul Jakov Smith, "Irredentism as Political Capital," 91–94, and *Taxing Heaven's Storehouse*, 46–47.
60 CB 235.41, 250.26, 250.53.
61 On Li Xian and other eunuch military supervisors, see Paul Jakov Smith, "Irredentism as Political Capital," 93, 119n97, 126. See also "Li Xian," *Song shi* 467.
62 CB 310.57.
63 Strings of cash (*guan qian*) was a unit of account that did not necessarily correspond with an exact number of coins. Nominally, one string was set at one hundred copper coins. However, the court regularly ordered the substitution of "short strings" of less than one hundred coins, and later of paper money.
64 CB 311.38.
65 CB 345.115.
66 Paul Jakov Smith, "Irredentism as Political Capital," 125–26.
67 On the *Offices of Zhou* as a statist text, see Puett, "Centering the Realm." On forest offices in the *Offices of Zhou*, see Miller, "Forestry and the Politics of Sustainability," 606–7. Wang Anshi knew the text well and wrote his own commentary, *A New Interpretation of the Offices of Zhou* [Zhouguan xinyi]; see Bol, "Wang Anshi and the *Zhouli*."
68 CB 251.58.
69 CB 237.64. An order in 1076 clarified that miscellaneous trees (*zamu*) on *individual properties* were included in calculating the corvée-replacement tax on each household, but common woodlots were not. CB 277.102.
70 Levine, *Divided by a Common Language*, 99–103; Levine, "Che-tsung's Reign," 521–29.
71 On tea and salt monopolies, see Paul Jakov Smith, *Taxing Heaven's Storehouse*, 195–98; Chien, *Salt and State*. On Cai Jing's policies more generally, see Chaffee, "Politics of Reform"; Ebrey, *Emperor Huizong*, 102–3.

72 In 1071, assistant magistrates were established in counties with more than twenty thousand primary households (*zhuhu*) to fulfill administrative tasks. CB 221.19.
73 SHY *zhiguan* 48.53–54.
74 SHY *zhiguan* 48.54.
75 Chaffee, "Politics of Reform," 54–55.
76 SHY *xingfa* 1.27–28.
77 SHY *zhiguan* 48.55.
78 These are from the 1201 *Qingyuan tiaofa*, which its modern editors note contains many regulations from the northern Song. QYTF 2.
79 This violation resulted in eighty strokes of the light cane. QYTF 911.
80 QYTF 685–86.
81 Hartman, "Cai Jing's Biography in the *Songshi*."
82 Rewards for planting trees on dikes were canceled in 1136, a decade after the Song retreated from northern China, under the logic that there was no longer a need to repair the Yellow River dikes. It is not clear if the other forestry programs were also canceled. QYTF 687. While absence of evidence is not evidence of absence, I have found no specific references to county forests after the retreat to southern China in 1126–27.
83 Tang Zhenwei, *Zhenglei bencao* 14.81a–b.
84 Fang Shao, *Qingxi kou gui*.
85 Zhou Bida, *Sheng zhang wengao*, quoted in *Jiaqing Yuhang xianzhi* 38.
86 See, e.g., SHY *xingfa* 2.124; Shiba, *Commerce and Society*, 83, 121–32.
87 Timber imports from Japan: von Glahn, "Ningbo-Hakata Merchant Network," 269–70. Timber and metal imports from Fujian and Guangdong: Shiba, "Ningbo and Its Hinterland."
88 Su Shi, *Dongpo zaji*, quoted in Chen Rong, *Zhongguo senlin shiliao*, 34–35.
89 "Products" [Wuchan], *Jiaqing Yuhang xianzhi* 38, quoting *Xianchun Lin'an zhi*; Zhu Xi, "Ten Thousand Fir Temple" [Wanshan si], *Huian xiansheng Zhu Wen gong wenji* 2. The latter is attested by an inscription from the Tiansheng reign (1023–32) prohibiting their cutting.
90 Li and Ritchie, "Clonal Forestry in China," 123.
91 Ye Mengde, *Bishu lühua* 2.
92 Yuan Cai, "Timely Planting of Mulberry and Timber" and "Advance Planning," *Yuanshi shifan* 2–3. See Ebrey, *Family and Property in Sung China*, referenced 116, translated 266.
93 "Local Products—Fruit and Timber" [Wuchan—guomu], *Chunxi Xin'an zhi* 2, quoted in Bian, *Ming Qing Huizhou shehui yanjiu*, 177–78.
94 LDQY 532–47 #412–22.
95 "Planting Firs" [Cha shan], *Nongsang jiyao* 6, quoting an earlier manual that is no longer extant.
96 Moore, "'Amsterdam Is Standing on Norway,' Part II"; Radkau, *Wood*, 142–44.

97 Germany: Scott, *Seeing Like a State*, chap. 1; Lowood, "Calculating Forester." Venice: Appuhn, *Forest on the Sea*, chaps. 4–5. France: Matteson, *Forests in Revolutionary France*.

CHAPTER TWO: BOUNDARIES, TAXES, AND PROPERTY RIGHTS

1 "Registers I" [Banji lei yi], *Chunxi Sanshan zhi* 10.
2 "Registers I," *Chunxi Sanshan zhi* 10 (my emphasis).
3 According to detailed figures from a single lineage in Huizhou, approximately two-thirds of forest acreage was planted with timber, and the remaining third was split between other commercial crops and graves. It is not clear how generalizable these figures are. Chen Keyun, "Cong 'lishi shanlin zhichan bu,'" 73–75.
4 For introductions to this key source genre, see Brook, *Geographical Sources of Ming-Qing History*; Dennis, *Local Gazetteers in Imperial China*; Hargett, "Song Dynasty Local Gazetteers," 405–12; Bol, "Rise of Local History," 37–41.
5 On problems with Ming population, tax, and landholding figures, see Ray Huang, *Taxation and Governmental Finance*; Heijdra, "Socio-economic Development of Rural China," 460–475; Ho, *Studies on the Population of China*.
6 Ray Huang, *Taxation and Governmental Finance*, 38–43.
7 Twitchett, *Financial Administration under the T'ang*.
8 Twitchett, *Financial Administration under the T'ang*, 31–40.
9 Hansen, *Negotiating Daily Life in Traditional China*, 75–95 and more generally. Hansen states, with some exaggeration, that "in 600, officials did not recognize contracts and used government registers to record land ownership. By 1400, the registers had fallen into disuse and contracts had become the only proof of ownership" (1).
10 CB 237.64. An order in 1076 clarified that miscellaneous trees (*zamu*) on *individual properties* were included in calculating the corvée-replacement tax on each household, but common woodlots were not. CB 277.102. See also chapter 1.
11 Wang Deyi, "Li Chunnian."
12 Wang Deyi, "Li Chunnian."
13 See the cases in *Minggong shupan qingming ji* 5–6, some of which are translated in McKnight and Liu, *Enlightened Judgments*, pt. 4.
14 Wang Deyi, "Li Chunnian." His account is based largely on "Miscellaneous Notes on Boundary [Surveys]" [Jingye zalü], SHY *shihuo* 70.
15 QYTF 684. These regulations are not dated. Based on their requirement that boundaries be recorded in the registers, they must date to after Li Chunnian's initial proposal of 1141 and before the publication of the *Qingyuan tiaofa shilei* in 1203.
16 JYFN 185.20.

17 There is circumstantial evidence suggesting both possibilities. Ji'an was one of the prefectures noted as having county forests in 1105, suggesting that these might be remnants of those forests. But the timing of this record, a mere decade after the Li Chunnian surveys, suggests that this was newly surveyed land, perhaps land seized from landowners who refused to submit to surveys, perhaps land initially marked as state-managed commons, and then sold due to difficulties in managements and the active market for forest plots. Five percent is a rough estimate. Figures are not available for twelfth-century Ji'an. For comparison, Ji'an had just under fifty thousand *qing* of registered land in 1582 (*Wanli Ji'an fuzhi* 10). The somewhat smaller prefecture of Huizhou had just under thirty thousand *qing* of registered land in 1175 (*Chunxi Xin'an zhi*). The figure for twelfth-century Ji'an was probably somewhere between these two numbers, meaning that the twenty-eight hundred *qing* of state land cited in this record would have represented somewhere between 5 and 9 percent of all Ji'an landholdings.

18 "The Importance of Clear Property Boundaries" [Tianchan jiezhi yi fenming], Yuan Cai, *Yuanshi shifan* 2.

19 Wang Deyi, "Li Chunnian."

20 "Xiaozong 3," *Song shi* 35; "Preparing Boundary Records" [Yu jingjie shiwu], Zhu Xi, *Huian xiansheng Zhu Wen gong wenji* 100; "Treatise on Registers" [Banji zhi], *Min shu* 39.

21 *Chunxi Xin'an zhi* 3–4; *Hongzhi Huizhou fuzhi* 2. While all six counties in Huizhou reported increases in acreage, the surveys were most pronounced at incorporating new landholdings from the three most heavily forested, peripheral counties—Qimen, Yi, and Jixi. In all three counties, forests (*shan*) made up more than 50 percent of reported acreage in 1315. Wuyuan was also heavily forested but appears to have been under-surveyed. See also appendix A.

22 "Registers," *Chunxi Sanshan zhi* 10.5b and vols. 10–14 more generally.

23 "Registers" [Banji men], *Jiading Chicheng zhi* 13.1a–b.

24 "Land Tax" [Tianfu zhi], *Zhizheng Jinling xinzhi* 7.

25 Ayurbarwada's full title is Ayurbarwada Buyantu Khan, Emperor Renzong of Yuan. Reforms during his reign included a revival of the civil service examinations in 1313 and several large compilation projects. For a general account, see Hsiao, "Mid-Yuan Politics," 513–20, 530–32.

26 Central secretariat manager of state affairs (*zhongshu pingzhang zhengshi*) was effectively the second-highest civil office in the Yuan, rank 1b. In the official histories, these fiscal reforms are named the Yanyou Reorganization (Yanyou Jingli) after Ayurbarwada's second reign period, lasting from 1314 to 1320.

27 "Reorganization" [Jingli], *Yuan shi* 93.

28 See, e.g., Schurmann, *Economic Structure of the Yüan Dynasty*, 24–26, 31.

29 "Landholdings" [Tiantu], *Zhishun Zhenjiang zhi* 5.

30 *Zhishun Zhenjiang zhi* 5; "Landholdings" [Tiandi], *Hongzhi Huizhou fuzhi* 2.

31 An increase of four thousand *qing*. To put this in context, only about 40 percent as much acreage was added in the 165 years between 1150 and 1315 as was

recorded during 1148–49 alone. There were also qualitative differences between the newly surveyed acreage in the 1140s and the "long" thirteenth century.

32 Zhenjiang: *Zhishun Zhenjiang zhi* 5; Ningbo: *Zhizheng Siming xuzhi* 6; Nanjing: *Zhizheng Jinling xinzhi* 7. These categories do not appear in earlier editions of these gazetteers. For Zhenjiang, compare *Jiading Zhenjiang zhi* (1224) 4. For Ningbo, compare *Yanyou Siming zhi* (1320) 12; *Baoqing Siming zhi* (1227) 5–6. For Nanjing, compare *Jingding Jiankang zhi* (1264) 40.

33 Various Ningbo counties reported rivers (*he*), streams (*xi*), canals (*cao*), and lakes (*hupo*). See *Zhizheng Siming xuzhi* 4. Various Nanjing counties reported floodplains (*caodao*), reed land (*ludi*), and reed pools (*ludang*). See *Zhizheng Jinling xinzhi* 7. Note that the translations for these land types are provisional. It is not entirely clear what the difference is between the three or four types of ponds/pools/lakes (*tang, chi, dang, hupo*). Based on the words used as modifiers, *tang* most likely referred to engineered ponds dug to store water or raise fish, while *dang* probably referred to seminatural ponds and pools. The use of *chi* in Ningbo and *tang* in Nanjing suggests that these were used as equivalents. *Hupo* suggests a larger natural lake, perhaps a share of fishing grounds in a lake or bay. While not appearing here, larger man-made reservoirs generally used the term *bei*.

34 I have only found direct evidence of this standardization in the four prefectures cited above, all in Jiangnan (and formerly the Song circuits of Jiangnan Dong or Zhejiang Xi). While officials were sent to Jiangxi and Henan, I have found no clear evidence of the results of their registration efforts aside from the short account and summary statistics in *Yuan History* 93. It appears that reforms did not take effect in the southern portion of Jiangzhe, which included Fujian (see discussion later in chapter).

35 Dardess, "End of Yüan Rule," 575–84.

36 Liang Fangzhong, *Mingdai fuyi zhidu*, 5–8.

37 Ho, *Studies on the Population of China*, 101–16.

38 Ray Huang, "Ming Fiscal Administration," 127.

39 Ray Huang, "Ming Fiscal Administration," 128.

40 A hastily compiled cadastre from Qimen County bears a Longfeng reign date, from the short-lived "Song restoration" of Han Lin'er. *Qimen shisi du wu bao yulin ce* [Fish-scale register of Qimen County sector 40 *bao* 5], in *Huizhou qiannian qiyue wenshu—Song-Yuan-Ming bian*, vol. 11. Based on evidence from contemporary deeds this register was probably the product of local *baojia* self-defense groups (LDQY 578–79 #449–50, 585 #455).

41 Comparing land registration figures for 1315, 1369, and 1392 in *Hongzhi Huizhou fuzhi* and *Huizhou fu fuyi quanshu*. The absence of forest registers in Qimen and Wuyuan was the result of tax breaks granted by a short-lived regional regime during the 1350s. See appendix A.

42 Zhejiang: Liang Fangzhong, *Mingdai fuyi zhidu*, 5–8. Jiangxi: Jin, *Mingdai lijia zhi*, 11–12.

43 Ho, *Studies on the Population of China*, 107–8.

44 Ray Huang, "Ming Fiscal Administration."
45 Jin, *Mingdai lijia zhi*, 11–12. Note that the rapidly surveyed northeast corner of Jiangxi, including Raozhou and Guangxin Prefectures, was part of East Jiangnan in the Song and Jiangzhe in the Yuan. Their institutional history is therefore more similar to more easterly parts of Jiangnan than to central and western Jiangxi.
46 Reported acreage figures start in 1391 in almost all extant Ming gazetteers from Jiangxi, the one exception being Fuzhou 撫州. Total acreage in Fuzhou was 24 percent higher in 1391 than in the mid-thirteenth century (probably 1260–64). Population figures were compiled at least once in the Yuan, but acreage figures were not, suggesting that Fuzhou 撫州—like Fuzhou 福州 and Quanzhou—may have relied on nominal acreage figures in the Yuan.
47 Liang Fangzhong, *Mingdai fuyi zhidu*, 5–8.
48 "Landholdings," *Zhengde Fuzhou fuzhi* 7–10.
49 "Landholdings," *Wanli Quanzhou fuzhi* 7.
50 "Landholdings," *Jiajing Guangdong tong zhi chugao* 23.
51 Ray Huang, "Ming Fiscal Administration," 128.
52 "Yellow Registers" [Huang ce], *Da Ming huidian* 20.
53 Liang Fangzhong, *Mingdai fuyi zhidu*, 18–22; Luan, *Ming dai huangce yanjiu*.
54 Note that these terms were generally not used in official documents, which called all cadastres *ji*. But they appear frequently in government-adjacent accounts, including unofficial histories and local gazetteers. The term "fish-scale diagrams" (*yulin tu*) appeared as early as the Southern Song.
55 *Ming shi* 77.
56 Ray Huang, *Taxation and Governmental Finance*, 11–29.
57 As early as 1393, parts of Zhejiang, Jiangxi, and Fujian were allowed to send their summer tax in cash instead of grain or cloth. Shortly thereafter, northern Jiangxi, Zhejiang, and Songjiang Prefecture were allowed to pay their fall tax in cotton instead of grain. Jin, *Mingdai lijia zhi*, 50, 61–62.
58 Semiofficial tax intermediaries included the heads of administrative villages (*lizhang*), who served on a decennial rotation and were primarily responsible for their villages' tax payments. In particularly wealthy areas, there were also special "tax captaincies" (*liangzhang*). The system of tax captaincies was only formalized in the Southern Metropolitan Region, Zhejiang, Jiangxi, Fujian, and Huguang; it was implemented to a lesser degree in Shandong, Shanxi, and Henan. Ray Huang, *Taxation and Governmental Finance*, 37; Jin, *Mingdai lijia zhi*, 72–73. See also Liang Fangzhong, *Mingdai liangzhang zhidu*.
59 This estimate is based on data from Jiangxi gazetteers. See appendix A.
60 On the likely reduction of tax rates following the 1581 surveys, see appendix A.
61 "Landholdings," *Bamin tong zhi* (1505) 21; "Landholdings," *Zhengde Fuzhou fuzhi* (1520) 7.
62 Because this acreage uses the fiscal rather than the areal *mu*, we cannot be sure how much area these registered forests actually covered, but the figures do roughly demonstrate the economic importance to private forests in the region.

63 Chen Quanzhi, "Jiangxi," *Pengchuang rilü* 1.
64 The importance of tung and camellia oil to the local economy is revealed by the taxes imposed on oil presses. "Excise Taxes" [Kecheng], *Zhengde Yuanzhou fuzhi* 2.
65 Dardess, "Ming Landscape," 348–49.
66 The growth of commercial forestry is suggested by the different ways timber is graded in the Ganzhou tariff. One category applies to free-floated timber (*qingshui liu*), which is not parsed by variety and is probably from wild growth. Other categories apply specifically to fir, tung, pine, etc. See "Monopoly Administration" [Quanzheng zhi], *Tianqi Ganzhou fuzhi* 13.
67 "Land Taxes," *Guangdong tong zhi chugao* 23. On Su Shi's pine-planting techniques, see chapter 1. For more on tenancy contracts, see chapter 4.
68 Qu Dajun, "Fir," *Guangdong xinyu*, translated in Elvin, *Retreat of the Elephants*, 77, with minor modifications.
69 "Fir," *Qianlong Hengyang xianzhi* 3.
70 "Customs" [Fengsu], *Qianlong Qiyang xianzhi* 30.
71 Fang et al., *Atlas of Woody Plants in China*, 22, 27.
72 Lee, "Forests and the State," 73–74.
73 Kain and Baigent, *Cadastral Survey*, 331–32; Warde, *Invention of Sustainability*, 183–92; Totman, *Green Archipelago*, 98. Even Venice, a prodigy in forest management, did not conduct comprehensive forest surveys until 1569. See Appuhn, *Forest on the Sea*, 159–63 and passim.
74 Lee, "Forests and the State," 71–75, 88–89.
75 Totman, *Green Archipelago*, chap. 6.
76 Radkau, *Wood*, 106–8, 175–76.

CHAPTER THREE: HUNTING HOUSEHOLDS AND SOJOURNER FAMILIES

1 I owe this insight to Maura Dykstra.
2 See Chien, *Salt and State*; Paul Jakov Smith, *Taxing Heaven's Storehouse*; von Glahn, *Country of Streams and Grottoes*.
3 On timber rafting, see chapter 7.
4 See, e.g., Liang Fangzhong, *Mingdai fuyi zhidu*; Ray Huang, *Taxation and Governmental Finance*.
5 See Twitchett, *Financial Administration under the T'ang*, esp. chap. 3.
6 Smelter households: *Song shi* 133.58, 138.53. Tea households: *Song shi* 35.8, 35.54, 36.33, 137.18–40; Paul Jakov Smith, *Taxing Heaven's Storehouse*. Saltern households: *Song shi* 34.59–61; Chien, *Salt and State*, 41–45.
7 Von Glahn, *Country of Streams and Grottoes*, esp. chap. 3.
8 See, e.g., *Baoyou chongxiu qinchuan zhi* 6.12b; CB 341.36.
9 Wittfogel, "Public Office in the Liao Dynasty"; Wittfogel and Fêng, *History of Chinese Society*; Franke, "Chinese Law in a Multinational Society."
10 Initially, one faction in the Mongol elite wanted to depopulate the north and turn it into pastures. In 1229 or 1230, an official named Begder put forward this

proposal. Yelü Chucai, a Khitan with experience at the Jin court, had recently been appointed the top revenue official for North China. Yelü argued that more revenue could be derived through the regular tax system, and in 1230 he dispatched revenue commissioners, largely former Jin civil servants, to the ten circuits of North China. This allowed the Mongols to begin collecting household-based taxes from the sedentary former Jin subjects in addition to the head tax on steppe nomads and forest peoples in the north. Allsen, "Rise of the Mongolian Empire," 375–78.

11 Mote, "Chinese Society under Mongol Rule," 650–56. "Demographics" [Hukou], *Zhiyuan Jiahe zhi* 6; "Demographics," *Changguozhou tuzhi* 3; "Demographics," *Zhishun Zhenjiang zhi* 3. The first specific mention of craft households in the Yuan History is from 1252 (*Yuan shi* 3). Stephen G. Haw claims that many of the *jiang* households were brought from Central Asia. Haw, "Semu Ren in the Yuan Empire," 2. The creation of military households is harder to pin down, but they are referenced in texts from the thirteenth century. See Hsiao, *Military Establishment of the Yüan Dynasty*, chap. 1. On Confucian households, see Mote, "Chinese Society under Mongol Rule," 645–48; Hymes, "Marriage, Descent Groups, and the Localist Strategy," 107–10.

12 Smelters: *Yuan shi* 5.1, 6, 8, 16–17. At least some smelter households were grouped under the master category of "artisan," but I am not convinced that this was always the case. Salterns: *Yuan shi* 43.65–71; *Siming zhi* (1320) 12.

13 Rossabi, "Reign of Kublai Khan," 448–49.

14 "Demographics," *Nanhai zhi* 6; *Changguozhou tuzhi* 3.

15 *Changguozhou tuzhi* 3.

16 *Zhizheng Jinling xinzhi* 8. Mote, "Chinese Society under Mongol Rule," 655.

17 See Bello, *Across Forest, Steppe, and Mountain*, esp. chap. 2; Schlesinger, *World Trimmed with Fur*.

18 The so-called system of four classes is overwhelmingly based on an interpretation of just two sources: the essay "Clans" [Shizu], *Chuogeng lu* 1, and "Examinations" [Xuanju zhi], *Yuan shi* 81. Yet this interpretation has been widely accepted in the historiography; e.g., Rossabi, "Muslims in the Early Yüan Dynasty," 65–88; Mote, "Chinese Society under Mongol Rule," 627–35. For a more detailed historiography of the concept, see Funada, "Genchō chika no shikimoku."

19 Funada, "Image of the Semu People"; Funada, "Semuren yu Yuandai zhidu, shehui," 162–74. Aspects of Funada's conclusions about Semu people have been critiqued by Stephen G. Haw (see Haw, "Semu Ren in the Yuan Empire"), but his general premise stands.

20 For example, in Nanjing, there were two major groupings: "northerners," which included Mongols, "various categories," and Hans, and "southerners," which were parsed into "military, postman, and artisan households" (i.e., those that owed specific labor service) and "undesignated households" (i.e., those that owed generic labor service). In Zhenjiang, households were divided into "locals" (*tuzhuo*), "sojourners" (*qiaoyu*)—including Mongols, Uighurs, Jurchens, and

"Han"—and "tenants" (*ke*). Far from a Mongol perspective, these evidence a southern bias that grouped "Han" farmers with Mongols as "northerners" or "sojourners." *Zhizheng Jinling xinzhi* 8; *Zhishun Zhenjiang zhi* 3.

21 *Ming Taizu shilu* 135, cited in Jin, *Mingdai lijia zhi*, 10. See also chapter 2.

22 Leading households were specified based on a combination of the number of working-age men (*ding*) and crop yield (*liang*). Some had fewer than ten *li* households, or fewer than ten tithings; others contained supernumerary ones—generally households without land. Cadastral villages were further grouped into hierarchies of wards (*tu* or *li*) and townships (*du*). See Brook, *Chinese State in Ming Society*, 19–35; Ray Huang, "Ming Fiscal Administration," 134–36.

23 These divisions were based on earlier subcounty divisions, including the Song's *baojia* system and the *she* organizations created in North China in the Yuan. Named cantons (*xiang*) were inherited directly from the Song and Yuan but fell out of official use in favor of numbered townships (*du*). Townships had origins in the *baojia* system of the 1070s but were first widely implemented in the Yuan and Ming. They were the main basis of land surveys, and extant cadastres are largely organized by *du*. Wards (*tu*) literally mean "maps" and probably originated from the divisions of aerial plot diagrams first produced during the twelfth-century boundary surveys. See Brook, *Chinese State in Ming Society*, 17–41.

24 Ray Huang, *Taxation and Governmental Finance*, 34–36.

25 Itō, *Sō Gen gōson shakai shiron*.

26 Faure, *Emperor and Ancestor*; Liu Zhiwei, *Zai guojia yu shehui zhijian*.

27 "Population" [Hukou] and "Salt and Tea Regulations" [Yanfa chafa], *Ming shi* 77, 80.

28 He and Faure, "Introduction: Boat-and-Shed Living," 6.

29 Yang Peina, "Government Registration in the Fishing Industry."

30 "Hunting and Gathering" [Bu cai], *Da Ming huidian* 191. A local example is found in "Land Tax" [Tianfu pian], *Jiajing Chizhou fuzhi* 4.

31 Liang Fangzhong, *Mingdai fuyi zhidu*, 96–97; "Fuel" [Chaitan] and "Reed Taxes along the River" [Yan jiang lu ke], *Da Ming huidian* 205, 208.

32 These examples are drawn from the *Jiangxi sheng fuyi quanshu*, *Yongzheng Zhejiang tongzhi*, and *Bamin tong zhi*. Despite different names, tribute and other goods levies were effectively forms of corvée. Jin, *Mingdai lijia zhi*, 73, quotes the "Supplement on Matters Related to Jiangxi Corvée Levies" [Jiangxi chaiyi shiyi fu], in Zhang Huang, *Tushubian* 90.51, which says: "All direct tax payments and expenses aside from those paid from the land tax are listed under the administrative village groups [*lijia*]. This means that all the village units of a county are responsible for them." See also Ray Huang, "Ming Fiscal Administration," 134–35.

33 Brook, *Confusions of Pleasure*, 47; Naquin, *Peking*, 109–10; Farmer, *Early Ming Government*, 128.

34 In 1441, 380,000 large timbers were left over from the Yongle reign (Lan, "Ming Qing shiqi de huangmu caiban," 93; Wuyuan Jiang, "Ming Qing chaoting

Sichuan caimu yanjiu," 244; *Ming Yingzong shilu* 65). If we assume this represented one-third of the original total, over a million timbers would have been shipped to Beijing. A contemporary poem notes that a force of eight hundred workers logged four hundred trees (Cao and Li, *Yunnan linye wenhua beike*, 20–21). This suggests a workforce of around two million.

35 Brook, *Confusions of Pleasure*, 47.
36 Von Glahn, *Fountain of Fortune*, 70–74.
37 "Direct Supply, Requisitions, and Construction" [Shanggong cai zao], *Ming shi* 82, translated in Elvin, "Three Thousand Years of Unsustainable Growth," 27, with minor modifications. See also "Hunting and Gathering," *Da Ming huidian* 191.
38 Elvin, "Three Thousand Years of Unsustainable Growth," 27.
39 For more detail on the decline of record keeping in the fifteenth century, see Heijdra, "Socio-economic Development of Rural China," 459–81; Ray Huang, *Taxation and Governmental Finance*; Liang Fangzhong, *Mingdai fuyi zhidu*; and the summary in von Glahn, *Economic History of China*, 286–89.
40 Heijdra, "Socio-economic Development of Rural China," 232–34, gives a great summary of the Japanese scholarship on this issue.
41 Based on a survey of sixteen gazetteers from Ming dynasty Jiangxi that recorded landholding figures for the fifteenth century, only one reported new land figures for either the 1421 or the 1431 survey (Ganzhou), and none reported new figures between 1431 and 1451. Only one of ten Jiangxi gazetteers has population figures between 1421 and 1451 (Ganzhou). The earliest survey for which new figures were recorded was 1461 (Ruizhou and Ganzhou), and the first for which the majority reported figures was 1491. Until the 1580s, these figures were overwhelmingly copies of earlier numbers.
42 Liang Fangzhong, *Mingdai fuyi zhidu*, 228–30. Deng Zhihua, "Ming zhongye," 2. Deng's article lacks page numbers, so I have numbered it sequentially from the first page of the article.
43 Deng Zhihua, "Ming zhongye," 1.
44 Liang Fangzhong, *Mingdai fuyi zhidu*, 279–80.
45 Liang Fangzhong, *Mingdai fuyi zhidu*, 268–69.
46 Hai Rui, "Eight Proposals from Xingguo [County]" [Xingguo ba yi], *Hai Rui ji*, 1. For a similar assessment from around the same time, see Liu Guangji, "Long Memorial on Corvée Levies" [Chaiyi shu], quoted in Liang Fangzhong, *Mingdai fuyi zhi*, 296.
47 Qian Qi, "Long Memorial on Pitying and Renewing the Counties" [Xuxin xian shu], *Kangxi Jiangxi tongzhi* 117.
48 *Guangxu Jiangxi tongzhi* 83, quoted in Liang Fangzhong, *Mingdai fuyi zhidu*, 294.
49 Liang Fangzhong, *Mingdai fuyi zhidu*, 274–75.
50 Liang Fangzhong, *Mingdai fuyi zhidu*, 290–91.
51 Liang Fangzhong, *Mingdai fuyi zhidu*, 290–96. See also Deng Zhihua, "Ming zhongye," 4–5.

52 Liang Fangzhong, *Mingdai fuyi zhidu*, 296–98.
53 Ray Huang, *Taxation and Governmental Finance*, 299–301. As Huang stresses, the surveys took until the late 1580s in some parts of the north and the results were highly uneven.
54 This striking anecdote is quoted from an unnamed source in Deng Zhihua, "Ming zhongye," 5.
55 *Jiajing Chizhou fuzhi* (1546) 4.
56 *Kangxi Jiangxi tongzhi* (1683) 12; *Jiangxi fuyi quanshu* (1622) 1. Ding is the fourth of the "heavenly stems" in the sexegenary cycle, so a more intuitive translation would be the letter "D" warehouse. For more, see "Inner Court Warehouses" [Neifu ku], *Da Ming huidian* 30; Liu Ruoyu, "Inner Court Offices and Duties" [Neifu yamen zhezhang], *Zhuozhong zhi* 16.
57 Based on figures from *Jiangxi sheng fuyi quanshu* [Jiangxi Province complete tax records] 1.
58 "Fir" [Shan], *Yongzheng Zhejiang tongzhi* 106, quoting an unnamed edition *Kaihua xianzhi*. See also "Local Practices" [Fengsu], *Qianlong Qiyang xianzhi* 4.
59 "Taxes" [Fushui], *Jiajing Jianping xianzhi* 118.
60 Gerritsen, "Fragments of a Global Past," 128–31; Zurndorfer, "Chinese Merchants and Commerce," 75, 80–84.
61 The literature on Huizhou merchants—especially by scholars in China and Japan—is extremely extensive. Selections include Bian, *Ming Qing Huizhou shehui yanjiu*; Du, *Order of Places*; Fu, *Ming Qing shidai shangren ji shangye ziben*, chap. 2; McDermott, *New Rural Order*, vol. 1; Zurndorfer, *Chinese Local History*.
62 On tariff regulations, see chapter 6.
63 "Fir," *Yongzheng Zhejiang tongzhi* 106.
64 Medley, "Ching-Tê Chên"; Vainker, *Chinese Pottery and Porcelain*, 176–78 and more generally.
65 Dillon, "Jingdezhen Porcelain Industry," 278–90; Dillon, "Jingdezhen as a Ming Industrial Center"; Gerritsen, "Fragments of a Global Past"; Yuan, "Porcelain Industry at Ching-Te-Chen"; Zurndorfer, "Chinese Merchants and Commerce," 80–84.
66 Dillon, "Jingdezhen Porcelain Industry," 278–83; Gerritsen, "Fragments of a Global Past," 143–47.
67 Zurndorfer, "Chinese Merchants and Commerce," 83.
68 McDermott, *New Rural Order*, 1:421–29; Du, *Order of Places*, 54–57. Anecdotes specifically concerning Huizhou timber merchants are collected in Lixing Tang, *Merchants and Society in Modern China*, table 2.1.
69 Leong, *Migration and Ethnicity*; Wing-hoi Chan, "Ethnic Labels in a Mountainous Region"; Coggins, *Tiger and the Pangolin*, 41–45. Leong's and Chan's studies largely overturn older scholarship that claimed that the Hakka came from North China, overwhelmingly based on Luo Xianglin's 1933 *Kejia yanjiu daolun* [An introduction to the study of the Hakka], which itself was based on a small handful of genealogies.

70 Pan 潘, Lan 藍, and Lü 呂—as well as Lei 雷—are the surnames most closely associated with a myth claiming descent from Panhu, which is associated with the Yao and may have been borrowed as part of the formation of the Hakka/She group identity. Wing-hoi Chan, "Ethnic Labels in a Mountainous Region," 272–74.

71 Chen Quanzhi, "Fujian," *Pengchuang rilü* 1.

72 The derivation of this term is controversial, and it was far from universal until modern times. Leong, *Migration and Ethnicity*, 62–68; Wing-hoi Chan, "Ethnic Labels in a Mountainous Region."

73 Leong, *Migration and Ethnicity*, 43–63. On their role in cultivating tobacco: Benedict, *Golden-Silk Smoke*, 37–45. On indigo: Wing-hoi Chan, "Ethnic Labels in a Mountainous Region," 275; Menzies, *Forest and Land Management*, 97–99; O, *Mindai shakai keizaishi kenkyū*, 135.

74 Schlesinger, *World Trimmed with Fur*.

75 Grove and Esherick, "From Feudalism to Capitalism," 409.

76 As Joseph McDermott established in a survey of the contractual evidence and the Chinese- and Japanese-language scholarship, there was far from a single type of bond servant. There were also multiple forms of tenancy, and the borders between the two were often unclear. See McDermott, "Bondservants in the T'ai-hu Basin"; Tanaka, "Popular Uprisings"; Rawski, *Agricultural Change and the Peasant Economy*, chap. 2; Grove and Esherick, "From Feudalism to Capitalism," 407–8.

CHAPTER FOUR: DEEDS, SHARES, AND PETTIFOGGERS

1 The "Huizhou archive" actually consists of thousands of documents collected in several dozen different locations, principally national historical institutions in Beijing and province-level institutions in Anhui, but with notable collections in lower-level archives, in other provinces, and in the United States and Japan. As Joseph McDermott notes, these archives were the results of multiple collection and preservation efforts beginning in the 1940s, and since the 1990s many documents have been reprinted. Despite the multiple ways that documents entered the archive and the large size of the archive overall, there are notable trends that suggest preservation bias. For example, extant forest deeds come overwhelmingly from just two of Huizhou's six counties, Xiuning and Qimen, and land registers are overwhelmingly from Xiuning and neighboring parts of other counties. See McDermott, *New Rural Order*, 1:16–38 and table 0.1.

2 LDQY 809 #653.

3 LDQY 809 #653.

4 LDQY 809 #653.

5 LDQY 809 #653.

6 LDQY 809 #653.

7 Several scholars note the problematic nature of applying Western legal terms and concepts to Chinese law. See, e.g., Ocko, "Missing Metaphor; Bourgon, "Uncivil Dialogue."
8 Zelin, "Rights of Property in Prewar China"; Gardella, "Contracting Business Partnerships."
9 Cohen, "Writs of Passage."
10 MNQY 27 #73.
11 MNQY 28 #74–75.
12 MNQY 28–30 #76–79.
13 Mote, "Rise of the Ming Dynasty," 42–43; "Biography of Han Lin'er" [Han Lin'er zhuan], *Ming shi* 122.
14 LDQY 578–79 #449–50.
15 *Qimen shisi du wu bao yulin ce* [Fish-scale register of Qimen County sector 40 bao 5], in *Huizhou qiannian qiyue wenshu—Song-Yuan-Ming bian*, vol. 11.
16 "Biography of Han Lin'er," *Ming shi* 122.
17 LDQY 585 #455.
18 Luan, *Ming dai huangce yanjiu*.
19 LDQY 754 #599 (1426); 759 #603 (1430); 760–63 #605–6 (1436).
20 This arrangement is noted in the sale of one such property in 1485: LDQY 785 #631.
21 LDQY 759 #603 (1430); 761–62 #606 (1436); 762 #607 (1437); 766 #611 (1441).
22 E.g., LDQY 767 #612 (1446); 773–74 #619 (1459); 777 #622 (1465).
23 Brook, *Chinese State in Ming Society*, 28–29.
24 LDQY 770 #615 (1456); 795 #640 (1502); 833 #673 (1556).
25 LDQY 798–99 #643 (1507); 828 #669 (1557).
26 LDQY 863 #698 (1570); 865 #700 (1571); 888 #719 (1581); 912 #737 (1596); 919 #741 (1601); 926–27 #748 (1607), and several others.
27 LDQY 903 #730 (1592); 969 #783 (1628).
28 Surveying forest deeds (*mai shan qi* or *mai shandi qi*) in LDQY: 1 of 8 properties were subdivided in the thirteenth century (12.5 percent); 9 of 26 (35 percent) in the fourteenth; and 20 of 23 in the fifteenth (87 percent). The small sample size suggests caution. These figures are for a single prefecture, and from a single collection of deeds, so there may also be selection bias at play. Nonetheless, the trend is clear.
29 It is not possible to determine what percentage of land was corporate owned in the Ming. Several works rely largely on the well-organized records of lineage trusts, which therefore have an outside influence on the scholarship. Yet the endowment of corporations to lineage temples was a relatively new innovation in the mid-Ming. It was only in the late Ming and the Qing that it became widespread. McDermott, *New Rural Order*, vol. 1, chap. 5; Miller, "Roots and Branches," chaps. 3–4.
30 From land reform documents of the 1950s, Chen Keyun estimates that more than 60 percent of forest acreage throughout Huizhou was lineage-owned,

corporate land. In some local contexts, this figure was as high as 85–90 percent. Yet she notes that this was not yet the case in the Ming. Chen Keyun, "Cong 'lishi shanlin zhichan bu,'" 78–80. This pattern was not restricted to Huizhou. During the 1930s Nationalist land reform in Nanchang, Jiangxi, the overwhelming majority of forest was lineage owned. This was also the case in Jinhua, Zhejiang, in the 1950s. *Nanchang Shi linye zhi*, 177; Zhong Chong, "Sekkō Shō Tōyō Ken Hokkō Bonchi ni okeru sō zoku no chiri," 361.

31 Yuan Cai, "Timely Planting of Mulberry and Timber," *Yuanshi shifan* 3; and see chapter 1.

32 A handful of deeds did specify physical partitions (e.g., LDQY 887 #718), but they were the exception rather than the rule.

33 The practice of measuring and enumerating trees was important to forestry as it developed in Europe after the sixteenth century. See Scott, *Seeing Like a State*, chap. 1; Lowood, "Calculating Forester"; Appuhn, *Forest on the Sea*, chaps. 4–5.

34 *Gongsi biyong* [Essentials for public and private use], LDQY 591 #460; Chen Xuru, *Chidu shuangyu*, LDQY 1006 #812.

35 Enumerated fruit and oilseed trees: LDQY 865 #700, 1036 #842. I have seen only two deeds enumerating timber trees: LDQY 969 #783 (1629); 994 #803 (1639). McDermott thinks the omission of tree counts may have been because it was difficult to predict how many seedlings would fail. In Japan, seedling success rates on similar plantations were between 0 and 73 percent with the norm below 50 percent. See McDermott, *New Rural Order*, 1:385, 388–89. Figures for Japan from Totman, *Green Archipelago*, 139–40.

36 Several deeds explicitly mentioned that shares had been divided between brothers. LDQY 532 #412, 558–59 #432, 574 #444. See also LDQY 555–56 #429, 574–75 #444–45.

37 E.g., LDQY 903 #730 (chestnuts); 908 #734 (chestnuts and bond servant houses).

38 McDermott, *New Rural Order*, 1:377–78, 380–81, 396–99, and passim.

39 E.g., LDQY 809 #653, 877–78 #710.

40 This landlord-planter division is attested indirectly in the late 1360s and the 1370s in deeds selling forest "bones," with "forest rental contracts" (*zushan qi*) becoming common by the mid-1400s. Chen Keyun, "Cong 'lishi shanlin zhichan bu,'" 80–81; McDermott, *New Rural Order*, 1:402–3; Yang Guozhen, *Ming Qing tudi qiyue wenshu yanjiu*, 148. There might be additional levies on tenants in the form of rice, chicken, silver, liquor, cash, or firewood. Chen Keyun argues that fixed rent rates rose or fell according to the amount of time, work, and additional rent a tenant might have to pay for supplementary crops of grain, etc. According to Yang Guozhen, the most common tenant/owner split was 50-50, but varied between 25 and 75 percent, which is also true in the contracts I have surveyed. According to McDermott's own work, the landlord rarely took less than 50 percent, and more commonly 70 percent—the same share of the rice crop generally taken by landlords.

41 LDQY 791 #636.

42 Chen Keyun, "Cong 'lishi shanlin zhichan bu,'" 82–83.
43 McDermott, *New Rural Order*, 1:373.
44 LDQY 1040–49 #846–55.
45 Chen Keyun, "Ming Qing Huizhou shanlin jingying zhong de 'lifen' wenti." See also, e.g., LDQY 1046–49 #853, 855.
46 McDermott, *New Rural Order*, 1:405–6.
47 LDQY 757–58 #601.
48 LDQY 775–76 #621.
49 McDermott, *New Rural Order*, 1:398.
50 E.g., LDQY 766 #611, 767 #612.
51 McDermott, *New Rural Order*, 1:389. McDermott calls these "total lists."
52 The use of decimal shares to ease tax accounting is implicit in the timing of these changes and is made explicit in several later deeds. LDQY 1210–11 #984 (1728); 1219 #992 (1733); 1513 #1238 (1786). On the single whip reforms, see chapter 3.
53 LDQY 881–82 #713. While calculated as acreage equivalents, given the small proportions involved it is inconceivable that these plots were actually divided.
54 The decimal shares in these segments may have originally been derived from fractional shares. The proportions are 0.083 (one-twelfth, rounded to three decimal places); 0.109 (an error for one-ninth?); 0.125 (one-eighth); and 0.042 (one-twenty-fourth, rounded to three places). This seller owned one-eighteenth share of these four plots, so the deed then calculated the decimal proportion as totaling 0.01995. He further owned a one-eighteenth share of a 0.29 share plot. LDQY 894–95 #724.These figures are given as acreage equivalents, but the initial figures appear to be proportions of one. It is unclear from context whether this meant that they reflected actual acreages or simply proportions of equal-size or equal-yield plots.
55 Needham and Wang, *Mathematics and the Sciences*, 108–10.
56 LDQY 1074–90 #880–89; earliest example is 1437. McDermott calls these "pacts."
57 LDQY 1045–47 #852–54 (1507); McDermott, *New Rural Order*, 1:393n79.
58 Bian, *Ming Qing Huizhou shehui yanjiu*, 178–81, 378–79, 389–90; McDermott, *New Rural Order*, 1:392–93.
59 McDermott, *New Rural Order*, 1:393.
60 McDermott has observed a single planter working as many as eleven plots, just enough to work each plot for three years (or two plots per year for six years) before returning to the first after thirty-some years for the timber harvest. McDermott, *New Rural Order*, 1:410–11.
61 E.g., LDQY 1043 #849 (1470).
62 McDermott, *New Rural Order*, 1:401.
63 McDermott, *New Rural Order*, 1:427–28.
64 LDQY 1047–48 #854.
65 To some degree, this was a product of design. Zhu Yuanzhang sought to make the *Great Ming Code* an unchanging legal document. But despite his wishes,

new precedents began to pile up in the late fifteenth century and were compiled in increasingly formal legal guides in the sixteenth century. See Langlois, "Code and ad hoc Legislation." Nonetheless, I have found essentially no new precedent on these articles and their subsections on forests and timber in any of the major Ming legal compilations, including the *Huang Ming tiaofa shilei zuan* [Categorized regulations of the August Ming], the *Jiajing xinli* [New precedents of the Jiajing reign], the *Jia Long xinli* [New precedents of the Jiajing and Longqing reigns], and the Wanli edition *Da Ming huidian* [Collected statutes of the Great Ming] included in the *Siku quanshu*.

66 Yonglin, *Great Ming Code*, xl–lv.
67 "Fraudulently Selling Fields and Houses" [Daomai tianzhai], *Da Ming lü*, Article 99. Compare to *Tang Code*, Article 405; *Song xingtong*, Article 405. Here and throughout, the *Great Ming Code* translation is modified from Yonglin, *Great Ming Code* (emphasis is mine).
68 "Stealing Wheat and Rice from Fields" [Dao tianye gumai], *Da Ming lü*, Article 294. Compare to *Tang Code*, Article 291; *Song xingtong*, Article 291.
69 "Discarding or Destroying Things Such as Utensils and Crops" [Qihui qiwu jiahao deng], *Great Ming Code*, Article 104. Compare to *Tang Code*, Article 442; *Song xingtong*, Article 442.
70 Lee, "Forests and the State," 75 and nn. 82–83.
71 Aoki, "Kenshō no chiiki-teki imēji." See also Miller, "Roots and Branches," chap. 2. The classic English-language study of pettifoggers is Macauley, *Social Power and Legal Culture*, but Macauley focuses on the Qing, when Fujian had largely superseded Jiangxi as the most notorious site of litigation.
72 Yang Yifan et al., editors' preface to *Lidai zhenxi sifa wenxian* [Rare legal documents from successive dynasties], 1–3. See also Will et al., *Official Handbooks and Anthologies*, sec. 4.3, "Magistrates Handbooks: Handbooks for Pettifoggers."
73 Nakajima, *Mindai goson no funso to chitsujo*. See also Dykstra, "Complicated Matters," esp. chaps. 3, 6, and 7. Note that *xishi* is generally translated as "petty matters." Dykstra translates it somewhat against the grain as "complicated matters." While the former is a more direct translation, the latter does provide some of the connotations of how it is sometimes employed.
74 While the suits in *Critical Points* were modified to remove identifying information, they are specific enough to suggest that they were adapted from real cases. In fact, several cases are similar enough to specific suits from late fourteenth- and fifteenth-century Huizhou to suggest that *Critical Points* accurately reflected the legal environment of mid-Ming Huizhou. For example, several cases in EBKQ 9–13 are quite similar to specific cases summarized in Nakajima, *Mindai goson no funso to chitsujo*, 78–79.
75 "In the Matter of Forcibly Seizing a Hereditary Property" [Qiangduo shiye shi], EBKQ 9–10.
76 "In the Matter of Tyrannically Seizing a Hereditary Property" [Baduo shiye shi], EBKQ 10.

77 "In the Matter of Plotting to Steal a Property with Clear Ownership" [Mou duo mingye shi], EBKQ 10–11.
78 "In the Matter of Destroying Shares and Occupying the Whole" [Mie fen tun zhan shi], EBKQ 11.
79 "In the Matter of Encouraging a Crowd to Seize a Property" [Gu zhong duo ye shi], EBKQ 11–12.
80 "In the Matter of Fabricating Shares with the Intent to Defraud" [Nie fen qi pian shi], EBKQ 13.
81 "In the Matter of Timber Theft and Assault" [Daomu shangren shi], EBKQ 52.
82 "In the Matter of Forest Wardens Stealing from Their Own Property" [Linshou zidao shi], EBKQ 52–53.
83 LDQY 1040 #846 gives a distance of three *chi*; 1048–49 #855 gives a distance of five *chi*. The upper end of the range appears to be more common. Xu Guangqi, *Nongzheng quanshu*, 38.7a, gives four to five *chi*. McDermott, *New Rural Order*, 1:389, gives the smaller estimate of two hundred to three hundred trees per *mu*. Even the larger spacing is quite close compared to modern plantations, where pines are typically two meters or more apart (fewer than two thousand poles per hectare), but it allows for substantial reduction of the crop by intentional thinning or due to die-offs.
84 LDQY 1043 #847, 1041 #849, 1046–47 #853. McDermott, *New Rural Order*, 1:396, 404, 416.
85 McDermott, *New Rural Order*, 1:395–96. LDQY 1044–45 #850–51.
86 On silvicultural practices in the ninth century, see chapter 1.
87 *Nongzheng quanshu* 38.7a. Translated in McDermott, *New Rural Order*, 1:384.
88 Richardson, *Forestry in Communist China*, 88. Richardson explicitly mentions the planting of *Cunninghamia* cuttings amid mature trees (termed "coppice with standards"). Li and Ritchie, "Clonal Forestry in China."
89 Chen Keyun, "Cong 'lishi shanlin zhichan bu,'" 73–75.
90 For a more comprehensive picture of forest transformation based on tax data, see chapter 2 and appendix A.
91 Ye et al., "Factor Contribution to Fire Occurrence." This is one of the few studies on vegetation's contribution to forest fire risk. It focuses on a single county in southern Zhejiang with vegetation, climate, and settlement patterns roughly comparable to those of most of Zhejiang, Fujian, and Jiangxi. In this study, vegetation was only the third most important risk factor, behind human activity and topography, but still accounted for nearly 15 percent of variation. Another recent study of Fujian considered vegetation but found it comparatively less important than factors like topography and settlement density. Guo et al., "Wildfire Ignition."
92 Barros and Pereira, "Wildfire Selectivity."
93 The need to protect young trees from livestock is repeatedly mentioned in references on planting and forest lawsuits. See, e.g., Su Shi as referenced in chapter 1. According to Chris Coggins, ungulates do not typically graze on fir

seedlings, so the primary threat would have been trampling. Coggins, *Tiger and the Pangolin*, 166–67.

94 Zhong and Hsiung, "Tree Nutritional Status"; Jian Zhang et al., "Soil Organic Carbon Changes"; Wang, Wang, and Huang, "Comparisons of Litterfall."

95 Menzies, *Forest and Land Management*, chaps. 4–5.

96 Fengshui is a system of thought that incorporates aspects of climate and terrain and more metaphysical notions of positive and negative influences. Historically, it was used principally for determining appropriate sites for houses and graves and their positioning in the landscape. Fengshui forests are a specific intervention to protect the microclimates around sensitive sites by planting or maintaining mature trees. See Coggins, *Tiger and the Pangolin*, chap. 8; Coggins, "When the Land Is Excellent"; Menzies, *Forest and Land Management*, chap. 5; Miller, "Roots and Branches," chap. 6.

CHAPTER FIVE: WOOD AND WATER, PART I: TARIFF TIMBER

1 Albion, *Forests and Sea Power*, chap. 6 and passim; Moore, "'Amsterdam Is Standing on Norway,' Part I" and "Part II"; Funes Monzote, *From Rainforest to Cane Field*, chaps. 2–3; Wing, *Roots of Empire*, chap. 2; Grove, *Green Imperialism*.

2 Albion, *Forests and Sea Power*; Matteson, *Forests in Revolutionary France*; Wing, *Roots of Empire*.

3 Appuhn, *Forest on the Sea*; Radkau, *Wood*, chaps. 2–3; Warde, *Ecology, Economy, and State Formation*.

4 Albion, *Forests and Sea Power*, 141–42; Fritzbøger, *Windfall for the Magnates*; Falkowski, "Fear and Abundance"; Teplyakov, *Russian Forestry and Its Leaders*, 3–5.

5 Imber, *Ottoman Empire*, 294–95; Lee, "Forests and the State"; Mikhail, *Nature and Empire*, chap. 3; Mikhail, *Under Osman's Tree*, chap. 8; Totman, *Green Archipelago*; Totman, *Lumber Industry*.

6 Moore, "Amsterdam Is Standing on Norway,' Part II"; Radkau, *Wood*, 112–18.

7 The Yangzi River basin, at 1.8 million square kilometers, is bigger than the entire Baltic Sea catchment of about 1.6 million square kilometers. The Rhine basin covers approximately 185,000 square kilometers, compared to over 750,000 for the Yellow River. No Chinese state ever controlled the entire catchments of both the Yellow and the Yangzi Rivers, but the Yuan, Ming, and Qing came close. By contrast, Holland never came anywhere near controlling the entirety of Rhine or Baltic timber markets, let alone the entire territory of their watersheds. Add in the greater productivity of forests in South China compared to northern Europe, and large Chinese empires like the Yuan and Ming probably controlled at least ten times the timber trade of Holland at its peak, although there are no comprehensive statistics to assess this claim.

8 See Twitchett, *Financial Administration under the T'ang*, chap. 3.

9 "Miscellaneous Taxes" [Zashui], *Tang huiyao* 84. See also *Xin Tang shu* 52.

10 There was a proportional in-kind tax collected on at least some mines, but mine products were more often taxed by production quotas or government purchase. SHY *shihuo* 34.20b, and 33–34 generally; CB 375.63, 389.64. On the Guangzhou tariff, see CB 275.11, 331.102, 334.56, 341.27, 483.13.
11 Bamboo and timber depots were initially established in both Jingdong and Jingxi Circuits (the circuits to the east and west of the capital), although after 1011 the eastern one was eliminated and the bamboo and timber tariff was concentrated at the Jingxi depot. SHY *shihuo* 55.120. Coal: SHY *shihuo* 54.11a. Bamboo slats: SHY *shihuo* 54.98.
12 SHY *shihuo* 55.3a.
13 SHY *shihuo* 54.15a–b.
14 Officials posted to the Jingxi timber depot: CB 258.65, 282.3. An official was posted to Jingdong in 1098, suggesting that the eastern depot was reopened at some point. CB 501.61. The collection of tariffs is indirectly attested in many other locations in the anecdotes cited herein.
15 *Sansi* literally means "three bureaus." It emerged after the An Lushan Rebellion when officials were appointed to serve concurrently in the General Accounts Bureau (Duzhi), the Board of Revenue (Hubu), and the Salt and Iron Commission (Yantie)—three offices that each controlled a large portion of official revenue. In the Song, they were merged into a single office that retained the old name.
16 CB 42.48, 97.113.
17 CB 97.113.
18 SHY *shihuo* 55.3a. Other similar orders were issued occasionally throughout the dynasty. See also CB 422.36.
19 CB 78.66.
20 CB 100.29.
21 SHY *shihuo* 17.10b, 14a–b, 17b, 24b, 25b, 30a–b; CB 62.145, 173.83, 252.6, 291.62.
22 Corruption in 980: CB 21.47, 51, 61. In 1017: SHY *shihuo* 17.17a; CB 71.166. In 1080: CB 304.47.
23 Shiba, "Business Nucleus," 110–16.
24 Shiba, *Commerce and Society*, 6–14, 93.
25 Mihelich, "Polders and the Politics of Land Reclamation" (figure is at 193); Shiba, "Environment versus Water Control."
26 Von Glahn, "Ningbo-Hakata Merchant Network," 251–62, 269–70. See also von Glahn, *Economic History of China*, 262–65, 270–73.
27 The few instances of official woodcutting that I have found served immediate strategic ends; they were not intended as sources of ordinary building timber.
28 SHY *shihuo* 17.33b, 17.34b.
29 SHY *shihuo* 17.35b, 18.1b, 30a; JYFN 199.9.
30 SHY *shihuo* 17.34b.
31 Zhao Yushi, *Bin tui lu* 9, cites two accounts of these events, one from Hong Mai, *Yijian wu zhi* [Record of the listener E], and another from *Fu xiu yuemu ji*.

32 SHY *shihuo* 17.35a; SHY *shihuo* 18.2b, 18.3b, 24a–b; JYFN 181.49; Chen Rong, *Zhongguo senlin shiliao*, 34.
33 SHY *shihuo* 50.10a–12b; JYFN 101.15.
34 JYFN 164.59, 199.9; SHY *bing* 6.18a–b.
35 SHY *shihuo* 17.34b.
36 JYFN 174.40.
37 SHY *shihuo* 18.9a.
38 SHY *shihuo* 18.9a.
39 SHY *bing* 6.19a, *shihuo* 18.4a.
40 SHY *bing* 6.20a.
41 SHY *shihuo* 17.41a–b.
42 Fan Chengda, *Canluan lu*, entry for 1173 (*guisi* [year in the hexadecimal cycle]) 1.3.
43 SHY *shihuo* 18.23b.
44 SHY *shihuo* 18.29b–30a.
45 Chen Rong, *Zhongguo senlin shiliao*, 34.
46 SHY *shihuo* 17.44b.
47 SHY *xingfa* 2.127.
48 SHY *shihuo* 18.27b–28a.
49 Schurmann, *Economic Structure of the Yüan Dynasty*, 160–62.
50 *Hongzhi Huizhou fuzhi* 3.318; *Hongzhi Huizhou fuzhi* 7.616.
51 Total receipts from the tax station were around thirty thousand strings of cash in the late eleventh century and about twenty-seven thousand strings in the early thirteenth century, most of which were from commercial taxes rather than the bulk goods tariff. In 1320, the tax office yielded around sixty-five thousand strings of cash, of which just fewer than three thousand were from the tariff. Based on the 1320 figures, about 5 percent of these total revenues came from the tariff on timber and bamboo. *Zhishun Zhenjiang zhi* 6.390.
52 *Hongwu Suzhou fuzhi* 8.365; *Hongzhi Taicang zhouzhi* 100; *Jiajing Taicang zhouzhi* 9.667; *Gu Su zhi* 15.996.
53 While details are not forthcoming, I suspect that this integration was a product of the Yanyou Reorganization (1314–20). See Hsiao, "Mid-Yuan Politics"; Schurmann, *Economic Structure of the Yüan Dynasty*, 24–26, 31; "Reorganization" [Jingli], *Yuan shi* 93. See also discussion on the reorganization in chapter 2.
54 Schurmann, *Economic Structure of the Yüan Dynasty*, 160–62.
55 *Hongwu Suzhou fuzhi* 8.365, 8.368, 9.381, 9.428; *Hongzhi Taicang zhouzhi* 100; *Jiajing Taicang zhouzhi* 9.667; "Tariffs" [Choufen] *Gu Su zhi* 15.
56 Liang Fangzhong, *Mingdai fuyi zhidu*, 96–97; "Fuel" [Chaitan], *Da Ming huidian* 205.
57 Xi Shu, preface to *Caochuan zhi* 1.
58 "Tariffs," *Da Ming huidian* 204; "Food and Commodities 5" [Shihuo wu], *Ming shi* 81.

59 Sarah Schneewind has called into question the extent of Hongwu's ability to enforce his edicts in the countryside. On the other hand, Richard von Glahn argues that Hongwu's edicts were highly destructive to the trade in the lower Yangzi region. For their extended debate on the issue of the extent of the Hongwu emperor's power, see Schneewind, "Ming Taizu *Ex Machina*," and von Glahn, "Ming Taizu *Ex Nihalo*?"
60 "Tariffs," *Da Ming huidian* 204; *Ming shi* 81.
61 *Caochuan zhi* 1.
62 "Ships" [Chuanshou], *Da Ming huidian* 200.
63 Li Min, "Record of the Board of Works Branch Office Name Inscription" [Gongbu fensi timing ji], *Jiajing Renhe xianzhi* 14.
64 "Military Farms Bureau" [Tuntian qingli si], *Da Ming huidian* 208.
65 "Reed Taxes along the River" [Fan yan jiang luke], *Da Ming huidian* 208.
66 "Fuel Disbursement Quotas" [Ji gai zhi chaitan], *Da Ming huidian* 208.
67 "Military Farms Bureau," *Da Ming huidian* 208; *Ming Taizu shilu* 207.5866.
68 "Tariffs," *Da Ming huidian* 204; "Ships," *Da Ming huidian* 200.
69 "Military Farms Bureau," *Da Ming huidian* 208.
70 "Tariffs," *Da Ming huidian* 204; "Ships," *Da Ming huidian* 200.
71 Fir was the only timber taxed at the lowest rate of one-thirtieth. Other timber varieties taxed at 20 percent included pine, blue sandalwood (*tanmu*), boxwood (*huangyang*), pearwood (*limu*), and the catchall "miscellaneous timber" (*zamu*). Pine and fir were the only two types of cut lumber listed in the tax schedule. Fuels included reed fuel (*luchai*), charcoal (*mutan*), mineral coal (*meitan*), and firewood (*muchai*). "Tariffs," *Da Ming huidian* 204. Note that these tax rates are not definitively associated with a date, although they follow the record of the establishment of the Nanjing tariffs in 1393. The source—the *Da Ming huidian*—was first compiled in the late fifteenth century and completed in 1507; I rely on the more widely available second edition completed in 1587. Therefore, while these rates probably reflect the tariff collected in the late fourteenth or early fifteenth century (as is certainly the case for the rates referenced for Beijing), they may instead reflect regulations of the late fifteenth or the sixteenth century. The general rate on commercial goods is given as one-thirtieth in the monograph "Food and Commodities 5," *Ming shi* 81.
72 It is also possible, and indeed likely, that the Ming benefited from greater construction efficiencies and self-imposed thrift that required fewer materials. Nonetheless, the contrast is great enough that the late fourteenth-century Nanjing timber market must have been substantially larger than the late twelfth-century Hangzhou market.
73 *Ming shi* 81; "Tariffs," *Da Ming huidian* 204.
74 "Tariffs," *Da Ming huidian* 204. The low rates on straw at Beijing, compared to very high rates at Nanjing, probably reflected the high costs of overland transport.
75 "Tariffs," *Da Ming huidian* 204.

76 "Customs Stations" [Guan], *Wanli Shaoxing fuzhi* 109.
77 "Material Quotas" [Liao e], *Caochuan zhi* 4.
78 "Tariffs," *Da Ming huidian* 204.
79 On administrative retrenchment in the mid-1400s, see chapters 2 and 3.
80 *Jiajing Zhejiang tongzhi* 13.
81 "Jiujiang Customs Station" [Jiujiang guan], *Guangxu Jiangxi tongzhi* 87.
82 "Jiujiang Customs Station," *Guangxu Jiangxi tongzhi* 87.
83 *Jiajing Nangong xianzhi* 107.
84 *Jiajing Zhejiang tongzhi* 13.
85 "Jiujiang Customs Station," *Jiajing Zhejiang tongzhi* 13.
86 "Construction and Development" [Jianzhi yange], *Jiajing Huguang tujing zhishu* 2021.
87 "Material Quotas," *Caochuan zhi* 4. The date of this last request is not provided in the source, but is most likely shortly prior to 1501, the date of the first edition of the text. For more on shipbuilding quotas, see chapter 6.
88 Li Min, "Record of the Board of Works Branch Office Name Inscription," *Jiajing Renhe xianzhi* 14.
89 In the late 1400s, Hangzhou collected four thousand taels' worth of timber and bamboo per annum. Revenue grew to fourteen thousand taels by the mid-1500s. *Jiajing Zhejiang tongzhi* 13.
90 For details on timber price inflation at the shipyards, see chapter 6.
91 Allowing for 70 percent inflation in timber prices, the 3.5-fold increase in total revenue would indicate that the volume of timber increased by just under 106 percent. These figures must be used with caution. The inflation figures are based on estimates from two different institutions, both based near Nanjing. These are almost certainly inexact. The tariff revenue figures are more reliable, but are from Hangzhou, which tapped a distinct timber market.
92 Linear size appears primitive, but this measure is still used to calculate shipping rates for packages and luggage size for airlines.
93 The text also specifies a rate of 17.55 taels for 3.6 linear *zhang*, which should be 17.503 based on the arithmetic. The very minor difference suggests an error in calculation rather than a different rate for larger rafts.
94 "Jiujiang Customs Station," *Guangxu Jiangxi tongzhi* 87.
95 "Ganzhou Customs Station" [Gan guan], *Guangxu Jiangxi tongzhi* 87.
96 *Tianqi Ganzhou fuzhi* 13.
97 See Meng Zhang, "Timber Trade along the Yangzi River," chap. 1. Zhang's forthcoming monograph is based on this research.

CHAPTER SIX: WOOD AND WATER, PART II: NAVAL TIMBER

1 Glete, *Warfare at Sea*.
2 Albion, *Forests and Sea Power*; Appuhn, *Forest on the Sea*; Bamford, *Forests and French Sea Power*; Grove, *Green Imperialism*; Moore, "'Amsterdam Is Standing on Norway,' Part I" and "Part II"; Wing, *Roots of Empire*.

3 On Ottoman sea power, see Brummett, *Ottoman Seapower and Levantine Diplomacy*; Casale, *Ottoman Age of Exploration*. On timber for shipbuilding, see Imber, *Ottoman Empire*, 294–95; Mikhail, *Under Osman's Tree*, 153–55, 270–71nn4–5, 272n9. On Korean sea power, see Lee, "Forests and the State"; Lee, "Postwar Pines."
4 Andrade, *Gunpowder Age*; Needham, Wang, and Robinson, *Physics*, 279–88; Needham et al., *Military Technology*.
5 In Chinese history, conquest almost always came from the north; the two major exceptions were the Ming in the late 1360s and the Nationalists in the late 1920s. The importance of the Yangzi River frontier for southern defense (and northern advance) was reflected as late as 1949, when the Nationalists chose to use their fleet to retreat to Taiwan rather than defending the river against the Communists. With almost no navy of their own, the Communists were able to piece together one from Nationalist defectors, cross the Yangzi, and complete their reunification of mainland China, much like the Mongols had done nearly seven hundred years earlier.
6 Chittick, "Dragon Boats and Serpent Prows"; Chittick, "Song Navy."
7 Sasaki, *Lost Fleet*, 42–46 and passim.
8 Chaffee, *Muslim Merchants of Premodern China*; Sen, *Buddhism, Diplomacy, and Trade*; Billy K. L. So, *Prosperity, Region, and Institutions*.
9 Billy K. L. So, *Prosperity, Region, and Institutions*, 335–36n199; Shiba, *Commerce and Society*, 9–14; Shiba "Ningbo and Its Hinterland," 129–35; Sasaki, *Lost Fleet*, 46–49.
10 Sasaki, *Lost Fleet*, 37–41; Lee, "Forests and the State," 68–77 and passim.
11 Min and Southern Tang were particular naval powers during the period of division. The first detailed description of warships dates to 759. Needham, Wang, and Lu, *Civil Engineering and Nautics*, 439–77; Schottenhammer, "China's Emergence as a Maritime Power," 455–56 and 455n62.
12 Lo, *China as a Sea Power*, 131–32.
13 Chittick, "Song Navy," 12–17.
14 "Armament Regulations" [Qijia zhi zhi], *Song shi* 197; Lo, *China as a Sea Power*, 129–30.
15 Lo, *China as a Sea Power*, 130–32; "Provincial Armies" [Xiangbing], *Song shi* 190.
16 "Provincial Armies," *Song shi* 190.
17 Due to their centrality to Song finances, *transport bureau* (*zhuanyun si*) and *transport commissioner* (*zhuanyun shi*) are sometimes translated as "finance bureau" and "fiscal commissioner."
18 Shiba, *Commerce and Society*, 6–14; SHY *shihuo* 50.2b, 50.3b–4b.
19 For example, in 1082, Li Xian, the eunuch official charged with overseeing the Xihe Logging Bureau, was also in charge of building warships to supply the Xihe garrisons. SHY *shihuo* 50.4b.
20 SHY *shihuo* 50.5b–6a. The superior jurisdictions of Hangzhou and Pingjiang were also ordered to stop issuing permission to cut timber unless approved by imperial writ.

21 SHY *shihuo* 50.6a–b.
22 SHY *shihuo* 50.6b. As originally ordered, 100 passenger ships at 100-timber size and 1,200 ships at 300-timber size would have used 370,000 timbers. With the reduction of the larger ships to 250 timbers, this would have saved 60,000 timbers.
23 For more on the Song retreat, see Tao, "Move to the South," 644–53.
24 Lo, *China as a Sea Power*, 133, 137–38; "Imperial Guard Part 1" [Jinjun shang], *Song shi* 187.
25 "Imperial Guard Part 1," *Song shi* 187. Names are modified from the translation in Lo, *China as a Sea Power*, 133.
26 At an estimated cost of 240,000 strings of cash. SHY *shihuo* 50.8a–9a; Lo, *China as a Sea Power*, 133–34.
27 SHY *shihuo* 50.11a.
28 Schottenhammer, "China's Emergence as a Maritime Power," 467.
29 Lo, *China as a Sea Power*, 138–43; Tao, "Move to the South," 653–55; Franke, "Chin Dynasty," 230–31.
30 SHY *shihuo* 50.12a.
31 SHY *shihuo* 50.14a–15a.
32 Lo, *China as a Sea Power*, 143–45.
33 On the peace of Shaoxing, see Franke, "Chin Dynasty," 233–35; Tao, "Move to the South," 677–84.
34 Tao, "Move to the South," 662–66.
35 Tao, "Move to the South," 665.
36 SHY *shihuo* 50.14a–15a. The name "sampan" comes from *sanban*, or "three boards," referring to small boats used primarily for fishing.
37 Lo, *China as a Sea Power*, 147–48; SHY *shihuo* 50.16a–17b.
38 SHY *shihuo* 50.17a–b. The figures differ slightly from those cited in Lo, *China as a Sea Power*, 148.
39 SHY *shihuo* 50.15a.
40 Franke, "Chin Dynasty," 539–40.
41 Lo, *China as a Sea Power*, 154–55; Franke, "Chin Dynasty," 241.
42 JYFN 96; Hok-Lam Chan, "Organization and Utilization of Labor Service," 657–58.
43 SHY *shihuo* 50.18a–b; Lo, *China as a Sea Power*, 157.
44 SHY *shihuo* 50.18b–20a.
45 Lo, *China as a Sea Power*, 159–63.
46 Lo, *China as a Sea Power*, 163–68; Franke, "Chin Dynasty," 242–43.
47 Franke, "Chin Dynasty," 243.
48 SHY *shihuo* 50.20a–b.
49 According to Ju-pang Lo's reconstruction, the total naval strength increased to over 30,000 men by 1190. While the figures for the 1130s are not complete, there were probably no more than 5,000 regular sailors and marines. Between the 1130s and the 1170s, individual garrisons at Fuzhou and Chizhou increased from 150 to 5,000 and 1,000, respectively. Conservatively, these figures suggest

that the troop strength of the Song navy increased at least five times over this interval, principally in the 1160s and 1170s. Lo, *China as a Sea Power*, 173–74.
50 My estimates, based on manpower figures from Lo, *China as a Sea Power*, 173–74.
51 SHY *shihuo* 50.31b, 33b–34b.
52 Lo, *China as a Sea Power*, 138.
53 SHY *shihuo* 50.9b–10b.
54 Lo, *China as a Sea Power*, 158.
55 Lo, *China as a Sea Power*, 179–80.
56 Shiba, *Commerce and Society*, 6–14, 93.
57 Billy K. L. So, *Prosperity, Region, and Institutions*, 84–85.
58 Shiba, "Ningbo and Its Hinterland," 129–35.
59 SHY *shihuo* 50.10a–b.
60 SHY *shihuo* 22a–23b.
61 Lo, *China as a Sea Power*, 213–17; Rossabi, "Reign of Khubilai Khan," 431–33; Davis, "Reign of Tu-tsung," 920–23. The exact size of the Yuan navy is not clear, but in late 1272 it was reorganized into four commands, each likely the size of Zhang Xi's original directorate of the navy (*shuijun zongguan*), which had four wings of about five hundred ships each. This suggests that the navy may have approached four thousand ships, the bulk of which were small rivercraft.
62 Lo, *China as a Sea Power*, 218.
63 Lo, *China as a Sea Power*, 218–20; "Biography of Bo Yan" [Bo Yan (zhuan)], *Yuan shi* 127.
64 Lo, *China as a Sea Power*, 221–22; "Biography of Bo Yan," *Yuan shi* 127.
65 Lo, *China as a Sea Power*, 223–25. For a more complete narrative of these events from the perspective of the Song court, see Davis, "Reign of Tu-tsung," 932–45.
66 Lo, *China as a Sea Power*, 225–26.
67 Lo, *China as a Sea Power*, 236–45; Rossabi, "Reign of Khubilai Khan," 434–35; Davis, "Reign of Tu-tsung," 946–61.
68 Henthorn, *Korea*, 154–60, 208.
69 Lo, *China as a Sea Power*, 248–52.
70 Lo, *China as a Sea Power*, 253–54; Henthorn, *Korea*, 208–9.
71 Lo, *China as a Sea Power*, 253–54; Henthorn, *Korea*, 208–9; Sasaki, *Lost Fleet*, 25–26, citing Rossabi, *Khubilai Khan*; Ōta, *Mōko shūrai*. Estimates of the number of ships range from 700 (Rossabi) to 900 (Ōta, Lo). Numbers of soldiers range from 23,000 total (Rossabi) to 30,000 total (Lo). Sources are in rough agreement on the number of sailors as 6,700–7,000.
72 Lo, *China as a Sea Power*, 255–58; Sasaki, *Lost Fleet*, 26–28; Rossabi, "Reign of Khubilai Khan," 437–42.
73 Lo, *China as a Sea Power*, 260–63.
74 Robinson, *Empire's Twilight*, 58.
75 Lo, *China as a Sea Power*, 264. After the 1270s, Koryŏ kings married extensively into the Mongol imperial house and positioned themselves as the khans' leading vassals. Sixiang Wang, personal communication.

76 Sasaki, *Lost Fleet*, 32; Lo, *China as a Sea Power*, 266–67.
77 Lo, *China as a Sea Power*, 268–73; Sasaki, *Lost Fleet*, 27–30.
78 Lo, *China as a Sea Power*, 277–79.
79 "Biography of Liu Xuan" [Liu Xuan (zhuan)], *Yuan shi* 168, modified from translation in Lo, *China as a Sea Power*, 281–82.
80 Lo, *China as a Sea Power*, 279–82.
81 Dreyer, "Military Origins of Ming China," 59–60, 64; Mote, "Rise of the Ming Dynasty," 36.
82 Dreyer, "Military Origins of Ming China," 60–63.
83 Mote, "Rise of the Ming Dynasty."
84 There are few direct accounts of this buildup, although Edward Dreyer notes that both Zhu and Chen derived much of their initial fleets from the fisherfolk of Lake Chao. Dreyer, "Military Origins of Ming China," 65–66, 69–70; Dreyer, "Poyang Campaign," 204–5.
85 Dreyer, "Poyang Campaign," 217.
86 Dreyer, "Poyang Campaign."
87 Hok-lam Chan, "Rise of Ming T'ai-tsu," 701–5.
88 Andrade, *Gunpowder Age*, 58–64.
89 Mote, "Rise of the Ming Dynasty," 37.
90 Ouyang Qu, preface to *Longjiang chuanchang zhi* [Treatise on the Longjiang shipyards].
91 Qie Bao, preface to *Chuanzheng xin shu* [New treatise on shipyard administration] 2–3; "Ships" [Chuanzhi], *Da Ming huidian* 200.
92 *Ming Taizu shilu* 207.5b. Chen Rong, *Zhongguo senlin shiliao*, 41. Jacques Gernet mistakenly reads this figure as 50 *million* trees (rather than 500,000), probably based on an error in a different edition of the source text. This larger figure leads Gernet to incorrectly interpret this plantation as anticipating the Zheng He fleets. See Gernet, *History of Chinese Civilization*, 399.
93 "Ships," *Da Ming huidian* 200.
94 *Caochuan zhi* 1.
95 "Tariff Administration" [Choufen zhi shui ban], *Caochuan zhi* 4.
96 "Material Quotas" [Liao e], *Caochuan zhi* 4.
97 Dreyer, *Zheng He*, 117–18; *Ming Taizong shilu* 20A.2b, 22.4a–b, 23.6b, 24.6b.
98 *Ming Taizong shilu* 27.4b–5a.
99 *Ming Taizong shilu* 43.3b.
100 Dreyer, *Zheng He*, 117–18.
101 Wilson, "Maritime Transformations of Ming China," 249–50. This figure may be an exaggeration. Ju-pang Lo points out that many coastal garrisons were not fully staffed. See Lo, *China as a Sea Power*, 331.
102 Levathes, *When China Ruled the Seas*, 75.
103 "Biography of Zheng He" [Zheng He (zhuan)], *Ming shi* 304.
104 Dreyer, *Zheng He*, 102.
105 Delgado, *Khubilai Khan's Lost Fleet*, 24–25.
106 Dreyer, *Zheng He*, 99.

107 Dreyer, *Zheng He*, 121.
108 First published in Levathes, *When China Ruled the Seas*, 21.
109 Goldstone, "Rise of the West—or Not?," 177.
110 Church, "Zheng He," 3–9; Dreyer, *Zheng He*, 104, 217–22.
111 The Liujiagang and Changle inscriptions of 1431 only mention "over a hundred ships." These are translated in Dreyer, *Zheng He*, 191–99, based on earlier translations by J. J. L. Duyvendak; figures are at 192 and 195. See also Church, "Zheng He," 10–11.
112 The rough consensus seems to be that 440-foot ships were possible but that the treasure ships may not have actually reached this size, topping out at perhaps half the recorded dimensions. See Dreyer, *Zheng He*, 102–16; Church, "Zheng He"; Church, Gebhardt, and Little, "Naval Architectural Analysis"; Levathes, *When China Ruled the Seas*, 80–82.
113 Dreyer, *Zheng He*, 121–22.
114 Dreyer, *Zheng He*, 50; Levathes, *When China Ruled the Seas*, 76.
115 See also Church, "Zheng He," 32–34.
116 In the late 1420s and early 1430s, the Yangzi River patrol fleet more than doubled in size, and the Longjiang shipyards continued to build large numbers of seagoing grain ships well into the 1450s. *Longjiang chuanchang zhi* 1, quoting *Da Ming huidian* and a 1428 edict (*Xuande san nian chi*).
117 *Longjiang chuanchang zhi* 1, quoting the [*Nanjing Gongbu*] *zhizhang tiaoli* [Regulations of official duties for the Nanjing Board of Works].
118 "Land Taxes" [Di ke], *Longjiang chuanchang zhi* 5.
119 "Material Quotas," *Caochuan zhi* 4.
120 *Longjiang chuanchang zhi* 1, quoting *Da Ming huidian*.
121 On the drawdown in fleet size, see Levathes, *When China Ruled the Seas*, 174–75.
122 Kwan-wai So, *Japanese Piracy in Ming China*, 52, 55, 61.
123 "Jiujiang Customs Station" [Jiujiang guan], *Guangxu Jiangxi tongzhi* 87.
124 "Material Quotas," *Caochuan zhi* 4.
125 "Material Quotas," *Caochuan zhi* 4. The date of this last request is not provided in the source, but is most likely shortly prior to 1501, the date of the first edition of the text.
126 *Longjiang chuanchang zhi* 1, quoting *Da Ming huidian*.
127 *Chuanzheng* 67.
128 *Chuanzheng* 11–15.
129 Calculated from the figures given in *Longjiang chuanchang zhi* 1 and *Chuanzheng* 67.
130 "Material Quotas," *Caochuan zhi* 4. The earliest preface to the text is dated 1501.
131 *Longjiang chuanchang zhi* 1, quoting *Da Ming huidian*.
132 *Longjiang chuanchang zhi* 1, quoting *Da Ming huidian*.
133 *Caochuan zhi* 1.
134 "Tariffs for Personnel Transports" [Choufen zuochuan], *Longjiang chuanchang zhi* 1.

135 "Established Regulations" [Cheng gui], *Longjiang chuanchang zhi* 1.
136 "Established Regulations," *Longjiang chuanchang zhi* 1.
137 *Chuanzheng* 66.
138 "Established Regulations," *Longjiang chuanchang zhi* 1; "Planks" [Danban], *Longjiang chuanchang zhi* 5.
139 *Chuanzheng* 67. The word for monopolize (*longduan*) literally means to "block a section" and probably derives from the practice of blocking a road or water route to control the price of a good.
140 "Established Regulations," *Longjiang chuanchang zhi* 1; *Chuanzheng* 68.
141 *Chuanzheng* 68–69.
142 "Timber Prices" [Mu jia], *Longjiang chuanchang zhi* 5.
143 *Chuanzheng* 70–73.
144 *Chuanzheng xin shu* 168–71.

CHAPTER SEVEN: BEIJING PALACES AND THE ENDS OF EMPIRE

1 Chinese buildings are made up of a series of bays (*jian*), each consisting of four vertical pillars (*zhu*) and four beams connecting them (*liangfang*; technically the front and back beams are called *fang* and the side beams are called *liang*). The size of the bays, in turn, determines the overall dimensions of the building. Liang Sicheng, *Zhongguo jianzhu shi*, 12–14.
2 Brook, *Confusions of Pleasure*, 47.
3 There are no precise counts of how many timbers were cut during the Yongle logging between 1406 and 1420. We do know that a reported 380,000 timbers cut in the Yongle era remained unused in 1441 (*Ming Yingzong shilu* 65). If we assume this represented one-third of the original total, over a million timbers would have been shipped to Beijing. A contemporary poem notes that a force of eight hundred workers logged four hundred trees (Cao and Li, *Yunnan linye wenhua beike*, 20–21). If this logger-to-log ratio persisted, the labor force supplying Beijing construction would have numbered in the millions.
4 *Jiajing Jianping xianzhi* 2.118; *Jiajing Ningbo fuzhi* 18.1830.
5 Anderson and Whitmore, "Introduction: 'The Fiery Frontier,'" 22–30; Herman, "Cant of Conquest."
6 Lan, "Ming Qing shiqi de huangmu caiban," 93.
7 Campbell, *What the Emperor Built*; Aurelia Campbell, personal communication.
8 "Shu Commandery" [Shu jun], *Han shu bu zhu* 28a.
9 "Chengdu Prefecture, Shu Commandery" [Chengdu fu Shu jun], *Xin Tang shu* 42.
10 SHY *xingfa* 2.124, 2.149.
11 Exchanges of timber for gifts to Dong tribes in Shaozhou in 1085 and in Chengzhou in 1086: CB 356.33, 377.50.
12 Gu Yewang, "Geographic Treatise" [Yudi zhi], quoted in *Taiping yulan, dibu* 13. See also Deng Deming, "Timber Visitors" [Muke], *Nankang ji*, quoted in *Taiping yulan, shengui bu* 4.

13 SHY *xingfa* 2.127.
14 "Timber Administration" [Muzheng zhi], *Jiaqing Zhili Xuyong tingzhi* 29.
15 Cao and Li, *Yunnan linye wenhua beike*, 18. Thanks to Aurelia Campbell for sharing this source with me.
16 "Construction 1" [Yingzao yi], *Da Ming huidian* 181.
17 Cao and Li, *Yunnan linye wenhua beike*, 18–19; Deng Pei, "Lun Ming-Qing shiqi zai Jinshajiang xiayou diqu jinxing de 'muzheng' huodong," 89. See also Campbell, *What the Emperor Built*.
18 *Ming Taizu shilu* 127.1b.
19 "Biography of [Zhu] Chun, Prince Xian of Shu" [Shu Xian wang Chun], *Ming shi* 117.
20 "Construction 1," *Da Ming huidian* 181.
21 "Sichuan Native Offices 1" [Sichuan tusi yi], *Ming shi* 311.
22 "Timber Administration," *Jiaqing Zhili Xuyong tingzhi* 29.
23 For general histories of these events, see Farmer, *Early Ming Government*; Dreyer, *Early Ming China*.
24 Farmer, *Early Ming Government*, 128; Dreyer, *Early Ming China*, 186; Naquin, *Peking*, 109–10.
25 "Food and Commodities 6" [Shihuo zhi liu], *Ming shi* 82.
26 "Timber Administration," *Wanli Sichuan zongzhi* 20; "Timber Administration," *Daoguang Zunyi fuzhi* 18; *Ming shi* 82; *Ming Taizong shilu* 65.1b.
27 "Timber Administration," *Yongzheng Sichuan tongzhi* 16.
28 Cao and Li, *Yunnan linye wenhua beike*, 20.
29 Cao and Li, *Yunnan linye wenhua beike*, 21.
30 Lan, "Ming Qing shiqi de huangmu caiban," 87.
31 *Jiajing Jianping xianzhi* 2.118; *Jiajing Ningbo fuzhi* 18.1830. Note that all of these references are retrospectives from the 1560s or later, by which time the corvée had been commuted to a silver payment.
32 *Ming shi* 81; "Tariffs" [Choufen], *Da Ming huidian* 207; "Materials" [Wuliao], *Da Ming huidian* 190.
33 *Ming Taizong shilu* 139.1b.
34 *Ming Taizong shilu* 146.2a.
35 *Ming Taizong shilu* 152.3a–b.
36 *Ming Taizong shilu* 172.2a.
37 *Ming Renzong shilu* 9a. It is unclear if this halted lumbering in the mountains as well, but the coincidence of this order with the end of Xie An's tenure in Sichuan suggests that it was in fact the end of these projects.
38 In 1425, the Hongxi emperor issued the edict that "wherever the government had placed restrictions [*jin*] on mountain workshops, gardens, forests, lakes, wetlands, kilns and foundries, fruit trees and beehives, all [was] to be returned to the common people." This was followed by further similar edicts under the Xuande emperor. Elvin, "Three Thousand Years of Unsustainable Growth," 27. See also *Da Ming huidian* 191; and chapter 3.

39 "Food and Commodities 6," *Ming shi* 82; *Ming Xuanzong shilu* 79. Until 1441, the court moved back and forth between Beijing and Nanjing. See Farmer, *Early Ming Government*, chap. 5.
40 "Construction 1," *Da Ming huidian* 181.
41 Lan, "Ming Qing shiqi de huangmu caiban," 93; *Ming Yingzong shilu* 65.
42 "Food and Commodities 6," *Ming shi* 82.
43 "Construction 1," *Da Ming huidian* 190.
44 "Sichuan Native Offices 2" [Sichuan tusi er], *Ming shi* 312.
45 "Sichuan Native Offices 2," *Ming shi* 312.
46 "Native Offices" [Tusi], *Ming shi* 310.
47 "Food and Commodities 6," *Ming shi* 82; Campbell, *What the Emperor Built*.
48 "Construction 1," *Da Ming huidian* 181; Campbell, *What the Emperor Built*.
49 Campbell, *What the Emperor Built*.
50 "Food and Commodities 6," *Ming shi* 82.
51 "Timber Administration," *Yongzheng Sichuan tongzhi* 16; *Daoguang Zunyi fuzhi* 18. The ad hoc nature of the timber supervisors was a function of both the irregular nature of requisitions and the general lack of mid-level regional administrators in the Ming hierarchy. See Hucker, *Censorial System of Ming China*.
52 Gui Youguang, "Obituary of Grand Master for Transmitting Proposals, Censorate Vice Censor-in-Chief of the Left Li [Xianqing]" [Tongyi dafu duchayuan zuo fu duyushi Li gong xingzhuang], *Zhenchuan xiansheng ji* 25. Thanks to Aurelia Campbell for sharing this source with me.
53 "Construction 1," *Da Ming huidian* 190.
54 "Construction 1," *Da Ming huidian* 190.
55 "Long Memorial on Large Timber" [Damu shu], *Wanli Guizhou tongzhi* 19.
56 "Food and Commodities 6," *Ming shi* 82.
57 "Food and Commodities 6," *Ming shi* 82.
58 "Long Memorial on Large Timber," *Wanli Guizhou tongzhi* 19.
59 "Food and Commodities 6," *Ming shi* 82.
60 Gui Youguang, "Obituary of Li Xianqing," *Zhenchuan xiansheng ji* 25.
61 "Timber Administration," *Yongzheng Sichuan tongzhi* 16; "Timber Administration," *Kangxi Junlian xianzhi* 3; "Timber Administration," *Kangxi Xuzhou fu Qingfu xian zhi* 2.
62 Gong Hui, *Xi cha huicao* [Essays on timber rafting in the western regions] 1.2a–3b. Thanks to Devin Fitzgerald for informing me about this source. See also "Timber Administration," *Yongzheng Sichuan tongzhi* 16.
63 *Xi cha huicao* 1.2a–3b.
64 *Xi cha huicao* 1.2a.
65 "Logging Administration," *Daoguang Zunyi fuzhi* 18.
66 Gui Youguang, "Obituary of Li Xianqing," *Zhenchuan xiansheng ji* 25.
67 "Native Offices," *Ming shi* 310.
68 "Sichuan Native Offices 2," *Ming shi* 312. *Ming shi* 316 gives the earlier date and *Ming shi* 312 the later.

69 "Guizhou Native Offices" [Guizhou tusi], *Ming shi* 316.
70 "Sichuan Native Offices 2," *Ming shi* 312.
71 "Sichuan Native Offices 2," *Ming shi* 312. The same record also appears as the "Biographies of the Bozhou Yang House" [Bozhou Yang shi], *Zuiwei lu* 34.33a.
72 Swope, "To Catch a Tiger."
73 "Obituary of Li Xianqing." It is not clear from this text whether Guizhou timber was purchased from merchants or cut by state labor teams, although the long memorial cited below suggests that in the 1540s it was still the latter.
74 On standards for timber sizing and pricing in the shipyards, see chapter 6.
75 "Long Memorial on Large Timber," *Wanli Guizhou tongzhi* 19.
76 Meng Zhang, *Sustaining the Market*, chap. 1.
77 "Timber Administration," *Yongzheng Sichuan tongzhi* 16; "Timber Administration," *Daoguang Zunyi fuzhi* 18.
78 Unfortunately, there do not appear to be any extant examples of these logging registers. Presumably, they shared features with both the cadastres detailed in chapter 2 and the lumber purchase forms discussed in chapter 6.
79 Menzies, *Forestry and Land Management*, chap. 8.
80 These figures are somewhat difficult to compare. The 1441 figures are for logs left over in storage, which may have come from any region and do not give an exact figure for total yields. The sixteenth- and seventeenth-century reports give figures for logs cut in the Sichuan-Guizhou region, with only the figure for 1685 reporting the number reaching the capital. The eighteenth-century figures give only the number reaching the capital, without reporting the number cut.
81 Meng Zhang, *Sustaining the Market*, chaps. 1 and 3. See also Zhang Yingqiang, *Mucai zhi liudong*.

CONCLUSION

1 Woodside, *Lost Modernities*.
2 The seminal work on this transition in early northeastern America is Cronon, *Changes in the Land*. There is a particularly extensive literature on wood rights in modern South and Southeast Asia. See, e.g., McElwee, *Forests Are Gold*; Peluso, *Rich Forests, Poor People*; Guha, *Unquiet Woods*.
3 Radkau, *Nature and Power*, 212–21.
4 See, e.g., Grove, *Green Imperialism*; Lowood, "Calculating Forester"; Warde, *Invention of Sustainability*.
5 For example, the distinction between white fir (*baishan*) and red fir (*chishan*) appears to map onto modern taxonomies separating *Cunninghamia* and *Cryptomeria*. See, e.g., "Products" [Wuchan], *Qianlong Ruijin xianzhi* 2. For officials promoting "best practices," see, e.g., "Encouraging the People to Plant Miscellaneous Grains on Empty Mountain Land in This County" [Xian you yushantu quan min zaizong zaliang], *Hunan shengli cheng'an* 7.5a–21b. On the recognition of erosion, see Osborne, "Local Politics of Land Reclamation."

6 Historians of China have begun to question this narrative of decline. See, e.g., Wensheng Wang, *White Lotus Rebels*. Nonetheless, there was a clear change in the tenor of statecraft in the nineteenth century, even before the Opium Wars and the Taiping Rebellion.
7 E.g., Chao, *Man and Land in Chinese History*; Philip C. C. Huang, *Peasant Family and Rural Development*.
8 Key works include Perdue, *Exhausting the Earth*; Marks, *Tigers, Rice, Silk, and Silt*; Vermeer, "Mountain Frontier" and "Population and Ecology"; Kuo-tung Ch'en, "Nonreclamation Deforestation." A useful summary of this scholarship is provided in Marks, *China*, chap. 5.
9 Averill, "Shed People"; Osborne, "Local Politics of Land Reclamation;" Osborne, "Highlands and Lowlands"; Benedict, *Golden-Silk Smoke*; Gardella, *Harvesting Mountains*; Leong, *Migration and Ethnicity*.
10 Ownby, *Brotherhoods and Secret Societies*.
11 Averill, *Revolution in the Highlands*.
12 Erbaugh, "Secret History of the Hakkas"; Leong, *Migration and Ethnicity*.
13 Averill, *Revolution in the Highlands*.
14 Bayly, *Birth of the Modern World*, chap. 12; Lee, "Forests and the State"; Matteson, *Forests in Revolutionary France*; Sahlins, *Forest Rites*.
15 See Miller, "Roots and Branches," chap. 6.

BIBLIOGRAPHY

ABBREVIATIONS

CB   Li Tao, *Xu zizhi tongjian changbian*
EBKQ   Erbi kenqing, in Yang Yifan et al., eds., *Lidai zhenxi sifa wenxian*
JYFN   Li Xinzhuan, *Jianyan yilai fannian yaolü*
LDQY   Zhang Zhuanxi, ed., *Zhongguo lidai qiyue huibian kaoyi*
MNQY   Yang Guozhen, ed., *Minnan qiyue wenshu zonglu*
QYTF   Yang Yifan and Tian Tao, eds., *Qingyuan tiaofa shilei, zhongguo zhenxi falü dianji xu bian*
SHY   *Song huiyao jigao*

PRIMARY SOURCES

Many of the following sources were accessed from digital repositories. To the extent possible, I have indicated the print edition underlying the digital version. For more information, see appendix B. To avoid repetition, I have not translated gazetteers that follow the standard title format. For example, the *Chongzhen Kaihua xianzhi* gives the reign era of the edition (Chongzhen, 1627–44), the place-name (Kaihua), the administrative level (county: *xian*, sub-prefecture: *zhou*, prefecture: *fu*, province: *tong*), and the word "gazetteer" (*zhi*). Nonstandard gazetteer titles are translated individually.

China Text Project, https://ctext.org.
Kanseki Repository, www.kanripo.org.
Wikisource, https://zh.wikisource.org.
World Digital Library, www.wdl.org.

Bamin tong zhi [Fujian provincial gazetteer]. Edited by Chen Dao. Ming Hongzhi edition (1487–1505). Erudition Local Gazetteers Database, First Collection.

Baoqing Siming zhi [Baoqing-era Ningbo gazetteer]. Edited by Hu Qu. Song Baoqing edition (1225–27). Erudition Local Gazetteers Database, First Collection.

Baoyou chongxiu Qinchuan zhi [Baoyou-era revised Qinquan gazetteer]. Edited by Bao Lian. Siku quanshu edition. Erudition Local Gazetteers Database, First Collection.

Bin tui lu [Record of retiring from a visit]. Zhao Yushi. Siku quanshu edition. Wikisource.

Bishu lühua [Notes while avoiding the summer heat]. Ye Mengde. Siku quanshu edition. Wikisource.

Canluan lu [Record of flying with immortals]. Fan Chengda. Siku quanshu edition. Wikisource.

Caochuan zhi [Treatise on transport ships]. Zhu Jiaxiang. Huai'an wenxian congkan edition. Wikisource.

Changguozhou tuzhi [Changguozhou illustrated gazetteer]. Edited by Guo Jian. Qing Xianfeng Siming liu zhi edition. Erudition Local Gazetteers Database, First Collection.

Chidu shuangyu [Double-fish charm of short forms]. Chen Xuru. In *Zhongguo lidai qiyue huibian kaoyi*, edited by Zhang Zhuanxi. Beijing: Beijing daxue chubanshe, 1995.

Chongzhen Kaihua xianzhi. Edited by Zhu Chaopan. Ming Chongzhen edition (1627–44). Erudition Local Gazetteers Database, First Collection.

Chuanzheng [Shipyard administration]. Tianyige Jiajing edition. In *Tianyige cang Mingdai zhengshu zhenben congkan*, edited by Yu Haoxu. Beijing: Xianzhuang shuju, 2010.

Chuanzheng xin shu [New treatise on shipyard administration]. Ni Dong. Siku quanshu edition. China Text Project.

Chunxi Sanshan zhi [Chunxi-era Fuzhou gazetteer]. Siku quanshu edition. Wikisource.

Chunxi Xin'an zhi. Edited by Zhao Buhuai. Qing Jiaqing 17 edition (1812). Erudition Local Gazetteers Database, First Collection.

Chuogeng lu [Record of a respite from plowing]. Tao Zongyi. Wikisource.

Da Ming huidian [Collected statutes of the Great Ming]. Edited by Li Dongyang et al. Siku quanshu edition. China Text Project.

Da Ming lü [Great Ming code]. Wikisource.

Daoguang Zunyi fuzhi. Edited by Huang Lezhi. Qing Daoguang edition. Erudition Local Gazetteers Database, First Collection.

Erbi kenqing [A brush-pen hatpin's critical points]. Xiao taoyuan juefei shanren. In *Lidai zhenxi sifa wenxian* [Rare legal documents from successive dynasties], edited by Yang Yifan et al. Beijing: Beijing shehui kexue wenxian chubanshe, 2012.

Gongsi biyong [Essentials for public and private use]. In *Zhongguo lidai qiyue huibian kaoyi*, edited by Zhang Zhuanxi. Beijing: Beijing daxue chubanshe, 1995.*Gu Su zhi* [Gazetteer of old Suzhou]. Wang Ao. Siku quanshu edition. China Text Project.

Guangdong tong zhi chugao [Guangdong provincial gazetteer, first draft]. Edited by Dai Jing. Ming Jiajing edition. Erudition Local Gazetteers Database, First Collection.

Guangdong xinyu [New comments on Guangdong]. Qu Dajun. Xuxiu Siku quanshu edition. China Text Project.

Guangxu Jiangxi tongzhi. Edited by Zeng Guofan. Qing Guangxu 7 edition (1881). Erudition Local Gazetteers Database, First Collection.

Hai Rui ji [Collected works of Hai Rui]. Hai Rui. Edited by Chen Yizhong. Beijing: Zhonghua shuju, 1962.

Han shu [History of the Han]. Ban Gu. Siku quanshu edition. Wikisource.

Han shu bu zhu. Ban Gu. Edited by Wang Xianqian and Yan Shigu. Shanghai: Shangwu yinshuguan, 1962.

Hongwu Suzhou fuzhi. Edited by Lu Xiong. Ming Hongwu 12 edition (1379). Erudition Local Gazetteers Database, First Collection.

Hongzhi Fuzhou fuzhi. Edited by Li Ji. Ming Hongzhi edition (1487–1505). In *Tianyige cang Mingdai difangzhi xuankan xubian*, edited by Zhu Dingling and Lu Guoqiang. Shanghai: Shanghai shudian, 1990.

Hongzhi Huizhou fuzhi. Edited by Peng Xiu. Ming Hongzhi edition (1487–1505). Erudition Local Gazetteers Database, First Collection.

Hongzhi Taicang zhouzhi. Edited by Li Duan. Qing Xuantong 1 edition (1909). Erudition Local Gazetteers Database, First Collection.

Hongzhi Yuezhou fuzhi. Edited by Liu Ji. Ming Hongzhi edition (1487–1505). In *Tianyige cang Mingdai difangzhi xuankan xubian*, edited by Zhu Dingling. Shanghai: Shanghai shudian, 1990.

Hou Han shu [History of the later Han]. Fan Ye. Siku quanshu edition. Wikisource.

Huang Ming tiaofa shilei zuan [Categorized regulations of the August Ming]. In *Zhongguo zhenxi falü dianji jicheng*, edited by Liu Hainian and Yang Yifan. Beijing: Kexue chubanshe, 1994.

Huian xiansheng Zhu Wen gong wenji [Collected works of Zhu Xi]. Zhu Xi. Jingshang haiyuanfenlou edition, edited by Rao Pingsu. Wikisource.

Huizhou fu fuyi quanshu. In *Mingdai shiji huikan*, edited by Tian Shengjin. Taibei: Taiwan xuesheng shuju, 1970.

Hunan shengli cheng'an [Hunan provincial regulations and precedents]. In *Zhongguo gudai defang falü wenxian, bing bian*, edited by Liu Ducai and Yang Yifan. Beijing: Beijing shehui kexue wenxian chubanshe, 2012.

Jia Long xinli [New precedents of the Jiajing and Longqing reigns]. In *Zhongguo zhenxi falü dianji jicheng*, edited by Liu Hainian and Yang Yifan. Beijing: Kexue chubanshe, 1994.

Jiading Chicheng zhi. Edited by Huang Ying. Taizhou congshu edition. Erudition Local Gazetteers Database, First Collection.

Jiading Zhenjiang zhi. Edited by Lu Xian. Qing weiyuan biecang edition. Erudition Local Gazetteers Database, First Collection.

Jiajing Chaling zhouzhi. Edited by Zhang Zhi. Ming Jiajing 4 edition (1525). In *Tianyige cang Mingdai difangzhi xuankan xubian*, edited by Zhu Dingling. Shanghai: Shanghai shudian, 1990.

Jiajing Changde fuzhi. Edited by Chen Hongmo. Ming Jiajing edition (1521-67).
Jiajing Chizhou fuzhi. Edited by Li Sihong. Ming Wanli 40 edition. Erudition Local Gazetteers Database, First Collection.
Jiajing Ganzhou fuzhi. Edited by Kang He. Ming Jiajing 15 edition (1536). In *Tianyige cang Mingdai difangzhi xuankan*, edited by Liao Lufen. Shanghai: Shanghai guji shudian, 1981-82. *Jiajing Guangxin fuzhi*. Edited by Zhang Shigao. Ming Jiajing edition (1521-67). In *Tianyige cang Mingdai difangzhi xuankan xubian*, edited by Zhu Dingling and Lu Guoqiang. Shanghai: Shanghai shudian, 1990.
Jiajing Guangdong tongzhi chugao [Guangdong provincial gazetteer, Jiajing draft edition]. Edited by Dai Jing. Ming Jiajing 14 edition (1535). Erudition Local Gazetteers Database, First Collection.
Jiajing Hengzhou fuzhi. Edited by Yang Pei. Ming Jiajing 15 edition (1536). In *Tianyige cang Mingdai difangzhi xuankan*, edited by Liao Lufen. Shanghai: Shanghai guji shudian, 1982.
Jiajing Huguang tujing zhishu [Jiajing-era Huguang illustrated gazetteer]. Edited by Xue Gang. Ming Jiajing 1 edition (1521). Erudition Local Gazetteers Database, First Collection.
Jiajing Jianning fuzhi. Edited by Xia Yulin. Ming Jiajing 20 edition (1541). In *Tianyige cang Mingdai difangzhi xuankan*, edited by Liao Lufen. Shanghai: Shanghai guji shudian, 1982.
Jiajing Jianping xianzhi. Edited by Lian Guang. Ming Jiajing edition (1521-67). Erudition Local Gazetteers Database, First Collection.
Jiajing Jiujiang fuzhi. Edited by Feng Cengnian. Ming Jiajing 15 edition (1536). In *Tianyige cang Mingdai difangzhi xuankan xubian*, edited by Zhu Dingling and Lu Guoqiang. Shanghai: Shanghai shudian, 1990.
Jiajing Nan'an fuzhi. Edited by Liu Jie. Ming Jiajing 15 edition (1536). In *Tianyige cang Mingdai difangzhi xuankan xubian*, edited by Zhu Dingling and Lu Guoqiang. Shanghai: Shanghai shudian, 1990.
Jiajing Nangong xianzhi. Edited by Ye Xuansong. Minguo 22 edition (1933). Erudition Local Gazetteers Database, First Collection.
Jiajing Ningbo fuzhi. Edited by Zhao Xizhe. Ming Jiajing 39 edition (1560). Erudition Local Gazetteers Database, First Collection.
Jiajing Renhe xianzhi. Edited by Shen Chaoxuan. Qing Guangxu ke wulin zhanggu congbian edition. Erudition Local Gazetteers Database, First Collection.
Jiajing Shaowu fuzhi. Edited by Xing Zhi. Ming Jiajing edition. In *Tianyige cang Mingdai difangzhi xuankan*, edited by Liao Lufen. Shanghai: Shanghai guji shudian, 1982.
Jiajing Taicang zhouzhi. Edited by Zhou Shizuo. Ming Chongzhen 2 reprint edition (1629). Erudition Local Gazetteers Database, First Collection.
Jiajing xinli [New precedents of the Jiajing reign]. In *Zhongguo zhenxi falü dianji jicheng*, edited by Liu Hainian and Yang Yifan. Beijing: Kexue chubanshe, 1994.
Jiajing Yanping fuzhi. Edited by Chen Neng. Ming Jiajing 4 edition (1525). In *Tianyige cang Mingdai difangzhi xuankan*, edited by Liao Lufen. Shanghai: Shanghai guji shudian, 1982.

Jiajing Yongfeng xianzhi. Edited by Guan Jing. Ming Jiajing 23 edition (1544). In *Tianyige cang Mingdai difangzhi xuankan*, edited by Liao Lufen. Shanghai: Shanghai guji shudian, 1982.
Jiajing Zhejiang tongzhi. Edited by Hu Zongxian. Ming Jiajing 40 edition (1561). In *Tianyige cang Mingdai difangzhi xuankan*, edited by Liao Lufen. Shanghai: Shanghai guji shudian, 1982.
Jiangxi sheng dazhi [Jiangxi provincial gazetteer]. Edited by Wang Zongmu. Reprint of Ming Wanli 25 edition (1595). Taipei: Chengwen chubanshe, 1989.
Jiangxi sheng fuyi quanshu [Jiangxi Province complete tax records]. In *Mingdai shiji huikan*, edited by Tian Shengjin. Taibei: Taiwan xuesheng shuju, 1970.
Jianyan yilai fannian yaolü [Essential records of the prosperous years since the Jianyan reign]. Li Xinzhuan. Siku quanshu edition. China Text Project.
Jiaqing Yibin xianzhi. Edited by Liu Yuanxi. Minguo reprint of Ming Longqing edition (1567–72). Erudition Local Gazetteers Database, First Collection.
Jiaqing Yuhang xianzhi. Edited by Zhang Ji'an. Minguo 8 reprint edition (1919). Erudition Local Gazetteers Database, First Collection.
Jiaqing Zhili Xuyong tingzhi. Edited by Zhou Weiye. Qing Jiaqing 17 edition (1812). Erudition Local Gazetteers Database, First Collection.
Jin shu [History of the Jin]. Fan Xuanling. Siku quanshu edition. Wikisource.
Jingding Jiankang zhi [Jingding-era Nanjing gazetteer]. Edited by Ma Guangzu. Qing Jiaqing 6 Jinling Sun Zhongqi ci edition (1801). Erudition Local Gazetteers Database, First Collection.
Jinling tuyong [Nanjing illustrated]. Zhu Zhifan. World Digital Library. Library of Congress Chinese Rare Book Collection.
Jishen lü [Record of investigating spirits]. Xu Xuan. Wikisource.
Jiu Tang shu [Old history of the Tang]. Liu Xu. Siku quanshu edition. Wikisource.
Kangxi Jiangxi tongzhi. Edited by Yu Chenglong. Siku quanshu edition. Wikisource.
Kangxi Junlian xianzhi. Edited by Ding Linsheng. Kangxi 25 manuscript edition (1685). Erudition Local Gazetteers Database, First Collection.
Kangxi Xuzhou fu Qingfu xian zhi. Edited by Ding Linsheng. Kangxi 25 edition (1685). Erudition Local Gazetteers Database, First Collection.
Lidai zhenxi sifa wenxian [Rare legal documents from successive dynasties]. Edited by Yang Yifan et al. Beijing: Beijing shehui kexue wenxian chubanshe, 2012.
Liuzhou wenchao [Notes from Liuzhou]. Liu Zongyuan. In *Tang Song ba dajia wenchao*, edited by Mao Dun. Wikisource.
Longjiang chuanchang zhi [Treatise on the Longjiang shipyards]. Li Zhaoxiang. Wikisource.
Longqing Linjiang fuzhi. Edited by Guan Daxun. Longqing 6 edition (1572). In *Tianyige cang Mingdai difangzhi xuankan*, edited by Liao Lufen. Shanghai: Shanghai guji shudian, 1982.
Mengxi bitan [Dream pool essays]. Shen Kuo. Siku quanshu edition. Wikisource.
Min shu. Edited by He Qiaoyuan. Ming Chongzhen edition (1567–72). Erudition Local Gazetteers Database, First Collection.

Ming Renzong shilu [Veritable records of Ming Renzong]. Zhongyang yanjiu lishi yuyan yanjiu suo reprint edition. Taibei: Zhonghua, 1962.
Ming shi [History of the Ming]. Zhang Yanyu. Siku quanshu edition. Wikisource.
Ming Taizong shilu [Veritable records of Ming Taizong]. Zhongyang yanjiu lishi yuyan yanjiu suo reprint edition. Taibei: Zhonghua, 1962.
Ming Taizu shilu [Veritable records of Ming Taizu]. Zhongyang yanjiu lishi yuyan yanjiu suo reprint edition. Taibei: Zhonghua, 1962.
Ming Xuanzong shilu [Veritable records of Ming Xuanzong]. Zhongyang yanjiu lishi yuyan yanjiu suo reprint edition. Taibei: Zhonghua, 1962.
Ming Yingzong shilu [Veritable records of Ming Yingzong]. Zhongyang yanjiu lishi yuyan yanjiu suo reprint edition. Taibei: Zhonghua, 1962.
Minggong shupan qingming ji [Enlightened judgments by famous judges]. Reprint edition edited by Zhongguo shehui kexue yuan lishi yanjiu suo Song Liao Jin Yuan shi yanjiu shi. Beijing: Zhonghua shuju, 1987.
Nanchang Shi linye zhi [Nanchang city forestry gazetteer]. Nanchang: Nanchang Shi difangzhi bianzuan weiyuanhui, 1991.
Nanhai zhi. Edited by Chen Dazhen. Yuan Dade edition (1297–1307). Erudition Local Gazetteers Database, First Collection.
Nanjing Gongbu zhizhang tiaoli [Regulations of official duties for the Nanjing Board of Works]. In *Jinling quanshu yi bian*, vol. 35. Nanjing: Nanjing chubanshe, 2010.
Nongsang jiyao [Essentials of agriculture and sericulture]. Siku quanshu edition. China Text Project.
Nongzheng quanshu [Complete book of agricultural administration]. Xu Guangqi. Siku quanshu edition. Wikisource.
Pengchuang rilü [Diary from a humble window]. Chen Quanzhi. Siku quanshu edition. China Text Project.
Qian fu lun [Comments of a recluse]. Wang Fu. Siku quanshu edition. Wikisource.
Qianlong Hangzhou fuzhi. Edited by Zheng Yun. Qianlong edition (1735–96). Erudition Local Gazetteers Database, First Collection.
Qianlong Hengyang xianzhi. Edited by Tao Xi. Qianlong 26 edition (1760). Erudition Local Gazetteers Database, First Collection.
Qianlong Qiyang xianzhi. Edited by Li Shi. Qianlong 30 edition (1764). Erudition Local Gazetteers Database, First Collection.
Qianlong Ruijin xianzhi. Edited by Guo Can. Qianlong 18 edition (1753). Erudition Local Gazetteers Database, First Collection.
Qimen shisi du wu bao yulin ce [Fish-scale register of Qimen County sector 40 *bao* 5]. In *Huizhou qiannian qiyue wenshu—Song-Yuan-Ming bian*, vol. 11, edited by Wang Yuxin and Zhou Zhaoquan. Shijiazhuang: Huashan wenyi chubanshe, 1993.
Qimin yaoshu [Essential arts to nourish the people]. Jia Sixie. Siku quanshu edition. Wikisource.
Qingxi kou gui [Tracks of the Qingxi bandits]. Fang Shao. Jinhua congshu edition.
Qingyuan tiaofa shilei [Precedents of the Qingyuan period arranged by topic]. In *Zhongguo zhenxi falü dianji xubian*, edited by Yang Yifan and Tian Tao. Ha'erbin: Heilongjiang remin chubanshe, 2002.

Shang shu [Book of documents]. Siku quanshu edition. Wikisource.
Shiji [Records of the Grand Historian]. Sima Qian. Siku quanshu edition. China Text Project.
Song huiyao jigao [Draft institutional history of the Song]. Xu Song. China Text Project.
Song shi [History of the Song]. Toqto'a. Siku quanshu edition. Wikisource.
Song shu [History of the Southern Dynasties Song]. Shen Yue. Siku quanshu edition. Wikisource.
Song xingtong [Song penal code]. Guoxue Baodian.
Songchao shishi [True history of the Song dynasty]. Li You. Siku quanshu edition. Wikisource.
Taiping guangji [Extensive records of the Taiping reign]. Edited by Li Fang. Siku quanshu edition. Wikisource.
Taiping yulan [Imperial encyclopedia of the Taiping reign]. Edited by Li Fang. Siku quanshu edition. Wikisource.
Tang huiyao [Institutional history of the Tang]. Wang Pu. Siku quanshu edition. China Text Project.
Tang lü shuyi [Tang Code with commentary]. Chansun Wuji. Siku quanshu edition. Wikisource.
Tianqi Ganzhou fuzhi. Edited by Yu Wenlong. Qing Shunzhi 17 edition (1660). Erudition Local Gazetteers Database, First Collection.
Tianqi Quzhou fuzhi. Edited by Lin Yingxiong. Ming Tianqi 2 edition (1568). Erudition Local Gazetteers Database, First Collection.
Tongzhi Wan'an xianzhi. Edited by Ouyang Jun. Qing Tongzhi 12 edition (1873). Erudition Local Gazetteers Database, First Collection.
Tushu bian [Illustrated encyclopedia]. Zhang Huang. Siku quanshu edition. Wikisource.
Wanli Guizhou tongzhi. Edited by Zhen Sichong. Ming Wanli 25 edition (1597). Erudition Local Gazetteers Database, First Collection.
Wanli Ji'an fuzhi. Edited by Yu Zhizhen. Ming Wanli 13 edition (1585). Erudition Local Gazetteers Database, First Collection.
Wanli Quanzhou fuzhi. Edited by Yang Sijian. Ming Wanli edition (1572–1620). Erudition Local Gazetteers Database, First Collection.
Wanli Shaoxing fuzhi. Edited by Xu Lianggan. Ming Wanli edition (1572–1620). Erudition Local Gazetteers Database, First Collection.
Wanli Sichuan zongzhi. Edited by Yu Huaizhong. Ming Wanli edition (1572–1620). Erudition Local Gazetteers Database, First Collection.
Wanli xinxiu Nanchang fuzhi. Edited by Fan Lai. In *Riben cang Zhongguo hanjian difangzhi congkan*. Beijing: Shumu wenxian chuban she, 1991.
Wenxian tongkao [Comprehensive investigations of documentary sources]. Ma Duanlin. Siku quanshu edition. Wikisource.
Xi cha huicao [Essays on timber rafting in the western regions]. Gong Hui. Tianyege edition. World Digital Library. Library of Congress, Chinese Rare Book Collection.

Xin Tang shu [New Tang history]. Edited by Ouyang Xiu and Song Qi. Siku quanshu edition. Wikisource.
Xinyu [New discourses]. Lu Jia. Siku quanshu edition. Wikisource.
Xu zizhi tongjian changbian [Extended continuation of the comprehensive mirror for aid in government]. Li Tao. Siku quanshu edition. China Text Project.
Yantie lun [Discourses on salt and iron]. Huan Kuan. Siku quanshu edition. Wikisource.
Yanyou Siming zhi. Edited by Ma Ze. Qing Xianfeng ke Siming liu zhi edition. Erudition Local Gazetteers Database, First Collection.
Yijian wu zhi [Record of the listener E]. Hong Mai. Siku quanshu edition. Wikisource.
Yongzheng Sichuan tongzhi. Edited by Huang Yangui. Siku quanshu edition. Erudition Local Gazetteers Database, First Collection.
Yongzheng Zhejiang tongzhi. Edited by Li Wei. Siku quanshu edition. Erudition Local Gazetteers Database, First Collection.
Yuan shi [History of the Yuan]. Song Lian. Siku quanshu edition. Wikisource.
Yuanshi shifan [Yuan's precepts for social life]. Yuan Cai. Siku quanshu edition. Wikisource.
Zhenchuan xiansheng ji. Gui Youguang. Sibu congkan edition. Wikisource.
Zhengde Fuzhou fuzhi. Edited by Ye Bo. Ming Zhengde 15 edition (1520). Erudition Local Gazetteers Database, First Collection.
Zhengde Jianchang fuzhi. Edited by Xia Liangsheng. Ming Zhengde 12 edition (1517). In *Tianyige cang Mingdai difangzhi xuankan*, edited by Liao Lufen. Shanghai: Shanghai guji shudian, 1982.
Zhengde Nankang fuzhi. Edited by Chen Lin. Ming Zhengde 10 edition (1515). In *Tianyige cang Mingdai difangzhi xuankan*, edited by Liao Lufen. Shanghai: Shanghai guji shudian, 1982.
Zhengde Raozhou fuzhi. Edited by Chen C. Ming Zhengde edition. In *Tianyige cang Mingdai difangzhi xuankan xubian*, edited by Zhu Dingling and Lu Guoqiang. Shanghai: Shanghai shudian, 1990.
Zhengde Ruizhou fuzhi. Edited by Xiong Xiang. Ming Zhengde edition (1506–1521). In *Tianyige cang Mingdai difangzhi xuankan xubian*, edited by Zhu Dingling. Shanghai: Shanghai shudian, 1990.
Zhengde Yuanzhou fuzhi. Edited by Yan Song. Ming Zhengde edition (1506–1521). Erudition Local Gazetteers Database, First Collection.
Zhenglei bencao [Collected classified materia medica]. Tang Zhenwei. Siku quanshu edition. Kanseki Repository.
Zhishun Zhenjiang zhi. Edited by Tuo Yin and Yu Xilu. Qing Daoguang 22 Dantu Baoshi edition (1822). Erudition Local Gazetteers Database, First Collection.
Zhiyuan Jiahe zhi. Edited by Dan Qing and Xu Shi. Qing Guangxu edition (1875–1908). Erudition Local Gazetteers Database, First Collection.
Zhizheng Jinling xinzhi. Edited by Zhang Xuan. Siku quanshu edition. Erudition Local Gazetteers Database, First Collection.

Zhizheng Siming xuzhi. Edited by Wang Yuangong and Xu Liang. Qing Xianfeng ke Siming liu zhi edition. Erudition Local Gazetteers Database, First Collection.
Zhongshu shu [Book on tree planting]. Guo Tuotuo. Quan Tang wen edition. Wikisource.
Zhouguan xinyi [A new interpretation of the Offices of Zhou]. Wang Anshi. Siku quanshu edition. Wikisource.
Zhuozhong zhi [Treatise on deliberations at court]. Liu Ruoyu. Wikisource.
Zuiwei lu [Record of my transgressions]. Cha Jizuo. Wuxing Liushi Jiayetang manuscript edition. Wikisource.

SECONDARY SOURCES

Abel, Clarke. *Narrative of a Journey in the Interior of China, and of a Voyage to and from That Country, in the Years 1816 and 1817: Containing an Account of the Most Interesting Transactions of Lord Amherst's Embassy to the Court of Pekin and Observations on the Countries Which It Visited*. London: Longman, Hurst, Rees, Orme, and Brown, 1818.

Albion, Robert Greenhalgh. *Forests and Sea Power: The Timber Problem of the Royal Navy, 1652–1862*. Cambridge, MA: Harvard University Press, 1926.

Allen, Timothy, and Thomas Hoekstra. *Toward a Unified Ecology*. 2nd ed. New York: Columbia University Press, 2015.

Allsen, Thomas. "The Rise of the Mongolian Empire and Mongolian Rule in North China." In *The Cambridge History of China*, vol. 6, *Alien Regimes and Border States, 907–1368*, edited by Herbert Franke and Denis C. Twitchett. Cambridge: Cambridge University Press, 1994.

Anderson, James A., and John K. Whitmore. "Introduction: 'The Fiery Frontier and the *Dong* World.'" In *China's Encounters on the South and Southwest: Reforging the Fiery Frontier over Two Millennia*, edited by James A. Anderson and John K. Whitmore. Leiden: Brill, 2014.

Andrade, Tonio. *The Gunpowder Age: China, Military Innovation, and the Rise of the West in World History*. Princeton, NJ: Princeton University Press, 2017.

Aoki, Atsushi. "Kenshō no chiiki-teki imēji: Jūichi-jūsan seiki kōsei shakai no hō bunka to jinkō idō o megutte" [The image of litigation: Regarding eleventh- to thirteenth-century Jiangxi society's legal culture and population movements]. *Shakai keizaishigaku* 65, no. 3 (1999): 3–22.

Appuhn, Karl. *A Forest on the Sea: Environmental Expertise in Renaissance Venice*. Baltimore: Johns Hopkins University Press, 2009.

Averill, Stephen C. *Revolution in the Highlands: China's Jinggangshan Base Area*. Lanham, MD: Rowman and Littlefield, 2006.

——— . "The Shed People and the Opening of the Yangzi Highlands." *Modern China* 9, no. 1 (1983): 84–126.

Barbieri-Low, Anthony. *Artisans in Early Imperial China*. Seattle: University of Washington Press, 2007.

Barros, Ana M. G., and José M. C. Pereira. "Wildfire Selectivity for Land Cover Type: Does Size Matter?" *PLoS ONE* 9, no. 1 (January 2014): e84760.

Barrow, John, and George Macartney. *Some Account of the Public Life, and a Selection from the Unpublished Writings, of the Earl of Macartney.* 2 vols. London: T. Cadell and W. Davies, 1807.

Bayly, C. A. *The Birth of the Modern World, 1780–1914.* Malden, MA: Wiley-Blackwell, 2003.

Bello, David A. *Across Forest, Steppe, and Mountain: Environment, Identity, and Empire in Qing China's Borderlands.* Cambridge: Cambridge University Press, 2016.

Benedict, Carol. *Golden-Silk Smoke: A History of Tobacco in China, 1550–2010.* Berkeley: University of California Press, 2011.

Bian Li. *Ming Qing Huizhou shehui yanjiu* [Research on Ming-Qing Huizhou]. Hefei: Anhui daxue chubanshe, 2004.

Biran, Michal. "Periods of Non-Han Rule." In *A Companion to Chinese History*, edited by Michael Szonyi, 129–43. Malden, MA: Wiley-Blackwell, 2017.

Birge, Bettine. *Women, Property, and Confucian Reaction in Sung and Yüan China.* Cambridge: Cambridge University Press, 2010.

Bol, Peter K. "The Rise of Local History: History, Geography, and Culture in Southern Song and Yuan Wuzhou." *Harvard Journal of Asiatic Studies* 61, no. 1 (2001): 37–76.

———. "Wang Anshi and the *Zhouli*." In *Statecraft and Classical Learning: The Rituals of Zhou in East Asian History*, edited by Benjamin Elman and Martin Kern, 229–51. Leiden: Brill, 2009.

Bond, William John, and Jon E. Keeley. "Fire as a Global 'Herbivore': The Ecology and Evolution of Flammable Ecosystems." *Trends in Ecology and Evolution* 20, no. 7 (August 2005): 387–94.

Bourgon, Jérôme. "Uncivil Dialogue: Law and Custom Did Not Merge into Civil Law under the Qing." *Late Imperial China* 23, no. 1 (June 2002): 50–90.

Brain, Stephen. *Song of the Forest: Russian Forestry and Stalinist Environmentalism, 1905–1953.* Pittsburgh: University of Pittsburgh Press, 2011.

Brook, Timothy. *The Chinese State in Ming Society.* New York: Routledge, 2004.

———. *The Confusions of Pleasure: Commerce and Culture in Ming China.* Berkeley: University of California Press, 1999.

———. *Geographical Sources of Ming-Qing History.* 2nd ed. Ann Arbor: Center for Chinese Studies, University of Michigan, 2002.

Brown, Robert. *The Miscellaneous Botanical Works of Robert Brown.* Edited by John Joseph Bennett. Vol. 1. London: Published for the Ray Society by R. Hardwicke, n.d.

Brummett, Palmira. *Ottoman Seapower and Levantine Diplomacy in the Age of Discovery.* Albany: State University of New York Press, 1993.

Campbell, Aurelia. *What the Emperor Built: Architecture and Empire in the Early Ming.* Seattle: University of Washington Press, 2020.

Cao Shanshou and Li Ronggao, eds. *Yunnan linye wenhua beike* [Yunnan forestry culture inscriptions]. Baoshan: Dehong minzu chubanshe, 2005.

Casale, Giancarlo. *The Ottoman Age of Exploration*. New York: Oxford University Press, 2011.

Chaffee, John W. "Huizong, Cai Jing, and the Politics of Reform." In *Emperor Huizong and the Late Northern Song: The Politics of Culture and the Culture of Politics*, edited by Patricia Buckley Ebrey and Maggie Bickford. Cambridge, MA: Harvard University Asia Center, 2006.

———. "The Impact of the Song Imperial Clan on the Overseas Trade of Quanzhou." In *The Emporium of the World: Maritime Quanzhou, 1000–1400*, edited by Angela Schottenhammer, 13–45. Leiden: Brill, 2001.

———. *The Muslim Merchants of Premodern China: The History of a Maritime Asian Trade Diaspora, 750–1400*. Cambridge: Cambridge University Press, 2018.

Chan, Hok-lam. "The Chien-Wen, Yung-Lo, Hung-Hsi, Hsuan-Te Reigns, 1399–1435." In *The Cambridge History of China*, vol. 7, *The Ming Dynasty, 1368–1644*, pt. 1, edited by Frederick W. Mote and Denis C. Twitchett. Cambridge: Cambridge University Press, 1988.

———. "The Organization and Utilization of Labor Service under the Jurchen Chin Dynasty." *Harvard Journal of Asiatic Studies* 52, no. 2 (1992): 613–64.

———. "The Rise of Ming T'ai-tsu (1368–98): Facts and Fictions in Early Ming Official Historiography." *Journal of the American Oriental Society* 95, no. 4 (1975): 679–715.

Chan, Wing-hoi. "Ethnic Labels in a Mountainous Region: The Case of She 'Bandits.'" In *Empire at the Margins: Culture, Ethnicity, and Frontier in Early Modern China*, edited by Pamela Kyle Crossley, Helen F. Siu, and Donald S. Sutton. Berkeley: University of California Press, 2006.

Chao, Kang. *Man and Land in Chinese History: An Economic Analysis*. Stanford, CA: Stanford University Press, 1986.

Ch'en, Kuo-tung. "Nonreclamation Deforestation in Taiwan, c. 1600–1976." In *Sediments of Time: Environment and Society in Chinese History*, edited by Mark Elvin and Ts'ui-jung Liu. Cambridge: Cambridge University Press, 1998.

Chen, Yuan Julian. "Frontier, Fortification, and Forestation: Defensive Woodland on the Song-Liao Border in the Long Eleventh Century." *Journal of Chinese History* 2, no. 2 (2018): 313–34. https://doi.org/10.1017/jch.2018.7.

Chen Keyun. "Cong 'lishi shanlin zhichan bu' kan Ming Qing Huizhou shanlin jingying" [A view of Ming Qing Huizhou forest business from the Li lineage forest account book]. *Jiang Huai luntan* 9 (January 1992): 73–84.

———. "Ming Qing Huizhou shanlin jingying zhong de 'lifen' wenti" [The question of "labor shares" in Ming Qing Huizhou forest business]. *Zhongguo shi yanjiu*, January 1987.

Chen Rong. *Zhongguo senlin shiliao* [Historical materials on Chinese forests]. Beijing: Zhongguo linye chubanshe, 1983.

Chien, Cecilia Lee-fang. *Salt and State: An Annotated Translation of the Songshi Salt Monopoly Treatise*. Ann Arbor: Center for Chinese Studies, University of Michigan, 2004.

Chittick, Andrew. "Dragon Boats and Serpent Prows: Naval Warfare and the Political Culture of South China's Borderlands." In *Imperial China and Its*

Southern Neighbours, edited by Victor H. Mair and Liam C. Kelley. Singapore: Institute of Southeast Asian Studies, 2015.

———. "The Song Navy and the Invention of Dragon Boat Racing." *Journal of Song-Yuan Studies* 41, no. 1 (2011): 1–28.

Church, Sally K. "Zheng He: An Investigation into the Plausibility of 450-Ft Treasure Ships." *Monumenta Serica* 53, no. 1 (December 2005): 1–43.

Church, Sally K., John Gebhardt, and Terry Little. "A Naval Architectural Analysis of the Plausibility of 450-Ft Treasure Ships." Paper prepared for the First International Conference of the Zheng He Society, Malacca, 2010.

Churchman, Catherine. "Where to Draw the Line? The Chinese Southern Frontier in the Fifth and Sixth Centuries." In *China's Encounters on the South and Southwest: Reforging the Fiery Frontier over Two Millennia*, edited by James A. Anderson and John K. Whitmore. Leiden: Brill, 2014.

Clark, Hugh R. *The Sinitic Encounter in Southeast China through the First Millennium CE*. Honolulu: University of Hawai'i Press, 2015.

Coggins, Chris. *The Tiger and the Pangolin: Nature, Culture, and Conservation in China*. Honolulu: University of Hawai'i Press, 2003.

———. "When the Land Is Excellent: Village Feng Shui Forests and the Nature of Lineage, Polity and Vitality in Southern China." In *Religion and Ecological Sustainability in China*, edited by James Miller, Dan Smyer Yu, and Peter van der Veer. London: Routledge, 2014.

Cohen, Myron L. "Writs of Passage in Late Imperial China: The Documentation of Practical Understandings in Minong, Taiwan." In *Contract and Property in Early Modern China*, edited by Madeleine Zelin, Jonathan K. Ocko, and Robert Gardella. Stanford, CA: Stanford University Press, 2004.

Cronon, William. *Changes in the Land: Indians, Colonists, and the Ecology of New England*. New York: Hill and Wang, 2003.

———. *Nature's Metropolis: Chicago and the Great West*. New York: W. W. Norton, 2009.

Crossley, Pamela Kyle, Helen F. Siu, and Donald S. Sutton, eds. *Empire at the Margins: Culture, Ethnicity, and Frontier in Early Modern China*. Berkeley: University of California Press, 2006.

Daniels, Christian, and Nicholas K. Menzies. *Agro-Industries and Forestry*. Pt. 3 of *Biology and Biological Technology*, vol. 6 of *Science and Civilisation in China*, edited by Joseph Needham. Cambridge: Cambridge University Press, 1996.

Dardess, John W. "A Ming Landscape: Settlement, Land Use, Labor, and Estheticism in T'ai-Ho County, Kiangsi." *Harvard Journal of Asiatic Studies* 49 (1989): 295–364.

———. "Shun-ti and the End of Yüan Rule in China." In *The Cambridge History of China*, vol. 6, *Alien Regimes and Border States, 907–1368*, edited by Herbert Franke and Denis C. Twitchett. Cambridge: Cambridge University Press, 1994.

Davis, Richard L. "The Reign of Tu-tsung and His Successors." In *The Cambridge History of China*, vol. 5, pt. 1, *The Sung Dynasty and Its Precursors, 907–1279*, edited by Denis C. Twitchett and Paul Jakov Smith. Cambridge: Cambridge University Press, 2009.

De Bary, William Theodore, and Irene Bloom, comps. *Sources of Chinese Tradition.* 2nd ed. Vol. 1. New York: Columbia University Press, 1999.
DeLanda, Manuel. *A New Philosophy of Society: Assemblage Theory and Social Complexity.* London: Continuum, 2006.
———. *A Thousand Years of Nonlinear History.* New York: Zone Books, 2000.
Delgado, James P. *Khubilai Khan's Lost Fleet: In Search of a Legendary Armada.* Berkeley: University of California Press, 2010.
Deng, Gang. *Maritime Sector, Institutions, and Sea Power of Premodern China.* Westport, CT: Greenwood Press, 1999.
Deng Pei. "Lun Ming-Qing shiqi zai Jinshajiang xiayou diqu jinxing de 'muzheng' huodong" [Discussion of Ming-Qing period logging administration activities in the lower Jinsha River area]. *Qinghai shizhuan xuebao* 2 (2006): 89–91.
Deng Zhihua. "Ming zhongye Jiangxi difang caizheng tizhi de gaige" [Local fiscal reforms in mid-Ming Jiangxi]. *Zhongguo shehui jingji shi yanjiu* 21, no. 1 (2001).
Dennis, Joseph R. *Writing, Publishing, and Reading Local Gazetteers in Imperial China, 1100–1700.* Cambridge, MA: Harvard University Asia Center, 2015.
Dillon, Michael. "Jingdezhen as a Ming Industrial Center." *Ming Studies*, no. 1 (January 1978): 37–44.
———. "Transport and Marketing in the Development of the Jingdezhen Porcelain Industry during the Ming and Qing Dynasties." *Journal of the Economic and Social History of the Orient* 35, no. 3 (1992): 278–90.
Dodson, John Richard, Shirene Hickson, Rachel Khoo, Xiao-Qiang Li, Jemina Toia, and Wei-Jian Zhou. "Vegetation and Environment History for the Past 14,000 Yr BP from Dingnan, Jiangxi Province, South China." *Journal of Integrative Plant Biology* 48, no. 9 (September 2006): 1018–27.
Dreyer, Edward. *Early Ming China: A Political History, 1355–1435.* Stanford, CA: Stanford University Press, 1982.
———. "Military Origins of Ming China." In *The Cambridge History of China*, vol. 7, *The Ming Dynasty, 1368–1644*, pt. 1, edited by Frederick W. Mote and Denis C. Twitchett, 58–106. Cambridge: Cambridge University Press, 1988.
———. "The Poyang Campaign, 1363: Inland Naval Warfare in the Founding of the Ming Dynasty." In *Chinese Ways in Warfare*, edited by Frank A. Kierman and John K. Fairbank. Cambridge, MA: Harvard University Press, 1973.
———. *Zheng He: China and the Oceans in the Early Ming Dynasty, 1405–1433.* New York: Pearson, 2006.
Du, Yongtao. *The Order of Places: Translocal Practices of the Huizhou Merchants in Late Imperial China.* Leiden: Brill, 2015.
Dykstra, Maura. "Complicated Matters: Commercial Dispute Resolution in Qing Chongqing from 1750 to 1911." Ph.D. diss., University of California, Los Angeles, 2014.
Ebrey, Patricia Buckley. *Emperor Huizong.* Cambridge, MA: Harvard University Press, 2014.
———. *Family and Property in Sung China: Yuan Ts'ai's Precepts for Social Life.* Princeton, NJ: Princeton University Press, 1984.

Elliott, Mark C. "*Hushuo*: The Northern Other and the Naming of the Han Chinese." In *Critical Han Studies: The History, Representation, and Identity of China's Majority*, edited by Thomas S. Mullaney, James Leibold, Stéphane Gros, and Eric Vanden Bussche. Berkeley: University of California Press, 2012.

Elvin, Mark. "The Environmental History of China: An Agenda of Ideas." *Asian Studies Review* 14, no. 2 (November 1990): 39–53.

———. "The Environmental Legacy of Imperial China." *China Quarterly*, no. 156 (1998): 733–56.

———. *The Pattern of the Chinese Past*. Stanford, CA: Stanford University Press, 1973.

———. *The Retreat of the Elephants: An Environmental History of China*. New Haven, CT: Yale University Press, 2004.

———. "Three Thousand Years of Unsustainable Growth: China's Environment from Archaic Times to the Present." *East Asian History* 6 (December 1993): 7–46. Essay is the basis of the Annual Lecture of the Centre for Modern Chinese Studies at St Antony's College Oxford, May 11, 1994.

Elvin, Mark, and Ts'ui-jung Liu, eds. *Sediments of Time: Environment and Society in Chinese History*. Cambridge: Cambridge University Press, 1998.

Endicott-West, Elizabeth. *Mongolian Rule in China: Local Administration in the Yuan Dynasty*. Cambridge, MA: Harvard University Asia Center, 1989.

Erbaugh, Mary S. "The Secret History of the Hakkas: The Chinese Revolution as a Hakka Enterprise." *China Quarterly*, no. 132 (1992): 937–68.

Falkowski, Mateusz. "Fear and Abundance: Reshaping of Royal Forests in Sixteenth-Century Poland and Lithuania." *Environmental History* 22, no. 4 (October 2017): 618–42.

Fang, Jingyun, Zehao Shen, Zhiyao Tang, Xiangping Wang, Zhiheng Wang, Jianmeng Feng, Yining Liu, Xiujuan Qiao, Xiaopu Wu, and Chengyang Zheng. "Forest Community Survey and the Structural Characteristics of Forests in China." *Ecography* 35, no. 12 (December 2012): 1059–71.

Fang, Jingyun, Zhiheng Wang, and Zhiyao Tang, eds. *Atlas of Woody Plants in China: Distribution and Climate*. New York: Springer, 2011.

Farmer, Edward L. *Early Ming Government: The Evolution of Dual Capitals*. Cambridge, MA: Harvard University Asia Center, 1976.

Faure, David. *Emperor and Ancestor: State and Lineage in South China*. Stanford, CA: Stanford University Press, 2007.

Fiskesjö, Magnus. "Rising from Blood-Stained Fields: Royal Hunting and State Formation in Shang China." *Bulletin of the Museum of Far Eastern Antiquities*, no. 73 (2001): 48–191.

Foster, John Bellamy. "Marx's Theory of Metabolic Rift: Classical Foundations for Environmental Sociology." *American Journal of Sociology* 105, no. 2 (September 1999): 366–405.

Franke, Herbert. "The Chin Dynasty." In *The Cambridge History of China*, vol. 6, *Alien Regimes and Border States, 907–1368*, edited by Herbert Franke and Denis C. Twitchett. Cambridge: Cambridge University Press, 1994.

———. "Chinese Law in a Multinational Society: The Case of the Liao (907–1125)." *Asia Major* 5, no. 2 (1992): 111–27.

Fritzbøger, Bo. *A Windfall for the Magnates: The Development of Woodland Ownership in Denmark c. 1150–1830.* Odense: University Press of Southern Denmark, 2004.

Fu Yiling. *Ming Qing shidai shangren ji shangye ziben* [Ming-Qing period merchants and merchant capitalism]. 1956. Reprint, Beijing: Zhonghua shuju, 2007.

Funada Yoshiyuki. "Genchō chika no shikimoku—jin ni tsuite" [Semuren under the Yuan dynasty]. *Shigaku zasshi* 108, no. 9 (1999): 1593–1618.

———. "The Image of the Semu People: Mongols, Chinese, and Various Other Peoples under the Mongol Empire." Paper presented at the roundtable "The Nature of the Mongol Empire and Its Legacy," Centre for Studies in Asian Cultures and Social Anthropology, Austrian Academy of Sciences, Vienna, November 6, 2010.

———. "Semuren yu Yuandai zhidu, shehui—chongxin tantao menggu, Semu, Hanren, Nanren huafen de weizhi" [Semu people and the system and society in the Yuan: Reexamining the classification of the Mongols, Semu, Hanren, and Nanren]. In *Yuanshi Luncong*, vol. 9, edited by Liu Yingsheng. Beijing: Zhongguo guangbo dianshi chuban she, 2004.

Funes Monzote, Reinaldo. *From Rainforest to Cane Field in Cuba: An Environmental History since 1492.* Translated by Alex Martin. Chapel Hill: University of North Carolina Press, 2008.

Gadgil, Madhav, and Ramachandra Guha. *This Fissured Land: An Ecological History of India.* Berkeley: University of California Press, 1993.

Gardella, Robert. "Contracting Business Partnerships in Late Qing and Republican China: Paradigms and Patterns." In *Contract and Property in Early Modern China*, edited by Madeleine Zelin, Jonathan K. Ocko, and Robert Gardella. Stanford, CA: Stanford University Press, 2004.

———. *Harvesting Mountains: Fujian and the China Tea Trade, 1757–1937.* Berkeley: University of California Press, 1994.

Gernet, Jacques. *Buddhism in Chinese Society.* Translated by Franciscus Verellen. New York: Columbia University Press, 1998.

———. *A History of Chinese Civilization.* Translated by J. R. Foster and Charles Hartman. 2nd ed. Cambridge: Cambridge University Press, 1996.

Gerritsen, Anne. "Fragments of a Global Past: Ceramics Manufacture in Song-Yuan-Ming Jingdezhen." *Journal of the Economic and Social History of the Orient* 52, no. 1 (2009): 117–52.

———. *Ji'an Literati and the Local in Song-Yuan-Ming China.* Leiden: Brill, 2007.

Giersch, C. Patterson. "From Subjects to Han: The Rise of Han as Identity in Nineteenth-Century Southwest China." In *Critical Han Studies: The History, Representation, and Identity of China's Majority*, edited by Thomas S. Mullaney, James Leibold, Stéphane Gros, and Eric Vanden Bussche. Berkeley: University of California Press, 2012.

Girardot, N. J., James Miller, and Xiaogan Liu, eds. *Daoism and Ecology: Ways within a Cosmic Landscape*. Cambridge, MA: Center for the Study of World Religions, Harvard Divinity School, 2001.

Glete, Jan. *Warfare at Sea, 1500–1650: Maritime Conflicts and the Transformation of Europe*. New York: Routledge, 2000.

Golas, Peter J. *Mining*. Pt. 13 of *Chemistry and Chemical Technology*, vol. 5 of *Science and Civilisation in China*, edited by Joseph Needham. Cambridge: Cambridge University Press, 1999.

Goldstone, Jack A. "The Rise of the West—or Not? A Revision to Socio-economic History." *Sociological Theory* 18, no. 2 (2000): 175–94.

Grew, Bernd-Stefan, and Richard Hölzl. "Forestry in Germany, c. 1550–2000." In *Managing Northern Europe's Forests: Histories from the Age of Improvement to the Age of Ecology*, edited by K. Jan Oosthoek and Richard Hölzl, 15–65. Oxford, UK: Berghahn Books, 2018.

Grove, Linda, and Joseph W. Esherick. "From Feudalism to Capitalism: Japanese Scholarship on the Transformation of Chinese Rural Society." *Modern China* 6, no. 4 (1980): 397–438.

Grove, Richard H. *Green Imperialism: Colonial Expansion, Tropical Island Edens and the Origins of Environmentalism, 1600–1860*. Cambridge: Cambridge University Press, 1996.

Guha, Ramachandra. *The Unquiet Woods: Ecological Change and Peasant Resistance in the Himalaya*. Expanded ed. Berkeley: University of California Press, 2000.

Guo, Futao, Zhangwen Su, Guangyu Wang, Long Sun, Fangfang Lin, and Aiqin Liu. "Wildfire Ignition in the Forests of Southeast China: Identifying Drivers and Spatial Distribution to Predict Wildfire Likelihood." *Applied Geography* 66 (January 2016): 12–21.

Hansen, Valerie. *Negotiating Daily Life in Traditional China: How Ordinary People Used Contracts, 600–1400*. New Haven, CT: Yale University Press, 1995.

Hardin, Garrett. "The Tragedy of the Commons." *Science* 162, no. 3859 (December 13, 1968): 1243–48.

Hargett, James M. "Song Dynasty Local Gazetteers and Their Place in the History of *Difangzhi* Writing." *Harvard Journal of Asiatic Studies* 56, no. 2 (1996): 405–42.

Harrell, Stevan. *Ways of Being Ethnic in Southwest China*. Seattle: University of Washington Press, 2001.

Hartman, Charles. "A Textual History of Cai Jing's Biography in the *Songshi*." In *Emperor Huizong and the Late Northern Song: The Politics of Culture and the Culture of Politics*, edited by Patricia Buckley Ebrey and Maggie Bickford. Cambridge, MA: Harvard University Asia Center, 2006.

Hartwell, Robert. "A Cycle of Economic Change in Imperial China: Coal and Iron in Northeast China, 750–1350." *Journal of the Economic and Social History of the Orient* 10, no. 1 (1967): 102–59.

———. "Demographic, Political, and Social Transformations of China, 750–1550." *Harvard Journal of Asiatic Studies* 42, no. 2 (1982): 365–442.

———. "Financial Expertise, Examinations, and the Formulation of Economic Policy in Northern Sung China." *Journal of Asian Studies* 30, no. 2 (February 1971): 281–314.

———. "Markets, Technology, and the Structure of Enterprise in the Development of the Eleventh-Century Chinese Iron and Steel Industry." *Journal of Economic History* 26, no. 1 (1966): 29–58.

———. "A Revolution in the Chinese Iron and Coal Industries during the Northern Sung, 960–1126 A.D." *Journal of Asian Studies* 21, no. 2 (February 1962): 153–62.

Haw, Stephen G. "The Semu Ren in the Yuan Empire—Who Were They?" Paper presented at the "Mobility and Transformations: New Directions in the Study of the Mongol Empire" joint research conference of the Institute for Advanced Studies and the Israel Science Foundation, Jerusalem, 2014.

He, Xi, and David Faure, eds. *The Fisher Folk of Late Imperial and Modern China: An Historical Anthropology of Boat-and-Shed Living*. New York: Routledge, 2016.

———. "Introduction: Boat-and-Shed Living in Land-Based Society." In *The Fisher Folk of Late Imperial and Modern China: An Historical Anthropology of Boat-and-Shed Living*, edited by Xi He and David Faure. New York: Routledge, 2016.

Heijdra, Martin. "The Socio-economic Development of Rural China during the Ming." In *The Cambridge History of China*, vol. 8, *The Ming Dynasty, 1368–1644*, pt. 2, edited by Denis C. Twitchett and Frederick W. Mote. Cambridge: Cambridge University Press, 1998.

Henthorn, William E. *Korea: The Mongol Invasions*. Leiden: Brill, 1963.

Herman, John E. "The Cant of Conquest: Tusi Offices and China's Political Incorporation of the Southwest Frontier." In *Empire at the Margins: Culture, Ethnicity, and Frontier in Early Modern China*, edited by Pamela Kyle Crossley, Helen F. Siu, and Donald S. Sutton. Berkeley: University of California Press, 2006.

Ho, Ping-ti. "The Introduction of American Food Plants into China." *American Anthropologist* 57, no. 2 (April 1955): 191–201.

———. *Studies on the Population of China, 1368–1953*. Cambridge, MA: Harvard University Press, 1959.

Hsiao, Ch'i-Ch'ing. "Mid-Yuan Politics." In *The Cambridge History of China*, vol. 6, *Alien Regimes and Border States, 907–1368*, edited by Herbert Franke and Denis C. Twitchett. Cambridge: Cambridge University Press, 1994.

———. *The Military Establishment of the Yuan Dynasty*. Cambridge, MA: Harvard University Asia Center, 1978.

Huang, Philip C. C. *The Peasant Family and Rural Development in the Yangzi Delta, 1350–1988*. Stanford, CA: Stanford University Press, 1990.

Huang, Ray. "The Ming Fiscal Administration." In *The Cambridge History of China*, vol. 8, *The Ming Dynasty, 1368–1644*, pt. 2, edited by Denis C. Twitchett and Frederick W. Mote. Cambridge: Cambridge University Press, 1998.

———. *Taxation and Governmental Finance in Sixteenth-Century Ming China*. Cambridge: Cambridge University Press, 2009.

Hucker, Charles O. *The Censorial System of Ming China*. Stanford, CA: Stanford University Press, 1966.

Hulsewe, A. F. P. *Remnants of Ch'in Law: An Annotated Translation of the Ch'in Legal and Administrative Rules of the 3rd Century B.C. Discovered in Yün-meng Prefecture, Hu-pei Province, in 1975*. Leiden: Brill, 1985.

Hung, Kuang-chi. "When the Green Archipelago Encountered Formosa: The Making of Modern Forestry in Taiwan under Japan's Colonial Rule (1895–1945)." In *Environment and Society in the Japanese Islands: From Prehistory to the Present*, edited by Bruce L. Batten and Philip C. Brown. Corvallis: Oregon State University Press, 2015.

Hymes, Robert. "Marriage, Descent Groups, and the Localist Strategy in Sung and Yüan Fu-Chou." In *Kinship Organization in Late Imperial China, 1000–1940*, edited by Patricia Buckley Ebrey and James L. Watson. Berkeley: University of California Press, 1986.

Imber, Colin. *The Ottoman Empire, 1300–1650: The Structure of Power*. New York: Palgrave Macmillan, 2004.

Itō Masahiko. *Sō Gen gōson shakai shiron: Minsho Rikōsei taisei no keisei katei* [Historical essay on Song-Yuan village society: The formation of the early Ming *lijia* system]. Tokyo: Kyūko Shoin, 2010.

Jiang, Wenying, et al. "Natural and Anthropogenic Forest Fires Recorded in the Holocene Pollen Record from a Jinchuan Peat Bog, Northeastern China." *Palaeogeography, Palaeoclimatology, Palaeoecology* 261, nos. 1–2 (April 2008): 47–57.

Jiang Wuyuan, "Ming Qing chaoting Sichuan caimu yanjiu" [Research on Ming and Qing dynasty logging in Sichuan]. In *Zhongguo Zijincheng xuehui lunwenji, di er ji*, edited by Yu Zhuoyun and Zhu Chengru. Beijing: Zijincheng chubanshe, 2002.

Jin Zhongbo. *Mingdai lijia zhi yu fuyi zhidu zhi guanxi ji qi bianqian* [The Ming dynasty *lijia* system, the tax system, their relationship, and changes]. Taipei: Zhongguo wenhua daxue shixue yanjiu suo, 1985.

Johnson, Wallace, trans. *The T'ang Code*. Vol. 2, *Specific Articles*. Princeton, NJ: Princeton University Press, 1997.

Jørgensen, Dolly. "The Roots of the English Royal Forest." In *Anglo-Norman Studies 32: Proceedings of the Battle Conference 2009*, edited by C. P. Lewis, 114–28. Woodbridge, UK: Boydell Press, 2010.

Kain, Roger J. P., and Elizabeth Baigent. *The Cadastral Map in the Service of the State: A History of Property Mapping*. Chicago: University of Chicago Press, 1992.

Keightley, David N. *Sources of Shang History: The Oracle-Bone Inscriptions of Bronze Age China*. Berkeley: University of California Press, 1985.

Kim, Nam. "Sinicization and Barbarization: Ancient State Formation at the Southern Edge of Sinitic Civilization." In *Imperial China and Its Southern Neighbours*, edited by Victor H. Mair and Liam C. Kelley. Singapore: Institute of Southeast Asian Studies, 2015.

Lan Yong. "Ming Qing shiqi de huangmu caiban" [Imperial logging requisitions in the Ming-Qing era]. *Lishi yanjiu* 6 (1994): 86–98.

Langlois, John D. "The Code and ad hoc Legislation in Ming Law." *Asia Major* 6, no. 2 (1993): 85–112.

Lau, Ulrich, and Thies Staack. *Legal Practice in the Formative Stages of the Chinese Empire: An Annotated Translation of the Exemplary Qin Criminal Cases from the Yuelu Academy*. Leiden: Brill, 2016.

Lee, John S. "Forests and the State in Pre-industrial Korea, 918–1897." Ph.D. diss., Harvard University, 2017.

———. "Postwar Pines: The Military and the Expansion of State Forests in Post-Imjin Korea, 1598–1684." *Journal of Asian Studies* 77, no. 2 (May 2018): 319–32.

Leong, Sow-Theng. *Migration and Ethnicity in Chinese History: Hakkas, Pengmin, and Their Neighbors*. Edited by Tim Wright. Stanford, CA: Stanford University Press, 1997.

Levathes, Louise. *When China Ruled the Seas: The Treasure Fleet of the Dragon Throne, 1405–1433*. 1994. Reprint, New York: Oxford University Press, 1997.

Levine, Ari Daniel. "Che-tsung's Reign (1085–1100) and the Age of Faction." In *The Cambridge History of China*, vol. 5, pt. 1, *The Sung Dynasty and Its Precursors, 907–1279*, edited by Denis C. Twitchett and Paul Jakov Smith. Cambridge: Cambridge University Press, 2009.

———. *Divided by a Common Language: Factional Conflict in Late Northern Song China*. Honolulu: University of Hawai'i Press, 2008.

Lewis, Mark Edward. *China between Empires*. Cambridge, MA: Harvard University Press, 2009.

———. *China's Cosmopolitan Empire: The Tang Dynasty*. Edited by Timothy Brook. Cambridge, MA: Belknap Press of Harvard University Press, 2012.

———. *Sanctioned Violence in Early China*. Albany: State University of New York Press, 1989.

Li, Minghe, and Gary A. Ritchie. "Eight Hundred Years of Clonal Forestry in China: I. Traditional Afforestation with Chinese Fir (*Cunninghamia lanceolata* (Lamb.) Hook.)." *New Forests* 18, no. 2 (September 1999): 131–42.

Li, Ren-Yuan. "Making Texts in Villages: Textual Production in Rural China during the Ming-Qing Period." Ph.D. diss., Harvard University, 2014.

Li, Xiaoqiang, John Dodson, Jie Zhou, and Xinying Zhou. "Increases of Population and Expansion of Rice Agriculture in Asia, and Anthropogenic Methane Emissions since 5000 BP." *Quaternary International* 202, nos. 1–2 (June 2009): 41–50.

Liang Fangzhong. *Mingdai fuyi zhidu* [Tax system of the Ming dynasty]. In *Liang Fangzhong Wenji* [Collected works of Liang Fangzhong]. Beijing: Zhonghua shuju, 2008.

———. *Mingdai liangzhang zhidu* [The tax captaincy system of the Ming dynasty]. Shanghai: Shanghai renmin chubanshe, 1957.

Liang Sicheng. *Zhongguo jianzhu shi* [A history of Chinese architecture]. Tianjin: Baihua wenyi chuban she, 1998.

Liu, Kam-Biu, and Hong-lie Qiu. "Late-Holocene Pollen Records of Vegetational Changes in China: Climate or Human Disturbance." *Tao* 5 no. 3 (September 1994): 393–410.

Liu, Ts'ui-jung. "Han Migration and the Settlement of Taiwan: The Onset of Environmental Change." In *Sediments of Time: Environment and Society in*

Chinese History, edited by Mark Elvin and Ts'ui-jung Liu. Cambridge: Cambridge University Press, 1998.

Liu Zhiwei. *Zai guojia yu shehui zhijian: Ming Qing Guangdong diqu lijia fuyi zhidu yu xiangcun shehui* [Between state and society: Ming Qing Guangdong local *lijia* and tax systems and village society]. Beijing: Renmin daxue chubanshe, 2010.

Lo, Jung-pang. *China as a Sea Power, 1127–1368: A Preliminary Survey of the Maritime Expansion and Naval Exploits of the Chinese People during the Southern Song and Yuan Periods.* Edited by Bruce A. Elleman. Singapore: National University of Singapore Press, 2012.

Lowood, Henry E. "The Calculating Forester: Quantification, Cameral Science, and the Emergence of Scientific Forestry Management in Germany." In *The Quantifying Spirit in the Eighteenth Century*, edited by Tore Frängsmyr, J. L. Heilbron, and Robin E. Rider. Berkeley: University of California Press, 1990.

Luan Xiancheng. *Ming dai huangce yanjiu*. Beijing: Zhongguo she hui ke xue chu ban she, 1998.

Luo Xianglin. *Kejia yanjiu daolun* [An introduction to the study of the Hakka]. Xingning: Xishan shucang, 1933.

Macauley, Melissa. *Social Power and Legal Culture: Litigation Masters in Late Imperial China*. Stanford, CA: Stanford University Press, 1998.

Mann, Charles C. *1493: Uncovering the New World Columbus Created*. New York: Vintage, 2012.

Marks, Robert B. *China: Its Environment and History*. Lanham, MD: Rowman and Littlefield, 2011.

———. *Tigers, Rice, Silk, and Silt: Environment and Economy in Late Imperial South China*. Cambridge: Cambridge University Press, 1998.

Matteson, Kieko. *Forests in Revolutionary France: Conservation, Community, and Conflict, 1669–1848*. Cambridge: Cambridge University Press, 2015.

Mazumdar, Sucheta. "The Impact of New World Food Crops on the Diet and Economy of China and India, 1600–1900." In *Food in Global History*, edited by Raymond Grew, 58–78. Boulder, CO: Westview Press, 1999.

McDermott, Joseph. "Bondservants in the T'ai-hu Basin during the Late Ming: A Case of Mistaken Identities." *Journal of Asian Studies* 40, no. 4 (1981): 675–701.

———. *The Making of a New Rural Order in South China*. Vol. 1, *Village, Land, and Lineage in Huizhou, 900–1600*. Cambridge: Cambridge University Press, 2014.

McDermott, Joseph, and Shiba Yoshinobu. "Economic Change in China, 960–1279." In *The Cambridge History of China*, vol. 5, pt. 2, *Sung China, 960–1279*, edited by John W. Chaffee and Denis C. Twitchett. Cambridge: Cambridge University Press, 2015.

McElwee, Pamela D. *Forests Are Gold: Trees, People, and Environmental Rule in Vietnam*. Seattle: University of Washington Press, 2016.

McKnight, Brian E., and James T. C. Liu, trans. *The Enlightened Judgments: Ch'ing-Ming Chi, the Sung Dynasty Collection*. Albany: State University of New York Press, 1999.

McNeely, Jeffrey A., Kenton Miller, Russell A. Mittermeier, Walter V. Reid, and Timothy B. Werner. *Conserving the World's Biological Diversity*. Gland, Switzerland: International Union for Conservation of Nature and Natural Resources; Washington, DC: World Resources Institute, Conservation International, World Wildlife Fund-US, and World Bank, 1990.

McNeill, J. R. *Mosquito Empires: Ecology and War in the Greater Caribbean, 1620-1914*. New York: Cambridge University Press, 2010.

Medley, Margaret. "Ching-Tê Chên and the Problem of the 'Imperial Kilns.'" *Bulletin of the School of Oriental and African Studies, University of London* 29, no. 2 (1966): 326-38.

Menzies, Nicholas K. *Forest and Land Management in Imperial China*. New York: Palgrave Macmillan, 1994.

———. "Strategic Space: Exclusion and Inclusion in Wildland Policies in Late Imperial China." *Modern Asian Studies* 26, no. 4 (October 1992): 719-33.

Mihelich, Mira Ann. "Polders and the Politics of Land Reclamation in Southeast China during the Northern Song Dynasty (960-1126)." Ph.D. diss., Cornell University, 1979.

Mikhail, Alan. *Nature and Empire in Ottoman Egypt: An Environmental History*. Cambridge: Cambridge University Press, 2012.

———. *Under Osman's Tree: The Ottoman Empire, Egypt, and Environmental History*. Chicago: University of Chicago Press, 2017.

Miller, Ian M. "Forestry and the Politics of Sustainability in Early China." *Environmental History* 22, no. 4 (October 2017): 594-617.

———. "Roots and Branches: Woodland Institutions in South China, 800-1600." Ph.D. diss., Harvard University, 2015.

Moore, Jason W. "'Amsterdam Is Standing on Norway,' Part I: The Alchemy of Capital, Empire and Nature in the Diaspora of Silver, 1545-1648." *Journal of Agrarian Change* 10, no. 1 (January 2010): 33-68.

———. "'Amsterdam Is Standing on Norway,' Part II: The Global North Atlantic in the Ecological Revolution of the Long Seventeenth Century." *Journal of Agrarian Change* 10, no. 2 (April 2010): 188-227.

———. "Transcending the Metabolic Rift: A Theory of Crises in the Capitalist World-Ecology." *Journal of Peasant Studies* 38, no. 1 (January 2011): 1-46.

Mostern, Ruth. *"Dividing the Realm in Order to Govern": The Spatial Organization of the Song State (960-1276 CE)*. Cambridge, MA: Harvard University Press, 2011.

———. "Sediment and State in Imperial China: The Yellow River Watershed as an Earth System and a World System." *Nature and Culture* 11, no. 2 (June 2016): 121-47.

Mote, Frederick W. "Chinese Society under Mongol Rule." In *The Cambridge History of China*, vol. 6, *Alien Regimes and Border States, 907-1368*, edited by Herbert Franke and Denis C. Twitchett. Cambridge: Cambridge University Press, 1994.

———. "The Rise of the Ming Dynasty." In *The Cambridge History of China*, vol. 7, *The Ming Dynasty, 1368-1644*, pt. 1, edited by Frederick W. Mote and Denis C. Twitchett, 11-57. Cambridge: Cambridge University Press, 1988.

Mullaney, Thomas S., James Leibold, Stéphane Gros, and Eric Vanden Bussche, eds. *Critical Han Studies: The History, Representation, and Identity of China's Majority*. Berkeley: University of California Press, 2012.
Nakajima Gakushō. *Mindai goson no funso to chitsujo: Kishu monjoo shiryo to shite* [Disputes and order in Ming dynasty villages: Using Huizhou documents as sources]. Tokyo: Kyūko shoin, 2002.
Naquin, Susan. *Peking: Temples and City Life, 1400–1900*. Berkeley: University of California Press, 2000.
Needham, Joseph, Ho Ping-Yü, Lu Gwei-Djen, and Wang Ling. *Military Technology: The Gunpowder Epic*. Pt. 7 of *Chemistry and Chemical Technology*, vol. 5 of *Science and Civilisation in China*, edited by Joseph Needham. Cambridge: Cambridge University Press, 1987.
Needham, Joseph, and Wang Ling. *Mathematics and the Sciences of the Heavens and the Earth*. Vol. 3 of *Science and Civilisation in China*, edited by Joseph Needham. Cambridge: Cambridge University Press, 1959.
Needham, Joseph, Wang Ling, and Kenneth Girdwood Robinson. *Physics*. Pt. 1 of *Physics and Physical Technology*, vol. 4 of *Science and Civilisation in China*, edited by Joseph Needham. Cambridge: Cambridge University Press, 1962.
Needham, Joseph, Wang Ling, and Lu Gwei-Djen. *Civil Engineering and Nautics*. Pt. 3 of *Physics and Physical Technology*, vol. 4 of *Science and Civilisation in China*, edited by Joseph Needham. Cambridge: Cambridge University Press, 1971.
O Kŭm-sŏng. *Mindai shakai keizaishi kenkyū: Shinshisō no keisei to sono shakai keizaiteki yakuwari* [Research in Ming dynasty society and economy: The formation of the gentry stratum and their social and economic roles]. Translation of *Chungguk kŭnse sahoe kyŏngjesa yŏn'gu*. Tokyo: Kyūko Shoin, 1990.
Ocko, Jonathan K. "The Missing Metaphor: Applying Western Legal Scholarship to the Study of Contract and Property in Early Modern China." In *Contract and Property in Early Modern China*, edited by Madeleine Zelin, Jonathan K. Ocko, and Robert Gardella. Stanford, CA: Stanford University Press, 2004.
Oosthoek, K. Jan, and Richard Hölzl, eds. *Managing Northern Europe's Forests: Histories from the Age of Improvement to the Age of Ecology*. Oxford, UK: Berghahn Books, 2018.
Osborne, Anne. "Highlands and Lowlands: Economic and Ecological Interactions in the Lower Yangzi Region under the Qing." In *Sediments of Time: Environment and Society in Chinese History*, edited by Mark Elvin and Ts'ui-jung Liu. Cambridge: Cambridge University Press, 1998.
———. "The Local Politics of Land Reclamation in the Lower Yangzi Highlands." *Late Imperial China* 15, no. 1 (1994): 1–46.
Ostrom, Elinor. *Governing the Commons: The Evolution of Institutions for Collective Action*. Cambridge: Cambridge University Press, 1990.
Ōta K. *Mōko shūrai: So no gunjishiteki kenkyū* [Mongol invasion: The study of its military history]. Tokyo: Kinseisha, 1997.
Ownby, David. *Brotherhoods and Secret Societies in Early and Mid-Qing China: The Formation of a Tradition*. Stanford, CA: Stanford University Press, 1996.

Peluso, Nancy Lee. *Rich Forests, Poor People: Resource Control and Resistance in Java*. Berkeley: University of California Press, 1994.
Peluso, Nancy Lee, and Peter Vandergeest. "Genealogies of the Political Forest and Customary Rights in Indonesia, Malaysia, and Thailand." *Journal of Asian Studies* 60, no. 3 (2001): 761–812.
Perdue, Peter C. *Exhausting the Earth: State and Peasant in Hunan, 1500–1850*. Cambridge, MA: Harvard University Asia Center, 1987.
Pomeranz, Kenneth. *The Great Divergence: China, Europe, and the Making of the Modern World Economy*. Rev. ed. Princeton, NJ: Princeton University Press, 2001.
———. *The Making of a Hinterland: State, Society, and Economy in Inland North China, 1853–1937*. Berkeley: University of California Press, 1993.
Puett, Michael. "Centering the Realm: Wang Mang, the *Zhouli*, and Early Chinese Statecraft." In *Statecraft and Classical Learning: The Rituals of Zhou in East Asian History*, edited by Benjamin Elman and Martin Kern. Leiden: Brill, 2009.
Pyne, Stephen J. *Fire: Nature and Culture*. London: Reaktion Books, 2012.
Qi Xia and Qiao Youmei. *Zhongguo jing ji tong shi*. Beijing: Jing ji ri bao chu ban she, 1998.
Rackham, Oliver. *The History of the Countryside: The Classic History of Britain's Landscape, Flora and Fauna*. 1986. Reprint, London: Phoenix, 2001.
Radkau, Joachim. *Nature and Power: A Global History of the Environment*. Translated by Thomas Dunlap. Cambridge: Cambridge University Press, 2008.
———. *Wood: A History*. Translated by Patrick Camiller. Cambridge, UK: Polity, 2012.
Rawski, Evelyn Sakakida. *Agricultural Change and the Peasant Economy of South China*. Cambridge, MA: Harvard University Press, 1972.
Ren, Guoyu. "Decline of the Mid- to Late Holocene Forests in China: Climatic Change or Human Impact?" *Journal of Quaternary Science* 15, no. 3 (March 2000): 273–81.
Richards, John F. *The Unending Frontier: An Environmental History of the Early Modern World*. Berkeley: University of California Press, 2006.
Richardson, S. D. *Forestry in Communist China*. Baltimore: Johns Hopkins University Press, 1966.
Robinet, Isabelle. *Taoism: Growth of a Religion*. Translated by Phyllis Brooks. Stanford, CA: Stanford University Press, 1997.
Robinson, David M. *Empire's Twilight: Northeast Asia under the Mongols*. Cambridge, MA: Harvard University Asia Center, 2009.
———. "Politics, Force and Ethnicity in Ming China: Mongols and the Abortive Coup of 1461." *Harvard Journal of Asiatic Studies* 59, no. 1 (1999): 79–123.
Rossabi, Morris. *Khubilai Khan: His Life and Times*. 20th anniversary ed., with a new preface. Berkeley: University of California Press, 2009.
———. "The Muslims in the Early Yüan Dynasty." In *China under Mongol Rule*, edited by John D. Langlois. Princeton, NJ: Princeton University Press, 1981.

———. "The Reign of Khubilai Khan." In *The Cambridge History of China*, vol. 6, *Alien Regimes and Border States, 907–1368*, edited by Herbert Franke and Denis C. Twitchett. Cambridge: Cambridge University Press, 1994.

Sahlins, Peter. *Forest Rites: The War of the Demoiselles in Nineteenth-Century France*. Cambridge, MA: Harvard University Press, 1998.

Sanft, Charles. "Environment and Law in Early Imperial China (Third Century BCE–First Century CE): Qin and Han Statutes concerning Natural Resources." *Environmental History* 15, no. 4 (2010): 701–21.

Sasaki, Randall James. *The Origins of the Lost Fleet of the Mongol Empire*. College Station: Texas A&M University Press, 2015.

Schafer, Edward H. "The Conservation of Nature under the T'ang Dynasty." *Journal of the Economic and Social History of the Orient* 5, no. 3 (1962): 279–308.

———. "Hunting Parks and Animal Enclosures in Ancient China." *Journal of the Economic and Social History of the Orient* 11, no. 3 (1968): 318–43.

Schlesinger, Jonathan. *A World Trimmed with Fur: Wild Things, Pristine Places, and the Natural Fringes of Qing Rule*. Stanford, CA: Stanford University Press, 2017.

Schneewind, Sarah. "Ming Taizu *Ex Machina*." *Ming Studies*, no. 1 (January 2007): 104–12.

Schoppa, R. Keith. *Song Full of Tears: Nine Centuries of Chinese Life around Xiang Lake*. Boulder, CO: Basic Books, 2002.

Schottenhammer, Angela. "China's Emergence as a Maritime Power." In *The Cambridge History of China*, vol. 5, pt. 2, *Sung China, 960–1279*, edited by John W. Chaffee and Denis C. Twitchett. Cambridge: Cambridge University Press, 2015.

Schurmann, Herbert Franz. *Economic Structure of the Yüan Dynasty*. Cambridge, MA: Harvard University Press, 1956.

Scott, James C. *The Art of Not Being Governed: An Anarchist History of Upland Southeast Asia*. New Haven, CT: Yale University Press, 2010.

———. *Seeing Like a State: How Certain Schemes to Improve the Human Condition Have Failed*. New Haven, CT: Yale University Press, 1999.

Sen, Tansen. *Buddhism, Diplomacy, and Trade: The Realignment of India-China Relations, 600–1400*. Lanham, MD: Rowman and Littlefield, 2015.

Shiba, Yoshinobu. "The Business Nucleus of the Southern Song Capital of Hangzhou." In *The Diversity of the Socio-economy in Song China, 960–1279*, edited by Shiba Yoshinobu. Tokyo: Toyo Bunko, 2011.

———. *Commerce and Society in Sung China*. Translated by Mark Elvin. Ann Arbor: Center for Chinese Studies, University of Michigan, 1969.

———. "Environment versus Water Control: The Case of the Southern Hangzhou Bay Area from the Mid-Tang through the Qing." In *Sediments of Time: Environment and Society in Chinese History*, edited by Mark Elvin and Ts'ui-jung Liu. Cambridge: Cambridge University Press, 1998.

———. "Ningbo and Its Hinterland." In *The City in Late Imperial China*, edited by G. William Skinner. Stanford, CA: Stanford University Press, 1977.

Shin, Leo K. *The Making of the Chinese State: Ethnicity and Expansion on the Ming Borderlands*. Cambridge: Cambridge University Press, 2012.

Sivaramakrishnan, K. *Modern Forests: Statemaking and Environmental Change in Colonial Eastern India*. Stanford, CA: Stanford University Press, 1999.
Smith, Bruce D. "The Ultimate Ecosystem Engineers." *Science* 315, no. 5820 (March 11, 2007): 1797–98.
Smith, Paul Jakov. "Introduction: Problematizing the Song-Yuan-Ming Transition." In *The Song-Yuan-Ming Transition in Chinese History*, edited by Paul Jakov Smith and Richard von Glahn. Cambridge, MA: Harvard University Asia Center, 2003.
———. "Irredentism as Political Capital: The New Policies and the Annexation of Tibetan Domains in Hehuang (the Qinghai-Gansu Highlands) under Shenzong and His Sons, 1068–1126." In *Emperor Huizong and the Late Northern Song: The Politics of Culture and the Culture of Politics*, edited by Patricia Buckley Ebrey and Maggie Bickford. Cambridge, MA: Harvard University Asia Center, 2006.
———. *Taxing Heaven's Storehouse: Horses, Bureaucrats, and the Destruction of the Sichuan Tea Industry, 1074–1224*. Cambridge, MA: Harvard University Asia Center, 1991.
So, Billy K. L. *Prosperity, Region, and Institutions in Maritime China: The South Fukien Pattern, 946–1368*. Cambridge, MA: Harvard University Asia Center, 2001.
So, Kwan-wai. *Japanese Piracy in Ming China during the 16th Century*. Lansing: Michigan State University Press, 1975.
Sun Xiangjun and Chen Yinshuo. "Palynological Records of the Last 11,000 Yrs in China." *Quaternary Science Reviews* 10 (1991): 537–44.
Swope, Kenneth M. "To Catch a Tiger: The Suppression of the Yang Yinglong Miao Uprising (1587–1600) as a Case Study in Ming Military and Borderlands History." In *New Perspectives on the History and Historiography of Southeast Asia: Continuing Explorations*, edited by Michael Arthur Aung-Thwin and Kenneth R. Hall. Abingdon, Oxon: Routledge, 2011.
Szonyi, Michael. *The Art of Being Governed: Everyday Politics in Late Imperial China*. Princeton, NJ: Princeton University Press, 2017.
Tackett, Nicolas. *The Origins of the Chinese Nation: Song China and the Forging of an East Asian World Order*. Cambridge: Cambridge University Press, 2017.
Tanaka Masatoshi. "Popular Uprisings, Rent Resistance, and Bondservant Rebellions in the Late Ming." In *State and Society in China: Japanese Perspectives on Ming-Qing Social and Economic History*, edited by Linda Grove and Christian Daniels. Tokyo: University of Tokyo Press, 1984.
Tang, Lixing. *Merchants and Society in Modern China: Rise of Merchant Groups*. Abingdon, Oxon: Routledge, 2017.
Tang, Zhiyao, Zhiheng Wang, Chengyang Zheng, and Jingyun Fang. "Biodiversity in China's Mountains." *Frontiers in Ecology and the Environment* 4, no. 7 (September 2006): 347–52.
Tao, Jing-shen. "The Move to the South and the Reign of Kao-Tsung (1127–1162)." In *The Cambridge History of China*, vol. 5, pt. 1, *The Sung Dynasty and Its Precursors, 907–1279*, edited by Denis C. Twitchett and Paul Jakov Smith. Cambridge: Cambridge University Press, 2009.

Teplyakov, V. K. *A History of Russian Forestry and Its Leaders*. Darby, PA: Diane Publishing, 1998.
Totman, Conrad. *The Green Archipelago: Forestry in Preindustrial Japan*. Athens: Ohio University Press, 1998.
———. *The Lumber Industry in Early Modern Japan*. Honolulu: University of Hawai'i Press, 1995.
Twitchett, Denis C., ed. *The Cambridge History of China*. Vol. 3, *Sui and T'ang China, 589–906*, pt. 1. Cambridge: Cambridge University Press, 1979.
———. *Financial Administration under the T'ang Dynasty*. Cambridge: Cambridge University Press, 1971.
Twitchett, Denis C., and Tilemann Grimm. "The Cheng-t'ung, Ching-t'ai, and T'ien-Shun Reigns, 1436–1464." In *The Cambridge History of China*, vol. 7, *The Ming Dynasty, 1368–1644*, pt. 1, edited by Frederick W. Mote and Denis C. Twitchett. Cambridge: Cambridge University Press, 1988.
Twitchett, Denis C., and Frederick W. Mote, eds. *The Cambridge History of China*. Vol. 8, *The Ming Dynasty, 1368–1644*, pt. 2. Cambridge: Cambridge University Press, 1998.
Vainker, S. J. *Chinese Pottery and Porcelain*. London: British Museum Press, 2005.
Vermeer, Eduard B. "The Mountain Frontier in Late Imperial China: Economic and Social Developments in the Bashan." *T'oung Pao* 77, no. 4/5 (1991): 300–329.
———. "Population and Ecology along the Frontier in Qing China." In *Sediments of Time: Environment and Society in Chinese History*, edited by Mark Elvin and Ts'ui-jung Liu. Cambridge: Cambridge University Press, 1998.
von Glahn, Richard. *The Country of Streams and Grottoes: Expansion, Settlement, and the Civilizing of the Sichuan Frontier in Song Times*. Cambridge, MA: Harvard University Asia Center, 1987.
———. *The Economic History of China: From Antiquity to the Nineteenth Century*. Cambridge: Cambridge University Press, 2016.
———. *Fountain of Fortune: Money and Monetary Policy in China, 1000–1700*. Berkeley: University of California Press, 1996.
———. "Imagining Pre-modern China." In *The Song-Yuan-Ming Transition in Chinese History*, edited by Paul Jakov Smith and Richard von Glahn. Cambridge, MA: Harvard University Asia Center, 2003.
———. "Ming Taizu *Ex Nihilo*?" *Ming Studies*, no. 1 (January 2007): 113–41.
———. "The Ningbo-Hakata Merchant Network and the Reorientation of East Asian Maritime Trade, 1150–1350." *Harvard Journal of Asiatic Studies* 74, no. 2 (December 2014): 249–79.
———. "Towns and Temples: Urban Growth and Decline in the Yangzi Delta, 1100–1400." In *The Song-Yuan-Ming Transition in Chinese History*, edited by Paul Jakov Smith and Richard von Glahn. Cambridge, MA: Harvard University Asia Center, 2003.
Wagner, Donald B. "The Administration of the Iron Industry in Eleventh-Century China." *Journal of the Economic and Social History of the Orient* 44, no. 2 (2001): 175–97.

Walsh, Michael. *Sacred Economies: Buddhist Monasticism and Territoriality in Medieval China*. New York: Columbia University Press, 2010.
Wang, Qingkui, Silong Wang, and Yu Huang. "Comparisons of Litterfall, Litter Decomposition, and Nutrient Return in a Monoculture *Cunninghamia lanceolata* and a Mixed Stand in Southern China." *Forest Ecology and Management* 255 (2008): 1210–18.
Wang, Wensheng. *White Lotus Rebels and South China Pirates: Crisis and Reform in the Qing Empire*. Cambridge, MA: Harvard University Press, 2014.
Wang Deyi. "Li Chunnian yu Nan Song tudi jingjie" [Li Chunnian and southern Song land boundaries]. *Shihuo yuekan* 2, no. 5 (1972). Included in *Songshi yanjiu ji* (Taibei: Guoli bianyi guan, 1974). Digital version accessed at Zongguo nongye lishi yu wenhua [China's agricultural history and culture], http://agri-history.ihns.ac.cn/history/nansong1.html.
Warde, Paul. *Ecology, Economy and State Formation in Early Modern Germany*. Cambridge: Cambridge University Press, 2010.
———. "Fear of Wood Shortage and the Reality of the Woodland in Europe, c. 1450–1850." *History Workshop Journal* 62, no. 1 (October 2006): 28–57.
———. *The Invention of Sustainability: Nature and Destiny, c. 1500–1870*. Cambridge: Cambridge University Press, 2018.
Wiens, Herold J. *China's March toward the Tropics: A Discussion of the Southward Penetration of China's Culture, Peoples, and Political Control in Relation to the Non-Han-Chinese Peoples of South China and in the Perspective of Historical and Cultural Geography*. Hamden, CT: Shoe String Press, 1954.
Will, Pierre-Etienne, et al. *Handbooks and Anthologies for Officials in Imperial China: A Descriptive and Critical Bibliography*. Leiden: Brill, 2020. Selections available online from Legalizing Space in China, http://lsc.chineselegalculture.org, accessed March 23, 2017.
Williams, Michael. *Deforesting the Earth: From Prehistory to Global Crisis, an Abridgment*. Chicago: University of Chicago Press, 2006.
Wilson, Andrew R. "The Maritime Transformations of Ming China." In *China Goes to Sea: Maritime Transformation in Comparative Historical Perspective*, edited by Andrew S. Erickson, Lyle J. Goldstein, and Carnes Lord. Annapolis, MD: Naval Institute Press, 2009.
Wing, John T. *Roots of Empire: Forests and State Power in Early Modern Spain, c. 1500–1750*. Leiden: Brill, 2015.
Wittfogel, Karl A. "Public Office in the Liao Dynasty and the Chinese Examination System." *Harvard Journal of Asiatic Studies* 10, no. 1 (1947): 13–40.
Wittfogel, Karl A., and Chia-shêng Fêng. *History of Chinese Society: Liao, 907–1125*. Philadelphia: American Philosophical Society, 1949.
Woodside, Alexander. *Lost Modernities: China, Vietnam, Korea, and the Hazards of World History*. Cambridge, MA: Harvard University Press, 2006.
Wright, Tim. "An Economic Cycle in Imperial China? Revisiting Robert Hartwell on Iron and Coal." *Journal of the Economic and Social History of the Orient* 50, no. 4 (2007): 398–423.

Yang Guozhen. *Ming Qing tudi qiyue wenshu yanjiu* [Research on Ming-Qing land contracts]. Beijing: Renmin daxue chubanshe, 2009.

———, ed. *Minnan qiyue wenshu zonglu* [Collection of contractual documents from southern Fujian]. Xiamen: Xiamen daxue chubanshe, 1990.

Yang Peina. "Government Registration in the Fishing Industry in South China during the Ming and Qing." In *The Fisher Folk of Late Imperial and Modern China: An Historical Anthropology of Boat-and-Shed Living*, edited by Xi He and David Faure. New York: Routledge, 2016.

Ye, Tao, Yao Wang, Zhixing Guo, and Yijia Li. "Factor Contribution to Fire Occurrence, Size, and Burn Probability in a Subtropical Coniferous Forest in East China." *PLoS ONE* 12, no. 2 (February 16, 2017): e0172110.

Yonglin, Jiang, trans. *The Great Ming Code / Da Ming lü*. Seattle: University of Washington Press, 2014.

Yuan, Tsing. "The Porcelain Industry at Ching-Te-Chen 1550–1700." *Ming Studies*, no. 1 (January 1978): 45–54.

Zelin, Madeleine. "A Critique of Rights of Property in Prewar China." In *Contract and Property in Early Modern China*, edited by Madeleine Zelin, Jonathan K. Ocko, and Robert Gardella. Stanford, CA: Stanford University Press, 2004.

Zhang, Jian, et al. "Stability of Soil Organic Carbon Changes in Successive Rotations of Chinese Fir (*Cunninghamia lanceolata* (Lamb.) Hook) Plantations." *Journal of Environmental Sciences* 21 (2009): 352–59.

Zhang, Ling. "Changing with the Yellow River: An Environmental History of Hebei, 1048–1128." *Harvard Journal of Asiatic Studies* 69, no. 1 (2009): 1–36.

———. *The River, the Plain, and the State: An Environmental Drama in Northern Song China, 1048–1128*. Cambridge: Cambridge University Press, 2016.

Zhang, Meng. "Financing Market-Oriented Reforestation: Securitization of Timberlands and Shareholding Practices in Southwest China, 1750–1900." *Late Imperial China* 38, no. 2 (December 2017): 109–51.

———. *Sustaining the Market: Long-Distance Timber Trade in China, 1700–1930*. Seattle: University of Washington Press, forthcoming.

———. "Timber Trade along the Yangzi River: Market, Institutions, and Environment, 1750–1911." Ph.D. diss., University of California, Los Angeles, 2017.

Zhang Yingqiang. *Mucai zhi liudong: Qingdai Qingshuijiang xiayou diqu de shichang, quanli yu shehui* [The movement of timber: Markets, rights, and society in the lower Qingshui River region in the Qing dynasty]. Jinping, Guizhou: Shenghuo dushu xinzhi sanlian shudian, 2006.

Zhang Zhuanxi, ed. *Zhongguo lidai qiyue huibian kaoyi* [Collection and translation of Chinese historical contracts]. Vol. 1. Beijing: Beijing daxue chubanshe, 1995.

Zhao, Yan. "Vegetation and Climate Reconstructions on Different Time Scales in China: A Review of Chinese Palynological Research." *Vegetation History and Archaeobotany* 27, no. 2 (March 2018): 381–92.

Zhong, An-Liang, and Wen-Yue Hsiung. "Evaluation and Diagnosis of Tree Nutritional Status in Chinese-Fir (*Cunninghamia lanceolata* (Lamb.) Hook)

Plantations, Jiangxi, China." *Forest Ecology and Management* 62 (December 1993): 245–70.

Zhong Chong. "Sekkō Shō Tōyō Ken Hokkō Bonchi ni okeru sō zoku no chiri—zokufu zhiryō no bunseki o chū shin to shite" [Geography of lineage in the North River basin of Dongyang County, Zhejiang—based on analysis of genealogical materials]. *Jimbun chiri* 57, no. 4 (2005): 353–73.

Zhou Weiquan. *Zhongguo gudian yuanlin shi* [History of Chinese classical gardens]. Beijing: Qinghua daxue chubanshe, 1990.

Zurndorfer, Harriet. *Change and Continuity in Chinese Local History: The Development of Hui-Chou Prefecture, 800 to 1800.* Leiden: Brill, 1997.

———. "Chinese Merchants and Commerce in Sixteenth Century China: The Role of the State in Society." In *Leyden Studies in Sinology: Papers Presented at the Conference Held in Celebration of the Fiftieth Anniversary of the Sinological Institute of Leyden University, December 8–12, 1980,* edited by Wilt Lukas Idema, 75–86. Leiden: Brill, 1981.

INDEX

Abel, Clarke, 3–4
Albion, Robert Greenhalgh, 117, 139
An Guoheng, 153
An Lushan Rebellion, 213n15
Annam, present-day Vietnam, 130
Averill, Stephen C., 167

Baltic Sea, 212n7
bamboo: market for, 70; plantations of, 40, 60, 75, 93, 95; state monopolies on, 105; taxes and tariffs on, 99, 100, 104, 106, 107, 109, 112; uses for, 4, 149. *See also* China fir; *nanmu*; pine
Beijing: connection to Yellow Sea, 119; under the Ming, 15, 65, 130, 141, 144, 146; supply of timber to, 110, 113, 114, 150; tariffs collected at, 215n74; under the Yuan, 125, 144
Bello, David A., 13
biome modification: by fire, 22, 23, 36, 192nn6,7; by tree planting, 11, 13, 22–23, 35
Book of Tree Planting ("hunchback Guo"), 26, 35
Bozhou native office, present-day Zunyi, Guizhou, 152
A Brush-Pen Hatpin's Critical Points (Erbi kenqing), 91–94, 210n74
Buddhism, 24
Bureau of Military Farms (Tuntian Qingli Si), 108

cadastres. *See* forest surveys; land surveys
Cai Jing, 16, 33–34, 36, 43, 62, 162
Cai Kejian, 68

Campbell, Aurelia, 142
Caochuan zhi (Treatise on transport ships), 134, 138
Champa, present-day Vietnam, 128
Chan, Hok-lam, 130
Chan, Wing-hoi, 205n69
Changsha, Hunan, 127
Chaozhou, Guangdong, 48
Cheju Island, 126, 127
Chen Keyun, 84–85, 94–95, 207n30, 208n40
Chen Xu, 133–34
Chen Youliang, 129, 130, 220n84
Chengdu, Sichuan, 144
China fir: distinction between white fir and red fir, 225n5; as dominant tree in South China plantations, 4, 55, 56, 70; Latin name, 190n17; native range, 12; in shipbuilding, 118, 119; silviculture of, 87, 211n88; sizes and grading, 113; susceptibility to fire, 95, 211n91; tariffs on, 109, 115, 215n71. *See also* bamboo; *nanmu*; pine
China's March toward the Tropics (Wiens), 165
Chizhou, Anhui, 69, 94, 103, 218n49
Chŏlla Province, Korea, 126, 127
Chu kingdom, 122
Chuanzheng xin shu (New treatise on shipyard administration), 138
Coggins, Chris, 211n93
Colbert, Jean-Baptiste, 36, 162
Collected Statutes of the Great Ming (Da Ming huidian), 171, 215n71

Columbus, Christopher, 131
commercial forestry: and concepts of landownership, 41–42, 56–57; environmental and social costs of, 8–9, 75, 95–96, 161, 164; and expanding state control, 5–6, 13–14; legal framework for, 38–39; varieties cultivated for, 4–5, 25, 40, 55, 60, 70, 110. *See also* tree planting
Communist Revolution, 17–18, 167, 217n5
Complete Book of Agricultural Administration (Xu Guangqi), 94
corvée labor: attempts to escape, 74–75; drafted by noble and monastic estates, 25; during Qin and Han dynasties, 24; reforms of system of, 67, 68, 76, 161; replacement tax on, 195n69; for shipbuilding, 120, 123, 124, 139; supplying government with part-time workers, 58; tribute and levies as form of, 203n32; for woodcutting and logging expeditions, 10–11, 62, 65–66, 100, 194n33. *See also* labor
Cunningham, Allan, 190n17
Cunningham, James, 7, 190n17
Cunninghamia lanceolata. See China fir

Da Ming huidian (Collected statutes of the Great Ming), 171, 215n71
Da Ming lü (Great Ming Code), 49, 89–90, 93, 209n65
Dadu, present-day Beijing, 125, 144
Dai Jin, 147
Daoism, 24, 145
Dashenggang, Jiangsu, 108
DeLanda, Manuel, 189n4
Deng Xiaoping, 167
Dengzhou, Shandong, 125
Dingzhou, Hebei, 30
Dong people, 222n11
Dongting Lake, 11, 122
Dreyer, Edward, 132, 220n84
Dykstra, Maura, 210n73

East China Sea, 120
Elvin, Mark, 10, 165–66, 190n29
England, 98
environmental degradation: erosion and sedimentation, 8, 17, 29, 166; and loss of "ecosystem services," 164; loss of wild habitat, 8, 10, 60, 75, 165–66; reduction in biodiversity, 11, 13; susceptibility to wildfire, 95, 211n91

Erbaugh, Mary S., 167
Erbi kenqing (A brush-pen hatpin's critical points), 91–94, 210n74
Essays on Timber Rafting in the Western Regions (Gong Hui), 140, 149*fig.*, 150–51, 152*fig.*, 153*fig.*, 154*fig.*
Essential Arts to Nourish the People (Jia Sixie), 25
European forestry, 6–7, 9, 98, 164–65, 208n33

Fang Guozhen, 129, 130
fengshui, 96, 168, 212n96
fir. *See* China fir
forest, as term, 6–7, 161, 169. *See also* woodlands
forest deeds: as evidence of ownership, 41, 80, 81–82; of the Fang family, 84; as historical evidence, 10, 35, 206n1, 207n28; in shareholding arrangements, 19, 84–87, 93, 208nn32,40, 209n54; of a single Quanzhou property, 80–81; of the Tan family, 77–79; and tax law, 82, 92–93. *See also* landowners
forest surveys: categories in, 52; and the Chinese property system, 40–44, 89–90, 161, 162; in Europe and Northeast Asia, 6, 56, 201n73. *See also* land surveys
forestry. *See* commercial forestry
Forests and Sea Power (Albion), 117, 139
France, 36, 98
fuel: commodification of, 30; for industrial purposes, 24, 70, 72, 106; labor for cutting, 8, 10, 64, 69; levies and tariffs on, 58, 64, 65, 100, 107, 109–10, 114; from open-access woodlands, 8, 27, 32, 95–96, 164; reed, 64, 100, 107, 109, 215n71; tree planting for, 25, 55; use of coal as, 29, 169
Fujian Province: forest fire risk in, 211n91; forest registration in, 51; Hakka people of, 14, 61, 71, 73; highland peoples of, 73; land surveys of, 13, 44, 48, 52, 173; logging in, 132; maritime traders from, 119; non-agrarian goods from, 64–65; during the Qing dynasty, 210n71; shipbuilding in, 119, 123, 124, 131; taxation in, 67, 75, 130, 200nn57,58; tea production in, 70; timber trade in, 72; topography, 11; tree plantations in, 95, 161
Funada Yoshiyuki, 202n19
Fuzhou, Fujian, 44, 48, 200n46, 218n49
Fuzhou, Jiangxi, 200n46

258 | INDEX

Gan River, 11
Ganzhou, Jiangxi, 55, 112–13, 175*table*, 176, 201n66, 204n41
Ge Gaiyi, 68
German principalities, 36, 56, 98
Gernet, Jacques, 220n92
Goldstone, Jack A., 131
Gong Hui, 140, 150–51
Grand Canal: and Beijing's timber supply, 141; building of transport ships for, 108, 121; and Hangzhou's timber supply, 101–2; Ming restoration of, 15, 65, 66; position of Kaifeng relative to, 28; presence of Huizhou merchants along, 72; Yellow Sea as alternative to, 119, 129; Yuan defeat of Song navy at, 126
The Great Divergence (Pomeranz), 166
Great Ming Code (Da Ming lü), 49, 89–90, 93, 209n65
Gu Zuo, 144
Guangdong Province: fir plantations in, 55; forest registration in, 51, 52; Hakka people of, 14, 61, 71, 73; land surveys of, 13, 44, 48; and logging expenses, 148; maritime traders from, 119; naval fleet in, 120; reform of corvée system in, 67; shipbuilding in, 124; tax forgiveness in, 103; timber trade and production in, 72, 161; topography, 11
Guanghua, Hubei, 125
Guangxi Province: forest registration in, 51, 52; forest surveys in, 13, 44; land surveys in, 48; presence of Huizhou merchants in, 72; taxation in, 103; tree plantations in, 55, 161
Guangxin, Jiangxi, 52, 70, 175, 200n45
Guangzhou, Guangdong, 34, 48, 99, 121, 124
Gui E, 68
Guizhou Province: depletion of old growth forests in, 142, 156; falling outside the state's reach, 48; Ming-era logging in, 147, 148, 155, 157, 225nn73,80; spread of commercial silviculture to, 159, 161; timber tributes from native officials in, 146

Hai Rui, 68
Hakka people: common surnames of, 72, 206n70; crops cultivated by, 17, 176; diasporic distribution, 74*map*; and major civil conflicts, 17–18, 166–67; as marginal, itinerant labor force, 14, 61, 72–73, 76, 89; older theory of origins of, 205n69. *See also* non-Han peoples
Han dynasty, 22, 23–24, 32, 142–43

Han Lin'er, 81, 129, 199n40
Han River, 125
Han Shantong, 81
Han Wendi, 193n17
Han Yong, 67
Hangzhou: as capital of Southern Song, 28, 38; capture by Jin armies, 122; customs station, 108, 111, 113, 133, 139; natural environment surrounding, 34, 101; tariffs collected at, 104, 109, 216nn89,91; timber trade in, 71, 72, 101–2, 114, 115, 215n72. *See also* Southern Song dynasty; Zhejiang Province
Hansen, Valerie, 197n9
Hartwell, Robert, 194n42
Haw, Stephen G., 202nn11,19
Hebei Province, 127
Henan Province, 45, 199n34, 200n58
Hengyang County, Hunan, 55
Hezhou, Guangxi, 31, 123
Ho, Ping-ti, 171
Holland, 36, 98, 162–63, 212n7
Hong Xiuquan, 167
Hongwu emperor. *See* Zhu Yuanzhang (Hongwu Emperor)
household registration, 49, 59, 60, 61–68, 73–76
Huai River, 121
Huai'an, Jiangsu, 133
Huainan, present-day Anhui and Jiangsu, 44, 103
Huang, Ray, 171, 205n53
Huang Yingnan, 43
Huangmu Ting (Imperial Timber Pavilion), 135
Hubei Province, 44, 103, 157, 159. *See also* Huguang Province
Huguang Province: building of transport ships in, 110; land surveys of, 48; logging costs in, 148; and Ming building projects, 130, 144, 146, 147, 155, 157; taxation in, 200n58. *See also* Hunan Province
Huizhou, present-day Anhui: archival records for, 50, 77, 206n1; forest labor in, 61, 73; as "hotbed of litigation," 91, 210n74; lineage ownership of forests in, 207n30; logging restrictions in, 30; merchants from, 14, 71–72, 115; in range of China fir, 12; taxable acreage in, 44, 46, 81–82, 172–73, 197n3, 198nn17,21; timber tariffs in, 106; tree plantations in, 35, 83, 94–95; during Yuan-Ming interregnum, 47, 81

Hunan Province: breakaway kingdom of Chu, 122; forest registration in, 51, 161; land surveys of, 44; logging in, 104–5, 155, 157; shipbuilding in, 121; tariff collection in, 111; tree plantations in, 55, 70; tributaries of the Yangzi in, 11, 122. *See also* Huguang Province

Huzhou, Zhejiang, 35, 111

Imperial Timber Pavilion (Huangmu Ting), 135

India, 24

Japan, 9–10, 15, 34, 98, 126–27, 190n28, 208n35

Java, 15

Jeju Island, 126, 127

Jeolla Province, Korea, 126, 127

Ji Gongzhi, 126, 127

Jia Sixie, 25

Ji'an, Jiangxi, 70, 198n17

Jianchang, Jiangxi, 175*table*, 176

Jiangnan region: as cradle of human-planted forests, 35, 159, 161; forest registration in, 51, 52–53; history and geography of, 11–12; land surveys of, 44, 45, 46, 47, 48, 49, 199n34; timber tariffs in, 106, 107, 109, 115; waterways throughout, 102. *See also* South China

Jiangxi Province: forest fire risk in, 211n91; forest registration in, 51, 53–54; Hakka people of, 14, 61, 71, 73; as a "hotbed of litigation," 91, 210n71; land surveys of, 13, 45, 47, 48, 173, 199n34, 204n41; logging in, 144; non-agrarian goods from, 65; in the range of China fir, 12; shipbuilding in, 110, 121, 130; during Song and Yuan dynasties, 200n45; taxation in, 67–69, 75, 200nn57,58; tree plantations in, 35, 95, 161; tributaries of the Yangzi in, 11

Jiangzhe, present-day Zhejiang and Fujian, 45, 200n45

Jiangzhou, Jiangxi, 103

Jianning, Fujian, 174

Jianzhou, Fujian, 104

Jin dynasty: conquest of North China, 15, 28–29, 38, 45, 101, 105, 121; defeat of Liao dynasty, 62; naval power, 117, 120, 122, 123, 125, 128; rise of Prince of Hailing, 122–23, 162; treaty with Southern Song, 42

Jingdezhen, Jiangxi, 70, 71–72, 106

Jingdong Circuit, present-day Shandong, 44, 213nn10,14

Jingxi Circuit, present-day Henan, 213n10

Jingzhou, Hubei, 111

Jinhua, Zhejiang, 207n30

Jiujiang, Jiangxi, 110, 111, 112, 175

Jixi County, Anhui, 172, 173*fig.*, 198n21

Jurchen people. *See* Jin dynasty

Kaifeng: as Northern Song capital, 28, 38; shipbuilding at, 125; size of, 194n46; timber and coal supplies to, 29, 31, 100, 113, 114. *See also* Northern Song dynasty

Kaihua County, Zhejiang, 70

Ke Xian, 67

Khitan people, 15, 28, 62

Kim Panggyong, 126

Korea: forest surveys, 56; Hideyoshi's campaign against, 154; imbalance of mountain forests and lowland farms in, 167–68; naval power, 119–20; oversight of forests in, 9, 10, 36, 90, 98; and Yuan dynasty, 125, 126–27, 128, 139, 219n75

Kublai Khan, 62, 125, 126–27, 128, 131–32, 162. *See also* Yuan dynasty

labor: bond servant, 84, 87, 88, 93, 206n76; and commodification of forest products, 25–27, 59; contractual, 84–85, 87, 88–89, 93, 94, 162, 164; itinerant, 34, 61, 89; for logging operations, 144–45, 148–51, 203n34; in shareholding arrangements, 83, 84, 85, 87–89; and silver tax, 69–70. *See also* corvée labor

land surveys: categories of land types in, 44, 46, 49, 52, 171, 199n33; and landownership, 41, 92; Li Chunnian's method of, 37–38, 42–43, 49, 51, 56; and non-agrarian landscapes, 43–44; and tax evasion, 66–67; by Zhang Juzheng in 1581, 51, 82; Zhang Lü's reform of, 38, 45–46. *See also* forest surveys; landowners

landowners: and Chinese property system, 40–41, 55; effect on open-access woodlands, 57, 59, 60, 75, 166; investment in tree plantations, 4–5, 35, 41–42, 56–57, 60; registration of properties, 42–43, 51, 81; in shareholding arrangements, 82–89, 92–93, 96, 209n54; theft from, 55, 87–88, 90, 92–93, 96. *See also* forest deeds; labor; land surveys

Leong, Sow-Theng, 167, 205n69

Li Chunnian, 37–38, 42–43, 49, 51, 56, 198n17

Li Gang, 121, 123

Li Xian, 31–32, 162, 217n19
Li Xianqing, 147, 148, 151, 155
Liang Fangzhong, 171
Liao dynasty, 15, 28, 62
Liaodong Peninsula, 119–20, 127
Liaoning Province, 70
Linjiang, Jiangxi, 70, 175
Liu Bing, 146
Liu Guangji, 68, 69
Liu Zongyuan, 26
Lo, Ju-pang, 218n49, 220n101
logging: bans and restrictions on, 30–31, 36, 217n20; and depletion of old-growth woodlands, 18, 26–27, 141, 142, 147, 155–59; for imperial construction, 16, 65, 140–42, 162; labor for, 89, 141, 144, 147–51, 222n3; for shipbuilding, 115, 127, 132; and shipping routes, 54, 97–98; and the spread of silviculture, 51, 113. *See also* environmental degradation; woodlands
Longjiang chuanchang zhi (Treatise on the Longjiang shipyards), 138
Longjiang customs station, Nanjing, 108, 115, 134–35, 143
Longjiang shipyards, Nanjing, 130, 131, 132, 133, 221n116
Lu Jie, 152
Luo Xianglin, 205n69

Macartney, George Macartney, Earl, 3–4
Macauley, Melissa, 210n71
Mahu, 144
Manchu people, 16
Manchuria, 75
Mao Zai, 155
Marks, Robert B., 10
McDermott, Joseph, 8, 85, 88, 172, 206nn76,1, 208nn35,40, 209n60
Mencius, 23
Meng Zhang, 159
merchants: connections with landowners, 16, 36, 84; geographical networks, 34; from Huizhou, 14, 71–72, 115; licensing of, 104; and naval expansion, 124, 135, 139; and official corruption, 103; shipping routes, 98, 135; the state's reliance on, 155; taxes and tariffs on, 103, 112. *See also* timber trade
Min River, 132
Minde, 143–44
Ming dynasty: administration of forests, 16, 57, 224n51; brief history of, 15–16, 212n7,

217n5; Hongxi reign, 66, 223n38; Hongzhi reign, 146; Jiajing reign, 146, 147; land surveys of, 38, 52, 63, 66–67, 171–76, 200n46, 203n23; landownership regulations, 82; legal code, 49, 89–90, 93, 209n65; logging operations during, 140–42, 157, 158*map*, 222n3, 223n37; naval power, 118, 119, 120, 129–38; oversight of non-agrarian trades, 61, 71, 73–74; policy of self-sufficiency, 107, 114; retrenchment and reform during, 18, 132, 146; shareholding arrangements in, 83, 207n29; shipbuilding administration during, 134–35, 139; taxation in, 67–71, 107–13, 114, 133, 171; timber production during, 115; village system under, 63–65, 203n22; Wanli reign, 152; Xuande reign, 66, 110, 131, 132, 223n38; Zhengde reign, 146; Zhengtong reign, 132. *See also* Zhu Di (Yongle Emperor); Zhu Yuanzhang (Hongwu Emperor)
Möngke Khan, 126
Mongol people. *See* Yuan dynasty
Mongolia, 75
Mozi, 23

Nan Zhili. *See* Southern Metropolitan Region
Nan'an, Jiangxi, 112, 174
Nanchang, Jiangxi, 127, 129, 175, 207n30
Nanjing: capture by Jin armies, 122; fuel supply of, 107; garrisons at, 131, 132, 133, 134, 135; household categories in, 202n20; land registers in, 46, 47, 199n33; shipbuilding at, 139; tariffs collected at, 109, 113, 114, 139, 215n74; timber trade in, 111, 115, 215n72; timber tributes to, 144
Nanling Mountains, 55, 56
nanmu: for palace construction, 143, 155; for shipbuilding, 135; state procurements of, 148, 156; as tribute timber, 142, 144, 146, 147. *See also* bamboo; China fir; pine
Nationalist Party, 207n30, 217n5
naval power, 117–39; important fronts in, 118–20; during Ming dynasty, 118, 119, 120, 129–38; during Song dynasty, 120–24; types of ships in, 120, 121, 124; during Yuan dynasty, 125–28. *See also* shipbuilding
New Comments on Guangdong, 55
New Treatise on Shipyard Administration (*Chuanzheng xin shu*), 138
Ni Dong, 138
Ningbo, Zhejiang, 34, 46, 52, 63, 121, 124, 199n33

INDEX | 261

Nongzheng quanshu (Xu Guangqi), 94
non-Han peoples: and Daoist techniques, 24; displacement of, 9; highland settlement, 12; and logging operations, 143, 144; payment of timber tributes, 141–42, 146–47, 151–52, 159; relation to the state, 13–14, 72–73; and Song dynasty, 28–29. *See also* Hakka people
North China: land surveys of, 42; maritime routes in, 119; relationship with South China, 12; rule by Jin dynasty, 45; species of timber in, 110; and Yuan dynasty, 105, 128, 203n23. *See also* Beijing; South China
North China Plain, 28, 29, 30, 36, 98
Northern Song dynasty: brief history, 15, 28; forest policy, 30–34; Huizong reign, 33; naval power, 121, 139; Shenzong reign, 32; timber supply, 29, 100–101, 114, 124; Zhenzong reign, 31; Zhezong reign, 32. *See also* Song dynasty; Southern Song dynasty
Nuremberg, 56

Offices of Zhou (Zhouli), 32
Ottoman Empire, 98
Outlaws of the Marsh (Shuihu Zhuan), 34
Ownby, David, 167

Pan Jian, 147
Pang Shangpeng, 68
Peng Shiqi, 147
pine: geographical range, 110, 114; grown in Korea and Europe, 56, 118; as a plantation tree, 4, 26, 94, 109; planting methods, 35, 55, 94, 211n83; producing pine tar, 70; susceptibility to fire, 95; taxation on, 215n71; used in palace construction, 155; used in shipbuilding, 118, 120, 139. *See also* bamboo; China fir; *nanmu*
Pingjiang, present-day Suzhou, Jiangsu, 217n20
Pingluan, Hebei, 128
Pingxiang County, Jiangxi, 54
Pomeranz, Kenneth, 166
porcelain industry, 71–72
Poyang Lake, 11, 12, 16, 53, 118, 129–30, 175
Precepts for Social Life (Yuan Cai), 21
Prussia, 36

Qian Qi, 68
Qianshan mountains, 128
Qiantang River, 101–2, 104, 106

Qimen County, Anhui, 81, 172, 173, 198n21, 199nn40,41, 206n1
Qin dynasty, 22, 23–24, 32, 142
Qing dynasty: control of Yangzi River basin, 212n7; forest surveys, 176; interpretation of timber tribute, 159; Kangxi reign, 155; logging operations during, 142, 155–56, 158*fig*.; pettifogging litigation during, 210n71; Qianlong reign, 155–56; shareholding arrangements in, 207n29; social unrest during, 166–67; taxation system, 63, 75, 113; Yongzheng reign, 155–56
Qingjiang, present-day Huai'an, Jiangsu, 130, 132, 133, 134, 135
Qinglin mountains, 31
Qiyang County, Hunan, 55
Quanzhou, Fujian, 34, 48, 70, 80, 124, 127, 200n46

Raozhou, Jiangxi, 52, 94, 173–74, 175, 200n45
Red Turban Rebellion, 15, 46, 81, 107, 129. *See also* Yuan dynasty
Retreat of the Elephants (Elvin), 10, 165–66
Rhine River, 212n7
Richardson, S. D., 94, 211n88
Roman law, 26
Rong Ni, 103
Ruizhou, Jiangxi, 174, 175, 204n41

Sacred Timber Depot (Shenmu Chang), 145, 146
Sanshan Gazetteer, 37
Sansi (State Finance Commission), 100, 101, 213n15
Schafer, Edwin H., 26–27
Schlesinger, Jonathan, 75
Schneewind, Sarah, 215n59
Scott, James C., 13, 163
Seeing Like a State (Scott), 163
Shaanxi Province, 67
shan, as term, 7, 9, 19
Shandong Province, 68, 126, 130, 200n58
Shang dynasty, 192n6
Shang Yang (Lord Shang), 23
Shanglin Park, 24, 193n15
Shanxi Province, 144, 145, 200n58
Shaoxing, Treaty of, 42
Shaoxing, Zhejiang, 52, 110
She Lu, 146
She people, 73, 76, 206n70

Shenmu Chang (Sacred Timber Depot), 145, 146
shipbuilding: ancillary materials for, 109, 130; different types of lumber for, 118, 120, 134–35; guides to administration of, 134, 138; labor for, 121, 123, 128, 130; and price inflation, 133–34; timber tariffs and, 103, 108, 162; of transport ships, 110, 121, 132, 218n22; types of ships built, 118, 136*fig*. *See also* naval power
Shipyard Administration (Chuanzheng), 138
Shu Yinglong, 155
Shuihu Zhuan (Outlaws of the Marsh), 34
Shuixi native office, present-day Bijie, Guizhou, 153
Sichuan Province: declining stands of old growth in, 142, 155, 156, 157, 159; imperial administration of logging in, 142–43, 225n80; land surveys of, 44; saying about mountains in, 151; timber for palace construction from, 145, 146, 147, 223n37; timber for shipbuilding from, 130, 132; timber tributes from, 143–44
Sima Guang, 32
Sima Qian, 193n17
Smith, Paul Jakov, 17
Sombart, Werner, 6
Song dynasty: *baojia* system, 203n23; brief history, 15; iron production during, 194n42; naval power, 117, 118, 119, 120–24, 125; oversight of forests and non-agrarian trades during, 16, 61, 62, 73; penal code of, 90; timber trade during, 109; wood crisis during, 4, 6, 9, 27–36, 38–39, 143. *See also* Northern Song dynasty; Southern Song dynasty
Songjiang, Jiangsu, 200n57
South China: land surveys of, 42; landholding practices and institutions, 39, 62–63; logging in, 141; relationship with North China, 12; shipbuilding in, 123, 131; timber trade in, 97, 101–2, 110, 124; topography, 11; tree plantations in, 70–71, 75, 94, 141, 160–61; Yuan control of, 45, 62–63, 105, 127, 128. *See also* Jiangnan region; North China
Southeast Asia, 15, 119, 128, 138
Southern Metropolitan Region: land surveys of, 47, 52; shipbuilding for, 132, 133; silviculture in, 95; taxation in, 68, 130, 200n58

Southern Song dynasty: control of Quanzhou, 80; corruption in, 103; establishment, 15, 28, 126; and forest management, 36, 38–39, 41, 57; Gaozong reign, 42; land surveys of, 42–44, 47, 50–51, 200n54; naval power, 121, 124, 139, 218n49; restrictions on Han logging, 104–5, 143; spread of litigation during, 91; timber trade during, 16, 102–5, 114, 115. *See also* Hangzhou
Spain, 98
State Finance Commission (Sansi), 100, 101, 213n15
Su Shi, 35, 55
Suzhou, Jiangsu, 106, 107, 121
Szonyi, Michael, 13

Taihe County, Jiangxi, 55
Taiping, present-day Wuhu, Anhui, 111
Taiping Rebellion, 17–18, 167, 226n6
Taiwan, 10, 217n5
Taizhou, Zhejiang, 44, 124
Tan family deed, 77–79, 84
Tang dynasty: fall, 28; landownership in, 41; legal code, 25–27, 59, 90; taxation during, 61, 99; wood policies of, 25–27, 32, 143
Tangut people, 15, 28, 31
tariff system, 97–116; attempt to eliminate, 107–8; conversion to cash payments, 104, 106; corruption in, 101, 103; exemptions from, 102–3, 104, 114; fractional, in-kind, 97–101, 109, 133; historical continuity, 113–16; method of calculation, 112; as oversight on wood markets, 162; revenues from, 106–7, 110–11; across varieties of wood, 109, 110, 114–15, 201n66, 215n71
taxation: and decimal accounting, 86–87, 209n52; evasion of, 66, 68, 82, 122; of forests, 7–8, 38–39, 51; in form of levies, 58–59, 61–62, 75; and land titles, 79–82; of non-agrarian goods, 61–63, 73–75, 213n10; on seagoing vessels, 121–22; in silver, 67–71, 164; "single whip method," 60, 68–69, 75–76, 82; and village system, 64
Tibetan people, 31
timber production: commodification of trees in, 5, 21, 22, 30; competition from other crops, 17, 166; and processing, 113; role of highland peoples in, 13–14; shareholding arrangements and, 84, 85, 88, 89; stages of, 16, 17, 94; from wild growth, 26–27, 41, 113

INDEX | 263

timber trade: and cash economy, 17, 22, 30, 102; futures market in, 8; geographical expansion of, 7, 34–35, 36; linking North and South China, 12, 98; price inflation in, 133–34, 216n91; and salt trade, 112; standardization of grades and measures in, 13, 134–35; state involvement in, 32, 105; and state penetration of uplands, 13–14. *See also* commercial forestry; merchants; tariff system; taxation
Tingzhou, Fujian, 44, 73
Tongzhou, Beijing, 123, 145
Toyotomi Hideyoshi, 154
Treatise on the Longjiang Shipyards (Longjiang chuanchang zhi), 138
Treatise on Transport Ships (Caochuan zhi), 134, 138
tree planting: in clear-cut areas, 51, 55; and concepts of landownership, 41; effects on the environment, 11, 17, 22–23, 35, 60, 75, 95; grants of forest title and, 39–40, 50–51, 56; methods, 94, 211n88; ordered by Zhu Yuanzhang, 16; and reduction in open-access woodlands, 61, 164; as a response to wood crises, 22–23, 24, 27; role of upland peoples in, 72–73; rotation of plots in, 78, 209n60; spread of, 54–56, 57, 71, 159, 161; and timber production targets, 34; writings on, 21, 25, 26, 162. *See also* commercial forestry
Tuntian Qingli Si (Bureau of Military Farms), 108
Tushan mountains, 128

Venice, 6, 36, 98, 162–63, 201n73
Vietnam, 15, 128
von Glahn, Richard, 16–17, 215n59

Wagner, Donald B., 194n42
Wang Anshi, 32, 41, 62, 196n72
Wang Li, 111
Wang Shao, 31
Wang Yangming, 112
Wang Zhi, 112
Wang Zongmu, 68
Wanyan Liang (Prince of Hailing), 122–23, 162
Weihe, Shandong, 130, 132, 133, 134
Wenzhou, Zhejiang, 124
Wiens, Herold J., 165
Wŏnjong, King of Korea, 126–27

wood crises: Qin and Han responses to, 22, 23–24; Song dynasty, 4, 6, 9, 27–36, 38–39, 143
woodlands: conversion to forests, 51, 57, 75, 141, 160–61, 169; distinguished from *forests*, 160–61; "ecosystem services" provided by, 164; in land surveys, 40, 43, 44; legal views of, 25–26, 90; levies on products of, 61, 69; open access to, 13, 17, 37–38, 41, 59, 90, 95–96; social costs of loss of, 164, 166–67. *See also* commercial forestry; logging
Woodside, Alexander, 162
Wuhu, present-day Anhui, 111, 133
Wuyi Mountains, 71, 72
Wuyuan County, Jiangxi, 172, 173, 198n21, 199n41

Xi Xia dynasty, 15, 28, 31
Xia Shi, 67
Xiang River, 11
Xiangyang, Hubei, 125, 126
Xie An, 144, 223n37
Xihe Circuit, 31
Xihe Logging and Timber Purchase Bureau, 32, 217n19
Xin'an Gazetteer, 44
Xiuning County, Anhui, 172, 173fig., 206n1
Xu Guangqi, 94
Xu Jie, 68
Xuancheng, Anhui, 94

Yang Guozhen, 208n40
Yang Yao, 122
Yang Yinglong, 152–55
Yangzhou, Jiangsu, 103, 127
Yangzi River: compared to other major river basins, 212n7; forest registration along highlands of, 52; logging along, 18, 34, 141, 142, 144, 147; naval importance, 118–19, 121, 129, 217n5, 221n116; as northern border of South China, 11–12; shipbuilding along, 124, 132, 139; and supply of fuel to Nanjing, 107; taxation on households along, 109; timber trade along, 8, 13, 72, 108, 113, 119, 162; tree plantations along, 3, 8, 70, 159; tributaries of, 11
Yanshan, Jiangxi, 70
Yanyou Reorganization, 45, 172, 198n26, 214n53
Yanzhou, Zhejiang, 104
Ye Mengde, 35, 36

Yellow River, 29, 36, 196n82, 212n7
Yellow Sea, 119–20, 127–28
Yelü Chucai, 62, 201n10
Yi County, present-day Anhui, 172, 173*fig.*, 198n21
Yibin County, Yunnan, 143
Yongle emperor. *See* Zhu Di (Yongle Emperor)
Yongning native office, present-day Ninglang County, Yunnan, 146
Yongshun native office, present-day Yongshun County, Hunan, 147, 152
Youyang native office, present-day Enshi, Hubei, 152, 153
Yuan Cai, 21, 23, 35, 36, 43, 83
Yuan dynasty: *baojia* system, 81, 199n40, 203n23; brief history of, 15, 81; conflicts, 114, 117; control of Fujian Province, 52, 80; fall of, 15, 46, 81, 107, 129; grain transport during, 129; and history of forest management, 57, 162–63; land surveys of, 38, 45–46, 48, 50, 172–73, 200n46, 203n23; naval power, 117–18, 119, 120, 125–28, 139, 219n61; and non-Han peoples, 141; oversight of non-agrarian trades, 61, 62, 63, 64, 71, 73–74, 202n11; size of empire, 212n7; taxation in, 45, 62, 63, 64, 105–7, 114; timber production during, 115
Yuanzhou, Jiangxi, 55, 70, 175*table*, 176
Yun-Gui Plateau, 56
Yunnan Province, 143, 148, 157

Zaiweibing, 153
Zhang Juzheng, 51, 69, 75, 82, 172, 173–74
Zhang Lü, 38, 45–46, 51
Zhang Shicheng, 129, 130
Zhang Xi, 125, 219n61
Zhang Xuan, 126
Zhangzhou, Fujian, 44, 73
Zhejiang Province: coastal pirates in, 129; forest fire risk in, 211n91; forest registration in, 51, 52; land surveys of, 44, 45, 47, 48; logging in, 121, 144; non-agrarian goods from, 65; in range of the China fir, 12; shipbuilding in, 110, 122, 128; taxation in, 68–69, 104, 130, 200nn57,58; tea production in, 70; topography, 11; tree plantations in, 35, 95, 159, 161. *See also* Hangzhou
Zhending, Hebei, 110
Zheng He expeditions, 15, 65, 66, 118, 131–32, 139, 221nn111,112. *See also* naval power; shipbuilding
Zhenjiang, Jiangsu, 46, 103, 106, 202n20, 214n51
Zhou Rudou, 68
Zhouli (Offices of Zhou), 32
Zhu Chun, 143, 144
Zhu De, 167
Zhu Di (Yongle Emperor): ascent to power, 109, 163; construction projects, 65–66, 141, 144, 147; logging under, 147, 151, 156, 162, 203n34, 222n3; naval expansion under, 130–32; retrenchment after the reign of, 18, 67, 82, 110, 145–46; tariffs under, 110. *See also* Ming dynasty
Zhu Qing, 126
Zhu Xi, 35
Zhu Ying, 67
Zhu Yuanzhang (Hongwu Emperor): in battle of Poyang Lake, 129–30, 220n84; defeat of Han Lin'er, 81; land surveys under, 46–47, 49–50, 172; orders for tree planting, 16, 162; policy of self-sufficiency, 107–8, 143, 215n59; successor, 109; village system, 63–65. *See also* Ming dynasty

WEYERHAEUSER ENVIRONMENTAL BOOKS

Seeds of Control: Japan's Empire of Forestry in Colonial Korea, by David Fedman

Fir and Empire: The Transformation of Forests in Early Modern China, by Ian M. Miller

Communist Pigs: An Animal History of East Germany's Rise and Fall, by Thomas Fleischman

Footprints of War: Militarized Landscapes in Vietnam, by David Biggs

Cultivating Nature: The Conservation of a Valencian Working Landscape, by Sarah R. Hamilton

Bringing Whales Ashore: Oceans and the Environment of Early Modern Japan, by Jakobina K. Arch

The Organic Profit: Rodale and the Making of Marketplace Environmentalism, by Andrew N. Case

Seismic City: An Environmental History of San Francisco's 1906 Earthquake, by Joanna L. Dyl

Smell Detectives: An Olfactory History of Nineteenth-Century Urban America, by Melanie A. Kiechle

Defending Giants: The Redwood Wars and the Transformation of American Environmental Politics, by Darren Frederick Speece

The City Is More Than Human: An Animal History of Seattle, by Frederick L. Brown

Wilderburbs: Communities on Nature's Edge, by Lincoln Bramwell

How to Read the American West: A Field Guide, by William Wyckoff

Behind the Curve: Science and the Politics of Global Warming, by Joshua P. Howe

Whales and Nations: Environmental Diplomacy on the High Seas, by Kurkpatrick Dorsey

Loving Nature, Fearing the State: Environmentalism and Antigovernment Politics before Reagan, by Brian Allen Drake

Pests in the City: Flies, Bedbugs, Cockroaches, and Rats, by Dawn Day Biehler

Tangled Roots: The Appalachian Trail and American Environmental Politics, by Sarah Mittlefehldt

Vacationland: Tourism and Environment in the Colorado High Country, by William Philpott

Car Country: An Environmental History, by Christopher W. Wells

Nature Next Door: Cities and Trees in the American Northeast, by Ellen Stroud

Pumpkin: The Curious History of an American Icon, by Cindy Ott

The Promise of Wilderness: American Environmental Politics since 1964, by James Morton Turner

The Republic of Nature: An Environmental History of the United States, by Mark Fiege

A Storied Wilderness: Rewilding the Apostle Islands, by James W. Feldman

Quagmire: Nation-Building and Nature in the Mekong Delta, by David Biggs

Seeking Refuge: Birds and Landscapes of the Pacific Flyway, by Robert M. Wilson

Toxic Archipelago: A History of Industrial Disease in Japan, by Brett L. Walker

Dreaming of Sheep in Navajo Country, by Marsha L. Weisiger

Shaping the Shoreline: Fisheries and Tourism on the Monterey Coast, by Connie Y. Chiang

The Fishermen's Frontier: People and Salmon in Southeast Alaska, by David F. Arnold

Making Mountains: New York City and the Catskills, by David Stradling

Plowed Under: Agriculture and Environment in the Palouse, by Andrew P. Duffin

The Country in the City: The Greening of the San Francisco Bay Area, by Richard A. Walker

Native Seattle: Histories from the Crossing-Over Place, by Coll Thrush

Drawing Lines in the Forest: Creating Wilderness Areas in the Pacific Northwest, by Kevin R. Marsh

Public Power, Private Dams: The Hells Canyon High Dam Controversy, by Karl Boyd Brooks

Windshield Wilderness: Cars, Roads, and Nature in Washington's National Parks, by David Louter

On the Road Again: Montana's Changing Landscape, by William Wyckoff

Wilderness Forever: Howard Zahniser and the Path to the Wilderness Act, by Mark Harvey

The Lost Wolves of Japan, by Brett L. Walker

Landscapes of Conflict: The Oregon Story, 1940–2000, by William G. Robbins

Faith in Nature: Environmentalism as Religious Quest, by Thomas R. Dunlap

The Nature of Gold: An Environmental History of the Klondike Gold Rush, by Kathryn Morse

Where Land and Water Meet: A Western Landscape Transformed, by Nancy Langston

The Rhine: An Eco-Biography, 1815–2000, by Mark Cioc

Driven Wild: How the Fight against Automobiles Launched the Modern Wilderness Movement, by Paul S. Sutter

George Perkins Marsh: Prophet of Conservation, by David Lowenthal

Making Salmon: An Environmental History of the Northwest Fisheries Crisis, by Joseph E. Taylor III

Irrigated Eden: The Making of an Agricultural Landscape in the American West, by Mark Fiege

The Dawn of Conservation Diplomacy: U.S.-Canadian Wildlife Protection Treaties in the Progressive Era, by Kurkpatrick Dorsey

Landscapes of Promise: The Oregon Story, 1800–1940, by William G. Robbins

Forest Dreams, Forest Nightmares: The Paradox of Old Growth in the Inland West, by Nancy Langston

The Natural History of Puget Sound Country, by Arthur R. Kruckeberg

WEYERHAEUSER ENVIRONMENTAL CLASSICS

Environmental Justice in Postwar America: A Documentary Reader, edited by Christopher W. Wells

Making Climate Change History: Documents from Global Warming's Past, edited by Joshua P. Howe

Nuclear Reactions: Documenting American Encounters with Nuclear Energy, edited by James W. Feldman

The Wilderness Writings of Howard Zahniser, edited by Mark Harvey

The Environmental Moment: 1968–1972, edited by David Stradling

Reel Nature: America's Romance with Wildlife on Film, by Gregg Mitman

DDT, Silent Spring, and the Rise of Environmentalism, edited by Thomas R. Dunlap

Conservation in the Progressive Era: Classic Texts, edited by David Stradling

Man and Nature: Or, Physical Geography as Modified by Human Action, by George Perkins Marsh

A Symbol of Wilderness: Echo Park and the American Conservation Movement, by Mark W. T. Harvey

Tutira: The Story of a New Zealand Sheep Station, by Herbert Guthrie-Smith

Mountain Gloom and Mountain Glory: The Development of the Aesthetics of the Infinite, by Marjorie Hope Nicolson

The Great Columbia Plain: A Historical Geography, 1805–1910, by Donald W. Meinig

CYCLE OF FIRE

Fire: A Brief History, 2nd ed., by Stephen J. Pyne

The Ice: A Journey to Antarctica, by Stephen J. Pyne

Burning Bush: A Fire History of Australia, by Stephen J. Pyne

Fire in America: A Cultural History of Wildland and Rural Fire, by Stephen J. Pyne

Vestal Fire: An Environmental History, Told through Fire, of Europe and Europe's Encounter with the World, by Stephen J. Pyne

World Fire: The Culture of Fire on Earth, by Stephen J. Pyne

ALSO AVAILABLE:

Awful Splendour: A Fire History of Canada, by Stephen J. Pyne

Printed in the USA
CPSIA information can be obtained
at www.ICGtesting.com
CBHW030218240224
4636CB00001B/4